Symbolism in the Fourth Gospel

Symbolism
in the Fourth Gospel

MEANING, MYSTERY, COMMUNITY

Craig R. Koester

FORTRESS PRESS   MINNEAPOLIS

SYMBOLISM IN THE FOURTH GOSPEL
Meaning, Mystery, Community

Library of Congress Cataloging-in-Publication Data

Koester, Craig R., 1953–
    Symbolism in the Fourth Gospel: meaning, mystery, community / Craig R. Koester.
        p.   cm.
    Includes bibliographical references and indexes.
    ISBN 0-8006-2893-4 (alk. paper) :
    1. Bible. N.T. John—Criticism, interpretation, etc.
2. Symbolism in the Bible. I. Title.
BS2615.6.S97K64   1995
226.5'06—dc20   94–31476
                                                                                CIP

The paper used in this publication meets the minimum requirements of American National Standard for Information Sciences—Permanence of Paper for Printed Library Materials, ANSI Z329.48–1984. ∞™

Manufactured in the U.S.A.   AF 1-2893

            2   3   4   5   6   7   8   9

For my parents
Richard and Gloria Koester

Contents

Abbreviations

Abbreviations of biblical books, other ancient sources, and periodical literature are taken from the *Journal of Biblical Literature* 107 (1988): 579–96. The list included here offers the short titles of works frequently cited.

Ashton, *Understanding*	John Ashton, *Understanding the Fourth Gospel* (Oxford: Clarendon, 1991).
Barrett, *Gospel*	C. K. Barrett, *The Gospel according to St. John,* 2d ed. (Philadelphia: Westminster, 1978).
Brown, *Community*	Raymond E. Brown, *The Community of the Beloved Disciple* (New York: Paulist, 1979).
Brown, *Epistles*	Idem, *The Epistles of John,* AB 30 (Garden City, N.Y.: Doubleday, 1982).
Brown, *Gospel*	Idem, *The Gospel according to John,* AB 29–29A (Garden City, N.Y.: Doubleday, 1966–70).
Bultmann, *Gospel*	Rudolf Bultmann, *The Gospel of John* (Philadelphia: Westminster, 1971).
Culpepper, *Anatomy*	R. Alan Culpepper, *Anatomy of the Fourth Gospel: A Study in Literary Design* (Philadelphia: Fortress, 1983).
de Jonge, *Jesus: Stranger*	M. de Jonge, *Jesus: Stranger from Heaven and Son of God. Jesus Christ and the Christians in Johannine Perspective,* SBLSBS 11 (Missoula, Mont.: Scholars, 1977).
Dodd, *Interpretation*	C. H. Dodd, *The Interpretation of the Fourth Gospel* (Cambridge: Cambridge University Press, 1953).

Martyn, *Gospel of John* — J. Louis Martyn, *The Gospel of John in Christian History: Essays for Interpreters* (New York: Paulist, 1978).

Martyn, *History and Theology* — Idem, *History and Theology in the Fourth Gospel*, 2d ed. (Nashville: Abingdon, 1979).

Meeks, *Prophet-King* — Wayne A. Meeks, *The Prophet-King: Moses Traditions and the Johannine Christology*, NovTSup 14 (Leiden: Brill, 1967).

Rensberger, *Johannine Faith* — David Rensberger, *Johannine Faith and Liberating Community* (Philadelphia: Westminster, 1988).

Schnackenburg, *Gospel* — Rudolf Schnackenburg, *The Gospel according to St. John* (New York: Herder/Seabury/Crossroad, 1968–82).

Schürer, *History* — Emile Schürer, Geza Vermes, Fergus Millar, and Matthew Black, *The History of the Jewish People in the Age of Jesus Christ*, rev. ed. (Edinburgh: T. & T. Clark, 1973–87).

Preface

The symbolic language of John's Gospel has long engaged the imagination of its readers. The evocative references to light and darkness, bread, living water, and other images have elicited a steady stream of exegetical, theological, and artistic comment. Paradoxically, the same qualities that contribute to the wide appeal of John's Gospel actually compound the difficulty of interpretation, since the leading symbols do not readily allow themselves to be defined; they convey multiple meanings simultaneously. In the following pages, therefore, I seek to distinguish and to explore the interaction between various aspects of meaning in Johannine symbols. At the same time I want to avoid reducing these multifaceted symbols to flat propositional statements or, conversely, suggesting that they are so indeterminate that they can mean anything the interpreter wishes.

Johannine symbolism cannot be treated adequately within the confines of one discipline; it demands consideration of the literary, the sociohistorical, and the theological aspects of the text. From a literary perspective I have built on the work of many predecessors, while giving renewed attention to the way we recognize symbols in the text, to the structure of the symbolism, and to its relationship to the literature of antiquity. When treating sociohistorical matters, I challenge the idea that Johannine Christianity was an introverted sect whose symbolic language would have been opaque to the uninitiated. I argue that Johannine symbolism would have been accessible to a spectrum of readers, helping to foster a sense of Christian identity that was distinct from the world while motivating the Christian community to a missionary engagement with the world. In terms of theological emphasis, I give special attention to the Johannine presentation of Jesus' death, and I stress the centrality of the cross for understanding symbolic language throughout the Gospel.

This study took shape with several audiences in mind. One audience consists of the biblical scholars and theologians interested in the Johannine writings and in symbolic language. The need for a monograph on Johannine symbolism has often been voiced (for example, by Wayne A. Meeks, "The Man from Heaven in Johannine Sectarianism," *JBL* 91 [1972] 44–72, esp. 47; Robert Morgan, *Biblical Interpretation* [Oxford: Oxford University Press, 1988], 228–29). My hope is that this book can help to fill a lacuna in the field while opening up avenues for further research. A second audience consists of my students, with whom I have studied John's Gospel over the years. When done well, exegetical study both stimulates and disciplines thought. Here I venture modeling responsible scholarship while seeking to capture the interest of a new generation of biblical interpreters for a lifetime of engagement with the Fourth Gospel. A third audience is the church. Many pastors have found it daunting to preach and teach from John's Gospel because of the multilayered quality of its language. This study can serve as a guide to some of the most perennially popular aspects of the Gospel. I have tried to write in an accessible way, placing the most technical matters in the notes and organizing the book so that readers interested in particular symbols can find them easily.

Some of the most rewarding aspects of research and writing are conversations with colleagues, and many have shared valuable insights with me during the course of this project. Here I want to thank those who helped shape it at the outset and who read all or portions of the manuscript at various stages: Raymond E. Brown, Gerhard O. Forde, Terence E. Fretheim, Donald Juel, Robert Kysar, J. Louis Martyn, Todd W. Nichol, Peter Ochs, Fernando F. Segovia, and Paul R. Sponheim. I also want to express my appreciation to Luther Seminary in St. Paul, Minnesota, and Lutheran Brotherhood, who made possible a sabbatical leave in which to complete the manuscript, and to Daniel Hardy and the staff at the Center of Theological Inquiry for their support and the hospitality they extended to me and my family. Thanks are also due to the library staffs at Luther Seminary and Princeton Theological Seminary for their help at many points. Finally, I want to acknowledge my gratitude to Fortress Press, especially for the late John Hollar's interest in the project and for Marshall Johnson's editorial help in bringing it to completion.

1

Symbol, Meaning, and Mystery

The study of Johannine symbolism takes us to a problem that lies at the heart of all theological reflection: How do people know God? In the language of the Fourth Gospel, God is "from above" and people are "from below," and to ordinary human eyes God's presence is veiled, his activity elusive. John's prologue says that "no one has ever seen God" (1:18a), a comment on the human condition that provides no exceptions. Throughout the Gospel Jesus will address listeners who do not know God, who have never heard God's voice and have never seen God's form (5:27; 7:28; 8:19). A cleft separates the human from the divine.[1] Yet the Gospel also says that Jesus made God known (1:18b). He could reveal God because he came from heaven and did not speak on his own authority, but uttered the words of God in God's own name (3:34; 5:43; 8:28).

Jesus descended to bear witness to what he had seen and heard above, but when he crossed the chasm and entered the world, he spoke with human beings who found him to be as inscrutable as God himself. The prologue acknowledges that "the world knew him not" (1:10), and the first scene ends with John the Baptist's unsettling declaration that the one God has sent now stands in your midst "and him you do not know" (1:26). Jesus' divine origin was hidden from human eyes; it could not be discerned "by appearances" (7:24). In the peculiar economy of the Gospel, Jesus must make God known, but God must also make Jesus known. No

1. The importance of the distinction between the "above" and the "below" for understanding Johannine symbolism is widely recognized. See Wayne A. Meeks, "The Man from Heaven in Johannine Sectarianism," *JBL* 91 (1972) 44–72; Culpepper, *Anatomy*, 200; C. K. Barrett, *Essays on John* (Philadelphia: Westminster, 1982), chaps. 1 and 5. C. H. Dodd associates the dichotomy with Platonic categories in *Interpretation*, 139–43. On the relationship of this cleft to religious symbolism generally, see Philip Wheelwright, *Metaphor and Reality* (Bloomington: Indiana University Press, 1962) 130.

one comes to the Father except through Jesus (14:6), and no one comes to Jesus without being drawn by the Father (6:44).

According to the Fourth Gospel, people are drawn to Jesus, and so to God, through testimony.[2] The words spoken by and about Jesus, together with the actions he performed, are the vehicles through which revelation is given. Jesus came from above, but he could not reveal divine truths in heavenly language. Human beings belong to the earth and speak in worldly terms (3:31), therefore Jesus used familiar earthly images to convey his message. A teacher named Nicodemus slipped along the shadowed streets of Jerusalem to meet Jesus, and Jesus told him that entry into the kingdom of heaven was "birth" and that the Spirit was a wind blowing across the human landscape (3:3-8). Nicodemus stammered his incredulity, but Jesus responded, "If I have told you earthly things and you do not believe, how can you believe if I tell you heavenly things?" (3:12). The question goes to the crux of the issue: Those who belong to the world cannot comprehend unmediated heavenly truths. But as the Gospel unfolds we see that people can come to know Jesus and God when their own language, the language of the world, becomes a vehicle for divine communication.

Earthly images could be used to bear witness to divine realities because the earth is God's creation. This is one of the main theological underpinnings of Johannine symbolism. In the beginning, God uttered the Word that brought all things into being, and without this Word "was not anything made" (1:3).[3] To be sure, the creation itself yielded no sure knowledge of God, and when the creative Word became flesh in Jesus, people refused to receive him (1:10). Yet once in the world, Jesus called upon things that could be seen, touched, and tasted to bear witness to the unseen God who sent him, so that the commonplace—bread made from barley meal, streams of cool water, and a glimmer of light—became vehicles of revelation. The Gospel declares that "no one has ever seen God," but that the only Son "has made him known" (1:18) by using images from the creation to bear witness to the Creator; that is, through symbolic speech and actions.

A second and related problem is how revelation given at particular times and places can have broader, even universal, significance. The agent of revelation was Jesus, an individual who encountered a limited number of people in Roman Palestine during a career that lasted perhaps three

---

2. On the place of this theme, see my article "Hearing, Seeing, and Believing in the Gospel of John," *Bib* 70 (1989) 327–48.

3. On the relation of creation to symbolism in John, see John Painter, "Johannine Symbols: A Case Study in Epistemology," *Journal of Theology for Southern Africa* 27 (1979) 26–41, esp. 32–34; Culpepper, *Anatomy,* 200–201.

years. The Gospel recounts the actions he performed and the words he spoke, while seeking to show that their significance transcends their immediate context. When Jesus fed a crowd beside the Sea of Galilee, he spoke about the bread that comes down from heaven to give life not just to his immediate listeners but "to the world" (6:33), and when he opened the eyes of one man born blind, he announced that he was "the light of the world" (9:5).

The Gospel writer sought to disclose the abiding significance of what Jesus had said and done in the conviction that Jesus himself continues to abide among people through the Spirit or "paraclete" (14:15-17, 23). Like the belief that the world is God's creation, a sense of the ongoing work of the Spirit undergirds Johannine symbolism theologically. The Spirit did not bring new revelation on the same order as Jesus had already given but manifested Jesus' presence and disclosed the significance of his words and actions to people living after his ministry on earth had ended (14:26). The Gospel presents the paradox that the divine is made known through what is earthly and the universal is disclosed through what is particular. This gives Johannine symbolism a tensive, dialectical quality that conveys transcendent reality without finally delimiting it. The Gospel's testimony, given in symbolic language, is a vehicle for the Spirit's work; and it is through the Spirit that the testimony becomes effective, drawing readers to know the mystery that is God.[4]

JOHANNINE SYMBOLISM IN ITS
LITERARY CONTEXT

The ability of symbols to communicate things that cannot be expressed adequately by other means has attracted the interest of people working across a spectrum of scholarly disciplines. Each has its own ways of understanding what symbols are and what they do, and many would not share the fourth evangelist's theological assumptions.[5] We will draw questions

4. On the relation of the Spirit to the Gospel's levels of meaning, see esp. Martyn, *History and Theology*, 143–51. On the role of paradox see Ashton, *Understanding*, 550–53; Judith Lieu, *The Second and Third Epistles of John* (London: T. & T. Clark, 1986) 215–16.

5. For example, sociologists Peter Berger and Thomas Luckmann identify a symbol as any significative theme that spans spheres of reality (*The Social Construction of Reality: A Treatise in the Sociology of Knowledge* [New York: Doubleday, 1967] 40). Psychologist Carl Jung viewed symbols as the visible manifestations of the archetypes present in the human psyche. See Jolande Jacobi, *Complex/Archetype/Symbol in the Psychology of C. G. Jung* (Princeton, N.J.: Princeton University Press, 1959) 74–79. The most thoroughgoing attempt to use insights from psychology to interpret ancient symbols is Erwin R. Goodenough, *Jewish Symbols in the Greco-Roman Period* (New York: Pantheon, 1953–68) 4.25–62. Literary critic Northrop Frye extended the term *symbol* to any unit of any literary structure that can be isolated for critical attention (*Anatomy of Criticism: Four Essays* [Princeton, N.J.: Princeton University Press, 1971] 71). For a survey of approaches to symbolism in various disciplines, see F. W. Dillistone, *The Power of Symbols in Religion and Culture* (New York: Crossroad, 1986) 99–151.

and insights from various areas of research, while keeping the focus on the Fourth Gospel and trying to let our general observations about symbolism conform as much as possible to the distinctive contours of the text. Symbols can affect people with an immediacy that cannot be replicated in more discursive speech; yet as symbols capture the imagination, they engage readers in an ongoing process of reflection. We begin this process of reflection by exploring patterns in the Gospel's symbolism and their role in communicating the Gospel's message.[6]

Defining Johannine Symbolism

A symbol, in the most general sense, is something that stands for something else. Here, however, we will focus the definition: A symbol is an image, an action, or a person that is understood to have transcendent significance. In Johannine terms, symbols span the chasm between what is "from above" and what is "from below" without collapsing the distinction. Images are things that can be perceived by the senses, such as light and darkness, water, bread, a door, a shepherd, and a vine. The actions that function symbolically in John's Gospel include nonmiraculous actions, like driving merchants out of the Jerusalem temple and washing feet, as well as miraculous "signs," like turning water into wine and raising Lazarus from the dead. The person who makes God known is Jesus, and those he meets represent types of belief and unbelief. Sometimes life, freedom, and truth have been called symbols because in John's Gospel they refer to divine realities. Because, however, these concepts do not involve images that can be perceived by the senses, they will not be considered symbols here.[7]

---

6. Northrop Frye, *Anatomy of Criticism*, 85–87. On the importance of working from the particular, see Walter Hinderer, "Theory, Conception, and Interpretation of the Symbol," *Perspectives in Literary Symbolism* (ed. J. Strelka; Yearbook of Comparative Criticism 1; University Park, Pa.: Pennsylvania State University, 1968) 81–127, esp. 91–92. Our approach differs from that of Paul Diel, who seeks to "decipher" the symbols in the Gospel in light of his own psychological theory of motivations, which was developed independently of the text. See Paul Diel and Jeannine Solotareff, *Symbolism in the Gospel of John* (San Francisco: Harper & Row, 1988). On "deciphering" see also Diel's *Symbolism in the Bible: Its Psychological Significance* (San Francisco: Harper & Row, 1986) x, 91, 136.

7. For a similar definition of *symbol* see Thomas Fawcett, *The Symbolic Language of Religion: An Introductory Study* (London: SCM, 1970) 30. Cf. Takashi Onuki, *Gemeinde und Welt im Johannesevangelium: Ein Beitrag zur Frage nach der theologischen und pragmatischen Funktion des johanneischen "Dualismus"* (WMANT 56; Neukirchen-Vluyn: Neukirchener, 1984) 46. In his study of Johannine symbolism, Günter Stemberger understood symbols to be shortened expressions that are open to the absolute and dynamic. Accordingly, he considered concepts like life and death, slavery and freedom, and love and hate to be symbols along with light, darkness, and water (*La symbolique du bien et du mal selon Saint Jean* [Paris: Seuil, 1970] 15–21). John Ashton makes "life" the central symbol, with light, water, bread, etc. as subsidiary symbols (*Understanding*, 516).

Johannine symbolism is concentric, with Jesus at its heart; he has a unique role as the one who reveals God. The Gospel's images and actions, in turn, help to show who Jesus is. These symbols, as we have defined them, include things that differ from each other in important ways.[8] For example, a sign like turning water into wine brings the power of God into the realm of human experience in a manner different from a nonmiraculous action like cleansing the temple or a statement like "I am the light of the world." Nevertheless, we will include the images, the actions, and representative figures in our study of the Gospel's symbolism because they function similarly in the text. Each conveys something of transcendent significance through something accessible to the senses.

Given this range of symbolic elements, a useful distinction can be made between core and supporting symbols. Core symbols occur most often, in the most significant contexts in the narrative, and contribute most to the Gospel's message.[9] For example, the repeated statements identifying Jesus as "the light of the world" (1:9; 3:19; 8:12; 9:5; 12:46) establish light as a core symbolic image with darkness as its counterpart. Other elements such as day and night and sight and blindness play an important supporting role in the text through their relationship to light. A recurring cluster of core and supporting images creates a motif. While the core symbols usually stand at the center of a narrative, the supporting images in a motif often remain in the background. For example, when Jesus proclaims, "I am the light of the world" (8:12), light is the core symbol on which attention focuses. In the passing observation that Nicodemus came to Jesus "by night" (3:2), however, the darkness is merely suggestive and its full import not readily apparent. Some core symbols, like the vine (15:1-17), appear only once in the Gospel, and their significance is evident in a single context. The supporting elements in a motif, however, occur repeatedly, and their effect is cumulative. The implications of Nicodemus's coming "by night," for example, unfold gradually, as images for darkness recur in the narrative.[10]

Transcendent realities are conveyed most clearly through core symbols. The Gospel begins by announcing that human beings receive "light" from

8. Some theologians reserve the term *symbol* for that which participates in the reality for which it stands. See, e.g., Paul Tillich, *Systematic Theology* (Chicago: University of Chicago Press, 1951–63) 1.239; Sandra Schneiders, "History and Symbolism in the Fourth Gospel," *L'Evangile de Jean: Sources, redaction, théologie* (ed. M. de Jonge; BETL 44; Gembloux and Louvain: Duculot and Louvain University, 1977) 371–76, esp. 372. On the value of distinguishing various kinds of symbols, see Culpepper, *Anatomy*, 197.

9. See Hinderer, "Theory, Conception, and Interpretation of the Symbol," esp. 98. Cf. Culpepper, *Anatomy*, 189; Victor Turner, *The Forest of Symbols: Aspects of Ndembu Ritual* (Ithaca, N.Y.: Cornell University Press, 1967) 30–32.

10. William Freedman, "The Literary Motif: A Definition and Evaluation," *Novel* 4 (1971) 123–31, esp. 124–25. Cf. Culpepper, *Anatomy*, 183.

the Word that was with God and was God (1:1-5), and later references to
"the light of the world" recall Jesus' divine origin (e.g., 3:19; 12:46). Similarly, when Jesus said, "I am the bread of life," he added that he had
"come down from heaven" and sharply distinguished himself from other
forms of bread. He reminded his listeners that their ancestors ate a bread
called manna in the wilderness and died but said that he was a kind of
bread that would provide life everlasting (6:48-51b). Supporting symbols
do not convey transcendent realities as directly as the core symbols do, but
they help to reveal the significance of the core symbols, as will be seen
later.[11] Supporting symbols also help to disclose the wider or universal
dimensions of the text. Many individuals in the Gospel, for example, speak
for groups of people and even humanity generally; they are important
representative figures.

Some of the core symbols are expressed in the form of metaphors. To
speak metaphorically is to speak of one thing in terms appropriate to
another.[12] A metaphor has two parts, both of which are sometimes present
in a single sentence. When Jesus says, "I am the bread of life," it is clear
that he is speaking (a) of himself (b) in terms of bread. In other cases, a
metaphorical statement may provide only an image without specifying
what the image refers to; the referent must be supplied from the context.
When Jesus invited people to come to him and drink, declaring, "out of
his heart shall flow rivers of living water," he spoke metaphorically, but
only by taking his statement in its larger context can readers tell that
"living water" refers to the Spirit (7:37-39).

Symbols and metaphors are not identical, but they are related on a
continuum. One difference is that metaphors are expressed verbally, while
symbols may be either verbal or nonverbal. Bread initially functions symbolically in actions like breaking five loaves, giving them to a crowd of five
thousand people, and gathering up the fragments left over. Later, bread
also functions symbolically in the metaphorical statement "I am the bread
of life" (6:11-13, 35). Another difference is that symbols, as we have defined them, involve images from the realm of sense perception, while the

11. Culpepper, *Anatomy,* 187.
12. Metaphor has been the subject of much debate. Metaphor has usually been understood as a way of speaking. See Aristotle, *Poetics* 21.7–15 1457b; *Rhetoric* 3.2.8–15 1405ab; and
a current treatment, Janet Martin Soskice, *Metaphor and Religious Language* (Oxford: Clarendon, 1985) 15–23. Emphasis has recently been given to metaphor as a way of thinking; e.g.,
Sallie McFague, *Metaphorical Theology: Models of God in Religious Language* (Philadelphia: Fortress, 1982) 31–42; Mary Gerhart and Alan Melvin Russell, *Metaphoric Process: The Creation of
Scientific and Religious Understanding* (Fort Worth: Texas Christian University Press, 1984) 95–
120. Without denying the thought process undergirding metaphor, we will focus on its verbal
expression.

elements of a metaphor may be more abstract. Statements like "I am the resurrection and the life" and "I am the way, the truth, and the life" are metaphorical in form but do not include symbols in the sense used here. Bread and water can be seen and touched, but general terms like *the resurrection* and *the way* are less tangible, and *truth* and *life* as such cannot be visualized. We will focus on images that can be perceived by the senses.[13]

If symbols consist of an image and a referent, they also need an interpreter to make the connection. All three elements must be present for an image actually to function symbolically; the symbol must mean something for someone.[14] The primary images in John's Gospel are taken from the fabric of daily life, and in most life situations they have no special meaning. A splash of cool water on our faces helps chase sleep from our eyes in the morning, and the aroma of fresh bread wafting through a bakery door sets our mouths watering, but unless we connect the water and the bread with transcendent realities, they are simply refreshing, not symbolic. In themselves water and bread are potential symbols; they "actually become symbolic when they are *seen* to point beyond themselves."[15]

A challenge for interpreters is to discern which images in John's Gospel should be understood symbolically. The text depicts the disastrous and often comic results of someone's failure to detect the figurative nature of some of Jesus' sayings. We can chuckle when Nicodemus is tripped up by the prospect of being "born" again, sputtering about the impossibility of entering his mother's womb a second time. But as we make our way through the narrative, we may find that our own footing is not so sure. We may be confident that a statement like "people loved darkness rather than light" (3:19) is symbolic, but does this mean that all references to darkness and night are symbolic? Mary Magdalene arrived at Jesus' tomb in the dark on Easter morning (20:1), and Jesus appeared to his disciples later that evening (20:19). If we discern symbolic significance in the darkness in

13. On the distinction between metaphor and symbol, see Paul Ricoeur, "Metaphor and Symbol," *Interpretation Theory: Discourse and the Surplus of Meaning* (Fort Worth: Texas Christian University Press, 1976) 45–69, esp. 63–69; Wheelwright, *Metaphor and Reality*, 92–110. Metaphor is sometimes extended to nonverbal communication, but in John's Gospel the metaphors are expressed verbally. See also the discussion in the previous note.

14. Already suggested by Augustine, *On Christian Doctrine* 2.1.1, which contains a helpful discussion of figurative speech. Cf. R. A. Markus, "Augustine on Signs," *Augustine: A Collection of Critical Essays* (ed. R. A. Markus; Garden City, N.Y.: Anchor, 1972) 61–91, esp. 74.

15. Painter, "Johannine Symbols: A Case Study in Epistemology," 33. Cf. Philip Wheelwright, "The Archetypal Symbol," *Perspectives in Literary Symbolism* (ed. J. Strelka; Yearbook of Comparative Criticism 1; University Park, Pa.: Pennsylvania State University Press, 1968) 214–43, esp. 215; Xavier Léon-Dufour, "Towards a Symbolic Reading of the Fourth Gospel," *NTS* 27 (1980–81) 439–56, esp. 440.

these passages, are we astute interpreters of the text, or have we fallen prey to mere fantasy?

As we attempt to identify symbols in John's Gospel, we will bear in mind that something can be both symbolic and historical. We can discern symbolic significance in images, events, or persons without undercutting their claims to historicity, and we can recognize that certain images, events, and people are historical without diminishing their symbolic value. Historically, it seems certain that Jesus died on a cross, yet the cross became the primary symbol for the Christian faith. Peter and Jesus' mother were people who actually lived in Palestine in the first century, yet both came to have symbolic significance for the church. Accordingly, Mary Magdalene may well have come to Jesus' tomb while it was still dark; the question we will pursue is whether darkness has symbolic significance in this context.[16]

Recognizing Johannine Symbols

The symbols that are easiest to identify are expressed in the form of metaphors. Metaphors can be recognized because an incongruity or contradiction results when a person speaks of one thing in terms of another.[17] For example, the statement "I am the bread of life" (6:35), taken at face value, means that Jesus is claiming to be a baked mixture of flour and water, which is absurd. This incongruity or absurdity at the literal level forces readers to make sense of the statement in a nonliteral way.[18] As soon as readers realize that Jesus is not claiming to be a baked mixture of flour and water, they begin asking in what sense he is analogous to bread. As the discourse proceeds, it becomes clear that Jesus is not like bread in his physical makeup but is like bread in that he sustains life. Understood on that level, the metaphor is intelligible.

When Jesus declared, "I am the bread of life," the incongruity was readily apparent within the statement itself, but sometimes the incongruity appears only when the statement is read in a broader context. For example, the statement "I am the good shepherd" (10:11) could be true in a literal sense, since some people do tend sheep for a living. But the statement appears in a passage dealing with Jesus' relationship to a group

---

16. On the connection between history and symbolism, see Sandra Schneiders, "History and Symbolism in the Fourth Gospel," 371–76; Léon-Dufour, "Towards a Symbolic Reading of the Fourth Gospel," 439; idem, "Spécificité symbolique du langage de Jean," *La communauté johannique et son histoire* (ed. J.-D. Kaestli, J.-M. Poffet, J. Zumstein; Geneva: Labor et Fides, 1990) 121–34.

17. On incongruity and the recognition of metaphor, see Paul Ricoeur, "The Metaphorical Process as Cognition, Imagination, and Feeling," *Critical Inquiry* 5 (1978) 143–59; Eva Feder Kittay, *Metaphor: Its Cognitive Force and Linguistic Structure* (Oxford: Clarendon, 1987) 40–95.

18. Ricoeur, "Metaphor and Symbol," 50.

of people, and here it would be a mistake to think that Jesus is claiming to be an expert in animal husbandry. The statement only becomes meaning- ful when understood figuratively.[19]

The characters in the Gospel story often react to the incongruous as- pect in Jesus' statements, making metaphors easier for readers to identify. A Samaritan woman found Jesus sitting alone beside a well, and he asked her for a drink. The woman demurred, but Jesus told her that if she had asked, he would have given her "living water" (4:10). The woman immedi- ately objected, since the well was deep and Jesus did not even have a bucket. Her objection in turn provided an opportunity for Jesus to elabo- rate further on the meaning of his statement. He distinguished the "living water" he was offering from ordinary well water, which quenches thirst only temporarily, and he told the woman to think of the water as a reality that springs up within a person and leads to eternal life.

The core symbols in John's Gospel are often expressed in metaphors, but the supporting symbols are not; they are often imbedded in the fabric of the narrative, making them more difficult to identify. Some supporting symbols are connected to a core symbol in the same literary context. Jesus' encounter with Nicodemus is paradigmatic in this regard. The episode begins when Nicodemus comes to Jesus "by night" (3:2), a detail that seems insignificant when taken by itself. The full symbolic force of the night emerges only later, when Jesus says, "the light has come into the world, and people loved darkness rather than light, because their deeds were evil" (3:19-21). The clear symbolic use of darkness at the end of the scene indicates that the "night" at the beginning of the scene also should be understood symbolically.

An image need not be connected with a core symbol in the same episode to function symbolically; it may acquire symbolic overtones as part of a recurring cluster of images, or motif, that is related to core symbols elsewhere in the Gospel. William Freedman has suggested that the ele- ments of a motif can be identified by their frequency and their appear- ance at unlikely points in the narrative. An effective motif also will appear at significant points in the story and will include elements that fit together in a coherent whole.[20] When attempting to identify elements that may function symbolically as part of a motif, we do well to say that some are almost certainly symbolic and that others are only possibly symbolic.

---

19. The observation that some metaphors may be true both literally and figuratively was made by Ted Cohen, "Figurative Speech and Figurative Acts," *Philosophical Perspectives on Metaphor* (ed. M. Johnson; Minneapolis: University of Minnesota Press, 1981) 184. His exam- ple is "no man is an island."

20. Freedman, "The Literary Motif," 126–28.

At the last supper, for example, Jesus gave a morsel to Judas, who immediately departed to betray Jesus; and the text says "it was night" (13:30). The image of darkness is not further developed in this episode, but darkness and night frequently played symbolic roles earlier in the Gospel, most recently in 12:46. Moreover, it would be odd to mention the night only when the betrayer goes out rather than in the description of the setting at the beginning of the episode if night has no symbolic import. Taken symbolically, the reference to night is highly effective, since it occurs precisely when Jesus' betrayal is set in motion and brings to their culmination the connections between darkness and hostility toward Jesus found earlier in the Gospel. Therefore the reference to "night" in 13:30 almost certainly functions symbolically.

More problematic is the Easter story, in which "Mary Magdalene came to the tomb early, while it was still dark, and saw that the stone had been taken away from the tomb," so she ran to tell two disciples that Jesus' body had been stolen (20:1-2). The image of darkness is not clearly developed within this scene. The episode begins with darkness and ends when Mary sees Jesus (20:18), but her "seeing" is not explicitly connected with images of light. To say that it was "dark" as well as "early" seems redundant, which could suggest that the darkness is significant; but references to darkness, which were prominent in the first half of the Gospel, are rare after the departure of the betrayer in 13:30. There is a reminder that Nicodemus had come to Jesus by night (19:39), the disciples huddle behind closed doors on Easter "evening" (20:19), and finally Peter organizes a fruitless nighttime fishing venture (21:3). Recognition of Jesus is not correlated with light in these scenes, however, apart from the mention of "morning" in 21:4. Most important, these images are not associated with sin and evil as they were earlier in the Gospel (cf. 3:19-21; 12:35; 13:30). Although the darkness surrounding Mary's visit to the tomb may reflect incomprehension, the symbolic import of the image is at most an intriguing possibility, not a certainty.

The symbolic character of actions in the Gospel can be identified in the same ways as the symbolic character of other images. Symbolic actions regularly exhibit an element of incongruity; that is, they contradict ordinary patterns of behavior. For example, people in the first century normally washed their own feet or sometimes had them washed by a slave, and the washing was done when a person entered the house. Therefore when Jesus the master began to wash the feet of his disciples during the middle of a meal, it was a clear break with social convention. Peter's objection, "Lord, do you wash my feet?" (13:6) confirms the incongruity of the action. The significance of the act is elaborated in Jesus' comments to his disciples.

The foot-washing scene contains both core and supporting symbols. The text says that Jesus "rose from supper, laid down his garments, and wrapped a towel around himself. Then he poured water into a basin, and began to wash his disciples' feet" (13:4-5). The core symbol is the act of foot washing; the main supporting symbol is the removal of Jesus' clothing. Like the foot washing itself, the removal of clothing contradicts social convention; people simply did not behave that way at meals. The Greek words used in this scene are also unusual; instead of the usual words for taking off (*ekdyein*) and putting on (*endyein*) clothing, the text says that Jesus "laid down" (*tithenai*, 13:4) and "took up" (*lambanein*, 13:12) his garments, using verbs found elsewhere for laying down and taking up his life (10:17-18). By removing his clothing, therefore, Jesus supports and heightens the sense of scandalous self-giving conveyed by the foot washing and anticipates his final act of self-giving in death by crucifixion.

The accounts of the miraculous signs in the Gospel also provide clues to the symbolic character of these actions. Like nonmiraculous symbolic actions, the signs do not fit within normal patterns of behavior. If a wedding guest surprised his host with a gift of 120 to 180 gallons of wine, for example, the gesture would have been unusual. But when Jesus transformed that much water into wine at a wedding, the action was extraordinary. The significance of the act is introduced by a conversation in which Jesus' mother comments that the wine has run out and Jesus brusquely replies that his "hour" has not yet come (2:3-4). As the narrative unfolds it becomes clear that the "hour" is the hour of Jesus' death. The meaning is further elaborated in a concluding comment, which says that the miracle of the wine manifested Jesus' "glory," a term referring to the power and presence of God (2:11).

The primary symbol in this episode is the transformation of water into wine, and the supporting symbols are the stone jars that held the water. The text states that the jars were "for the Jewish rites of purification" (2:6). If the statement is given full weight and the jars are understood to represent Jewish rituals, then the transformation of water into wine signals the beginning of a new order, which will transform and replace Jewish practices. The likelihood that the jars do play a representative role in the Cana story (2:1-12) increases when it is read together with the account of temple cleansing that follows (2:13-22), since the temple cleansing anticipates the replacement of the Jerusalem temple by the crucified and risen "temple" of Jesus' body. Understanding the jars as representative of Jewish rituals is also congruent with subsequent portions of the narrative where Jesus uses images from Jewish festival practices to convey something about himself and his mission.

Persons in the Gospel also can function symbolically, often in a complex way. A character's symbolic role is sometimes signaled by using plural forms of speech for individuals, which introduces an element of incongruity into the narrative. The encounter between Jesus and Nicodemus is, again, paradigmatic. Jesus and Nicodemus appear to be alone in this scene; no one else speaks or is said to be present. Jesus begins speaking to Nicodemus in the first person singular but suddenly shifts to the first person plural in the middle of the conversation, saying, "Truly, truly, I say to you, *we* speak of what *we* know, and bear witness to what *we* have seen" (3:11). The abrupt change to "we" suggests that Jesus now speaks both for himself and his followers, as he does elsewhere (9:4), since his followers will continue to bear witness to him after his ministry on earth has ended. As the narrative unfolds, a second dimension emerges: Jesus speaks not only for his followers, he speaks for God. Jesus has come from above and "utters the words of God" (3:32-34). The remainder of the Gospel unpacks what it means for Jesus to be God's unique representative, the one in whom God's Word is embodied (cf. 1:14).

Nicodemus plays an important supporting role in the text. Although he appears to be alone, he speaks in the plural: "Rabbi, *we* know that you are a teacher come from God" (3:2). Jesus initially responds to him with singular forms of address but shifts to the Greek plural in the middle of the conversation, saying, "*you people* do not receive our testimony"; although "I have told *you people* earthly things," "*you people* do not believe" (3:11-12). Nicodemus's representative role is complex, like that of Jesus. He is first "a man of the Pharisees" and "a ruler of the Jews" (3:1), thus representing the Jewish authorities who regularly refuse to believe in Jesus elsewhere in the Gospel. Second, he speaks for people who believed when they saw the miraculous signs Jesus did, but whose faith was untrustworthy (2:23-25; 3:2). As a representative of both groups, Nicodemus stands over against the true believers for whom Jesus speaks in 3:11. The scope of Jesus' words continues to widen, however, so that by the end of the discourse he speaks of the entire world as a realm of darkness estranged from God. Thus it finally appears that Nicodemus, who had come "by night," represents a benighted world, squinting with incomprehension at the light of God that has appeared in Jesus.

The Structure
of Johannine Symbolism

As the narrative unfolds, the particular images, actions, and characters vary, but certain patterns remain constant. Wayne Meeks, drawing on the work of Edmund Leach, compared the recurring patterns in John's Gospel to a technique used in electronic communications. Sometimes a communicator must try to convey a message despite persistent static on the airwaves. In such cases, the message is repeated often, in as many different ways as possible. "From the repeated impact of varying signals, the basic *structure* which they have in common gets through."[21] Similarly, interpreters of the Fourth Gospel must pay attention to the underlying structure of its symbolic system in order to discover what the author is trying to convey. The Gospel says that Jesus has come from above to declare to the world what he has heard from God, but the cleft separating the human from the divine creates interference in the channels of communication. Nevertheless, repetition of a similar idea in differing forms ensures that the basic message will get through.

The fundamental structure of Johannine symbolism is twofold. The primary level of meaning concerns Christ; the secondary level concerns discipleship. The movement from Christology to discipleship is apparent in symbolic images and actions throughout the Gospel. The clearest examples are the "I am" sayings of Jesus. The first half of John 6:35 reads, "I am the bread of life," which makes a statement about Jesus. The second half reads, "He who comes to me shall not hunger and he who believes in me shall never thirst," which says something about the believer. Similarly, 8:12 begins, "I am the light of the world," which is a christological statement, and continues, "he who follows me will not walk in darkness, but will have the light of life," which says something about Jesus' followers. Other examples of the movement from Christology to discipleship are: "I am the door—if anyone enters by me he will be saved" (10:9); "I am the good shepherd; I know my own—and my own know me" (10:14); "I am the vine—you are the branches" (15:5). In each case the image itself refers to Jesus, and a particular aspect or effect of the image is applied to his followers.

Elsewhere the image itself is applied first to Jesus and second to the disciples. In 12:24 Jesus says, "Unless a seed falls into the earth and dies, it remains alone, but if it dies it bears much fruit." The primary level of meaning is christological. The preceding verse announced that the hour of Jesus' glorification had come, and the image of the seed helps readers understand that Jesus' ministry will come to fruition only through his death (12:23). On a secondary level, the image of the seed refers to Christian life, introducing sayings about the need to die to the self through service to Christ, which blossoms into life everlasting (12:25-26). Here the same image—the seed—says something first about Christ and second about Christians.

---

21. "The Man from Heaven in Johannine Sectarianism," 48. Discerning the structure of symbols from a history-of-religions perspective has been a significant part of the work of Mircea Eliade. See his "Methodological Remarks on the Study of Religious Symbolism," *The History of Religions: Essays in Methodology* (ed. M. Eliade and J. M. Kitagawa; Chicago: University of Chicago Press, 1959) 86–107.

This twofold pattern can help to clarify the meaning of Jesus' confusing comment, "out of his heart shall flow rivers of living water," in which water refers to the Spirit (7:37-39). The passage is perplexing because it can be punctuated in two different ways. According to one version, the water or Spirit flows from Jesus' heart; according to the other version, it flows from the believer's heart.[22] The apparent ambiguity, however, is another instance where the same image has a primary and a secondary level of meaning.[23] On the primary level the text refers to Jesus. He is the source of the living water promised to the Samaritan woman (4:10); water will flow from his side as he hangs on the cross (19:34); and on Easter he will be the one to infuse the disciples with the Spirit signified by water (20:22). On a secondary level the text refers to the disciples. Those who receive the Spirit or "drink" from Jesus will have the Spirit's living water well up out of their own hearts, as Jesus promised the Samaritan woman (4:14).

The same movement from Christology to discipleship appears in the symbolic actions. The account of Jesus washing his disciples' feet includes two interpretations of the action. The first is christological and foreshadows the salvific character of Jesus' death. Jesus tells Peter, "If I do not wash you, you have no part in me," adding that this "washing" provides a complete cleansing (13:8, 10). The second interpretation presents the foot washing as a model of discipleship. Jesus says, "If I then, your Lord and Teacher, have washed your feet, you also ought to wash one another's feet. For I have given you an example, that you also should do as I have done to you" (13:14). The movement from Christology to discipleship in this text reflects the same symbolic structure found throughout the Gospel.[24]

The miraculous signs follow a similar pattern. Perhaps the clearest example is the story of the blind beggar in John 9. The episode begins when Jesus smears mud on the man's eyes and tells him to wash in the pool of Siloam. The man does so and is healed. On a primary level the miracle is christological; by enlightening the eyes of a man blind from birth, Jesus demonstrates that he is truly "the light of the world" (9:5). On a secondary

22. The RSV of 7:37b-38 reads, "If anyone thirst, let him come to me and drink. He who believes in me, as the scripture has said, 'Out of his heart shall flow rivers of living water.'" Here the Scripture quotation applies to the believer. According to the alternative given in the footnote, the text reads, "If anyone thirst let him come to me, and let him who believes in me drink. As the scripture has said, 'Out of his heart shall flow rivers of living water.'" Here the Scripture applies to Jesus. The NRSV reads, "Out of the believer's heart shall flow rivers of living water," which obscures the christological dimension of the text.

23. Edwyn Clement Hoskyns, *The Fourth Gospel* (ed. F. N. Davey; 2d ed.; London: Faber, 1947) 320–22.

24. Many interpreters have concluded that each interpretation of the foot washing reflects a different redactional level. See the discussion in Brown, *Gospel*, 2.559–62. Nevertheless, the movement from Christology to discipleship is consonant with the rest of the Gospel.

level the passage is about discipleship. Much of the chapter explores what it means to "see the light," both physically and through the eyes of faith. The haze begins to lift when the beggar's eyes are healed, and it continues to dissipate as he perceives and testifies that Jesus is a prophet, who is from God, finally worshiping Jesus as the Son of man (9:17, 33, 38).[25]

Each symbolic image and action has distinctive facets of meaning, and attention to the unique connotations of each image will be vital for interpretation. Nevertheless, by concentrating the primary meaning of each image on Jesus and the secondary dimension on his followers, the Gospel repeatedly compels readers to come to terms with the reality of God in the person of Jesus and to understand the meaning of their own lives in relation to him.

JOHANNINE SYMBOLISM IN ITS CULTURAL CONTEXT

The symbols in John's Gospel are conveyed in language that was an integral part of a cultural context, and understanding the symbolism means entering into that context. The evangelist wrote the Gospel in Greek for a Greek-speaking audience, assuming that those who saw the letters on the page or heard the words spoken aloud could connect them with known realities. As words are read or heard by someone who knows the language, they evoke certain associations in the reader or hearer. The text can, of course, be translated into other languages, but in this process the connotations of words and expressions inevitably change, and we do well to identify the range of meanings associated with the Greek expressions used in the text. For the earliest readers, these associations would have come from the broad cultural matrix of the Greco-Roman world and their more particular ethnic and religious heritage, as well as from other portions of the Gospel. As various associations come to mind, readers must discern which seem appropriate to the literary context and which do not. There is an interplay between text and reader as the associations evoked by the text simultaneously inform the reader's understanding of the passage and are adjusted to fit the literary context.[26]

---

25. John 9 is widely recognized as a two-level drama, which on one level recounts an incident from the ministry of Jesus, but on another level tells the story of the later church. See Martyn, *History and Theology*, 30.

26. The cultural context of Johannine symbols was stressed by Dodd, *Interpretation*, 137. Cf. G. B. Caird, *The Language and Imagery of the Bible* (London: Duckworth, 1980) 50. On the process of reading and its relationship to a cultural context, see recently Bruce J. Malina, "Reading Theory Perspective: Reading Luke-Acts," *The Social World of Luke-Acts: Models for Interpretation* (ed. J. H. Neyrey; Peabody, Mass.: Hendrickson, 1991) 3–23.

The Dynamics
of Johannine Symbolism

The importance of the cultural context can be illustrated by considering one of the Gospel's leading images. In John 10:11, Jesus is identified by the Greek word *poimēn*. The evangelist assumed that readers would understand that this combination of letters referred to someone who tended sheep, a person English speakers would call a shepherd. For those who knew Greek, the word *poimēn* would have evoked a cluster of associations from several sources. First, the broadest level was life experience. A shepherd was a common sight throughout the Greek-speaking world in the first century. The word might prompt readers to think of a figure with a weather-beaten face, dressed in coarse homespun clothing, with a wooden staff in one hand as he led a flock of sheep or goats out to pasture.

Second, associations might come from a reader's particular ethnic and religious heritage. According to the Jewish Scriptures, some of the leading figures in Israel's history had been shepherds. God appeared to Moses while he was tending sheep (Exod. 3:1-6), and David learned the art of war by defending his flocks against predators (1 Sam. 17:34-35). The term *poimēn* was used also metaphorically for Israel's leaders, a future Davidic king, and even for God in both biblical and extrabiblical Jewish writings.[27] The Greek classics, which were the mainstay of education throughout the Greco-Roman world, used shepherd as a metaphor for leaders like Agamemnon the king. Philosophers and orators often compared the art of governing a people to the art of shepherding a flock.[28]

Third, the Gospel itself establishes a certain cluster of associations around the word *poimēn*. Each time the image reappears it evokes and develops the associations found elsewhere in the narrative. John 10:1-5 introduces the image of the shepherd by describing how a shepherd enters the sheepfold, calls the sheep by name, and leads them out to pasture. In 10:7-18 Jesus identifies himself as the good shepherd, who lays down his life for his sheep. In 10:22-30 he adds that no one will snatch the sheep out of his hand. At the conclusion of the Gospel, Jesus enjoins Peter to "feed my lambs. . . . Tend my sheep. . . . Feed my sheep" (21:15-17). The emphatic use of shepherd imagery suggests that Peter's task must be

27. *Shepherd* is used for leaders in Jer. 23:1-4; Ezek. 34:1-6; for a future Davidic king in 34:23; and for God in 34:11; cf. Ps. 23:1. Shepherding is connected with teaching in *2 Bar.* 77:13-17, leadership in Jth. 11:19 and 4 Ezra 5:18, the Davidic messiah in *Pss. Sol.* 17:40; and with Moses' role as a leader in *Bib. Ant.* 19:3; Philo's *Life of Moses* 1.60–62; *Mekilta* "Beshallah" 7.125 (Lauterbach ed., vol. 1, p. 252).

28. E.g., Homer, *Iliad* 2.243, 254; Plato, *Republic* 345c–e; Epictetus, *Discourses* 3.22.35. See Erwin R. Goodenough, "The Political Philosophy of Hellenistic Kingship," *Yale Classical Studies* (ed. A. M. Hermon; New Haven, Conn.: Yale University Press, 1928) 1.55–102, esp. 60–62, 84.

understood in light of what Jesus said earlier in the Gospel about what it means to be a shepherd. Jesus makes a prophetic statement that reinforces the connection by anticipating that Peter, like Jesus the good shepherd, would lay down his life (21:18-19).

Thus far we have considered what the word *poimēn* might mean on the cognitive level, but symbols also evoke associations on the affective level.[29] For some people, especially in the western part of the Greco-Roman world, the image of a shepherd awakened nostalgia for the idyllic life of the shepherds who "lie there at ease under the awning of a spreading beech and practise country songs on a light shepherd's pipe."[30] For others, shepherds aroused suspicion, since they were often perceived as rough, unscrupulous characters, who pastured their animals on other people's land and pilfered wool, milk, and kids from the flock.[31] On the affective level, therefore, shepherding initially might attract or repel, or convey a sense of peace or uneasiness, depending on the reader's background.

The Gospel text appropriates and transforms both the affective and cognitive associations readers might bring to the text. At the affective level, the text softens the suspicion often leveled at shepherds by acknowledging that those who came before Jesus were indeed "thieves and robbers" (10:8) but Jesus himself is the good shepherd. The title "good shepherd," in turn, evokes the more positive attitudes toward shepherding, but the context tempers sentimentality by presenting a pastoral landscape that echoes with the cry of a wolf, not the gentle airs of a shepherd's flute. At the cognitive level, readers must discern what Jesus means when he says, "I am the good shepherd." If the context makes clear that Jesus is not claiming expertise in animal husbandry, the common use of the term *shepherd* for a leader, together with the references to the shepherd leading the sheep in John 10:3-4, suggests that he is claiming a special leadership role. The literary context then transforms the usual understanding of the shepherd metaphor by connecting it with Jesus' crucifixion. Responsible leaders, like good shepherds, were expected to seek the welfare of the sheep and even risk their lives for the flock, but only Jesus, *the* good shepherd, would lay down his life for the sheep. Similar types of interaction between the text and readers occur with other symbolic images and actions.

29. Fawcett, *The Symbolic Language of Religion*, 34; Hinderer, "Theory, Conception, and Interpretation of the Symbol," 97; Caird, *The Language and Imagery of the Bible*, 17; Ricoeur, "The Metaphorical Process as Cognition, Imagination, and Feeling," 155–59.

30. Virgil, *Eclogues* 1.1–5. Cf. the texts in J. M. Edmonds, *The Greek Bucolic Poets* (LCL; London: Heinemann; New York: Putnam, 1923).

31. See Joachim Jeremias, *Jerusalem in the Time of Jesus: An Investigation into Economic and Social Conditions during the New Testament Period* (Philadelphia: Fortress, 1969) 305, and *"poimēn, ktl.,"* *TDNT* 6.488–89; Ramsey MacMullen, *Roman Social Relations 50 B.C. to A.D. 284* (New Haven, Conn., and London: Yale University Press, 1974) 1–4.

The Spectrum
of Johannine Readers

Modern readers of the Gospel must rely on ancient texts to provide a window into the setting in which the Gospel was composed and first read. The problem is that the Greek-speaking world of the late first century included many different kinds of potential readers for the Fourth Gospel. Johannine imagery has affinities with imagery in an astonishing range of ancient sources, including the Dead Sea Scrolls and Hellenistic Jewish texts, Greco-Roman sources, and later gnostic writings.[32] We can focus our interpretive work by turning to the immediate audience for whom the Gospel was composed: the community of Johannine Christians. We will explore the social function of the Gospel's symbols in our final chapter, here attempting only to make a preliminary identification of the cultural backgrounds of the people who were part of the Johannine community at the time the Gospel was completed. This can help us discern what sorts of associations they would have brought to their reading of the text and how the text would have appropriated and transformed these associations.

Some have argued that Johannine Christians lived within a kind of introverted community and that the Fourth Gospel is a "closed system of metaphors" whose meaning is clear to insiders but opaque to the uninitiated. The Gospel's language has been called an "enchanting barrier" that "advertises a treasure within and yet seems designed to make the treasure all but inaccessible" to newcomers.[33] We will seek to show the opposite, arguing that the final form of the Gospel presupposes a *spectrum* of readers who came from various backgrounds and approached the text from somewhat different points of view. The Gospel would have been accessible to the less-informed readers yet sophisticated enough to engage those who were better informed.

There are two types of reasons for thinking that the final form of John's Gospel presupposes a spectrum of readers. First, literary studies have pointed out that some portions of the Gospel assume that readers are well informed about Jewish festivals like Passover and the feast of Booths, and that they can follow intricate debates based on the Scriptures and Jewish traditions. Yet other passages assume that some readers are not so well informed, patiently interpreting the meaning of words like *rabbi* and *messiah* (1:38, 41) and explaining that Jews used stone jars for purification

32. See George W. MacRae, "The Fourth Gospel and *Religionsgeschichte*," *CBQ* 32 (1970) 13–24, esp. 14–15.
33. See Meeks, "The Man from Heaven in Johannine Sectarianism," 68; Rensberger, *Johannine Faith,* 137. Norman Petersen refers to Johannine language as "an anti-language" that is "the language of an anti-society" (*The Gospel of John and the Sociology of Light: Language and Characterization in the Fourth Gospel* [Valley Forge, Pa.: Trinity, 1993] 19).

rituals and did not associate with Samaritans (2:6; 4:9b). The tension between passages presupposing a highly informed readership and those addressed to a less-informed readership suggests that the audience of the completed Gospel included various types of people.[34] Second, historical studies have shown that the Gospel and the community in which it was composed developed over a period of time. Although the literary history of the text and the social history of the community cannot be reconstructed with certainty at each juncture, it seems probable that the final form of the Gospel engaged Christians of different backgrounds: Jewish, Samaritan, and Greek.[35]

Jewish Christians almost certainly were at the center of the audience for which John's Gospel was written. The opening scenes present Jesus as a rabbi and as the Messiah or "Christ" foretold in the Jewish Scriptures. The titles Son of God and King of Israel, which appear on the lips of Nathanael, also recall Jewish tradition (1:35-51). Jesus continues to be called a rabbi throughout the Gospel, suggesting that the title would have been significant for readers, and the evangelist regularly uses "the Christ" as a Jewish messianic expression rather than making "Christ" a part of Jesus' name. The central portion of the Gospel explicates Jesus' identity in terms of the Jewish festivals of the Sabbath, Passover, Booths, and Dedication or Hanukkah (John 5–10), and the major symbols in these chapters—bread, water, and light—are closely connected with their use in Jewish rituals at these festivals.

The central conflict in the Gospel involves the Jewish authorities on one side and Jesus and his followers on the other. Especially significant is the story of the man born blind, who was repeatedly questioned concerning Jesus by some of the Jewish leaders and eventually expelled from the local synagogue (9:22). Conflict with the synagogue and fear of expulsion was apparently a factor in the context in which the Gospel was written, because in the evangelist's summary comments on Jesus' public ministry he cited fear of being put out of the synagogue as one of the chief reasons people refused to confess their Christian faith (12:42). Moreover, the farewell discourses explicitly forewarned that Christians would continue to

---

34. Culpepper, *Anatomy*, 221, 225.

35. The sketch of Johannine Christianity presented here closely follows that formulated by Brown, *Community*, 25–58. Cf. Schnackenburg, *Gospel*, 3.203–17; John Painter, "The Farewell Discourses and the History of Johannine Christianity," *NTS* 27 (1980–81) 525–43, esp. 525. The centrality of Jewish Christians, with some Samaritans at a later stage, is also advocated by J. Louis Martyn, although he does not agree that Greeks were a factor in the community for which the Gospel was written (*Gospel of John*, 90–121). Martyn is followed by Wayne Meeks, "Breaking Away: Three New Testament Pictures of Christianity's Separation from the Jewish Communities," *"To See Ourselves as Others See Us": Christians, Jews, "Others" in Late Antiquity* (ed. J. Neusner and E. S. Frerichs; Chico, Calif.: Scholars, 1985) 93–115, esp. 94–105; cf. Ashton, *Understanding*, 166–74.

face the threat of expulsion after Jesus had returned to the Father (16:2), which suggests that the experience of Jewish Christians in the postresurrection period was similar to the experience of the man born blind.

The readers of the Gospel who came into the Christian community from the synagogue would have been a part of the broad section of the Jewish population that was influenced by the teachings of the Pharisees and the rabbis without actually belonging to a Jewish party. Although affinities exist between John's Gospel and some of the Dead Sea texts—such as the dualistic use of light and darkness—the Gospel does not allude to any teachings peculiar to the Dead Sea sect, and there is little reason to think that the Johannine community included members from this group. Moreover, Jesus is pictured as teaching "in synagogues and in the temple, where all Jews come together" (18:20), and some of the symbols assume that many of the readers would have been familiar with temple ritual; but the members of the Dead Sea sect did not gather in synagogues used by other Jews and actually boycotted the Jerusalem temple. John's Gospel, unlike the other Gospels, never mentions the Sadducees or any of their distinctive teachings but simply assumes the importance of the prophetic writings and Psalms and belief in resurrection, which the Sadducees did not acknowledge. We will therefore look for texts that reflect views that were commonly held among Jewish people in the first century and were not limited to one Jewish party.

Moving outward from this Jewish Christian nucleus, there appear to have been a number of Samaritan Christians within the Johannine circle. According to John 4, a village of Samaritans was converted through the witness of a woman who had spoken to Jesus beside Jacob's well, bringing them to meet Jesus for themselves. This remarkable episode contains an interlude intimating that Jesus' ministry in Samaria actually presaged the future missionary activity of the disciples in the region. Although the disciples played no role in bringing the Samaritan villagers to faith, Jesus spoke as if they had already engaged in successful missionary activity. He said, "I sent you to reap that for which you did not labor; others have labored, and you have entered into their labor" (4:38).[36]

Evidence outside the Fourth Gospel says that Jesus either avoided Samaria or was unwelcome there during his lifetime, but that after the resurrection Christians did engage in missionary activity in Samaria with some success (Acts 8:4-25).[37] The detailed knowledge of Samaritan topog-

36. On the interpretation of this verse see Teresa Okure, *The Johannine Approach to Mission: A Contextual Study of John 4:1-42* (WUNT 31; Tübingen: Mohr/Siebeck, 1988) 160.
37. On Jesus and his disciples avoiding Samaria, see Matt. 10:5; Luke 9:52-53; 17:11. A more positive view of the Samaritans is reflected in Luke 10:33; 17:11-19.

raphy apparent in the Fourth Gospel suggests that Johannine Christians actually were active in Samaria at some point. The narrative refers to the obscure village of Sychar and rightly assumes that Jacob's well was located by a road that skirted grain fields and that it was within eyesight of "this mountain," Mount Gerizim, where the Samaritans worshiped (John 4:20, 35). The Gospel also mentions the area of Aenon near the village of Salim (3:23) and a town called Ephraim (11:54), both of which were probably in the region of Samaria. There are few extant Samaritan sources from this period; apart from the Samaritan version of the Pentateuch, the Samaritan texts we have are from the fourth century and later. We will attempt to make cautious use of these texts, however, together with other sources that mention Samaritan beliefs in order to explore how the Gospel's symbolism would have been perceived by Samaritan Christians.

At the horizon of the Gospel are the Greeks, who appear at the culmination of the Johannine account of Jesus' public ministry. As Jesus approached Jerusalem on a donkey with the crowds waving palms around him, the Pharisees lamented, "You see that you can do nothing; look, the world has gone after him." The evangelist immediately commented that "among those who went up to worship at the feast were some Greeks" (12:19-20). Since these Greeks came to Jerusalem for the festival, some interpreters have identified them as proselytes; yet there are good reasons to think that they represent gentile interest in Jesus. The use of the term *Greeks,* which regularly designated non-Jews in sources of this period, and their arrival at precisely the moment when the whole "world" was going after Jesus, indicate that they should be understood to be people who were not of Jewish background, even though they had come to Jerusalem for the festival.[38]

Significantly, these Greeks, unlike the Jewish people mentioned earlier in the narrative, did not actually get to see Jesus. Instead, they approached Philip, the disciple who bore the name of Alexander the Great's father and came from Bethsaida on the boundary between Galilee and the surrounding regions (12:21-22). Philip conveyed their request to Jesus, who announced that the arrival of the Greeks signaled the hour of his glorification, when he would be lifted up in death to draw "all people" to himself (12:23, 32-33). The sign above the cross proclaimed Jesus' kingship in

---

38. See further H. B. Kossen, "Who Were the Greeks of John XII 20?" *Studies in John Presented to Professor Dr. J. N. Sevenster on the Occasion of His Seventieth Birthday* (NovTSup 24; Leiden: Brill, 1970) 97–110; Johannes Beutler, "Greeks Come to See Jesus (John 12,20f)," *Bib* 71 (1990) 333–47; Brown, *Community,* 55–58. The presence of a significant gentile Greek component in Johannine Christianity is disputed by Martyn because there seems to be no trace in the Gospel of conflict over their inclusion in the community (*Gospel of John,* 120). This issue will be taken up in chapter 7.

Greek and Latin as well as Hebrew (19:20), reaffirming the significance of his death for both Jews and Gentiles. Although the Greeks who appeared in chapter 12 did not get to see Jesus before he was lifted up, the text looks beyond Jesus' death and resurrection to the time when Greeks would be drawn to Jesus through the work of disciples like Philip, whom Jesus would send into the world as he himself had been sent by God into the world (17:18-21).

Other sources confirm that the proclamation of the gospel to the Greeks was not a feature of Jesus' ministry but was an important facet of early Christian missionary work. Some years after Jesus' resurrection, the Christian message was extended to the Greeks at Antioch (Acts 11:20-21), and congregations that included Greeks were gradually formed at many places in the Mediterranean world. An apparent allusion to this missionary activity among the Greeks is found in John 7:35, where the Jewish leaders, who were puzzled by Jesus' remarks about going to the one who sent him, asked, "Surely he doesn't intend to go to the Dispersion among the Greeks and teach the Greeks does he?" Their question refers to the dispersion of Jews living outside Palestine in regions where most of the population would be considered Greek, which would include the area from Macedonia and Greece through Asia Minor and into Syria (cf. Mark 7:26). Grammatically, the Pharisees' question expects a negative answer, which would be correct in a sense, since Jesus was not speaking about a trip around the eastern Mediterranean but of his return to God. Yet in another sense their question actually demands a positive answer, since after Jesus returned to God he would "teach the Greeks" through the work of his disciples.

The Greeks in the audience envisioned by the evangelist cannot be firmly identified with a distinctive philosophical school or religious group. The Gospel's references to *logos,* freedom, and friendship, for example, have affinities with Stoic and Platonic teachings, but all of these concepts had fairly wide currency and none was limited to one philosophical school. Significantly, many aspects of the Gospel show a broad familiarity with Greco-Roman culture. The evangelist divided scenes, portrayed characters, and used dramatic irony in ways similar to the Greek tragedians and followed Greco-Roman rhetorical patterns in some of the discourses. By relating the Gospel's symbolism to what was commonplace in the Greco-Roman world, we may discern some of the connotations that would have been perceived by the Greeks, as well by Jewish and Samaritan Christians within the Johannine community, who shared this same broad cultural context. Although images like those in John's Gospel sometimes appear in later gnostic sources, these comparisons are useful mainly as a way of observing how the Gospel could be read and appropriated from a gnostic perspective.[39]

Christian sources other than the Fourth Gospel may offer additional information about the perspective of the evangelist and his readers. Comments at the end of the Gospel and its epilogue indicate that the author or authors knew more about Jesus than they recorded (20:30), and the narrative itself seems to assume that readers would know about at least some aspects of Jesus' ministry before reading the text. For example, readers were apparently expected to know about Jesus' death and resurrection, the imprisonment of John the Baptist, the prominence of the twelve disciples, and Mary's anointing of Jesus' feet.[40] The practice of baptism was well known to the readers (3:22), although it is not clear that they were equally familiar with the celebration of the Lord's Supper. Possible allusions to the sacraments will be considered when discussing specific passages; a summary is included in the postscript after chapter 7.

The fourth evangelist wrote independently of the other New Testament Gospels. While it is possible that he and his readers were familiar with other "books" about Jesus (21:25), we cannot assume that they knew one or more of the other extant Gospels.[41] We will use various writings to try to discern common early Christian perspectives that can elucidate the meaning of some of John's symbols, but we will not try to establish a direct connection between these texts and the Fourth Gospel. The Johannine Epistles constitute a special case. They were almost certainly composed within the same Christian community as the Gospel, probably sometime after the Gospel was completed.[42] Although the outlook of the epistles is not identical with that of the Gospel, the many similarities in language

---

39. The view that the Gospel's relationship to Gnosticism is basic for interpretation has been stressed in various ways by Bultmann (*Gospel*, 7–9), Luise Schottroff (*Der Glaubende und die feindliche Welt: Beobachtungen zum gnostischen Dualismus und seiner Bedeutung für Paulus und das Johannesevangelium* [WMANT 37; Neukirchen-Vluyn: Neukirchener, 1970]), Helmut Koester (*Ancient Christian Gospels: Their History and Development* [London: SCM; Philadelphia: Trinity, 1990] 244–71) and others. On the problems with gnostic comparisons see Brown, *Gospel*, 1.LII–LVI; Meeks, *Prophet-King*, 258–85. On the value of gnostic comparisons mainly for understanding the Gospel's role in the second century and later periods, see Brown, *Community*, 147–55; D. Moody Smith, *Johannine Christianity: Essays on Its Setting, Sources, and Theology* (Columbia: University of South Carolina Press, 1984) 24–25.

40. Culpepper, *Anatomy*, 211–23.

41. See the thorough survey of the discussion by D. Moody Smith, *John among the Gospels: The Relationship in Twentieth-Century Research* (Minneapolis: Fortress, 1991).

42. Most interpreters now consider the Gospel to have been written before the epistles. See the summary of the discussion in Brown, *Epistles*, 14–35. Judith Lieu has more recently cautioned against positing a direct dependence of the epistles upon the Gospel (*The Second and Third Epistles of John*, 166–216). A recent study positing the priority of the epistles is Charles H. Talbert, *Reading John: A Literary and Theological Commentary on the Fourth Gospel and Johannine Epistles* (New York: Crossroad, 1992).

make them helpful for comparison when exploring the connotations of Johannine imagery.

The present form of the Fourth Gospel envisions a spectrum of readers, and we must do the same in our interpretive work. We will ask how familiarity with Jewish traditions can inform the interpretation of the Gospel's symbolism, but we will also consider how readers approaching the text from a Samaritan or Greek perspective would discern the meaning of the symbols. This approach focuses our work without finally delimiting it. By asking how the Gospel could communicate with this spectrum of readers, we may better discern how it can continue to engage others along the reading spectrum, including the most diverse audience of all: those who read the Fourth Gospel today.

INTERPRETING JOHANNINE SYMBOLISM

A genuine symbol does not conceal a message that "only needs to be unmasked for the images in which it is clothed to become useless," as Paul Ricoeur observed.[43] The images stimulate and direct an ongoing process of reflection, rather than giving an answer that obviates the need for further thought. The "symbol gives; but what it gives is an occasion for thought, something to think about."[44] The expansive, multifaceted character of Johannine symbols and their ability to evoke responses from a wide range of readers present special problems for interpretation. The symbols can speak to people on both cognitive and affective levels; but even at the cognitive level, where we will focus our attention, they often mean several things at once. The phenomenon of multiple meanings, sometimes called polyvalence or plurisignation, distinguishes the symbols in John's Gospel from symbols like those used on a map, which must have a single well-defined meaning to be effective. A map will contain a key that explains that one image stands for a school building and another for a post office; but in John's Gospel images like light, water, and the miraculous signs can signify several things simultaneously.

Interpreting Johannine Symbols

Interpreting a Johannine symbol involves identifying and explicating the various dimensions of meaning conveyed by the image.[45] The Gospel nar-

---

43. *The Symbolism of Evil* (Religious Perspectives 17; New York: Harper & Row, 1967) 348. Paul Diel, in contrast, insists that symbolic and mythical language has a precise vocabulary and grammar, which he attempts to "decipher" in his studies of symbolism. See his *Symbolism in the Bible*, x, 54–55, 91, 136.

44. Ricoeur, *The Symbolism of Evil*, 348. Cf. Hinderer, "Theory, Conception, and Interpretation of the Symbol," 91–98.

45. Hinderer, "Theory, Conception, and Interpretation of the Symbol," 98.

rative itself is the best guide to doing this. The story of the blind beggar, for example, traces how the man came to understand what it meant for Jesus to heal him. At first he simply said that the "man called Jesus" had performed the healing (9:11). Later he concluded that Jesus was a prophet (9:17) who had come from God (9:33), and finally he worshiped Jesus as the divine Son of man (9:35-38). It is especially important to note that all of these statements are true and that no single statement captures the full significance of the event. To say the event showed only that Jesus was a man, only that he was a prophet, or only that he was worthy of worship would distort the meaning. There is a progression from the lower to the higher aspects of Jesus' identity, but this is not a movement from false-hood into truth. The Johannine perspective is paradoxical. Each of the beggar's statements revealed a new facet of meaning without negating what he had said before. If the disclosure of Jesus' divinity at the end of the episode moves beyond traditional understandings of messiahship, the earlier affirmations of his identity as a man, a prophet, and Messiah main-tain his ties to humanity and to the particular traditions of Israel (see pp. 39–44).[46]

Interpretation of the symbolism also entails recognizing false under-standings of an image or action. Symbols can mean a number of things, but they do not mean just anything, and the literary context of an image or action can help us identify interpretations that are simply wrong. As the man born blind progressively unpacked the meaning of his healing, the Jewish authorities voiced their own erroneous understanding of the event. Jesus had healed the man on the Sabbath, and Jewish law forbade making clay or performing cures on the Sabbath unless an illness was life threat-ening, which was not the case with congenital blindness. Accordingly, some of the authorities maintained that Jesus was not from God, for he did not keep the Sabbath (9:16), and they concluded that the sign proved Jesus was a sinner (9:24). With touches of humor the evangelist makes clear that these interpretations are absurd and stem from ignorance, not insight.

The lines between true and false interpretations of an image or action are not always sharply defined, however, which complicates the interpre-tive task. Philip Wheelwright has observed that many symbols have "a bright focussed center of meaning together with a penumbra of vagueness that is intrinsically ineradicable; which is to say, the vagueness could not be dispelled without distorting the original meaning."[47] Often the ambigu-

---

46. While focusing on cosmology, Adele Reinhartz notes the value in exploring connec-tions between the historical, ecclesiological, and cosmological levels of meaning in *The Word in the World: The Cosmological Tale in the Fourth Gospel* (SBLMS 45; Atlanta: Scholars, 1992) 1–6, 99–100.

47. "The Archetypal Symbol," 220.

ity is created by the plethora of associations an image or action evokes. The associations may come from other portions of the narrative, from the reader's particular cultural background, or from the broad field of life experience. Some of these associations will seem appropriate in the literary context, others will appear inappropriate, and still others will be indeterminate, not clearly to be included or excluded. Their influence may be felt rather than seen; they whisper instead of speaking.

Interpretation begins at the "bright focussed center of meaning" and moves outward into the "penumbra of vagueness." Interpreters must distinguish the aspects of meaning that seem certain from those that seem probable and from those that are simply intriguing possibilities. Aspects of meaning can be considered certain when they are made explicit in the immediate literary context. The probable elements of meaning appear when an image or action can readily be connected with other parts of the Gospel or read in the light of material that seems to be presupposed by the text. The intriguing possibilities emerge when connections with other portions of the text seem more distant or the image or action is considered in terms of associations that were commonplace in the Greek-speaking world in which the Gospel was composed.

Consider the bread of life discourse (6:25-59) as an example of how this works. (a) The literary context explicitly connects bread with life, so that when Jesus calls himself "bread," it is clear that he is speaking of his ability to give and sustain life. The nature of the life he gives is also explicated in the context—it is eternal life, a life not bounded by death. All of those specific connections are made in the text and must be integral to our understanding of the bread. (b) We move outward to another ring of associations by exploring connections between the bread of life discourse and the account of the feeding of the five thousand that preceded it. We can also consider the traditions about Passover and manna that the text seems to presuppose. Both Passover and manna are mentioned in the chapter, and many readers probably would have known more about them than is actually stated in the narrative. By comparing John 6 with biblical and extrabiblical stories about manna and Passover, our understanding of the bread imagery will be enhanced. (c) We move outward still further to ask what role bread played in the lives of people in the Greek-speaking world in the first century. Such commonplace associations are not explicitly mentioned in the text but help to create the ineradicable "penumbra of vagueness" that contributes the image's power.

Two criteria can help us distinguish viable interpretations from those that are implausible. One is that an interpretation must make disciplined use of the literary context in which the image appears. The symbol must be assessed in light of the immediate literary context, its development within the Gospel as a whole, and its relationship to other symbols in the Gospel.[48] The other criterion is that an interpretation must give attention to the cultural and social setting in which the Gospel was composed. For example, the fourth evangelist assumed that his readers would know Greek and would understand that the word *artos* referred to a baked mixture of flour and water, something English speakers call bread. Since bread does not mean the same thing in every culture, sensitivity to cultural nuances must inform interpretation. In the Greco-Roman world, bread was a staple food, but in many parts of tropical Asia rice is the staple and bread is a luxury, a substance often associated with immigrants from Europe. Jesus' claim to be the bread of life must be understood in its proper context: He was claiming to be basic to life, not an imported luxury item.

Meaning and Mystery

The Gospel of John becomes meaningful when the various aspects of its message fit into a coherent whole and are integrated with the rest of what the readers know, helping to create a coherent way of understanding life. The Gospel's cogency is threatened when readers perceive that one part contradicts another or violates what they already hold to be true. For the text to become meaningful again, a way must be found to resolve the contradiction. Symbols are a major way in which the Gospel brings potentially discordant elements into agreement with each other. It has often been noted that the root meaning of the word *symbol* is "to put together," and in John's Gospel the symbols help to disclose how apparently contradictory ideas can be brought together.

One of the Gospel's central claims is that Jesus is both Messiah and the person in whom people encounter God. From a traditional Jewish perspective this assertion contained a blasphemous contradiction: The messiah was to be a human being, and no one could claim that a human being was God. Jesus' hearers impatiently demanded, "How long will you keep us in suspense? If you are the Christ, tell us *plainly*" (10:24). Yet Jesus could not answer their question directly. If he said, "Yes, I am the Christ," that would be misleading, since many of his hearers assumed that the Christ would be an earthly ruler, someone like King David (6:15; 7:42). When Jesus said, "I and the Father are one," however, that too was misinterpreted and his hearers thought he was trying to usurp the place of God (10:30-33).

Jesus told them, "I am the good shepherd," which helps overcome what appears to be a fundamental contradiction in the Gospel's message by holding together the human and divine dimensions of Jesus' identity. In

---

48. Culpepper, *Anatomy*, 188–89.

the Old Testament, the prophets castigated the unjust "shepherds" who ruled Israel, promising that God would "set up over them one shepherd, my servant David, and he shall feed them: he shall feed them and be their shepherd" (Ezek. 34:23). The term *shepherd* became a fitting title for the Davidic messiah. In the same passage God also declared, "I myself will be the shepherd of my sheep, and I will make them lie down, says the Lord God" (Ezek. 34:15). Other Old Testament passages similarly refer to God as a shepherd. The title good shepherd encompassed the divine and messianic facets of Jesus' identity in a single image.[49]

Another disturbing aspect of the Gospel's message is the clash between Jesus' claim to have come from God and the reality of unbelief. Jesus was accepted by some but rejected by many others, and it seemed incongruous to think that the one whom God had sent to give life to the world would evoke such conflicting responses. The Gospel helps make sense of these divergent reactions, however, by calling Jesus "the light of the world." Paradoxically, light can produce both sight and blindness; readers would know this on the basis of their own experience. When the sun rises over a darkened earth, the light enables people to see, but the glare of the noonday sun blinds those who look into it. Similarly, some people recognize who Jesus is and others misunderstand him (9:39), but such divergent reactions do not undercut the truth of Jesus' claims any more than blindness negates the reality of the sun's light.

As symbols yield this kind of coherence, however, they continue to resist full explication. The symbol "carries something indeterminate, and, however we try, there is a residual mystery that escapes our intellects."[50] Many of the images that function symbolically in John's Gospel are as familiar as daily bread, yet the familiarity does not dispel the mystery; it conveys the mystery. The cleft between that which is "from above" and that which is "from below" remains; symbolic language provides a way to span the distance without collapsing the distance. The symbols in the Fourth Gospel direct people to Jesus, a man of ordinary flesh and blood, but one who embodied the otherness of God.

The symbolic aspects of the Gospel work together with other facets of the text that reflect both the disjunctions and the connections between the physical and the transcendent. Ricoeur has pointed out that a metaphorical statement produces "the appearance of kinship where ordinary vision does not perceive any relationship." Speaking of one thing in terms appropriate to another "causes a new, hitherto unnoticed, relation of

---

49. On the messianic and divine aspects of the shepherd image, see Jeremias, "*poimēn*," *TDNT* 6.487–88.

50. William York Tyndall, "Excellent Dumb Discourse," *The Theory of the Novel* (ed. P. Stevick; New York: Free Press, 1967) 342; quoted by Culpepper, *Anatomy*, 183.

meaning to spring up between the terms that previous systems of classification had ignored or not allowed."[51] The metaphor makes similar that which is dissimilar. "'Remoteness' is preserved within 'proximity.' To see *the like* is to see the same in spite of, and through, the different. This tension between sameness and difference characterizes the logical structure of likeness."[52]

The sense of disjunction is especially apparent in metaphors like "I am the light of the world" (8:12). Here it is clear that Jesus is not claiming to be light in a physical sense; that is, he is not does not emit luminous beams that are visible to the eyes. Instead, the context indicates that Jesus is claiming to be the source of enlightenment concerning God. Other passages, however, reveal a closer connection between the physical and spiritual levels of meaning. Nicodemus came to Jesus "by night," and Judas departed to betray Jesus when "it was night" (3:2; 13:30); in these instances the darkness is both a physical and a spiritual reality. Similarly, after Jesus anointed the eyes of a blind beggar, the man received both physical sight and the insight of faith in Jesus.

The way people in the Gospel misunderstand what Jesus says accents this interplay between the disjunctions and the connections in levels of meaning.[53] In some instances, people must reject one way of understanding what Jesus says in order to embrace another. The figures in the story typically seize upon the wrong interpretation, revealing its absurdity to the readers of the text, and their misunderstanding provides an opportunity for Jesus to point to the viable way of understanding what he said. When Jesus met the Samaritan woman beside Jacob's well, for example, he offered her "living water." She initially thought that he was speaking about fresh water to drink but soon realized that the idea was incongruous since Jesus had no bucket with which to draw. As the conversation progresses, it becomes clear to readers, if not to the woman herself, that Jesus is speaking not about water in the physical sense but about a spiritual reality, something that leads to everlasting life.

Other instances of misunderstanding involve an expression with two meanings that must be taken together, and Jesus' hearers fail to comprehend him not by seizing upon the wrong meaning but by seizing upon only one meaning. When Jesus approached Jerusalem before his passion, he was greeted by a cheering throng waving palm branches, and he told them that the hour had come for the Son of man to be "lifted up" (12:32). The expression "lift up" (*hypsoun*) can mean either to elevate something

---

51. "Metaphor and Symbol," 51.
52. "The Metaphorical Process as Cognition, Imagination, and Feeling," 148.
53. On the role of misunderstanding in John's Gospel, see the summary of the discussion in Culpepper, *Anatomy*, 152–65.

in a physical sense or to exalt someone in honor and glory. In one sense, Jesus' comment anticipated that he would be "lifted up" physically onto the cross to die. The crowd rightly understood that Jesus was referring to death but could not see what death—and especially death by crucifixion, a form of punishment usually reserved for slaves and brigands—had to do with messiahship (12:33-34). Yet in this and other contexts, the evangelist prepares readers to see that the "lifting up" was not only Jesus' elevation on the cross but also his exaltation in glory (cf. 3:14; 8:28). The cross was both the culmination of Jesus' work on earth and the inauguration of his return to glory in heaven. An expression like "lift up" emphasizes the connection, rather than the contrast, between the physical and the divine levels of meaning.

The contrast between levels of meaning is sharpest in the Gospel's pervasive use of irony.[54] An ironic passage is one where on the surface level something appears to be true but in reality the opposite is true. A Johannine definition of irony is found in Jesus' enjoinder, "Do not judge by appearances, but judge with right judgment" (7:24). Nicodemus, for example, appeared to know who Jesus was and called him "a teacher come from God," but Nicodemus's subsequent comments revealed that he really did not know what he was talking about (3:2, 10). The other Jewish leaders judged that Jesus was guilty of breaking the law by healing on the Sabbath, but Jesus pointed out that in reality they performed surgery on the Sabbath by circumcising people and were actually trying to violate the law by trying to murder him (7:19-23). In such cases of irony, readers are expected to reject the false understanding of something in order to embrace a true understanding.

A vital tension exists between the aspects of the Gospel that stress the *contrast* between levels of meaning and those that disclose the *connections* between levels of meaning. Irony warns that appearances are deceiving and that truth often runs contrary to ordinary perceptions. Metaphors in turn demand that readers abandon the literal, often physical interpretation of a statement in order to discern its true meaning. Yet the symbols also show how divine realities can be made known through images that people can see, taste, and touch; and together with wordplays like "lift up," they reveal how the human and the divine, the physical and the spiritual, can be encompassed in a single image.

These facets of the narrative work together to draw readers beyond the realm of the senses to divine realities, without permitting truth to be

54. On the nature and function of irony see the overview in Culpepper, *Anatomy*, 165–80; Paul Duke, *Irony in the Fourth Gospel* (Atlanta: John Knox, 1985); Gail R. O'Day, *Revelation in the Fourth Gospel: Narrative Mode and Theological Claim* (Philadelphia: Fortress, 1986) 11–32.

equated with sense perception or to be so divorced from sense perception that communication is no longer possible. Symbols invite a reader to see that "beyond the verge of what he can express, there is an area which can be glimpsed, never surveyed."[55] They convey transcendent realities without delimiting them. The "bright focussed center of meaning" with the ineradicable "penumbra of vagueness" typical of Johannine symbols presents readers with a reality that can be expressed, but not fully defined, in human terms. In the Gospel's own words, the Spirit of God is a wind that can be perceived but not captured; we "hear the sound of it," but it "blows where it wills" (3:8). Through symbols the mystery of God is encountered but not fully comprehended.

Interpretation of Johannine symbolism discloses many facets of the Gospel's meaning, but it cannot finally demonstrate its truth. John Ashton has commented that in John's Gospel "all truth is self-authenticating," for there is "nothing *outside* Jesus' revelation which he can call upon for support."[56] Perhaps a better way to put it is that truth must be divinely authenticated. The symbols in John's Gospel refer to Jesus and through Jesus to God, making claims that readers cannot verify by embarking on their own ascent into heaven or by appealing to canons of historical, social, or literary criticism. Verification can come only from God's side of the divide. A symbol's truth is confirmed when people are drawn through its witness into the faith in Jesus that brings knowledge of God. Interpreters can identify a symbol's structure and literary function, describe its social and cultural context, and explore ways it interacts with readers. But no one comes to know God in faith unless he or she is "drawn"; and from a Johannine perspective that must be done "from above."

---

55. Edward K. Brown, *Rhythm in the Novel* (The Alexander Lectures, 1949–50; Toronto: University of Toronto Press, 1950) 58. Quoted by Culpepper, *Anatomy*, 190.

56. *Understanding*, 525. Cf. Bultmann, *Gospel*, 163, 386; Martyn, *History and Theology*, 130.

2

Symbolic and
Representative Figures

Symbolism in John's Gospel centers on Jesus, the person in whom God is revealed. The images in Jesus' discourses and the actions he performs make known who he is; and he makes known who God is. Jesus said, "He who believes in me, believes not in me, but in him who sent me. And he who sees me sees him who sent me" (12:44-45). Because the unseen reality of God is made known in a person who can be seen and heard and touched, Jesus himself is often considered to be the Gospel's primary symbol. The people Jesus encounters play a vital supporting role in the narrative. Alan Culpepper has called them "the prism which breaks up the pure light of Jesus' remote epiphany into colors the readers can see."[1] The supporting characters rarely interact with each other; they draw out facets of Jesus' identity through their responses to his words and actions. They present a spectrum of possible responses to Jesus, helping to attract readers to positive exemplars of faith, to move them beyond inadequate faith responses, and to alienate them from characters who reject Jesus.

Jesus is the one person in the Gospel who reveals and embodies God. The problem is the particularity of this claim. Throughout the Gospel everyone who meets Jesus recognizes that he is a flesh-and-blood human being, and they call him a rabbi, a Jew, or simply a man. What they persistently debate, however, is whether Jesus is the Messiah and whether he is divine. A major conflict was sparked when Jesus claimed that he could work on the Sabbath because God worked on the Sabbath. His Jewish listeners understood this to be an attempt to usurp God's own

---

1. *Anatomy*, 104. See also Raymond F. Collins, "The Representative Figures of the Fourth Gospel," *Downside Review* 94 (1976) 26–46, 118–32. Reprinted in *These Things Have Been Written: Studies in the Fourth Gospel* (Louvain: Peeters; Grand Rapids, Mich.: Eerdmans, 1990) 1–45.

prerogatives, and they persecuted Jesus for trying to make himself equal with God (5:17-18). Later they demanded that he tell them plainly if he was the Christ, and he replied that he and his Father were one. Therefore they attempted to stone him for blasphemy, charging that he, a mere man, was trying to make himself God (10:30-33). Rudolf Bultmann rightly commented that the problem is that God's glory is not to be seen alongside Jesus' flesh nor through his flesh as through a window; it is to be seen in the flesh and nowhere else. "The revelation is present in a peculiar *hiddenness.*"[2]

The fourth evangelist faced the formidable challenge of disclosing the divine reality concealed by Jesus' humanity. In time some would question whether Jesus had been a person who had lived "in the flesh" (1 John 4:2; 2 John 7), but this was not the question that confronted the writer of John's Gospel. The evangelist assumed that both Jesus' followers and his foes recognized his humanity—and this assumption is mirrored in dialogues throughout the Gospel. The issue that drives the Gospel is whether Jesus was anything more than a Jewish man from Galilee who was executed by crucifixion on the outskirts of Jerusalem. The Gospel was written to show that the man Jesus was also the Christ and the Son of God. The other people in John's Gospel can best be called representative figures, since they do not reveal God as Jesus does. Instead, their responses to Jesus represent different ways of relating to God. Like Jesus, each of these figures is a distinctive individual. Yet the evangelist seeks to show that what is true for them is true also for others. Their particular encounters with Jesus disclose matters of universal significance.

CHARACTER PORTRAYAL

It can be difficult to interpret the characters in John's Gospel without undervaluing or overestimating their symbolic and representative traits. Interpretation must be done within an appropriate frame of reference. The importance of this interpretive frame can be demonstrated by briefly considering the ancient allegorical interpretations of John's Gospel. These seem strange to most modern readers in part because they rely on a frame of reference that we deem foreign to the text. In the third century, for example, Origen formulated one interpretation of the cleansing of the temple (John 2:14-16) within an ecclesiastical frame of reference, identifying the merchants selling their wares with the church leaders of his own time who betrayed those entrusted to their care for the sake of personal gain. Then he shifted to a philosophical frame of reference, suggesting

2. *Gospel,* 63.

that the merchants signified fleshly tendencies in the soul, which must be driven out by the whip of Christ's teachings.[3]

The Portrayal of Jesus

Several observations about character portrayal in John's Gospel can help establish a context for our own interpretations of its symbolism. First, the literary context usually provides indications of the main facets of Jesus' identity. (a) The people he meets usually identify him in human terms at the beginning of the conversation, calling him a man, a Jew, or a rabbi. All of these terms are appropriate for Jesus and do not exclude other facets of his identity. (b) As conversations progress, there is often discussion about Jesus' status as prophet and Messiah. The term *prophet* was used for special messengers of God and could be applied to many individuals. The title "the Messiah" and its Greek equivalent "the Christ" were usually reserved for a single figure whom God was expected to send. (c) Conversations often end with references to the divine aspects of Jesus' identity, especially his role as Son of God or Son of man. These two titles are not fully equivalent, but both are used in the Gospel in ways that reflect divinity.

Second, the text may refer or allude to ideas that were commonplace in the context in which it was composed. Often these references are made in disputes about Jesus' parentage and place of origin. (a) The text may suggest connections between Jesus and messianic expectations found in the Scriptures and Jewish traditions, sometimes countering the attempts of Jesus' opponents to discredit him for not meeting these expectations. (b) The text also seeks to show that God was Jesus' Father and that heaven was his place of origin by speaking of Jesus in language often used for God. Much of this language stems from Scripture and Jewish tradition, but we will also note similarities with the language used for God elsewhere in the Greco-Roman world. The Gospel both appropriates and transforms common patterns of thought.

Third, the text may present ways of understanding Jesus' identity that reflect later Christian understandings of who Jesus was. The Gospel itself notes that there were many things about Jesus that his disciples did not understand at first but grasped only after he had risen from the dead (2:22; 12:16). During the last supper, Jesus told the disciples that the Father would send them the Holy Spirit, who would teach and remind them of what Jesus had said and done (14:26). The Fourth Gospel is the product of this postresurrection reflection, disclosing the significance of Jesus in terms that were familiar in the late first century but that may not have been well known one or two generations earlier.

3. "Origen's Commentary on the Gospel of John" 10.16; *The Ante-Nicene Fathers,* vol. 10, pp. 393–94.

The Portrayal of Other Persons

The identity of the supporting characters emerges in a corresponding fashion. First, the literary context provides important clues to their significance. (a) The people Jesus meets have distinctive traits that identify them as individuals: a ruler of the Jews, a woman who had five husbands, a blind beggar. No two of them are alike. Their representative roles do not negate their individuality but actually develop out of their most distinctive traits. (b) An individual may represent a group of people. This representative role may be suggested by the introduction to an episode, which sometimes identifies a character with a particular group of people. The person in turn may act as the spokesperson for the group by using the first person plural, "we," and Jesus will often reply in the second person plural, *hymeis*, which we will translate as "you people." (c) The literary context may indicate that an individual and the group he or she represents actually reveal something more widely characteristic of human beings in relationship to God. In cases where the individual or group is explicitly identified with "the world," their responses to Jesus are usually duplicated by other people in the narrative so that they come to typify a certain faith stance.

Second, attention to the context in which the Gospel was composed can yield additional information about how typical a character would have seemed to first-century readers. Like other ancient sources, the Fourth Gospel often ascribes to people the characteristics of their ancestors and place of origin.[4] (a) Conversations with Jews and Samaritans frequently mention their "fathers," such as Abraham, Jacob, and the wilderness generation. The traits commonly associated with these ancestors reappear in the people Jesus meets. (b) Places of origin are often noted in the text, and traits typically associated with regions, cities, and other sites are reflected in the characters that come from these places. The evangelist drew on characteristics that some readers would already have associated with sites in Palestine but also described places and their inhabitants in ways that would have seemed typical of places elsewhere in the Greco-Roman world. Moreover, he shaped the perspective of his readers by repeatedly ascribing certain characteristics to the people of a given locale, so that even those without prior knowledge of the place would come to associate certain traits with its people.

Third, characters in the Gospel often represent viewpoints that were typical of people living in the late first century, at the time the Gospel was composed. The Gospel tells of persons who encountered Jesus during his

4. See Bruce J. Malina, "Is There a Circum-Mediterranean Person? Looking for Stereotypes," *BTB* 22 (1992) 66–87, and "Dealing with Biblical (Mediterranean) Characters: A Guide for U.S. Consumers," *BTB* 19 (1989) 127–41, esp. 129. In addition to the texts mentioned there see Acts 7:51; 26:6; Philo, *Life of Moses* 2.44.

ministry in the early part of the first century but who also speak to issues confronting people living one or two generations later.[5] Some of these issues are presaged in the farewell discourses, which warned that Jesus' disciples would be persecuted and expelled from the synagogue after he had returned to the Father (16:2). The conclusion of the Thomas episode speaks directly to the intended readers of the Gospel, who, like Thomas, were confronted with the necessity of believing without having seen Jesus (20:29-31). The final chapter deals with the crisis that erupted within the community when the Beloved Disciple died before Christ returned (21:20-23). These passages provide windows into the Johannine context and help us to discern how figures from the early first century remained significant for subsequent generations.

Character Portrayal
in Antiquity

The fourth evangelist's way of depicting the people would have helped make his Gospel accessible to those familiar with character portrayal in the ancient world. Interpreters have often noted that the evangelist seems to respect certain canons of Greek drama, even though most figures in the story are Jewish. The evangelist followed the practice of dividing scenes so that only two active characters appear on stage at any one time. For example, Jesus speaks to the Samaritan woman alone, but she exits when the disciples return, and the disciples fall silent when the townspeople arrive (4:27-28, 31-39). Later the man born blind appears successively with his neighbors and the Pharisees, exits when his parents are brought on stage, then returns to appear with his accusers alone (9:8, 13, 18, 24; cf. 11:20, 28). Groups of people typically speak with a single voice, functioning like the chorus in a drama. The Gospel's pervasive use of dramatic irony, in which the contrast between appearance and reality is underscored by the unwitting speeches of the characters, also resembles the irony in Greek tragedy more closely than that found in any other ancient literature. For such irony to be fully effective, audiences needed to know at the outset how the play would end. Information conveyed in a prologue usually placed the audience in a position to see truths concealed from the figures on stage. Similarly, the Fourth Gospel's prologue gives readers an omniscient perspective from which they can understand things the people in the Gospel story cannot. Like a drama, the Gospel moves relentlessly toward the conclusion intimated at the beginning; only the Gospel is

5. The idea that the Gospel reflects the faith of the community in which it was composed was used in various ways by Julius Wellhausen, Alfred Loisy, and Rudolf Bultmann and more recently was developed into an overall approach to the Gospel by Martyn (*History and Theology*) and Brown (*Community*).

driven not by the impersonal workings of fate but by the purposeful will of God.[6]

Aristotle considered character portrayal (*ēthos*) a constituent element of Greek tragedy, second only to plot in importance. Character was revealed when someone chose or avoided a course of action in circumstances where the choice was not obvious, that is, in a situation where everyone's choice would not be the same.[7] The *dramatis personae* in many Greek tragedies were understood to have been real people, but they were portrayed as "types." Drama, like history, could deal with things that actually happened, but the dramatist's concern was to convey general truths by showing how a certain type of person would speak or act in a given situation.[8] Similarly, character is revealed in the Fourth Gospel when people respond positively or negatively to the words and deeds of Jesus, the meaning of which is often not obvious. Moreover, the character of a particular person often conveys a general truth about a group or type of people or about the human condition.

Like Aristotle, the orator Dio Chrysostom, a younger contemporary of the fourth evangelist, understood that Homer and the tragedians included only select elements of a story in their works.[9] He assumed that Homer never spoke without a purpose and depicted "the dress, dwelling, and manner of life of people so as to accord with their character [*ēthos*]." Through character portrayal Homer instructed people about a suitable manner of a life.[10] Dio proposed to do the same by describing different types of people in his oratory.[11] In a similar way, the fourth evangelist included a select group of persons in his Gospel and depicted their manner and physical surroundings in accordance with their character. Through positive and negative examples he directed readers toward his own stated goal, that they might believe in Jesus and have life in his name (20:30-31).

The evangelist's approach to character portrayal would have been familiar to a broad spectrum of readers. Many would have been accustomed to looking for the general truths conveyed through individual characters in a drama. Yet as they entered the world of the Gospel they would also

6. On the chorus speaking as one person and the function of irony in Greek drama, see Philip Whaley Harsh, *A Handbook of Classical Drama* (Palo Alto, Calif.: Stanford University Press, 1944) 13, 20–22, 30, 165. On the Fourth Gospel's use of dramatic conventions see Martyn, *History and Theology*, 26; Paul Duke, *Irony in the Fourth Gospel* (Atlanta: John Knox, 1985) 140 and the literature he cites on 192 n. 5.

7. Aristotle, *Poetics* 6.19–24, 1450b. See also the notes by W. Hamilton Fyfe in Aristotle, *The Poetics* (LCL; Cambridge: Harvard University Press; London: Heinemann, 1965) 28–29.

8. *Poetics* 9.1–10, 1451b. See also the notes by Fyfe, ibid., 34–35; Harsh, *A Handbook of Classical Drama*, 5.

9. *Discourses* 61.8.

10. *Discourses* 2.39; cf. 2.44, 48.

11. *Discourses* 4.88–89.

have encountered much that was strange. As Erich Auerbach has observed, the Scriptures address their readers in a manner different from the Greek classics: "Far from seeking, like Homer, merely to make us forget our own reality for a few hours, it seeks to overcome our reality: we are to fit our own life into its world, feel ourselves to be elements in its structure of universal history." The transcendent and universal realities conveyed through Jesus and those he meets extend a claim upon the Gospel's readers, "and if we refuse to be subjected we are rebels."[12]

Ancient audiences generally assumed that the characters who strode across the stage were portraying actual persons and events from the past, especially in the tragedies that dealt with traditional subjects. At the same time, people like Aristotle and Dio Chrysostom recognized that authors carefully selected and crafted their material in order to convey a coherent message. The interplay between fidelity to tradition and the freedom to shape or even create new material varied among authors. Aristotle, for example, took the general truths conveyed by dramatists more seriously than the particular facts recounted by historians and even counseled authors to shape a cogent plot outline before inserting the names of particular characters.[13] By way of contrast, Thucydides, the premier Greek historian, valued historical evidence more highly and insisted that his evidence was superior to that presented by the poets, which people accepted uncritically. Nevertheless, while trying to preserve a general sense of what people had said, even Thucydides exercised some freedom in making speakers say what seemed appropriate to him on a given occasion.[14]

The intended readers of the Fourth Gospel almost certainly would have assumed that the narrative depicted actual people and events from the past. At the same time, they were told that the evangelist selected and shaped his material to convey a coherent message (20:30-31). The relationship between his fidelity to tradition and creative freedom remains disputed. Some have argued that in certain passages, especially in those not found in the other Gospels, the evangelist created characters and scenes to convey a symbolic meaning.[15] Others find the Gospel to be a more restrained presentation and elaboration of traditional materials that were only decades old, not centuries old as in Greek tragedies. A comparison of the four New Testament Gospels shows that none of the evangelists was content merely to repeat the tradition, as J. Louis Martyn has pointed out. Each revered the tradition enough to preserve it yet exercised the

---

12. *Mimesis: The Representation of Reality in Western Literature* (Princeton, N.J.: Princeton University Press, 1953) 15.
13. *Poetics* 9.1–10, 1451b; 17.5–8, 1455b.
14. *Peloponnesian War* 1.21.
15. See the discussion in Schnackenburg, *Gospel,* 2.244.

freedom to reshape it and make it his own.[16] We will acknowledge that the persons depicted in John's Gospel can be both historical and symbolic without attempting to assess the extent to which the evangelist shaped the tradition he received. We may speak, for example, about the symbolic significance of Jesus and Peter without denying that they actually lived in first-century Palestine; and we may recognize that Jesus and Peter were actual persons without diminishing their importance as symbols. Our attention will focus on what the Gospel presents to its readers.

JESUS

The principal figure in John's Gospel is Jesus, God's representative. The prologue says, "In the beginning was the Word and the Word was with God and the Word was God" (1:1), setting up a tension that persists throughout the Gospel. The Word was "with" God, which suggests that the two are not identical; and as the narrative unfolds there are indications that Jesus is subordinate to God. He does only what the Father has told him to do, he does nothing on his own authority. He prays to the Father, not to himself, and he returns to the Father, "for the Father is greater than I" (14:28). Yet the prologue also says that the Word "was God," which points to their oneness. Jesus says, "I and the Father are one" (10:30), uses the expression "I Am" to suggest that he could use God's own name for himself, and is finally called "My Lord and my God" by Thomas (20:28). Both the differences and the unity between Jesus and God are affirmed in the narrative, and the tension is not resolved. Jesus' identity will be discussed at length in subsequent chapters, but here we will consider several texts that help to establish a frame of reference within which these facets of his person and role can be understood.

Basic affirmations about Jesus were made by those who first followed him. When Andrew and another disciple of John the Baptist followed Jesus, they were asked what they were looking for and said, "'Rabbi' (which means Teacher), 'where are you staying?'" (1:38). Jesus is often identified as a rabbi or teacher in John's Gospel, and Jesus accepts these titles. At the last supper he specifically told his disciples, "You call me Teacher and Lord; and you are right, for so I am" (13:13). The Gospel refers to teaching as a primary form of activity during the central part of Jesus' public ministry. He taught in the synagogue at Capernaum and the temple at Jerusalem (6:59; 7:14, 28; 8:20), and when questioned by the high priest, Jesus replied that he had always taught in synagogues and in the temple

16. "Attitudes Ancient and Modern toward Tradition about Jesus," *USQR* 23 (1968) 129–45; idem, *History and Theology*, 19.

where all Jews come together (18:19-20). Calling Jesus a rabbi was appropriate, but it did not exhaust his identity.

A second facet of Jesus' identity was discerned by Andrew, who told his brother, "We have found the Messiah" (1:41). The next day Philip echoed Andrew's messianic confession by declaring, "We have found him of whom Moses in the law and also the prophets wrote, Jesus of Nazareth, the son of Joseph" (1:45). Nathanael was skeptical when he heard Philip's claim, since Nazareth was an insignificant village that was not mentioned anywhere in the Scriptures. Nevertheless, he went to meet Jesus and soon became convinced that Jesus was the promised Messiah, hailing him as "Son of God" and "King of Israel" (1:49). The title "King of Israel" connects Jesus with expectations concerning the appearance of a royal messiah who would lead the people Israel. On the lips of Nathanael, the title "Son of God" also is messianic. The Scriptures said that the heir to David's throne would be a "son" to God, and Nathanael's confession associates Jesus with these promises.[17]

This passage directly states that Jesus was the royal Messiah promised in the Scriptures so that all readers would know about this aspect of his identity. The text also provides more subtle clues to his messiahship, engaging readers more familiar with the Scriptures and Jewish traditions in a process of deeper reflection about his relationship to Israel's heritage. Philip directed Nathanael's attention to the Law and the Prophets, and Jesus in turn directed his attention to the experience of being called under a fig tree. He said, "Before Philip called you, while you were under the fig tree I saw you" (1:48). This odd comment is an allusion to Zech. 3:10: "In that day, says the Lord of hosts, *a man will call his neighbor* under a vine and *under a fig tree.*" Although several Old Testament texts envision a future era of peace when people will sit securely under their vines and fig trees,[18] only the Zechariah passage speaks of one man "calling" another under a vine or fig tree; and Jesus accented the element of calling in his comment to Nathanael. According to Zechariah 3, the act of one man calling another under a vine and fig tree was to mark the arrival of the "Branch," who was widely understood to be the Davidic Messiah (3:8). Jewish writings from this period show that people understood that this messianic Branch was foretold both by Moses in the Law (Gen. 49:10) and in the Prophets (Jer. 23:6; 33:16; Zech. 3:8; 6:12-13), just as Philip had said in John 1:45. These same texts identified the messianic Branch as the heir of David, who would be considered Son of God and King of Israel—the

---

17. See 2 Sam. 7:14; Ps. 2:2, 6-7. On "Son of God," see Ashton, *Understanding*, 260–62.
18. See 1 Kings 4:25; Mic. 4:4; cf. 1 Macc. 14:12.

messianic titles used by Nathanael in John 1:49.[19] The text tells all readers *that* Jesus is Israel's Messiah, while directing readers familiar with the Scriptures to see *how* he is the Messiah: It enables them to see that Philip's experience of being called under a fig tree (Zech. 3:10) marks Jesus as the messianic Branch of David (Zech. 3:8).

The third aspect of Jesus' identity is divinity, which appears in Jesus' final comments to Nathanael. Jesus said, "Truly, truly I say to you, you will see heaven opened and the angels of God ascending and descending upon the Son of man" (1:51). The title "Son of man" was used in various ways outside John's Gospel. Sometimes it was simply an expression that meant "human being," and sometimes it referred to a figure that would come from heaven at the end of time. The Johannine sense of the title is established by its use in this literary context, where the Son of man is the link between heaven and earth. This sense continues to be apparent throughout the Gospel, where the Son of man himself is said to descend from and reascend into heaven (3:13; 6:62) and to execute divine judgment (5:27).

This fairly direct presentation of Jesus as the link between heaven and earth uses language that readers familiar with the Scriptures would have been able to connect with the story of Jacob. One night while Jacob slept, "he dreamed that there was a ladder set up on the earth and the top of it reached to heaven; and behold, the angels of God were ascending and descending on it" (Gen. 28:12). God stood at the top of the ladder, so that the ladder was associated with the manifestation of God's presence. Jesus' words about "the angels of God ascending and descending" echo this passage, playfully turning it into a text that identifies him as the one through whom the presence of God is manifested—something that was affirmed earlier in the prologue (John 1:14) and will be stated again later in the Gospel (12:45; 14:7).

Progressions like those found in this episode occur repeatedly in the Gospel, establishing a frame of reference within which Jesus can be understood.[20] The debates at the feast of Booths first deal with Jesus' status as a teacher (7:14-24), then as prophet and Messiah (7:25-52), and finally as divine Son of man (8:12-30). The story of the man born blind is nearly identical. Jesus is first called a "man" (9:11), then a prophet and Messiah (9:17, 22), and finally he is worshiped as the Son of man (9:35-38). The feeding of the five thousand presents a variant form of this pattern. Jesus

19. The Dead Sea text 4QFlorilegium identifies the Branch with the heir of David and Son of God mentioned in 2 Sam. 7:10-14 and 4QPBless connects the Branch with the Messiah who will come from Judah according to Gen. 49:10. For complete discussion see my "Messianic Exegesis and the Call of Nathanael (John 1.45-51)," *JSNT* 39 (1990) 23–34.

20. The importance of these progressions has often been noted. See, e.g., Martyn, *History and Theology*, 131–33.

was identified as a prophet and king by the crowd (6:14-15) then appeared in a kind of theophany to the disciples (6:20). The difference is that here Jesus fled before the crowd could actually make him king, and he sharply contrasted himself with the prophet Moses. We will see, however, that this is not a repudiation of his claims to be prophet and Messiah but a rejection of the way the crowd understood these roles.

The evangelist presents all the aspects of Jesus' identity—the human, the messianic, and the divine—without negating any one of them. Comprehension of who Jesus is does not simply entail recognition of his divinity; it involves reflection on the interplay between several genuine facets of his identity. Jesus was a man, but not only a man; he was prophet and Messiah, but not only prophet and Messiah; he was divine, but not only divine. Even at the end of the Gospel, the evangelist stated that he wanted readers to believe that the man Jesus is also the Christ and the divine Son of God (20:31). Each facet has its own integrity; the disclosure of his divinity is given through his humanity and is interpreted in light of the traditions of Israel.[21]

Another aspect of this phenomenon is the interconnection between the particular and the universal aspects of Jesus' identity. He was a Jew who fulfilled the messianic expectations peculiar to Israel, yet he was also of significance for all people. This interplay between the particular and the universal is especially apparent in Jesus' encounter with the Samaritan woman, which follows a progression nearly identical to that just noted, relating it to the Samaritan as well as the Jewish religious tradition.

At the beginning of the chapter, the woman recognized that Jesus was a Jewish man. When he asked her for a drink, she exclaimed, "How is it that you, a Jew, ask a drink of me, a woman of Samaria" (4:9). The ensuing conversation indicates that her perception of his national background was valid as far as it went. Jesus spoke as a Jew in the initial part of their conversation concerning the place of worship. He said, "You worship what you do not know; *we* worship what *we* know, for salvation is from the Jews" (4:22). The use of the plural in this context suggests that Jesus speaks for Jews generally, and the substance of his comment reflects common Jewish polemics against idolaters, who were said to engage in such worship because of their ignorance of the true God (e.g., Isa. 44:9, 18). From a Jewish perspective the Samaritans were idolaters because of the nature of their worship on Mount Gerizim, as we will explore subsequently. Jesus was a Jew who worshiped in Jerusalem and called the temple there his

---

21. Marinus de Jonge interprets the different aspects of Jesus' identity in a unilinear fashion, maintaining that the affirmations of divinity completely redefine messiahship (*Jesus: Stranger*, 49–116). On the importance of giving full weight to the messianic affirmations, see Ashton, *Understanding*, 238–79.

Father's house (John 2:16). In Jesus, salvation would come "from the Jews," although it would be received by others.

In the next stage of the conversation, Jesus is identified as a prophet and Messiah. Although Jesus first met the woman beside the well along the road, he already knew that she had previously had five husbands and was living with a sixth man who was not her husband. The kind of knowledge Jesus exhibited was extraordinary, and the woman rightly called him a prophet (4:19). He continued to speak as a prophet when he announced the coming of a form of worship in which people would not worship either on Mount Gerizim ("this mountain") or in Jerusalem but in Spirit and truth (4:21, 23). The woman expanded the discussion by referring to the Messiah who was coming to teach her people "all things," and Jesus replied that he was that Messiah (4:25-26). Returning to her townspeople, the woman reported that Jesus had told her "all things" about herself and wondered if he might indeed be the Messiah (4:29).

The way the narrative is told subsumes Samaritan expectations under the Jewish expression *Messiah*. Samaritans in the first century apparently did not use the term *Messiah* or await the coming of someone like David, who was a Jewish king. They did, however, expect a prophetic figure like Moses to appear. The Samaritan form of the Pentateuch gives special prominence to the promise that God would raise up a prophet like Moses (Deut. 18:18) by including it after the Ten Commandments (Exod. 20:21). A Moses-like figure did gain a following among the Samaritans in the mid-first century, promising to disclose on the Samaritans' sacred mountain, Gerizim, the location of the sacred vessels used in the Mosaic tabernacle. The woman's concern about worship and the emphasis that the Messiah would declare "all things" reflect the evangelist's familiarity with Samaritan hopes for a prophetic figure. The use of the terms *Messiah* and *Christ* may level some of the differences between Samaritan and Jewish beliefs, but it also shows that Jesus is the fulfillment of the hopes of both traditions.[22]

The episode climaxes when the townspeople acclaim Jesus as "Savior of the world" (4:42). This was not a messianic title but was often used for Caesar—the one who had dominion over the entire world. The reception the Samaritans granted Jesus was appropriate for such a dignitary. In the Greco-Roman world it was customary to greet a visiting dignitary by going out to meet him on the road and inviting him into the city. This final scene reveals that Jesus is not merely a national deliverer but a figure of

22. On Samaritan messianism see Josephus, *Ant.* 18.4.1 §§85–88. Cf. my *Dwelling of God: The Tabernacle in the Old Testament, Intertestamental Jewish Literature, and the New Testament* (CBQMS 22; Washington, D.C.: Catholic Biblical Association, 1989) 55–58. On the Samaritans and the term *messiah* see de Jonge, *Jesus: Stranger*, 102–6; Teresa Okure, *The Johannine Approach to Mission: A Contextual Study of John 4:1-42* (WUNT 31; Tübingen: Mohr/Siebeck, 1988) 121–27.

universal significance. By declaring that he was "*truly* the Savior of the world," the speakers seem to be excluding rival claimants—including Caesar. The full theological weight of the title becomes apparent when it is read in connection with other references to Christ saving the world. God sent the Son "that the world might be saved through him" (3:17), for Jesus "did not come to condemn the world, but to save the world" (12:47). Since the world was estranged from God, the misplaced worship of the Samaritans made them well suited to represent such a world. Nevertheless, the Samaritans came to that faith in Jesus through which the world is saved (3:18), rightly calling him their Savior.[23]

The Gospel shows how each level presents something that is true about Jesus and uses symbols that help bind together the human and divine aspects of Jesus' identity in a coherent whole. This episode also shows how affirmations about Jesus' particular identity as a Jew and Messiah provide a basis for confessing his universal significance. The medium is consistent with the message. In this passage, as elsewhere in the Gospel, we find that the higher levels of Jesus' identity are often expressed in terms that have affinities with currents both inside and outside Judaism. Salvation is *from* the Jews in the person of Jesus, the Jewish Messiah, but it is *for* the world he has come to save (4:22, 42).[24]

Jesus' primary role was as God's representative, but in a secondary way he also represented his disciples. We might expect the situation to be reversed, so that the disciples would serve as Jesus' representatives. After all, God sent Jesus into the world, and Jesus in turn sent his disciples into the world; those who received Jesus received God, and those who received the disciples received Jesus (13:20; 17:18; 20:21). But the conversation with Nicodemus abruptly shifts from the singular to the plural: "Truly, truly I say to you, *we* speak of what *we* know and bear witness to what *we* have seen, but you do not receive *our* testimony" (3:11). The shift indicates that Jesus speaks both for himself and for his followers, as he does when he tells them that "*we* must work the works of him who sent me while it is day" (9:4).[25]

The early followers of Jesus would have seen their own experience presaged in the experience of Jesus. The witness Jesus bore concerning his identity and mission evoked sharp opposition from the unbelieving world,

23. For more extensive treatment see my "'Savior of the World' (John 4:42)," *JBL* 109 (1990) 665–80.

24. On developments from a lower to a higher Christology, and from a more particular to a more universal outlook, see Brown, *Community,* 25–58 and his summaries of other scholars on pp. 171–82. See also MacRae, "The Fourth Gospel and *Religionsgeschichte*," 15, 24; Gail R. O'Day, *Revelation in the Fourth Gospel: Narrative Mode and Theological Claim* (Philadelphia: Fortress, 1986) 73.

25. See esp. Martyn, *History and Theology.*

just as it would for his disciples. Jesus is often depicted in courtroomlike settings, defending himself against the charges leveled by his accusers; his disciples were confronted with similar prospects. Alongside the rejection, Jesus also found some who believed his words, and his success among the Samaritan villagers foreshadows the fruit of the mission work of his disciples. In his secondary role as a representative of his followers, Jesus exemplifies true discipleship, by persevering (8:31), faithfully bearing witness to the world (15:27), and moving readers to do the same.

NICODEMUS AND
THE SAMARITAN WOMAN

The Fourth Gospel depicts encounters between Jesus and many people. We will not pause before each portrait in the gallery but will focus on a number of figures that enable us to discern how individuals and groups function in a representative or symbolic way. Often the individuals are paired in the narrative, which provides opportunities to assess their character through comparison and contrast.[26] The first pair consists of Nicodemus and the Samaritan woman, two figures whose representative significance is highly developed (3:1—4:42). The shadowy figure of Nicodemus is a useful paradigm since his representative role can be discerned almost entirely through indications contained in the text itself, without much consideration of information that readers would have to bring to the text. The Samaritan woman's traits blend elements made explicit in the narrative with allusions to other traditions.

Nicodemus

We have already noted some of Nicodemus's representative traits in our first chapter. When he comes to Jesus, he appears to be alone; no one else speaks or is said to be present. Nevertheless, Nicodemus begins the conversation by saying, "Rabbi, *we* know that you are a teacher come from God" (3:2), which suggests that he speaks for a group of people. Jesus responds to him in the singular but suddenly shifts to the plural in the middle of the conversation, charging that "*you people* do not receive our testimony. If I have told *you people* earthly things and you do not believe, how will *you people* believe if I tell *you people* heavenly things?" (3:11-12). Then, without pausing, Jesus broadens the scope of the conversation even further, to speak of the entire world's estrangement from God (3:19). It becomes evident that Nicodemus is not only an individual or the spokes-

---

26. On the use of juxtaposition in the Gospel as a whole, see my article "Hearing, Seeing, and Believing in the Gospel of John," *Bib* 70 (1989) 327–48.

person for particular groups but someone with traits characteristic of all humanity. We must explore in more detail how Nicodemus assumes these representative roles.

The narrative initially identifies Nicodemus as a representative of two groups of people. First, Nicodemus is introduced as "a man of the Pharisees" and "a ruler of the Jews" (3:1). Jesus acknowledges Nicodemus's representative status by calling him "the teacher of Israel" (3:10), but he indicates that the Jewish teacher's primary trait is an inability to understand the ways of God. In the first chapter of the Gospel, the Jews and Pharisees from Jerusalem (1:19, 24) sent representatives to inquire about John the Baptist's identity. John quickly denied he was the Christ, Elijah, or the prophet and told the delegation about the preeminent one who was already in their midst, although they did not know him (1:26). In the second chapter Jesus went up to Jerusalem and drove the merchants out of the temple. The Jews who witnessed the event demanded a sign from Jesus, but when he spoke of the destruction and rebuilding of the temple, they found him incomprehensible (2:20). Later chapters confirm that Nicodemus's inability to understand Jesus is characteristic of the Jewish authorities and Pharisees throughout John's Gospel (e.g., 8:13, 19, 21, 22).

Second, Nicodemus speaks for the people who believed in Jesus because of the signs he performed. After the cleansing of the temple, the evangelist commented that while Jesus was in Jerusalem for Passover, "many believed in his name when they saw the signs that he did" (2:23). Nicodemus immediately appears and expresses the faith of this group by saying, "Rabbi, we know that you are a teacher come from God, for no one can do these signs that you do unless God is with him" (3:2). Nicodemus's apparent perceptiveness quickly turns to confusion, however, when Jesus declares that one sees and enters the kingdom of God through new birth (3:9). On subsequent Passovers the crowds who believe because of the miracles appear again, but like Nicodemus they become baffled by Jesus' words. Perceiving Jesus through the lens of their own preconceptions, they are ready to make Jesus their king but not to accept that he will be exalted by death and enthroned on a cross (cf. 6:2, 15, 26, 52; 12:9-18, 34).

At the most fundamental level, however, Nicodemus and the groups with which he is identified represent humanity estranged from God. This universal dimension emerges in the introduction to the episode through a play on the individual and collective meanings of the word *man* (*anthrōpos*). Jesus did not trust himself to the crowds in Jerusalem "because he knew all men and needed no one to bear witness concerning man, for he himself knew what was in man" (2:24-25). The narrative continues, "Now there was a man" (3:1), a particular man named Nicodemus, who manifests the condition of "man" generally.

Nicodemus may have been a ruler of the Jews, a spokesperson for the Jewish crowds at Passover, and one who was apparently interested in the kingdom of God, which was a Jewish idea (3:3, 5; cf. 6:2, 15; 12:13, 18); but Jesus traced Nicodemus's origins back to the physical birth he had in common with all humanity. Jesus declared that the fundamental categories affecting "any person" (*tis*) were flesh and Spirit, physical birth and birth from above. The dialogue makes clear that Nicodemus and those he represents derive their basic identity from their earthly origins, from the physical birth that is the common point of origin for all human beings. Significantly, the idea of new birth was not common in first-century Judaism, and the notion would actually have been more familiar to readers acquainted with certain Hellenistic religious practices. C. K. Barrett observed that the "novelty of John's thought when compared with Judaism is not accidental," since the text shows that no one, not even a ruler of the Jews, can "move forward continuously into the kingdom. A moment of discontinuity, comparable with physical birth, is essential."[27] Jesus' abrupt remarks place the teacher of Israel alongside all other human beings who are born of the flesh and stand in need of rebirth by the power of God's Spirit.

The images of darkness surrounding Nicodemus reinforce the universal dimensions of his character. Nicodemus first approached Jesus "by night" (3:2), and by the end of the discourse their nocturnal meeting becomes a microcosm of the encounter between Jesus and the world. "'And this is the judgment, that the light has come into the world, and men [*anthrōpoi*] loved darkness rather than light, because their deeds were evil. For every one who does evil hates the light, and does not come to the light, lest his deeds should be exposed. But he who does what is true comes to the light, that it may be clearly seen that his deeds have been done in God'" (3:19-21). Nicodemus represents the world; and the Jewish authorities and the masses for whom he speaks are, appropriately, called "the world" elsewhere in this Gospel (8:23; 12:18-19). But this encounter leaves readers with unsettling questions. Does the world remain in darkness, or does it come out of the darkness to the light? It is clear that God loved the world and sent his Son to save the world, but the world's response is left open. After asking a final question that is never answered, Nicodemus falls silent and seemingly "fades off into the darkness whence he came,"[28] while Jesus reproves his failure to understand or believe. Nicodemus did "come" to Jesus (3:2), which is characteristic of those who do what is true, and his incomprehension was "exposed" by the light (3:20-21). But does that mean he "saw the light" or that he remained under

---

27. *Gospel*, 206–7. Schnackenburg overestimates the connections between spiritual birth and Jewish practice (*Gospel*, 1.370–71).

28. Brown, *Gospel*, 1.145.

divine judgment? The encounter is fraught with ambiguity, and the conclusion of the episode leaves readers in suspense.[29] Nicodemus will appear twice more in the Gospel, and we must save further comment on his character for the chapters on light and darkness and the crucifixion.

The Samaritan Woman

The Samaritan woman is Nicodemus's mirror opposite. Nicodemus was a man, a Jew, and a respected member of society who came to Jesus by night. She was a woman, a Samaritan, and a marginal member of society who encountered Jesus in broad daylight. Like the story of Nicodemus, the encounter with the Samaritan woman begins as a conversation between two individuals. Jesus meets the woman as he sits alone beside a roadside well; his disciples have gone into the town to buy food. No one else is present. Yet as the conversation progresses, the woman serves as the spokesperson of the Samaritan people. She and Jesus begin to address each other in plural forms of speech and the woman voices Samaritan national concerns. The horizon broadens still further until the Samaritan townspeople receive Jesus not just as a national deliverer but as Savior of the world.

The woman's role as spokesperson for the Samaritan people emerges in the first part of the conversation. Her name is not given; she is simply called "a woman of Samaria" or "the Samaritan woman" (4:7, 9). When Jesus asks her for a drink, she raises the issue of national differences, wondering, "How is it that you, a Jew, ask a drink of me, a woman of Samaria?" (4:9a). Jesus comments that if she had asked him, he would have given her living water. The woman's response shifts into the first person plural, as she says, "Surely you're not greater than *our* father Jacob, who gave *us* this well?" (4:12).

The setting beside the ancestral well and references to Jacob enhance the typical aspects of the woman's character. In the Old Testament several of the woman's ancestors, including Jacob and Rachel, first courted beside a well. The stories follow a pattern: A man traveling in a foreign land meets a young woman beside a well. She gives him water and hurries home to tell her family about the visitor. The man is invited to stay, and a betrothal is arranged.[30] Jesus assumed the role of bridegroom earlier in

---

29. See the helpful treatment by Jouette M. Bassler, "Mixed Signals: Nicodemus in the Fourth Gospel," *JBL* 108 (1989) 635–46.

30. The connections between Old Testament betrothal scenes and John 4 have long been noticed. See, e.g., David Friedrich Strauss, *The Life of Jesus Critically Examined* (Philadelphia: Fortress, 1972; German orig. 1835) 308. More recently see M.-E. Boismard, "Aenon près de Salem: Jean III.23," *RB* 80 (1973) 218–29, esp. 223–26; J. H. Neyrey, "Jacob Traditions and the Interpretation of John 4:10-26," *CBQ* 41 (1979) 419–37, esp. 425–26; C. M. Carmichael, "Marriage and the Samaritan Woman," *NTS* 26 (1979–80) 332–46; P. J. Cahill, "Narrative Art in John IV," *Religious Studies Bulletin* 2 (1982) 41–48; Duke, *Irony in the Fourth Gospel*, 101–3; M. Girard, "Jésus en Samarie (Jean 4,1-42): Analyses des structures stylistic et du process de symbolisation," *Eglise et Théologie* 17 (1986) 275–310, esp. 302–4.

the Gospel by providing wine for the wedding at Cana (2:1-11), and John
the Baptist identified Jesus as the bridegroom who had come to claim the
bride (3:29). In this story Jesus is traveling through Samaria, which was
foreign territory, where he meets one of Jacob's descendants, a woman
who had come to the well at midday as Rachel had (Gen. 29:7; John 4:6).
These typical traits suggest that the Samaritan woman, like Rachel, will be
receptive to the stranger. Despite her confusion over the meaning of "living water," she does ask Jesus for some (4:15).

At this point, however, a wrinkle appears in the story. Unlike the maidens
who usually appear in biblical betrothal scenes, the Samaritan woman previously had five husbands (4:16-18). The text does not say whether she was
divorced or widowed, but by almost any estimate a series of five husbands
seems excessive—the rabbis permitted a widow to marry a second or at most
a third time. Moreover, the woman was living with a sixth man, either out of
desire or necessity, in a relationship that was not a marriage. At best her
story is tragic; at worst it is sinful. Yet the peculiar details of the woman's life
actually enhance her role as a representative of the Samaritan people, which
began in 4:7-15 and will be developed further in 4:20-25.

The woman's personal history parallels her national history.[31] The Samaritans were not simply descendants of Jacob; their ancestry was mixed.
The Assyrians who conquered the region in 721 B.C. brought colonists
from five foreign nations into Samaria (2 Kings 17:24), and the issue of
intermarriage continued to cloud relations between Jews and Samaritans
in the first century. Josephus recalled that five nations had settled in
Samaria and charged that Samaritans claimed to descend from Joseph (cf.
John 4:5) only when the Jews were prospering, but insisted they were of
foreign descent when their Jewish neighbors were in trouble. Jewish writings from this period refer to the Samaritans as "Cuthians," a derogatory
reminder that Samaritans were the descendants of colonists brought in
from Cuthah and other places (*Ant.* 9.14.3 §288). Herod the Great continued the pattern of colonization that began under the Assyrians by settling
thousands of foreigners in the Samaritan capital, which he renamed
Sebaste, the Greek word for Augustus. The Samaritans lived alongside the
foreigners but did not intermarry with them as extensively as before.
The woman's personal history of marriage to five husbands and cohabita-
tion with a sixth parallels the colonial history of Samaria.

The woman responds to Jesus' insights about her personal life by calling Jesus a prophet and raising an issue of national importance—namely,
whether people should worship at the Jewish sanctuary in Jerusalem or
the Samaritan holy place at Gerizim. The conversation develops largely
through plural forms of speech.

31. For more extended discussion see my "'Savior of the World,'" 665–80. In addition to
the literature cited there, see Okure, *The Johannine Approach to Mission,* 88–89, 111–12.

The woman said to him, . . . "*Our* fathers worshiped at this mountain; and *you people* say that in Jerusalem is the place where it is necessary to worship." Jesus said to her, "Believe me, woman, the hour is coming when neither on this mountain nor in Jerusalem will *you people* worship the Father. *You people* worship what you do not know. *We* worship what we know, for salvation is from the Jews. But the hour is coming and now is when the true worshipers will worship the Father in Spirit and truth; for the Father seeks such people to worship him." (4:20-22)

The woman speaks for Samaritan worshipers, while Jesus, who considered the Jerusalem temple his Father's house (2:16), initially speaks for Jewish worshipers. By telling the woman, "You people worship what you do not know," Jesus voices the common Jewish contention that idolatry reflects ignorance (e.g., Isa. 44:9, 18; Wisd. of Sol. 13:1-2). The charge of idolatry was connected with the legacy of Jacob and with foreign colonization of Samaria, both of which were reflected in the woman's personal life. Jewish sources traced idolatry in Samaria back to the woman's ancestor Jacob, who buried the household gods Rachel had stolen from her father under the oak near Shechem, creating a deposit of idols at the foot of Mount Gerizim (Gen. 31:19, 34).[32] The foreigners who settled in the region after the Assyrian conquest exacerbated the problem by introducing the worship of their own deities. Herod the Great continued the pattern by erecting a renowned temple to Caesar in the Samaritan capital.

The conversation about worship begins to reveal the universal dimensions of the woman's character. Jesus placed the woman and the Samaritan people in the category of those who worship what they do not know: From a Jewish perspective this included most of humanity, and from a Johannine perspective it was typical of "the world." Yet such ignorance was not the final word, for Jesus announced that the worship established by "the fathers" would give way to worship inaugurated by God "the Father," which would be marked by Spirit and truth. The Samaritans worshiped what they did not know, but when the woman brought her townspeople to Jesus, they declared, "*We know* that this is *truly* the Savior of the world" (John 4:42). Their confession signals the return of a part of the unbelieving world to God (cf. 3:16-17; 12:45-46).

The faith of the townspeople points to the universal significance of Jesus because in him the differences between Jews and Samaritans are transcended. Jesus had spoken of worship that would not be tied to Gerizim or Jerusalem, and the woman had responded with a hope that remained both personal and national: "*I* know that Messiah is coming. . . . He will declare everything *to us*" (4:25). Nevertheless, when she reported that Jesus had told her "everything" about her personal life, her townspeople concluded that Jesus fulfilled and surpassed their national hopes, ac-

32. See also *Bib. Ant.* 25:10; *Gen. Rab.* 81:3.

claiming him "Savior of *the world*," an appellation associated not with Samaritan or Jewish messianic expectations but with the Roman emperor. The episode begins like the betrothal stories of Israel's ancestors but ends with the kind of civic reception that cities throughout the empire granted to Vespasian and Titus, the Roman generals who became emperors. People would stream out to the roadsides to greet them, then escort them into their town, calling them "savior and benefactor." By going out to meet Jesus on the road, inviting him into their town, and hailing him as the "Savior of the world," the people of Sychar witnessed to the universal scope of his power.[33]

THE ROYAL OFFICIAL AND
THE INVALID

The royal official from Capernaum and the paralytic at Bethzatha are not developed as fully as Nicodemus and the Samaritan woman, but they do play significant representative roles. Both figures span the boundaries between Jewish and non-Jewish worlds, and their stories are told in parallel fashion, which enables readers to reflect on their contrasting responses to Jesus (4:46—5:16).

The Royal Official

The story of the royal official is prefaced by a transitional scene that identifies him with the Galileans, introducing a tension that is resolved only later in the episode. On one hand, Jesus had gone to Galilee because of burgeoning opposition in Judea (4:1-3), and when he arrived the Galileans welcomed him (4:43-45), which seems positive; he also testified that "a prophet has no honor in his own country" (4:44), which seems to refer back to conflicts in Judea.[34] On the other hand, Jesus' remark could presage coming difficulties in Galilee, which most of the characters in the Gospel thought was Jesus' homeland.[35] It was true that the Galileans welcomed Jesus, but they did so "having seen all that he had done in Jerusalem at the feast, for they too had gone to the feast" (4:45), which suggests that they might exemplify the same unreliable miracle-faith Jesus encountered in Jerusalem (2:23-25). When the royal official arrives on the scene, Jesus seems to confirm this negative assessment by brusquely telling the

---

33. For detailed discussion see my "'Savior of the World,'" 665–67.

34. E.g., Barrett, *Gospel*, 246; Wayne A. Meeks, "Galilee and Judea in the Fourth Gospel," *JBL* 85 (1966) 159–96; Robert T. Fortna, *The Fourth Gospel and Its Predecessor: From Narrative Source to Present Gospel* (Philadelphia: Fortress, 1988) 311–12; Jouette M. Bassler, "The Galileans: A Neglected Factor in Johannine Community Research," *CBQ* 43 (1981) 243–57, esp. 248–49.

35. John 7:41, 52. Cf. Luke 4:24; Mark 6:4; Matt. 13:57; Brown, *Gospel*, 1.186–89; Schnackenburg, *Gospel*, 1.462; John W. Pryor, "John 4:44 and the *Patris* of Jesus," *CBQ* 49 (1987) 254–63.

man, "Unless *you people* see signs and wonders *you people* will not believe" (4:48).

Nevertheless, the royal official does emerge as a positive exemplar of faith. The setting helps align the Galilean official with the first disciples of Jesus. The episode begins and ends by reminding readers that Jesus had done a sign in Cana on his previous trip to Galilee (4:46, 54; cf. 1:43; 2:11). The disciples who accompanied Jesus on his first visit to Cana had believed in Jesus on the basis of what they had heard from or about him, and before going to Cana Jesus promised that his disciples would see "greater things" (1:51); the sign he performed confirmed his promise and the faith of his disciples (2:11). Like the first followers of Jesus, the royal official came to Jesus without having seen any miracles; he had only *heard* that Jesus had come to Galilee (4:47a). He pleaded with Jesus to come with him and heal his son, but his expectations were not met; Jesus simply promised that his son would live. The man believed Jesus' word without having seen a miracle and returned to Capernaum. He was met by servants who told him that his son was living, and the report of the sign confirmed Jesus' promise and the man's faith.

The official's national identity is surprisingly ambiguous, which helps him represent Christians of any background. The official seems to have some affinity with the Galileans who worshiped in Jerusalem, but unlike them his faith was confirmed by a sign, not based upon a sign. He is called a *basilikos,* a term that usually designated officials and soldiers employed by the king. Readers familiar with the history of the region would have known that Galilee was ruled by kings from the Herodian family, who were of Idumean rather than Jewish extraction and who ruled as Roman vassals. Some of their officials were Jewish, but many, especially in the military, were Gentiles who allied themselves with the Romans, which might suggest that this official was a Gentile.[36] The Herods are not mentioned in John's Gospel, however; the only kings mentioned are Jesus and Caesar. Therefore readers less familiar with the history of the region probably would assume the man was a non-Jewish royal official, like those found elsewhere in the empire. The man's identity is established primarily in terms of his faith, which was engendered by testimony, confirmed by further word of a sign, and could characterize Christians of any background.

The Invalid

The invalid in John 5:1-16 is the royal official's counterpart. In the first story the official came to Jesus and pleaded for healing; Jesus lamented the need for signs and wonders, yet the man persisted, was promised healing, and left

---

36. See the discussion in Francis J. Maloney, "From Cana to Cana (Jn. 2:1—4:54) and the Fourth Evangelist's Concept of Correct (and Incorrect) Faith," *Salesianum* 40 (1978) 817–43, esp. 835 n. 45; A. H. Mead, "The *basilikos* in John 4.46-53," *JSNT* 23 (1985) 69–72.

believing Jesus' word. In the second story Jesus came to the paralytic and offered healing; the man lamented his inability to benefit from the pool's signs and wonders, yet Jesus persisted and healed the man, who left not knowing Jesus' name. In the first story the official encountered servants who announced that healing had occurred; he checked on the time of healing, verifying that Jesus had done the healing, with the result that his whole household believed. In the second story the man encountered the Jewish authorities who announced that a Sabbath violation had occurred; Jesus checked on the man, verifying that he had done the healing, with the result that the Jewish authorities persecuted Jesus.

The paralytic's representative role is suggested by the introduction to the scene (5:1-5). The setting is described broadly at first, with Jesus going to Jerusalem for a festival. Next, attention is directed to a specific place in Jerusalem, to the pool known in Hebrew as Bethzatha, which had five porticoes. Readers are then taken inside the porticoes and shown the multitude of invalids lying there, including the blind, lame, and paralyzed. Finally, the author focuses on one particular invalid who had been ill for thirty-eight years. The man's situation was unique in some ways, yet he was also part of a much larger group.

Like the royal official, the paralytic's identity spanned the boundary between the Jewish and gentile worlds. His Jewish traits are clear. He was in Jerusalem, where the Jewish authorities became increasingly hostile to Jesus while the crowds exhibited an unreliable faith based on miracles. Like the crowd, the invalid was preoccupied with the miraculous, and when he was reprimanded by the Jewish authorities for a Sabbath violation, he readily reported his healer to the Jews. Yet the man also has striking affinities with the non-Jewish world. The pool at Bethzatha was in Jerusalem, but it was not a typical Jewish establishment. The shrine was built around a water source that bubbled intermittently and was thought to possess special healing powers. Sick people would sometimes be resident at the place for some time waiting for the water to stir. The invalid's comment in 5:7 suggests that a person who entered the water immediately would be healed, but that latecomers would not be helped. These practices are not well attested in Jewish sources, which commonly connected healing with prayer to God—and the God of Israel did not reserve his favor for those who were best able to help themselves.

The pattern at Bethzatha resembled the practices associated with the healing shrines of the gods Asclepius and Serapis, which were found throughout the eastern Mediterranean, as Antoine Duprez has observed.[37]

37. *Jésus et les dieux guérisseurs* (Cahiers de la *Revue Biblique* 12; Paris: Gabalda, 1970). See also W. D. Davies, *The Gospel and the Land* (Berkeley: University of California Press, 1974) 302–13.

Like the pool described in John 5, these sanctuaries were normally built beside natural water sources where people might remain for some time seeking the aid of the deity. Archaeological excavations have shown that the small grottos at Bethzatha were similar to those found at Asclepian sanctuaries elsewhere in the Roman Empire. Votive offerings to the god Serapis, dating from the second century, were discovered at Bethzatha, indicating how readily the shrine was adapted for pagan use. It is not clear that Greco-Roman deities were actually invoked at the pool prior to the destruction of Jerusalem, but at that time it was located outside the walls of Jerusalem where unorthodox practices were tolerated more readily than in the city.[38] It was also located near the Antonia fortress, the largest Roman military installation in the city, which would have been useful for the Gentiles stationed there. Many readers would not have known about Bethzatha itself, but the pattern described in the Gospel would have enabled them to discern the similarities between the practices associated with this pool and pools found elsewhere in the Greco-Roman world.

The story of the invalid gives a sharp word of warning to readers from Jewish and non-Jewish backgrounds. The invalid was intimidated by the Jewish authorities and, perhaps unwittingly, subjected his healer to persecution in his efforts to placate them. The man, like some of the first readers of the Gospel, lived in a situation where dual loyalties had become impossible. The story of the invalid showed that lack of commitment meant betrayal. At the same time, even readers who were not familiar with Bethzatha would have been able to detect the similarities between a place like Bethzatha and the healing shrines scattered across the ancient Mediterranean world. The deities associated with these shrines did not demand exclusive allegiance from worshipers, who could move from one religious cult to another with relative ease. Yet those who assumed that loyalty to Jesus was optional remained in sin and under the threat of judgment (5:14).

THE CROWDS

The primary interlocutors in the narrative thus far have been individuals, but in John 6–8 Jesus speaks almost exclusively with groups of people who play representative roles. John 6 relates a series of encounters between Jesus and a crowd in Galilee, and John 7–8 turns to the crowd that was in Jerusalem for the feast of Booths. The use of a group of people as a primary interlocutor in an episode was a feature of Greek drama, in which the chorus sometimes served as the main character's chief accompaniment or

---

38. Despite resistance, Herod even placed a golden eagle, which was forbidden by the law, on the great gate of the temple (*J.W.* 17.6.2 §151).

foil.[39] What is striking about the crowds in John's Gospel is that their identity subtly shifts as the episodes unfold, blurring the lines that distinguished the various factions within the crowd from each other, from the Jewish authorities, and even from those who seemed to believe in Jesus.

The Crowd in Galilee

The evangelist observed that the multitude followed Jesus in Galilee "because they saw the signs which he did on those who were diseased" (6:1-2). It was about the time of Passover, and Jesus fed the crowd with five barley loaves and two fish. They immediately acclaimed him a prophet and tried to make him their king, but Jesus eluded them and withdrew by himself. Each of these elements—the crowd's enthusiasm for signs, the Passover setting, and Jesus' negative reaction to their acclaim—helps readers discern the typical character of this group. They resemble the crowd Jesus encountered on the previous Passover, when he refused to trust those who believed because of the signs (2:23-25), and they are like the adoring masses who appear on the third and final Passover to laud Jesus as their king because of the signs, until Jesus again hides from them (12:12-18, 36).

The typical character of the crowd is enhanced by the story's geographical location, which was near the city of Tiberius. The introduction to the story of the feeding says that Jesus had gone "across the Sea of Galilee of Tiberius" (6:1), a peculiar designation that connects the episode not only with the region of Galilee but also with the city of Tiberius, which was the major urban center along the lake. Tiberius is mentioned again in the transitional scene that traces the movement of the crowd from the place where Jesus fed them to the town of Capernaum. The text says that "boats came from Tiberius [which was] near the place where they ate the bread after the Lord had given thanks" (6:23).[40] The crowd got into the boats and apparently followed the usual navigation route along the western

39. On the function of the chorus as an actor, see Harsh, *A Handbook of Classical Drama*, 20–22.

40. Interpreters often assume that the feeding took place on the east side of the lake rather than on the west side in the vicinity of Tiberius. See Schnackenburg, *Gospel*, 2.33; Barrett, *Gospel*, 285. Nevertheless, the narrative itself seems to presuppose that the feeding took place on the west side of the lake near Tiberius. The word *eggys* (near) sometimes modifies a verb in John's Gospel, as when Jesus is said to be "drawing near to the boat" (6:19). Therefore some understand 6:23 to mean that boats crossed from Tiberius on the western shore and "landed near the place" (NIV) where the feeding occurred on the eastern shore. But *eggys* probably means that the site of the feeding itself was near Tiberius. For example, *eggys* is used for a place called "Aenon [which is] near Salim" (3:23), and Jesus is said to have gone from the village of Bethany "to the region [which is] near the desert" (11:54). Several other occurrences of *eggys* in connection with places make this sense of the word clear by coupling it with a form of the word *to be:* Bethany "was near Jerusalem" (11:18), Golgotha "was near the city" (19:20), and the tomb "was near" the place of crucifixion (19:42). This is precisely the sense found in the original text of Sinaiticus, which said that "boats came from Tiberius, which was [*ousēs*] near where they ate the bread" (6:23).

shore of the lake to Capernaum, which was "across the sea" northward from Tiberius.[41]

The characteristics of the people of Tiberius were probably well known to some readers. Josephus called them a "promiscuous rabble," comprised of magistrates and poor folk "from any and all places of origin" (*Ant.* 18.2.3 §§36–38). The city, which was named for the emperor Tiberius, had been founded in about A.D. 19 by Herod Antipas, a Roman vassal. The king established it as his capital with a Hellenistic constitution but found it difficult to get Jews to settle there since he had built it on the site of a graveyard, and contact with the dead made people unclean according to Jewish law. Therefore, to find residents for his new city, Herod freed slaves and offered free land and houses to those who would settle there. A synagogue was established, but the memory of the city's unsavory origins tainted its reputation for some time.[42] During the war with Rome, some of the Tiberians supported the insurrectionists, but the city eventually opened its gates to Vespasian, whom they acclaimed savior and benefactor (*J.W.* 3.9.8 §459).[43]

Readers would not have to know the history of Tiberius, however, to see in the crowd traits that were typical of the masses in various Greco-Roman cities. Roman rulers regularly placated the populace with distributions of bread or grain. Cicero recalled that the practice was agreeable to the masses, since it provided food in abundance without work, but it was opposed by "loyal citizens" who thought it would induce idleness and drain the treasury. Juvenal lampooned citizens who dutifully accompanied the consul because of the free meal-ticket stashed in their wallets, and he mocked the fickle crowds who were willing to proclaim any lucky "carcass an equal successor to Augustus" but were devoted only to the "bread and circuses" with which their leaders mollified them. The notorious practice also spread to other cities, and Dio Chrysostom chided the people of Alexandria who were reputed to be a group "to whom you need only

---

41. The expression "across the sea" (*peran tēs thalassēs*, 6:1, 17, 22, 25) is often taken to mean that people were traveling east to west across the sea. Nevertheless, there are good reasons to think that it should be understood to mean travel across the stretch of water between the region of Tiberius and Capernaum, which are both on the western side of the lake. Jesus was in Jerusalem in chapter 5 and comes to Galilee in chapter 6; although the transition between the chapters is notoriously abrupt, the basic movement is from south to north. There is no reason to think that it suddenly becomes an east-to-west movement. A number of manuscripts actually say that "Jesus went across the Sea of Galilee to the region [*eis ta merē*] of Tiberius" (6:1). Evidence from Josephus indicates that there was regular boat travel between the towns on the western shore of the lake. Significantly, he says that those who traveled between Tiberius and the town of Taricheae—which was also on the western side and closer to Tiberius than Capernaum was—"crossed over" the lake (*diaper-aioun*; *Life* 304). Cf. Brown, *Gospel*, 1.232, 257–58.

42. *y. Sheb.* 9,38d; *Gen. Rab.* 79:6; *Eccl. Rab.* 10:8.

43. On the history of Tiberius see Schürer, *History*, 2.178–82; Str-B 2.467–77.

throw plenty of bread and a ticket to the hippodrome, since they have no interest in anything else."[44]

Like a typical crowd in a Greco-Roman city, the multitude in John 6 had no interest in anything but bread. Readers of the Gospel would need to know something about Moses traditions to understand why the crowd called Jesus a prophet (6:14), but the mob's eagerness to make Jesus king on the basis of a bread distribution would have been familiar to a broad spectrum of readers in the Greco-Roman world. The crowd exhibited the kind of loyalty that was based on eating their fill of the loaves (6:26), and Jesus repudiated it. He warned against their preoccupation with the food that perishes (6:27), and despite the complex allusions to Jewish traditions in the remainder of the discourse, his warning struck at an attitude that would have been well known to most readers.

In the next part of the episode, the crowd exhibits the traits of their Israelite ancestors, who are explicitly mentioned in the text. They demanded that Jesus work another bread miracle for them, recalling how "our fathers ate the manna in the wilderness" (6:31). The most memorable characteristic of the wilderness generation was their persistent "murmuring" against God and Moses. God delivered the people from bondage in Egypt by empowering Moses to perform great signs (Exod. 7:3-4; 10:1-2; Deut. 4:34),[45] but three days after passing through the sea they began murmuring for water (Exod. 15:24). God provided water, but the people murmured for food. So God fed them with manna each day until spies brought back an enormous cluster of grapes from the promised land. Then the people murmured because of the Canaanites there, and God thundered, "How long will this people despise me? And how long will they not believe in me, in spite of all the signs which I have wrought among them?" God vowed that the murmuring generation would die in the wilderness (Num. 14:11, 22-23, 26-30).

Jesus, like God, had fed the people with bread; but the people, like their ancestors, were not satisfied and murmured against him (John 6:41, 43). So Jesus bluntly reminded them that "your fathers ate manna in the wilderness—and they died" (6:49). The ominous implication is that those who exhibit the same murmuring tendencies will share a similar

44. Cicero, *Pro Sestio* 48 §103; Juvenal, *Satires* 10.44–46, 73–80; Dio Chrysostom, *Discourses* 32.31. See also Juvenal, *Satires* 7.174 and 8.118; Fronto, *Correspondence* (ed. and trans. C. R. Haines; LCL; Cambridge: Harvard University Press; London: Heinemann, 1963) 2.17. The philosopher Bion remarked that it was impossible to please a crowd except by turning into a cake (Dio Chrysostom, *Discourses* 66.26). For commentary on the practice, see E. Courtney, *A Commentary on the Satires of Juvenal* (London: Athlone, 1980) 104–5, 372, 472; E. G. Hardy, *The Satires of Juvenal* (2d ed.; London: Macmillan, 1891) 198–99, 232. See also Paul Veyne, *Bread and Circuses: Historical Sociology and Political Pluralism* (London: Penguin, 1990) 99–100.

45. Also Exod. 4:8, 9, 17, 28, 30; 8:23; Deut. 34:11; Ps. 78:43; 105:27.

fate. Yet Jesus contrasts the legacy of "the fathers" of Israel who died with the activity of God "the Father" who gives life (6:49-50, 58; cf. 4:20-24). The scope of God's activity extends beyond the traditional confines of Israel to give life "to the world" (6:33, 51), so that "anyone" who eats it may live forever. The crowd is offered life on the same basis that it is offered to any human being.

As the crowd becomes increasingly hostile to Jesus, the text suddenly identifies them as "the Jews" (6:41, 52). Prior to this, the Jews were firmly connected with Judea and Jerusalem, and a pattern emerged contrasting the negative response of people in Judea with the positive responses found elsewhere. In Jerusalem, Jesus met with skepticism from the Jews, unreliable faith from the crowd, and growing hostility from the Pharisees; but in Samaria the people acclaimed him Savior of the world. Similarly, the Galileans welcomed Jesus, and the royal official's household believed, but the invalid in Jerusalem reported Jesus to the Jewish authorities who persecuted him. The appearance of hostile Jews at Capernaum in Galilee breaks the carefully constructed contrasts between regions. Afterward Jesus continues to be threatened in Jerusalem and finds refuge outside Judea, but he also encounters unbelief from his own brothers in Galilee and belief from the beggar and from Martha and Mary in the vicinity of Jerusalem.

Jouette Bassler has observed that despite the careful geographical contrasts, the evangelist is primarily concerned not with the places in which Jesus is accepted or rejected but with the people who accept or reject him.[46] Historically, it seems certain that Jesus' first disciples came from Galilee and that Jesus was executed at Jerusalem in Judea—our sources are consistent on those points. The fourth evangelist made these positive and negative responses typical of the respective regions, then extended the regional affiliation to anyone who responded to Jesus in the way characteristic of the region. This movement from a notion of regional characteristics to more general faith responses may have been facilitated by the Johannine community's own experience of conflict with non-Christians from the synagogue and at least some success in mission among non-Jews in various places.

When the crowd at Capernaum manifested the same kind of animosity that Jesus encountered in Judea, the evangelist identified them as Jews (6:41, 52). Similarly, Nicodemus was initially identified with the Jewish authorities and the multitudes in Jerusalem, but when he expresses more openness to Jesus in the next chapter, the authorities wonder if he might actually be from Galilee (7:51-52). Jesus was not of Samaritan extraction,

46. "The Galileans: A Neglected Factor in Johannine Community Research," 252–57.

but in the heat of debate his opponents insisted, "Are we not right in saying that you are a Samaritan and have a demon?" (8:48-49). Pilate clearly was a Roman, but when interrogating Jesus he asked, "Am I a Jew?" (18:35), a question that could be answered affirmatively in light of his collusion with the Jewish authorities. Conversely, the blind beggar and Martha and Mary responded more positively to Jesus. Although they were Jewish and lived in the vicinity of Jerusalem, the expression "the Jews" is applied not to them but to the others in the story who were either hostile or manifested an unreliable faith in Jesus. "The Jews" is not a blanket appellation for the inhabitants of a region; it is used for those who exhibit certain types of faith responses (11:36-37, 45-46; 12:9, 17, 34).[47]

The evangelist shifts the crowd's identity again at the end of chapter 6. In almost kaleidoscopic fashion, the crowd of antagonistic "Jews" becomes a group of "disciples," whom we would expect to be the close associates of Jesus that were distinguished from the crowd earlier in the chapter (6:3, 8, 12, 16, 24). Yet at the end of the episode the so-called disciples "murmured" at Jesus and found it impossible to believe in him (6:60-65), just as the Jews in the previous scene had "murmured." Therefore, "many of his disciples drew back and no longer went about with him" (6:66), moving outside the sphere of true faith.

In contrast to this group, the Twelve—who are mentioned here for the first time in the Gospel—remain loyal. Jesus asked them, "You don't want to go away too, do you?" and Peter confessed that Jesus had the words of eternal life, for he was the Holy One of God (6:67-69). Yet the reality of unbelief was present even within the circle of the Twelve, for Jesus had chosen one of them, Judas, who was a devil and would betray him (6:70-71). Later Judas, moved by Satan, would go out from the circle of Jesus' followers and into the night (13:30), just as many in John 6 had departed.

Readers within the later Johannine community could easily have related this scene to a schism within their own community. According to 1 John 2:19, there were some who "went out" from the ranks of the faithful. This schism reflects a conflict with a transcendent dimension. The faithful, like Peter, were connected with Jesus "the Holy One,"[48] and they knew the truth (2:20-21). Those who had separated from them, like Judas, were antichrists associated with the devil and darkness (2:9, 18-19; 3:10). The epistles were probably written after the Gospel was completed and reflect a struggle with those who held to a highly spiritualized or docetic Christology. Although some have suggested that this section of the Gospel reflects the same conflict, the opponents throughout John 6—as elsewhere in the

---

47. On the traits of "the Jews" and the crowds, see Culpepper, *Anatomy*, 125–32.
48. On the identification of "the Holy One," see Brown, *Epistles*, 347–48.

Gospel—seem to have the opposite problem: an inability to move beyond the material level.[49] But even if specific issues changed, the kind of language used in John 6 continued to be used within the community during the period of the epistles in order to point to the transcendent dimensions of schisms and to keep readers among the faithful.[50]

The crowd in John 6 assumes various guises yet in each case proves false to Jesus. In the beginning they gaped after the signs like the multitudes in Jerusalem, then tried to turn him into a king of their own making. They clamored after bread like the typical masses from a Greco-Roman city but soon became hostile to Jesus like the Jewish authorities in Jerusalem. Finally, some who were called disciples broke away from Jesus, and a betrayer was even identified among the Twelve. On one level they are portrayed as the Jewish people who encountered Jesus early in the first century; on another level they represent types known throughout the Greco-Roman world; on still another level they reflect the fundamental conflict between the people of God and the demonic power manifested in unbelief.

The Crowd in Jerusalem

The representative quality of groups in John is even more pronounced in the disputes during the feast of Booths (John 7–8). Jesus' brothers told him to go to Judea to show himself "to the world." Jesus initially refused and identified those he would meet in Judea with "the world" that hated him (7:3, 4, 7). When Jesus later went to the feast, he met a world that at least initially seemed to be composed of various groups of people.[51] His most bitter opponents were the Pharisees and chief priests, who are sometimes called "the Jews" and who sought to arrest and kill Jesus (7:2, 11, 26, 32). "The crowd" is sometimes distinguished from the authorities, whom they feared (7:11-12, 25-26), but the line between these groups is blurry. Some in the crowd thought Jesus was a deceiver, and they, like the authorities, wanted to arrest him (7:43-44). Others thought Jesus was a good man, and some even believed in him; but even the believers are called "the Jews," and the text discloses that they, like the authorities, wanted to kill Jesus (8:31, 51). The primary trait of the crowd in the eyes of the chief priests and Pharisees was ignorance of the law (8:49), yet the

49. Those who argue that John 6:51c-58 opposes a docetic Christology include Georg Richter, "Formgeschichte," 43–48; H. Thyen, "Entwicklungen," 277; G. Bornkamm, "Eucharistische Rede," 163, 169; Schnackenburg, *Gospel*, 2.61. For the view that all of John 6 deals with a low Christology, see Rensberger, *Johannine Faith*, 71–73; cf. Brown, *Community*, 74–75, 78. Brown says that Jesus left the synagogue after 6:59, so the dispute in 6:60 is with another group (p. 74), but no departure is mentioned in the text; this chapter features a remarkable flow from one group to the next.

50. Brown, *Epistles*, 364 n. 4; 367 n. 14; 468–69; Barrett, *Gospel*, 302.

51. See Culpepper, *Anatomy*, 126, 129. On the typical cast of disputes among townspeople, cf. Chariton, *Chaereas and Callirhoe* 6.1.2–3.

Jewish leaders themselves apparently did not recall that the law provided for judicial hearings before someone could be condemned (8:51), which indicates that they were fundamentally no different from the uneducated masses. Initially there appear to be various groups in Jerusalem, but all of them prove to be part of "the world" in opposition to Jesus.

The interlocutors in these chapters exhibit many typical Jewish characteristics, but the conversations disclose their true identity in more universal terms. The Jewish authorities took issue with Jesus' credentials as a teacher of the law (7:14-24) and with the value of the testimony he bore to himself in relation to Mosaic regulations (8:13-20), but Jesus identified them as people who judge "according to the flesh" in ignorance of God (8:15, 19). The basic distinction was not between those who did and did not adhere to the Mosaic law but between Jesus who was from above and hearers who were from below. The contrast was cosmic in scope: His hearers were of this world; Jesus was not of this world (8:23).

The crowd exhibited distinctively Jewish traits at first, bickering over the qualifications needed for the prophet like Moses and the Messiah foretold in the Scriptures (7:27, 31, 40-43), but the scope of the discussion broadens so that they become representatives of a world hostile to God. Significant developments occur in the discussion of their Jewish ancestry. The argument began when Jesus announced, "If you continue in my word you are truly my disciples and you will know the truth and the truth will make you free" (8:31). The people replied that they were children of Abraham and had never been in bondage to anyone, a statement that is patently false. The children of Abraham had been in bondage once in Egypt, again in Babylon, and were under Roman domination in the first century. In the ensuing debate, Jesus reveals their true identity by discussing their ancestry in terms of slavery and freedom.

Jesus alluded to the fact that Abraham had two children, one slave and one free. Although they are not named here, readers familiar with the Scriptures would have known that Isaac was born of Sarah, the free woman, and Ishmael was born of the slave woman Hagar. Isaac was Abraham's heir, but Ishmael was expelled from Abraham's house, and Jewish tradition held that the expulsion occurred after Ishmael played with Isaac with malicious intent.[52] This tradition is echoed in the reminder that the slave does not continue in the house forever, but the son does, and that murderous intentions were characteristic of the slave son (8:34-38). Although Jesus' hearers claimed Abraham as their father, they did not manifest the traits of Abraham, who had received those whom God had sent; they were murderers like Ishmael (8:39-40; Gen. 18:1-5). Jesus' opponents denied

52. *Ant.* 1.12.3 §215; *Gen. Rab.* 53:11.

this parentage, insisting that they were not born of fornication like Ishmael was (John 8:41a).[53] In the second part of the debate, the crowd attempted to rebut Jesus by claiming, "We have one Father, even God" (8:41b). Jesus denied their assertion, countering that true children of God would love the one whom God had sent, while his opponents acted like their father the devil, who was a liar and a murderer from the beginning. They returned the accusation, charging that Jesus was the demonic one. Jesus retorted that he told the truth and that his hearers were liars because they claimed to know God when they did not. Their true murderous traits were finally revealed in their actions, for when Jesus recalled the name of God, "I Am," they picked up stones to throw at him. What began as a dispute between Jesus and a group of Jews was finally shown to be a conflict between the power of God and the power of the devil.

The particulars of the debate are Jewish, but the scope is universal, and it is worth asking how easily readers who were not of Jewish background could have understood this complex passage. Although references and allusions to the Old Testament and Jewish traditions pervade the text, the true nature of slavery and freedom was a standard topic in Greco-Roman rhetoric and philosophy. Jesus' statement "Everyone who commits sin is a slave to sin" (8:34) resembles a common philosophical tenet more closely than Jewish teachings. Socrates was said to have taught that truly free people acted according to what was best, while those who followed their passions were slaves.[54] The idea was common among the Stoics. Epictetus maintained that only the disciplined are free and that "no one who sins is free" but lives in slavery.[55]

The argument in John 8 follows a progression like that of a debate recounted by Dio Chrysostom, who was apparently emulating a well-known pattern.[56] The debate in Dio's discourse, like that in John's Gospel, deals with the problem of discerning who is a slave and who is free. One partner in the dispute declared that he was free but that his opponent was not free. The other partner denied it and returned the charge, insisting that his accuser was the illegitimate son of a slave, born of fornication (*Discourses* 15.2–3; John 8:41b). In the second phase of the dispute, one of the men observed that when suspicions arose concerning the origins of a prominent figure in a drama, the character's ancestry was often traced back to Zeus to avoid further investigation. The man asserted that his

---

53. Philo said that Ishmael was expelled from Abraham's house because he claimed to play on equal terms with the freeborn although he was a bastard (*Sobriety* 8).

54. Xenophon, *Mem.* 4.5.3–5; *Oec.* 1.22. See J. H. Bernard, *A Critical and Exegetical Commentary on the Gospel according to St. John* (ICC; Edinburgh: T. & T. Clark, 1928) 2.307.

55. Epictetus, *Discourses* 2.1.23–24. See Bultmann, *Gospel*, 438 n. 2.

56. In addition to the comments Dio makes, see Euripides, *Hippolytus* 424; Plutarch, *Moralia* 1c.

opponent could not claim to be free unless he too hastened to trace his lineage back to a god (*Discourses* 15.7, 12; John 8:41c). The man's opponent declined to claim divine ancestry, but Jesus' opponents did claim descent from God, which proved to be a demonic illusion.

Robert Fortna has observed that John's references to "the Jews" sweep away the distinctions between Pharisees, scribes, Sadducees, Herodians, and Zealots that appear in the other Gospels.[57] The Jewish groups that remain are characterized primarily by their various perceptions of Jesus. Yet the lines that separate the chief priests and Pharisees from the crowds, and that distinguish the different factions within the crowds from each other, are gradually eroded by Jesus' repeated self-revelation. The term "Jews" can be applied to the hostile authorities and to those who believed for a time, yet each wave of discourse blurs the distinction between the groups still further, so that all become part of the vast expanse of earth, in contrast to Jesus who has come from above.

THE MAN BORN BLIND
AND MARTHA, MARY, AND LAZARUS

The stories of the man born blind (John 9) and the raising of Lazarus (John 11) are not juxtaposed in the narrative, but they can be conveniently treated together. Both involve miracles that are recounted very briefly; each episode consists mainly of conversations that relate to the significance of the miracle—after it occurred in the case of the man born blind and before it occurred in the case of Lazarus. The main characters in each episode also prove to be followers of Jesus, and these incidents offer glimpses into the way the evangelist reflected the situation of the later Christian community in his portrayals of people.

The Man Born Blind

The blind beggar appears immediately after the heated exchange with the Jews in the temple. When asked about the man, Jesus made the odd comment, "*We* must work the works of him who sent me" (9:4). Although the story is primarily about the activity of Jesus, J. Louis Martyn has noted that the use of the plural suggests that the story can be read on a second level, reflecting the experience of Christians living at the time the Gospel was written.[58] Later in the Gospel Jesus speaks of the period after his return to the Father, when "he who believes in me will also do the works that I do" (14:12), and the blind man's encounter with Jesus seems to presage the encounter of other people with Jesus' disciples. This impres-

57. "Theological Use of Locale in the Fourth Gospel," 90.
58. *History and Theology,* esp. 24–62.

sion is strengthened in the remainder of the story. Unlike the miracle stories in the other Gospels in which Jesus remains the focus of attention, this episode concentrates on what happens to the man when Jesus is no longer present. The apparent absence of Jesus would correspond to the situation of people living one or two generations after the end of his earthly ministry.

The central part of the narrative tells how the beggar was repeatedly questioned by the Jewish authorities. The seriousness of the interrogation is reflected in the refusal of the man's parents to speak for him. They "feared the Jews, for the Jews had already agreed that if anyone should confess [Jesus] to be the Christ, he was to be put out of the synagogue" (9:22). The statement as it stands seems to be a creative anachronism. There is little evidence that a group of Jewish authorities made a formal agreement to expel Christian Jews from the synagogue during Jesus' own lifetime, but the farewell discourses do say that expulsion from the synagogue would be a threat for Jesus' disciples after his return to the Father (16:2).

As the authorities incessantly pressed their questions, the beggar became impatient and asked, "Why do you want to hear it again? You don't want to become his disciples *too,* do you?" (9:27). His question is sarcastic but implies that the beggar now considers himself one of Jesus' disciples. The authorities retorted, "You are his disciple, but we are disciples of Moses" (9:28). Martyn notes that this statement seems odd when placed in the lifetime of Jesus, since it recognizes that being a follower of Jesus is both antithetical to and, in a sense, comparable to being a follower of Moses. The comment seems to reflect a period later in the first century, when the leaders of the synagogue came to view the Christian movement as a distinguishable rival.[59] By the time the beggar is finally expelled from the synagogue (9:34), he exemplifies disciples who do not fall away under the threat of expulsion (16:1-2), and his example provides encouragement for others to maintain their loyalty to Christ despite opposition from local Jewish leaders.

There is still a third level to the story, in which the beggar represents humankind. The man remains anonymous and is introduced simply as "a man blind from birth" (9:1). The disciples assumed that his physical condition reflected God's judgment upon him, and they asked whether it was the man himself or his parents who had sinned with the result that he was born blind (9:2). The Pharisees who expelled him from the synagogue held a more contemptuous form of this view, telling the beggar, "You were born in utter sin" (9:34). The beggar's movement into faith, however, demonstrated that his physical birth did not determine his destiny before

59. Ibid., 39.

God, and the blindness that was his most distinctive trait was also his most representative one. Comments at the beginning and end of the chapter disclose the full scope of the episode: Jesus enlightened the eyes of an individual to show that he was "the light *of the world*" (9:5) and "came into this world . . . that *those* who do not see may see" (9:39ab). At the same time, the Jewish authorities who could see physically refused to recognize the power of God manifested in Jesus; by obstinately staring into "the light" they became blind to Jesus and to the God who had sent him. Jesus' concluding remarks also extended this response to people generally, warning that the coming of the light could mean that "those who see may become blind" (9:39c).

On one level this story relates what happened to one man during the ministry of Jesus in the early part of the first century. On another level it is the story of Jesus' followers and their conflicts with the Jewish authorities toward the end of the first century, long after Jesus had returned to the Father. On still another level it is the story of the world encountering God in the person of Jesus, some coming into the light of faith and others becoming blind in their unbelief, which is at the heart of sin.[60]

Martha, Mary, and Lazarus

Martha and Mary were apparently well-known individuals, whose role in Jesus' ministry is attested elsewhere (Luke 10:38-40). Each has distinctive qualities in John's Gospel, yet together with their brother, Lazarus, they are portrayed in a way that reflects the experience of Christians living at a later time. The story begins when "a certain man" called Lazarus lay ill in the village of Bethany near Jerusalem; Jesus was at another place called Bethany east of the Jordan River, about a day's journey away (10:40—11:1). Jesus received the message, "Lord, he whom you love is ill" (11:3), but he inexplicably delayed returning to Jerusalem, and Lazarus died. By calling Lazarus "he whom you love," the text suggests that his death was analogous to the death of "the disciple whom Jesus loved." The epilogue to the Gospel indicates that the Beloved Disciple's death created a crisis for the community because many had believed he would remain alive until Jesus returned; but when Jesus delayed in coming, the Beloved Disciple, like Lazarus, had died (21:20-23). The similarities do not warrant the idea that Lazarus and the Beloved Disciple were one and the same individual, and the story of Lazarus may have been composed even before the crisis of the Beloved Disciple's death.[61] Instead, these texts reflect the con-

60. On the relationship between the first-century polemical situation and the universal dimensions of this text, see Schnackenburg, *Gospel*, 2.244, 256.
61. On Lazarus and the Beloved Disciple, see Brown, *Gospel*, 1.XCV. Most scholars hold that John 21, which alludes to the Beloved Disciple's death, was added to the Gospel after the remainder of the text had been completed.

sternation felt in various Christian communities when believers died during Christ's apparent absence (cf. 1 Thess. 4:13-18).[62]

Jesus loved Lazarus, but the Gospel also says that he loved Martha, Mary (John 11:5), and all his followers (13:1, 34; 15:9, 12). The words "Lord, he whom you love is ill" could have been spoken by any Christian about any Christian who was sick. Moreover, Lazarus was called Jesus' "friend," and this was a term used for Jesus' disciples generally, especially during the postresurrection period (15:13-15; 3 John 15).[63] The representative character of Lazarus becomes fully apparent in Jesus' words to Martha. Although Jesus and Martha initially spoke about her brother, Jesus extended the promise of life to all believers. "He who believes in me, though he die, yet shall he live, and *everyone* who lives and believes in me shall never die" (11:25-26).

The two sisters are portrayed in a stylized way that enhances their representative roles. Off-stage at the beginning of the chapter, they send a joint message to Jesus about their brother's illness. Later, in good dramatic fashion, each woman makes her appearance in turn, greeting Jesus with the words "Lord, if you had been here my brother would not have died" (11:21, 32). The repetition gives these words a typical quality, since what was said by Martha could also be said by Mary and perhaps by others, especially since the term *brother* was commonly used for members of the postresurrection Johannine community (20:17; 21:23). The words of the two sisters, "Lord, he whom you love is ill" and "If you had been here my brother would not have died," could readily have been spoken by Christians later in the century when confronted by the death of someone within their community in a time when Jesus was physically absent from them.

Martha emerges as a paradigm of faith. Although her initial statement, "If you had been here," could be taken as a reproach, an added comment shows continuing trust in Jesus: "even now I know that whatever you ask from God, God will give you." After Martha expressed her trust, Jesus addressed her at the level of faith by assuring her that her brother would rise again. Martha affirmed her faith in resurrection, indicating that she understood it as a future hope. Jesus brought together her trust in him and her faith in the resurrection by saying, "I am the resurrection and the

---

62. See Collins, "The Representative Figures of the Fourth Gospel—I," 45–46; Culpepper, *Anatomy*, 140; Alois Stimpfle, *Blinde Sehen: Die Eschatologie im traditionsgeschichtliche Prozess des Johannesevangelium* (BZNW 57; Berlin: de Gruyter, 1990) 247–72. For a recent attempt to equate Lazarus with the Beloved Disciple, see Mark W. G. Stibbe, *John as Storyteller: Narrative Criticism and the Fourth Gospel* (SNTSMS 73; Cambridge: Cambridge University Press, 1992) 76–81.

63. R. Alan Culpepper, *The Johannine School: An Examination of the Johannine School Hypothesis Based on the Investigation of the Nature of Ancient Schools* (SBLDS 26; Missoula: Scholars, 1975) 272.

life" (11:25). In response, Martha confessed, "I believe that you are the Christ, the Son of God, he who is coming into the world" (11:27), which was the kind of confession the evangelist wanted the readers of the Gospel to make (20:31).

Mary presents a somewhat different response. Like Martha, she told Jesus, "Lord, if you had been here my brother would not have died" (11:29, 32), but she did not echo her sister's confidence that God would grant Jesus what he asked. Instead, Mary fell at his feet, weeping, and a group of "the Jews" accompanied her, joining in the weeping (11:31, 33). Up to this point Mary has been depicted as someone who trusted Jesus and was loved by Jesus, and there is little indication that here she represents "the Jews," who are usually portrayed negatively. Mary quickly came to Jesus on the road when she heard he had come, just as Martha had done, but the Jews followed her out of the village on the mistaken assumption that she was going to the tomb, not to Jesus (11:29, 31). When Jesus saw Mary and the others crying, he did become angry and troubled, but this cannot be taken as a judgment against Mary. Jesus' anger was not aroused by Mary's tears since he wept also (11:35). Later Jesus would become "troubled" at the prospect of his own imminent death (12:27; 13:21) and would seek to reassure his disciples, who were also "troubled" by it (14:1, 27). If Jesus' anger was prompted by unbelief, it was anger directed at the crowd that disparaged the genuineness of his love for Lazarus (11:36-38).[64] Mary does not articulate faith, but she is not censured by Jesus either, and the references to Mary anointing Jesus' feet, which bracket this episode (11:2; 12:3), suggest that the evangelist wanted her to be perceived in a positive way. Together the two women exemplify different responses to the death of someone loved by Jesus in a way that would address the concerns of the later community.

JESUS' DISCIPLES

The disciples of Jesus, who speak and act as a group throughout John's Gospel, are portrayed in ways that seem to reflect the later Christian community and believers generally. Unlike the other Gospels, the Fourth Gospel calls Jesus' closest associates not "the apostles" but "the disciples," a term that could be used for all believers. A group known as "the Twelve" is mentioned occasionally (6:67; 20:24), but the evangelist never lists the members of this group or suggests that they should be distinguished from other followers of Jesus. When an individual disciple speaks, it is usually in

64. On the difficulties surrounding the interpretation of Jesus' emotions in this passage, see Brown, *Gospel*, 1.425–26, 435; Schnackenburg, *Gospel*, 2.334–37.

the first person plural; and when Jesus responds to the disciple, he often does so in the second person plural, so that what he says to one applies to all.

The Beginnings of Discipleship

The paradigmatic character of the disciples becomes apparent in the way they come to faith. According to the first chapter, the disciples came to faith by hearing about Jesus from someone they knew. The process began with John the Baptist, who confessed that he initially did not recognize Jesus (1:31, 33) but was told by God that the one on whom the Spirit descended and remained would baptize with the Holy Spirit. The descent of the Spirit confirmed what God had said. Next John told two of his disciples, "Behold the Lamb of God"; they followed Jesus to see where he was staying. One of the first followers was Andrew, who told his brother Simon Peter, "*We* have found the Messiah," and he brought Peter to Jesus (1:40-42). Jesus himself told Philip, "Follow me," then Philip told Nathanael, "*We* have found him of whom Moses in the law and also the prophets wrote, Jesus of Nazareth, the son of Joseph" (1:43-45). This pattern differs from the other Gospels, which say that Jesus himself called all of his first disciples, but it would be congruent with the experience of a later generation of Christians, who came to faith through the witness of others (17:20).

The first disciple to be portrayed in some detail is Nathanael, who has an important representative role. His character is disclosed through allusions to his ancestor Jacob, who was noted for his guile because he stole the birthright from his brother Esau but who later was the first to bear the name "Israel" (Gen. 27:35; 32:28). When Nathanael heard Philip's claims about Jesus, he was dubious but went to see for himself, and Jesus greeted him as "a true Israelite," a descendant of Jacob whose willingness to come despite his initial reservations showed that he had "no guile" (1:47). Nathanael soon recognized that Jesus was the royal Son of God and king of Israel foretold in the Scriptures. Jesus accepted this confession, then shifted to the plural to promise Nathanael and others like him that "*you people* will see heaven opened and the angels of God ascending and descending upon the Son of Man," just as his ancestor Jacob caught a glimpse of the divine presence at Bethel (1:51; Gen. 28:12). Jesus' promise was confirmed when the disciples together saw his divine glory manifested at Cana, Nathanael's hometown (2:11; 21:2).

The representative character of the disciples' faith is reinforced by repetition of this pattern throughout the Gospel. Those who come to genuine faith do so on the basis of hearing testimony about Jesus or from Jesus. The Samaritan townspeople believed in Jesus because of what the woman and Jesus told them, even though they saw no miracles (4:39, 41). The royal official sought Jesus out because he had heard about him, believed Jesus' promise that his son would live, and had his faith confirmed by the news that his son had recovered (4:47, 50, 53). The blind beggar responded to Jesus' command to go and wash with a trusting obedience before he was healed; his initial trust was confirmed by the experience of healing, grew into a tenacious loyalty under interrogation, and finally issued into worship of Jesus as the Son of man (9:7, 27, 38). Martha responded to Jesus' words with a confession of faith, and before Jesus called Lazarus from the tomb he repeated that faith would enable her to see the glory of God revealed in the miracle (11:27, 40). In contrast to these figures, the people whose response to Jesus was dependent upon the miraculous—Nicodemus, the invalid at Bethzatha, and the crowds—all failed to understand Jesus.[65]

Witnesses to the Resurrection

This pattern of discipleship culminates in the story of Jesus' resurrection. Mary Magdalene was the one who discovered that Jesus' tomb had been opened. The only other time Mary appears in John's Gospel is at the cross, where she stands alongside three other women (19:25). The other Gospels say that several women accompanied her to the tomb on Easter morning, but in John's account she apparently went by herself; no other women are mentioned. After discovering the open tomb, she ran to two of the disciples and said, "They have taken the Lord out of the tomb and we do not know where they have laid him" (20:2). The use of the *we* seems odd in this context because Mary seemed to be alone, but given the frequent use of plurals elsewhere in the Gospel, Mary is apparently functioning as a representative figure.[66]

On one level Mary may be the spokesperson for the other women who followed Jesus during the course of his ministry; but on another level she could be voicing a fear that continued to haunt the Christian community at the time the Gospel was composed. The remainder of the chapter, and especially the incident with Thomas, attests to how difficult it was for people to believe that Jesus had risen from the dead. The passing decades did not make resurrection faith any easier. Other sources indicate that even toward the end of the century the notion that Jesus' body had been stolen remained a vigorous alternative to belief in his resurrection (Matt.

65. See further my "Hearing, Seeing, and Believing in the Gospel of John."
66. Many interpreters discern in the plural evidence of John's use of an older tradition similar to that of the Synoptics, in which several women went to the tomb. On source-critical analysis see Brown, *Gospel*, 2.995–1004. Most interpreters, however, overlook the frequency with which an individual speaks in the plural in John's Gospel and the Gospel writer's use of the plural to indicate representative significance. Helpful on this is Collins, "The Representative Figures of the Fourth Gospel," 122–24.

27:62-66; 28:11-15). Mary's repeated references to body snatching make her well suited to speak for all who had such nagging suspicions and to show how this belief can be transformed into faith in the risen Lord.

Mary was different from Christians of subsequent generations in that she was present beside Jesus' cross on Good Friday and his tomb on Easter. Yet like later Christians she recognized the risen Jesus because of what she heard. Her seeing did not guarantee believing. Mary saw the open tomb but concluded that Jesus' body had been stolen, not that he had been raised. Later she saw two angels sitting in the tomb, but they made no impression upon her; when they asked her why she was weeping, she repeated that Jesus' body had been stolen and turned away without waiting for their reply. Finally she saw the risen Jesus himself, assumed he was the gardener, and persisted in thinking that the body had been stolen. Although Mary had seen so much, she recognized Jesus only when he called her by name (20:16). Her experience was consistent with that of disciples throughout the Gospel who came to know Jesus on the basis of what they heard, and it reflects the experience of believers generally, who recognize Jesus as their Good Shepherd because he has called them by name (10:3).

Mary initially called Jesus Rabbouni or Teacher, as his other disciples had done during his public ministry (1:38, 49; 4:31; 9:2; 11:8), and she tried to hold on to him, apparently thinking that resurrection restored him to his previous mode of life (20:16-17). Jesus directed her away from his physical presence and sent her to the other disciples with the message, "I am ascending to my Father and your Father, to my God and your God" (20:17). Earlier in the Gospel Jesus had said that his return to the Father would culminate in the giving of the Holy Spirit (16:7), a promise that was fulfilled shortly after Mary told the other disciples what she had seen and heard (20:22). In many ways Mary is a singular figure, one of the few who saw the risen Lord; but she also marks the transition to life in the post-resurrection community, where Jesus would be present through the Spirit and believers could call God their Father and bear witness to Jesus.

Thomas appears at the end of John 20, helping to bring the matter of discipleship into the lap of the readers. Earlier in the Gospel Thomas acted as a representative for the disciples generally. He was first mentioned in connection with the raising of Lazarus, when the disciples were incredulous that Jesus wanted to return to Judea where people were seeking to kill him. When Jesus insisted, Thomas said, "Come, let *us* also go that *we* may die with him" (11:16). At the last supper, Jesus told his disciples about his imminent departure to the Father and assured them that they knew the way, but Thomas interjected, "Lord, *we* do not know where you are going; how can *we* know the way?" (14:5). At the conclusion of the

Gospel, however, he speaks for the people of subsequent generations who are addressed in 20:30-31; like them, he was not present when the risen Jesus first appeared (20:24-25).

Thomas's movement from skepticism to faith anticipates the way later Christians would come to resurrection faith. Although Thomas had accompanied Jesus to Bethany for the raising of Lazarus, the miracle of Lazarus's resurrection did not create in Thomas any readiness to believe in Jesus' resurrection. Thomas had, however, received two important pieces of testimony. One was given at the last supper, when Jesus told him, "If you had known me, you would have known my Father also; henceforth you know him and have seen him" (14:7). The other was given after the resurrection when the disciples told Thomas, "We have seen the Lord" (20:25). The appearance of the risen Jesus confirmed what Thomas had already heard, and his confession "My Lord and my God" (20:28) gave assent to the truth of the testimony. By calling Jesus "my Lord," Thomas affirmed what the disciples had said after the resurrection, and by calling Jesus "my God," he corroborated what Jesus had said at the last supper. Readers are given the same kind of testimony Thomas received and are invited to receive it without making signs and wonders into a precondition as Thomas had done.

Peter was probably the best known of Jesus' disciples among early Christians, and the final chapter of the Gospel gives special attention to his role. At the beginning of the Gospel he was introduced as "Simon the son of John" (1:41-42a), but when he met Jesus, he was immediately given the new name Cephas, which the text explains means "Peter" (1:42b). The meaning of the new name is not further elaborated in the text, unlike Matt. 16:18. Attention is focused on the giving of the name. The new name marked Peter as an individual, but one whose identity was given to him by Jesus and whose significance cannot be understood apart from Jesus. Although Peter was unique in many ways, he was called in a manner typical of believers in later generations; he came to Jesus because Andrew, a member of his family, witnessed to him (1:41). In this sense he is a representative disciple.

Peter's representative role is developed at the end of the bread of life discourse when many left Jesus after he spoke about eating his flesh and drinking his blood. Jesus asked the Twelve, "Do you people also want to go away?" and Peter served as the spokesperson for the group: "Lord, to whom shall *we* go? You have the words of eternal life; and *we* have believed and come to know that you are the Holy One of God" (6:67-68). The title "Holy One of God" does not appear elsewhere in John, but it apparently was known to Christians outside the Johannine tradition (Luke 4:34; Acts 3:14; cf. Mark 1:24), while Peter's emphasis on faith that is bound to the words of Jesus and leads to eternal life is thoroughly Johannine. Taken together, Peter's confession fuses elements from various Christian traditions, and it expresses a faith that could be professed not just by the Twelve but by Christians of all sorts.

At the last supper Peter again acts as a representative figure. When Jesus stooped to wash his feet, Peter objected in individual terms: "You shall never wash *my* feet," and Jesus responded in the singular, saying that the foot washing was necessary for Peter to have a share with him (13:6-8). Then in response to Peter's request for a more complete bath, Jesus suddenly spoke more broadly, saying that "*the one who has bathed* has no need except to wash the feet, but is clean all over. And *you people* are clean, but not every one of you" (13:10). What began as a conversation between Jesus and Peter about foot washing expanded into comments about the cleanness of the faithful generally.

Some interpreters have suggested that Peter represents a group of Christians distinct from the Johannine community because of the way the evangelist portrays Peter's relationship to the Beloved Disciple. Several scenes seem to give precedence to the Beloved Disciple, who was especially revered by Johannine Christians, rather than to Peter, who was highly regarded by the church at large.[67] The "disciple whom Jesus loved" was first mentioned at the last supper, where he lay beside Jesus. Peter was farther away and had to ask this disciple about the identity of the betrayer. At the time Jesus was arrested, Peter struck the high priest's slave with his sword and was rebuked by Jesus. Peter and another disciple, whom we should almost certainly understand to be the Beloved Disciple, followed Jesus to the high priest's house. Both entered the courtyard, but when Peter was asked if he was indeed one of Jesus' disciples, he denied it. The Beloved Disciple was the only male disciple present during the crucifixion, where he was entrusted with the care of Jesus' mother.

The situation after the resurrection is more complex. Peter and the Beloved Disciple ran to the empty tomb. The Beloved Disciple reached the tomb first, which seems significant, but Peter entered the tomb first, which might give him a certain precedence. More significant is that the Beloved Disciple was the first to believe when he saw the grave cloths, while nothing is said about Peter's faith. Yet neither one of them understood the connection between Jesus' resurrection and the Scriptures at that point, and both simply returned to their homes (20:8-9). The first one to announce that Jesus was alive was not the Beloved Disciple but

67. Brown takes Peter as a representative of "apostolic Christians" (*Community*, 81–88); cf. Collins, "The Representative Figures of the Fourth Gospel—II," 126–29. On Peter's relationship to the Beloved Disciple see *Peter in the New Testament* (ed. R. E. Brown, K. P. Donfried, J. Reumann; Minneapolis: Augsburg; New York: Paulist, 1973) 129–47.

Mary Magdalene. Later Peter led some of the disciples in a fishing expedition on the Sea of Tiberius, but they caught nothing until Jesus told them where to put down the nets. When they made a great catch of fish, the Beloved Disciple was the first to recognize Jesus, but Peter hurled himself into the sea and finally brought the net to shore.

The anonymous "disciple whom Jesus loved" was especially important for Johannine Christians, and his role will be discussed at the end of our sixth chapter. Although the Gospel that preserved his testimony sought to ensure that he would not be overshadowed by Peter, there are good reasons to think that Peter, like a number of other individuals in the Fourth Gospel, represents not just some Christians but all Christians, including those in the Johannine community. Peter's representative role was established by the typical way he became a disciple, by his confession, and by Jesus' remarks to him at the foot washing. At the same time, his failings cannot be confined to any one group of Christians. If the Beloved Disciple's unflinching response was ideal, denying Jesus as Peter did remained a haunting possibility for every Christian threatened by persecution, including those within the Johannine community (16:1-2). And if Peter was given a special pastoral role in the final chapter, his affirmation of love for Jesus is something the evangelist would want all readers to confess (21:15-19).

The people in John's Gospel have distinctive traits. No two are alike. Yet the fourth evangelist allows us to see in their most singular features something characteristic of groups of people and of humanity in relation to God. Their responses to Jesus' sayings and actions help to disclose facets of the Gospel's other symbols, drawing readers more fully into the mystery of Jesus, the revealer of God.

3

Symbolic Actions

The Johannine account of Jesus' ministry is structured around a series of symbolic actions. The most important are the seven miracles or "signs" that Jesus performed during his public ministry. The term *signs* (*sēmeia*) is appropriate for these miracles, since a sign is not an end in itself but a visible indication of something else. Several nonmiraculous actions also contribute to the Gospel's symbolism. Although the signs have a privileged place, both types of symbolic actions are woven together in the narrative and reveal facets of Jesus' identity in a manner perceptible to the senses. Jesus' ministry began at Cana, when the steward of a wedding feast savored the wine Jesus produced from ordinary water to reveal his divine glory (2:11). Afterward the bellowing of the animals Jesus drove from the temple and the clatter of coins he strewed upon the pavement presaged his death and resurrection (2:21). His ministry culminated when he manifested the glory of God by calling the dead man Lazarus to leave the stench of the tomb (11:39-44) and then reclined at supper as the aroma of the perfume dripping from his feet portended his own burial (12:3, 7).

The stories of Jesus' deeds were an integral part of early Christian preaching, and some of the accounts of his miracles may have been collected to enhance the church's missionary work.[1] According to John's

---

1. Many interpreters think that one of the literary sources used by the fourth evangelist was a collection of Jesus' signs that had been formed as an aid to proclamation. For a survey of proposals see Robert Kysar, *The Fourth Evangelist and His Gospel: An Examination of Contemporary Scholarship* (Minneapolis: Augsburg, 1975) 13–37. See also the more recent work of D. Moody Smith, *Johannine Christianity: Essays on Its Setting, Sources, and Theology* (Columbia: University of South Carolina Press, 1984) 62–79; Hans-Peter Heekerens, *Die Zeichen-Quelle der johanneischen Redaktion: Ein Beitrag zur Enstehungsgeschichte der vierten Evangeliums* (SBS 113; Stuttgart: Katholisches Bibelwerk, 1984); Robert T. Fortna, *The Fourth Gospel and Its Predecessor: From Narrative Source to Present Gospel* (Philadelphia: Fortress, 1988) 205–16; Urban C. von Wahlde, *The Earliest Version of John's Gospel: Recovering the Gospel of Signs* (Wilmington, Del.: Michael Glazier, 1989). Our study does not assume or preclude the existence of such a source.

statement of purpose, the signs were written down in order that people might believe "that Jesus is the Christ, the Son of God" (20:31). The problem, however, which is clearly reflected in John's Gospel itself, is that miracles were so easily misconstrued. A crowd wanted to make Jesus king after he fed them with bread and fish; but he fled from them. When they sought him out the next day, he reproved them for having eaten their fill while utterly failing to perceive what the sign conveyed (6:15, 26). Jesus healed a paralytic and a blind man, but when the Jewish authorities learned about it, they persecuted him for a breach of Sabbath law and denounced him as a sinner (5:16; 9:24). Eventually the raising of Lazarus so alarmed the authorities that they planned to execute Jesus, thinking that his miracles would incite people to rebel against Rome (11:47-50).

A fundamental problem for the evangelist was that even in the first century miracles had no universally acknowledged meaning. The same action could be understood in diverse and often conflicting ways by people who viewed it from different perspectives. The problem was compounded by the evangelist's use of the signs to show that "Jesus is the Christ," since there is little evidence that Jewish people in the first century expected the Messiah to be a miracle-worker.[2] Hopes centered on a figure who would liberate Israel from political oppression and rule the people with righteousness. The use of miracles to demonstrate that Jesus was "the Son of God" also presented problems. In the ancient world there were miracle-workers who were considered "divine men" by some, but their opponents regularly accused them of practicing magic. There was no consensus about the criteria that distinguished a divine man from a magician, and reports of the wonders performed by these men fueled debates over their status.[3] Miracles similar to those in John's Gospel were ascribed to a rabbi, the emperor, and a magician by other ancient sources.[4] In themselves the signs of Jesus were open to sharply differing interpretations.

2. See Martyn, *History and Theology*, 95–99; W. Nichol, *The Sēmeia in the Fourth Gospel: Tradition and Redaction* (NovTSup 32; Leiden: Brill, 1972) 79–81; Wolfgang J. Bittner, *Jesu Zeichen im Johannesevangelium: Die Messias-Erkenntnis im Johannesevangelium vor ihrem jüdischen Hintergrund* (WUNT 26; Tübingen: Mohr/Siebeck, 1987) 136–38.

3. Scholars have debated whether there was an established concept of a miracle-working "divine man" (*theios anēr*) in the Hellenistic world. See the discussion and critique of this paradigm by David L. Tiede, *Charismatic Figure as Miracle Worker* (SBLDS 1; Missoula: Scholars, 1972), and Carl H. Holladay, *Theios Anēr in Hellenistic Judaism: A Critique of the Use of This Category in Hellenistic Judaism* (SBLDS 40; Missoula: Scholars, 1977). A summary of the discussion is found in Howard Clark Kee, *Miracle in the Early Christian World: A Study in Sociohistorical Method* (New Haven, Conn.: Yale University Press, 1983) 297–99. See also Eugene V. Gallagher, *Divine Man or Magician: Celsus and Origen on Jesus* (SBLDS 64; Chico, Calif.: Scholars, 1982). On the use of this category for the study of John's Gospel, see Nichol, *The Sēmeia in the Fourth Gospel*, 48–51; D. Moody Smith, *Johannine Christianity*, 62–79.

4. Healing a boy at a distance (John 4:46-54) is ascribed to Rabbi ben Dosa in *b.Ber.* 34b; some thought him a prophet. Healing blind eyes with spittle was attributed to Vespasian in Tacitus, *Histories* 4.81; Suetonius, *Vespasian* 7.2. Cf. Dio Cassius, *Roman History* 65.8.1. The use

The nonmiraculous actions performed by Jesus and others also provoked conflicting reactions. Bystanders in the temple understandably pressed Jesus with questions after he violently drove away the animals sold for sacrifices and overturned the tables of the money changers. When Mary poured expensive perfume over Jesus' feet, Judas protested what he perceived to be foolish waste. Finally, when Jesus removed his robe and began to wash the disciples' feet, Peter vigorously objected to his master's behavior. The evangelist could not assume that the meaning of these actions would be any clearer to the readers of the Gospel than they were to the people he described in his text.

Despite these ambiguities, the fourth evangelist made the actions of Jesus an integral part of his text. Instead of relying solely on abstract forms of speech, he conveyed a message with transcendent and universal dimensions precisely by recounting and explicating actions that could be seen, heard, and felt.[5] Symbolic actions were valuable for his purpose because they were able to integrate several levels of meaning into a coherent whole; the challenge was to limit the polyvalence without eliminating it. To direct the readers' reflections, the Gospel provides a frame of reference that discloses several appropriate levels of meaning while excluding some possible misinterpretations. This interpretive frame is created in several ways.

First, the conversations and discourses accompanying each action point to various aspects of its significance. The people who witness or hear about one of Jesus' actions usually interpret it, and their perceptions may be more or less adequate or simply false. The evangelist frequently juxtaposes episodes and characters—as we noted in chapter 2—which helps to move readers away from wrong interpretations toward those that are more viable. Even more important are comments made by Jesus before or after a given action, since they focus attention on its most significant aspects.

---

of miracles in imperial propaganda was an innovation; see Tiede, *Charismatic Figure as Miracle Worker,* 91–92. Lucian told of a magician reputed to walk on water (cf. John 6:16-21) and "call moldy corpses back to life" (cf. 11:43-44) by spells; a man he healed picked up his mat and walked away (cf. John 5:9). See Lucian, *Lover of Lies* 11 and 13; cf. 26. On the definition of magic see David E. Aune, "Magic in Early Christianity," *ANRW* 2.23.2 (1980) 1507–57, esp. 1515; Susan Garrett, *The Demise of the Devil: Magic and the Demonic in Luke's Writings* (Minneapolis: Fortress, 1989) 1–36; P. Samain, "L'accusation de magie contre le Christ dans les evangiles," *ETL* 15 (1938) 449–90, esp. 471. On ascriptions of magic to Jesus see Justin, *Dialogue* 69.5; *Apology* 1.30; *b. Sanh.* 43a. The charge that Jesus was a deceiver and possessed by a demon seems to echo these debates (John 7:12, 20-21, 47; 8:48-52; 10:20-21). Cf. Martyn, *History and Theology,* 73–81.

5. The importance of the signs as a visible, rather than a purely abstract, mode of presenting Jesus has rightly been stressed by Udo Schnelle, *Antidocetic Christology in the Gospel of John: An Investigation of the Place of the Fourth Gospel in the Johannine School* (Minneapolis: Fortress, 1992) 175, 233–34. Marianne M. Thompson rightly commented that the discourses in the Gospel do not render the signs superfluous, since the discourses grow out of the signs (*The Humanity of Jesus in the Fourth Gospel* [Philadelphia: Fortress, 1988] 56–63). Cf. Ashton, *Understanding,* 522.

Second, the actions evoke, appropriate, and redefine associations that readers would bring to the text. Associations may come from the literary context, the Old Testament and Jewish traditions, and the wider Greco-Roman cultural context.[6] The focus of all of the symbolic actions in John's Gospel is christological, and the connotations evoked by an action can be correlated with the levels of Jesus' identity noted in the surrounding narrative, especially those of prophet, Messiah, and divine Son of man.

Third, allusions to Jesus' crucifixion and resurrection appear in connection with each of the symbolic actions in the Gospel. The passion plays a central role in some cases, while in others it is less prominent; but the repeated references, both direct and indirect, work cumulatively to make the passion and resurrection of Jesus the lens through which the actions in the Gospel must be viewed. The interpretive relationship moves both ways: Jesus' death and resurrection disclose the significance of his earlier actions, and his earlier actions help readers discern the meaning of his passion.

NEW WINE—NEW TEMPLE

Jesus' ministry began with two symbolic actions that are juxtaposed in the second chapter of the Gospel: transforming water into wine and halting trade in the temple. In many ways these acts are quite different. One was a miracle and the other was not; one was festive and the other violent. At Cana Jesus' mother and disciples responded favorably to him, but at Jerusalem the crowd reacted with skepticism and unreliable belief. Yet both episodes include conversations that help disclose the significance of these actions, and both utilize Jewish institutions to reveal something about who Jesus is: The water at Cana was contained in jars used for Jewish purification rites, and the Jerusalem temple was the central Jewish sanctuary. Both incidents also foreshadow the passion, directing readers to reflect on their significance in light of Jesus' death and resurrection.

Changing Water into Wine

The story of Jesus' first sign is told simply. While attending a wedding at Cana in Galilee, Jesus' mother told him that the wine had run out, and after a surprisingly brusque reply, Jesus asked the servants to fill the six stone jars standing nearby with water. Having done this, the servants ladled

---

6. Bittner rightly acknowledges that the meaning of a sign concerns its function in a context—both the literary and broader historical or cultural contexts. He also considers it important that signs have a clear (*eindeutig*) meaning. This presupposes that the perception must be possible, that the context of the actions is clear and known, and that other connections do not appear in the same context (*Jesu Zeichen im Johannesevangelium*, 271–74).

out some water and took it to the steward of the feast, who was startled to find that it was high-quality wine. The evangelist did not dwell on the miraculous elements of the story but focused attention on the transcendent significance of the sign, observing that through it Jesus "revealed his glory and his disciples believed in him" (2:11).

The characters in this episode help readers understand what it meant for Jesus to manifest his glory through the gift of wine. Jesus' mother related what she had observed: "They have no wine" (2:3). Although her comment may be an implicit request for Jesus to do something about the problem, there is no suggestion that she was demanding a miracle; she told the servants, "Do *whatever* he tells you" (2:5). Jesus responded by calling her "woman" (2:4a), a term that could be used without disrespect for other women, but not one that a son would use for his mother. He also told her, "What have you to do with me?" an expression that often conveyed irritation and established distance between the person speaking and the one being addressed.[7] Then he made the cryptic comment, "My hour has not yet come" (2:4b); and as the narrative unfolds, readers learn that "the hour" is the hour of Jesus' passion (7:30; 8:20). This peculiar interchange enables readers to see that Jesus' actions cannot be understood on the level of typical relations between mother and son but must be interpreted retrospectively in light of his death and resurrection.

The steward's reaction also helps to show that the sign cannot be understood in terms of ordinary human practices. After tasting the wine he exclaimed, "Every man serves the good wine first, and when people have drunk freely, then the poor wine; but you have kept the good wine until now" (2:10). The steward spoke from a perspective shaped by observations about human behavior. The ancients did not actually consider it good etiquette to serve poor quality wine to guests whose sense of taste had been dulled by drinking, but readers familiar with the ways of the world could readily appreciate the humorous realism in the remark.[8] The steward did not know where the wine had come from, but he rightly concluded that offering a superb wine late in the feast did not conform to what he knew of "every man."[9]

---

7. Jesus uses "woman" to address the Samaritan woman in 4:21 and Mary Magdalene in 20:15 (cf. Matt. 15:28; Luke 13:12), but there seems to be no precedent for a son addressing his mother this way. See Brown, *Gospel*, 1.99. On the expression "What have you to do with me?" cf. Judg. 11:12; 1 Kings 17:18; 2 Kings 3:13; 2 Chron. 35:21; Mark 1:24; 5:7.

8. An anecdote in *Esth. Rab.* 2:3 about a wealthy man who gave inferior wine to guests who had drunk too much helps illustrate how John 2:10 would have been heard by early readers. See Roger Aus, *Water into Wine and the Beheading of John the Baptist* (BJS 150; Atlanta: Scholars, 1988) 10.

9. Especially stressed by Birger Olsson, *Structure and Meaning in the Fourth Gospel: A Text-Linguistic Analysis of John 2:1-11 and 4:1-42* (CB 6; Lund: Gleerup, 1974) 62–63.

The disciples who glimpsed the glory revealed by the sign focus the meaning still further. Their frame of reference was shaped by the testimony they had heard from and about Jesus prior to their arrival in Cana. John the Baptist identified Jesus as the Lamb of God (1:36) and the disciples who followed Jesus soon announced that they had found the Messiah foretold in the Law of Moses and the prophetic writings (1:41, 45). Nathanael was initially skeptical about what he heard but went to meet Jesus for himself and came to acclaim Jesus as Son of God and king of Israel—titles traditionally associated with the Davidic Messiah (1:49). In the Gospel narrative, the wine miracle at Cana confirms the disciples' confession of faith in Jesus as the Messiah (see pp. 40–41).

The text couples the proclamation of Jesus' messiahship with the miracle of the wine without explicitly stating how they are related. Readers themselves must forge the link between the disciples' testimony and the miracle at Cana. Philip's confession directs attention to the Law and the Prophets. Readers familiar with the Scriptures would probably have known that one of the law's most important messianic passages said that a ruler would come from the tribe of Judah to command the obedience of the peoples: "Binding his foal to the vine and his ass's colt to the choice vine, he washes his garments in wine and his vesture in the blood of grapes; his eyes shall be red with wine" (Gen. 49:10-12). Several of the prophetic writings looked for a new outpouring of divine favor upon Israel, saying that in that day "the mountains shall drip sweet wine, and all the hills shall flow with it," and sometimes connecting abundant wine with the restoration of Davidic rule (Amos 9:11, 13; cf. Joel 3:18; Isa. 25:6). By the late first century, Jewish tradition associated this lavish outpouring of wine with the advent of the Messiah.[10]

Jesus accepted messianic titles from his disciples but intimated that his identity was not confined to Jewish expectations. Before going to Cana, he told them they would "see heaven opened, and the angels of God ascending and descending upon the Son of Man" (John 1:51). People might expect the Messiah to enjoy the kind of honor or glory normally granted to a ruler, but readers were told earlier that Jesus' glory was of another order: It was "glory as of the only Son from the Father" (1:14). This

10. According to *2 Bar.* 29:5, when the Messiah appears, "on one vine will be a thousand branches, and one branch will produce a thousand clusters, and one cluster will produce a thousand grapes, and one grape will produce a cor [=120 gal.] of wine." The Targum of Amos speaks of the restoration of "the kingdom of the house of David" in 9:11 instead of "the booth of David" as in the Masoretic text. The Targum also adds, "It shall rule over all the kingdoms and it shall destroy and make an end of the greatness of armies," which has messianic overtones. See also Brown, *Gospel*, 1.105; Nichol, *The Sēmeia in the Fourth Gospel*, 54; Martin Hengel, "The Interpretation of the Wine Miracle at Cana: John 2:1-11," *The Glory of Christ in the New Testament: Studies in Christology in Memory of George Bradford Caird* (ed. L. D. Hurst and N. T. Wright; Oxford: Clarendon, 1987) 83–112, esp. 100–101.

comment, together with Jesus' promise about the heavens opening, enables readers to see the sign as a demonstration of Jesus' divinity as well as his messiahship. There were, perhaps, some precedents for this in the Scriptures, which associated the outpouring of wine with God's own presence among his people (Joel 3:17-18; Isa. 25:6); yet such ideas go well beyond traditional messianic expectations.[11]

Jesus first manifested his glory in a Jewish setting, but in a way that anticipated a revelation to the wider Greco-Roman world. Cana was a Jewish community in Galilee,[12] the home of Nathanael, who had a Hebrew name and was called "a true Israelite" (John 1:47; 21:2). The hosts of the wedding provided stone jars "for the Jewish rites of purification" (2:6), and Jesus performed a sign that signaled the fulfillment of the Jewish expectations expressed earlier. Yet the sign also anticipates the coming of the Greeks prior to the passion. Before he revealed his glory by turning the water into wine, he told his mother, "My hour has not yet come" (2:4), and when the Greeks pressed to see him at the end of his ministry, he announced that "the hour has come for the Son of Man to be glorified" (12:20-23). These statements about the hour of Jesus' glorification provide an important literary connection between the miracle at Cana and the arrival of the Greeks, and we do well to ask how the wine miracle might presage the communication of the message of Jesus to those outside the Jewish tradition.

Greeks would not immediately have grasped the messianic significance of the sign, but they would readily have understood that the miraculous gift of wine revealed the presence of deity. Throughout the Mediterranean world, wine was associated with the god Dionysos, who was said to have been the first to cultivate the vine and ferment its fruit. He was the one who provided "a constant succession of banquets, merrymakings, galas, festivals."[13] Stories were told about how the god "left behind him in many places over the inhabited world evidences of his personal favor and presence" by wondrous benefactions of wine.[14] At Andros, on the festival called the *theodosia*, or "gift of God," a spring would flow with wine; and at Teos a fountain of wine would surge spontaneously from the earth. At Elis three empty jars were placed in a sealed room each year and on the following

---

11. The Davidic Messiah is associated with the manifestation of God's glory in *Pss. Sol.* 17:31, but it is not apparent that the glory is manifested in his person.

12. Cana was used as one of Josephus's bases of operation during the Jewish revolt against Rome (*Life* 16 §86). According to later sources, a group of Jewish priests eventually settled in Cana. See Samuel Klein, *Beiträge zur Geographie und Geschichte Galiläas* (Leipzig: Rudolf Haupt, 1909) 56–57; Karl Kundsin, *Topologische Überlieferungstoffe im Johannes-Evangelium: Eine Untersuchung* (FRLANT 22; Göttingen: Vandenhoeck & Ruprecht, 1925) 22–23.

13. Philo, *Embassy to Gaius* 83.

14. Diodorus Siculus, *Library of History* 3.66.3.

morning were always found full of wine. A spring at Haliartus flowed with sweet wine-colored water, and local legend said that the infant Dionysos had been washed there. In Euripides' play *The Bacchae*, both water and wine bubbled up from the earth at the touch of the god.[15]

The legends of Dionysos probably tell us little about how the story of the first Cana miracle originated, but they do help us understand how the story could *communicate* the significance of Jesus to Greeks as well as Jews.[16] The widespread associations between a miraculous gift of wine and the presence of a deity would have helped many readers to understand that the sign revealed the presence of God in the person of Jesus. The many Jewish elements in the Gospel account would not necessarily have screened out connotations from the wider Greco-Roman environment. Dionysos was said to have been born in Palestine, at Scythopolis, southeast of Cana. Before the Maccabean revolt, the Syrians introduced worship of Dionysos into Jerusalem for a time (2 Macc. 6:7); this did not continue, but Dionysos was venerated at Tyre, just north of Galilee. Some Greek and Latin authors even thought that Dionysos and the God of Israel were the same.[17] The miracle at Cana testifies to the messianic and divine aspects of Jesus' identity by evoking associations from a broad cultural and religious spectrum.

The pregnant reference to Jesus' "hour," however, demands that the sign be understood in light of Jesus' passion (John 2:4). Cana was the first (*archē*) of his signs, and the cross marked the culmination (*telos*) of his works. The presence of Jesus' mother at Cana and the cross—and only in these two places in John's Gospel (2:1-12; 19:25-27)—reinforces the idea that the glory manifested in the wine and in Jesus' death must be under-

15. On Andros see Pliny, *Natural History* 2.31; 31.16. On Teos see Diodorus Siculus, *Library of History* 3.66.1–4. On Elis see Pausanias, *Description of Greece* 6.26.1-2; Athanaeus, *Deipnosophists* 1.61 [34a]. On Haliartus see Plutarch, *Lysander* 28.4. See also Euripides, *Bacchae* 704–7. Further discussion in C. H. Dodd, *Historical Tradition in the Fourth Gospel* (Cambridge: Cambridge University Press, 1963) 224–25; Barrett, *Gospel*, 188–89.

16. Rudolf Bultmann concluded that the Cana story was originally a pagan legend that was applied to Jesus (*Gospel*, 118–19). Others have vigorously disputed this. See E. C. Hoskyns, *The Fourth Gospel* (ed. F. N. Davey; 2d ed.; London: Faber, 1947) 190–92; Schnackenburg, *Gospel*, 1.340. Our concern is with the hearing of the text, not its origin.

17. On Dionysos and Scythopolis see David Flusser, "Paganism in Palestine," *The Jewish People in the First Century* (ed. S. Safrai and M. Stern; Aasen/Maastricht: van Gorcum; Philadelphia: Fortress, 1987) 2.1065–1100, esp. 1067–69. On Dionysos in Tyre see Morton Smith, "On the Wine God in Palestine (Gen. 18, Jn. 2, and Achilles Tatius)," *Salo Wittmayer Jubilee Volume on the Occasion of His Eightieth Birthday* (Jerusalem: Academy for Jewish Research, 1974) 2.815–29. On perceived connections between the God of Israel and Dionysos, see Tacitus, *Histories* 5.5, and Plutarch, *Moralia* 671B–672B. On the interplay between Jewish and pagan connotations in the Cana story, see Barrett, *Gospel*, 188–89; Ingo Broer, "Noch einmal: Zur religionsgeschichtliche 'Ableitung' von Jo 2,1-11," *Studien zum Neuen Testament und seiner Umwelt* (ed. A. Fuchs; Linz, 1983) 103–23; Hengel, "The Wine Miracle at Cana," 108–12; Walter Lütgehetmann, *Die Hochzeit von Kana (Joh 2,1-11): Zu Ursprung und Deutung einer Wunderzählung im Rahmen johanneischer Redaktionsgeschichte* (BU 20; Regensburg: Pustet, 1990) 261–82.

stood together (see pp. 214–19). Perhaps even the comment that the wedding took place "on the third day" may point in this direction, since the three days from his crucifixion to resurrection are mentioned in the next scene as well (2:1, 19-20). Jesus' messiahship would lead to Golgotha, and his glorification would be accomplished through crucifixion and resurrection. The divine favor revealed by his gift of wine was a prelude to the gift of his own life.

Cleansing the Temple

The account of Jesus' actions in the Jerusalem temple forms the companion piece to the miracle at Cana. Jesus went to Jerusalem for the Jewish feast of Passover. He entered the temple and found merchants selling oxen, sheep, and pigeons, as well as money changers conducting their business. Making a whip out of cords, he drove the animals out of the temple, poured out the coins of the money changers, overturned their tables, and demanded that those selling pigeons take them away, telling them, "You shall not make my Father's house a house of trade" (2:16).

The Jews who witnessed the incident posed a question that focused attention on the issue of Jesus' authority rather than on the meaning of his action or his motivation for doing it. They asked, "What sign have you to show us for doing this?" (2:18). The text does not explain what sort of wonder-worker they might have expected to interfere with trade in the temple, but the evangelist had said earlier that "the Jews" in Jerusalem were looking for the Christ, Elijah, or the prophet to appear (1:19-21); therefore, we should probably assume that "the Jews" in the Jerusalem temple (2:20) were also looking for an eschatological figure.

Jesus responded to them by alluding to the eschatological renewal of worship in the temple, ordering them not to make it a house of trade. His words apparently echo the last chapter of Zechariah—a book used a number of times by John—which said that when God came to rule over all the earth, worship would be pure and holy, all nations would worship in Jerusalem, and there would be "no longer be a trader in the house of the Lord" (Zech. 14:20).[18] There is some evidence that people expected Israel's worship to be purified by someone sent from God. The prophet Malachi, for example, said that God would send a messenger who would come suddenly into the temple to purify the priesthood and its offerings (Mal. 3:1). Others looked for the Messiah to "purge Jerusalem and make it holy as it was even from the beginning."[19]

18. John 12:15 = Zech. 9:9; John 19:37 = Zech. 12:10. John 7:38 is reminiscent of Zech. 14:8.
19. *Pss. Sol.* 17:30. See Brown, *Gospel*, 1.121–23.

The messianic character of Jesus' words "Destroy this temple and in three days I will raise it up" (John 2:19) may have been apparent to readers familiar with Jewish traditions. According to various sources, a new and glorious temple would be erected in Jerusalem in the new age of salvation. Some texts do not identify the builder of the temple, and others anticipated that God would establish it.[20] Still other texts expected the Messiah to raise the new structure. According to 2 Sam. 7:12-13, the heir to David's throne would build Israel's house of worship; and Zech. 6:12 said that the temple would be built by the Davidic "Branch." The connection between the Messiah and the temple emerged while the temple was still standing but became more widespread after its destruction—the period in which the Fourth Gospel was composed.[21]

The interchange between Jesus and the crowd shows that his actions cannot be fully comprehended within the framework of traditional messianic expectations. They found Jesus' words incomprehensible, since they knew it had taken forty-six years to construct the building in which they stood, and it was ridiculous to think that Jesus could erect something similar in three days. Readers familiar with the well-known story of the Jewish revolt would have been especially aware that Jesus' words could not refer to a building, since the Romans had destroyed the temple in A.D. 70 and it still stood in ruins years later. A comment by the narrator provides readers with the perspective needed to interpret this incident by connecting it with Jesus' death and resurrection: When Jesus referred to the destruction and rebuilding of the temple, "he spoke of the temple of his body" (2:21). This comment leaves much unsaid. The text makes clear that Jesus' body is a temple but does not explain how he functions as a temple. Nevertheless, several aspects of meaning can be inferred from the literary and cultural context.

First, the text suggests that the function of sacrifice, which was integral to the Jerusalem temple, is fulfilled and replaced by Jesus. The animals and birds mentioned in 2:14 were prescribed by the Levitical code for sacrifices used for atonement and purification (Lev. 1:3-17). Because trans-

---

20. The builder of the temple is not clearly identified in Tob. 13:10; *T. Benj.* 9:2; *Sib. Or.* 3:294, 702-720, 772-774; 4QpPs 37 iii 11. Tob. 14:5 suggests that people might rebuild the sanctuary. God is the builder of the sanctuary according to *1 Enoch* 90:29; *Jub.* 1:15-17; 11QTemple xxix 8-10. On the complex relationship of Jesus' actions to contemporary Jewish expectations, see J. K. Riches, "Apocalyptic—Strangely Relevant," *Templum Amicitiae: Essays on the Second Temple Presented to Ernst Bammel* (JSNTSup 48; Sheffield: JSOT, 1991) 237–63, esp. 245–50.

21. The connection between 2 Samuel 7 and the messianic temple is made in 4QFlor i 1-9. The Targums on Zech. 6:12 and Isa. 53:5 refer to the Messiah as builder of the temple, as does *Sib. Or.* 5.422. The fourteenth benediction, which became an important feature of Jewish worship, associated the rebuilding of the temple with the advent of the Messiah (see Schürer, *History*, 2.454–63). For discussion of texts see Donald Juel, *Messiah and Temple: The Trial of Jesus in the Gospel of Mark* (SBLDS 31; Missoula: Scholars, 1977) 169–209.

porting livestock over distance was difficult, pilgrims regularly purchased them in Jerusalem. The daily sacrifices made on behalf of all Israel were paid for by the half-shekel tax levied on all Jews (Exod. 30:11-16). The money changers in the temple provided Tyrian coinage in exchange for Greek and Roman monies to facilitate payment of this tax. By temporarily disrupting the trade necessary for sacrifice, Jesus foreshadowed the permanent cessation of sacrificial worship in Jerusalem and its replacement by his own death. His action took place during the feast of Passover, when lambs were slain to commemorate Israel's deliverance from death and bondage; Jesus would be crucified at Passover two years later as "the Lamb of God who takes away the sin of the world" (John 1:29). If the transformation of the water at Cana identified Jesus' death as the new means of purification, the disruption of commerce in the temple anticipated the time when atonement and cleansing would be effected through his passion and resurrection.

Second, the temple in Jerusalem was the place where God made his name or glory to dwell. Although God's presence was not confined to the temple, it was generally understood that the sanctuary was, in some sense, God's dwelling place. The Scriptures related how God's glory had filled Israel's tabernacle in the wilderness (Exod. 40:34) and the temple that Solomon had built (1 Kings 8:10-11). The prophet Ezekiel said that the glory of God had left the first temple at the time of the Babylonian exile, but he envisioned its return at the time of Israel's restoration (Ezek. 10:18-19; 11:22-23; 43:1-5). After the exile, the temple was rebuilt, and many thought that God was present there as in former sanctuaries, though both Jewish and Roman sources say that the divine presence left the temple before it was destroyed in A.D. 70.[22] Even while the second temple stood, some were dissatisfied with it, but those who looked for a new sanctuary in the future expected God's glory to be manifested there.[23] Jesus' promise of a new temple suggests that God's glory would be manifested, not in a building, but in a person, as it had been at Cana.

Third, the crucified and risen Jesus would be a unifying symbol for God's people, as the temple had been before. Reverence for the Jerusalem temple helped to give a distinctive identity to Jews scattered across the

22. Josephus, *J.W.* 6.5.3 §299; Tacitus, *Histories* 5.13. See G. I. Davies, "The Presence of God in the Second Temple," *Templum Amicitiae: Essays on the Second Temple Presented to Ernst Bammel* (JSNTSup 48; Sheffield: JSOT, 1991) 32–36.

23. Second Maccabees 2:4-8 expresses a Maccabean hope that God's glory would appear in the second temple when it was purified. The writer of *1 Enoch* 89:73 thought the second temple was polluted from the time it was built but expected God to be present in the eschatological temple (90:34). The Dead Sea sect thought that the priests in Jerusalem had defiled the second temple (1QpHab xii 8-9), but 11QTemple xxix 8-10 apparently associates the manifestation of God's glory with the eschatological sanctuary.

Greco-Roman world and into Babylonia. The devout prayed in the direction of the sanctuary and sometimes prayed at the times sacrifices were offered. When possible, they made pilgrimages or sent delegations to the festivals there. Gentiles could participate in Jewish worship in a limited way but were forbidden to enter the parts of the sanctuary reserved for Jews.[24] When Jesus halted "trade" in the temple, he alluded to a portion of Scripture that envisoned all nations worshiping in Jerusalem (Zech. 14:16, 21; John 2:16). In his crucified and risen body the promise was fulfilled; he became a sanctuary that transcended and replaced other places of worship (cf. 4:21) and endured beyond the destruction of the Jerusalem temple (cf. 11:48) to unite the community of those called to worship in Spirit and truth.

TWO HEALINGS

The healing of the Galilean official's son and the invalid at Bethzatha are the second and third signs recounted in the Gospel (4:46—5:47). In the last chapter we observed that these passages show two contrasting responses to Jesus. Through the eyes of the people portrayed in these stories, we can see how differently Jesus' healing power was perceived within different frames of reference. The discourse that follows these signs is the first time the Gospel provides a lengthy commentary on Jesus' actions, enabling readers to see more clearly what they reveal about him.

Three Perspectives

The Galilean official's perspective was shaped by the testimony he heard about Jesus and the promise he heard from Jesus. The man was in Capernaum with a boy who was seriously ill when "he heard that Jesus had come from Judea to Galilee" (4:47). Although he wanted Jesus to accompany him to his son's bedside, Jesus simply told him the boy would live, and the man "believed the word that Jesus spoke to him and went his way" alone (4:50). While still on the journey, the man's servants reported that the boy was living, and their report confirmed that the man's faith in Jesus' word was well placed (4:51-53). Although the significance of the healing is not elaborated, the story of the official suggests that a faith based on hearing is the context within which Jesus' signs can rightly be perceived.

The invalid at Bethzatha, in contrast to the official, had a view of healing that bordered on the magical. He lay beside the pool waiting for a

24. On prayer toward the sanctuary, see 1 Kings 8:48; Dan. 6:10; *m. Ber.* 4:5-6; *t. Ber.* 3:16. See Schürer, *History,* 2.449 n. 106 on the orientation of synagogues toward Jerusalem and 2.309–13 on gentile participation in worship. On prayer at the time of sacrifice, see Jth. 9:1. On relations between the Diaspora and Jerusalem see generally S. Safrai and M. Stern, *The Jewish People in the First Century* (CRINT 1/1; Aasen: van Gorcum, 1974) 117–215. On the temple and unity see Josephus, *Ag. Ap.* 2.23 §193.

mysterious disturbance in the water in the belief that the first person entering the pool when the water was troubled would be healed, but that latecomers would not be helped. His chief complaint was that others always made it into the water ahead of him (5:7). Later legend ascribed the troubling of the water to an angel of the Lord (5:4), but this verse is not included in the best manuscripts of the Gospel and has rightly been deleted from most modern translations. As the text stands, there is no mention of God in the healing process connected with the pool. David Aune has observed that magical actions typically try to manage supernatural powers in a way that virtually guarantees results.[25] The invalid did not try to produce the troubling of the waters but seemed to assume that a well-timed entry into the pool would make healing almost automatic. His readiness to make Jesus responsible for his breach of the Sabbath law and to report Jesus to the authorities shows that he perceived healing as something that had simply happened to him, with no need for further commitment on his part.

The Jewish authorities interpreted the miracle from a perspective shaped by a traditional understanding of Jewish Sabbath regulations, which identified carrying something from one place to another as a form of work that violated the command to rest on the seventh day.[26] The man whom Jesus healed was found carrying his mat on the Sabbath contrary to the law, but the onus was placed on Jesus when the authorities learned he had given the command to carry the mat and had also healed on the Sabbath. Jewish law permitted healing on the Sabbath when someone's life was in danger, but since the man had been ill for thirty-eight years, this was not the case. Jesus could have waited a day to cure him.[27] Interpreted within the framework of Jewish Sabbath regulations, the healing of the invalid marked Jesus as a transgressor and provided grounds for legal action against him (John 5:16).

The Speech: Jesus' Unity
with the Father

The Galilean official was the one figure in these episodes who responded appropriately to the signs, and his perspective was shaped by what he heard from and about Jesus. The discourse in John 5:17-47 serves as a commentary on the healing miracles, seeking to shape the perspective of the readers by the power of its language so that they can see that the signs

---

25. "Magic in Early Christianity," 1515.
26. Exod. 20:8-11; *m. Shabb.* 7:2; 10:5.
27. Str-B 1.623-625.

bear witness to Jesus' unity with the Father (5:36).[28] Jesus contended that his works must be seen in the context of God's activity rather than of Jewish Sabbath regulations: "My Father is working still, and I am working" (5:17). From a Jewish perspective his claim was a blasphemous attempt to usurp God's prerogatives, an expression of the human desire to become like God, which was at the root of sin (cf. Gen. 3:5). Jesus, however, insisted that the reverse was true. He was not defying God's will but obeying God's will and carrying out the responsibilities God had given him.

He made his point by alluding to ordinary relations between fathers and sons.[29] In antiquity a son often learned a trade from his father. If the man was a weaver, the boy would watch him move the shuttle and learn by imitation. The son does "what he sees the father doing; for whatever he does, that the son does likewise" (John 5:19). A concerned father would show his son what to do and eventually entrust the boy with certain responsibilities (5:20, 22). Jesus used this analogy for the "trade" he had learned from God: giving life. Jewish scholars understood that God breathed life into Adam when the world began and would bring the dead to life again at the end (2 Macc. 7:23). They also acknowledged that God continued giving life on the Sabbath. Although the Scriptures said God rested on the seventh day (Gen 2:2), it was understood that "God never ceases making, but as it is the property of fire to burn and of snow to chill, so it is the property of God to make," even on the Sabbath.[30]

Jesus insisted that his works bore witness to the truth of his claims, thereby placing readers in a position to connect the signs with the discourse (John 5:36). Jesus declared that his actions conformed to God's actions, for "as the Father raises the dead and gives them life, so also the Son gives life to whom he will" (5:21). The signs demonstrated the truth of his claim. The Galilean official had asked Jesus to heal his son, for the boy "was at the point of death" (4:47), and Jesus told him "your son lives" (4:50, 53). Since it was God's work to give life to the dead, Jesus did the same by giving life to a boy on the threshold of death. Similarly, since it

28. The connection between the healing stories and the discourse has often been noted. See Hoskyns, *The Fourth Gospel*, 249; Bultmann, *Gospel*, 203; Dodd, *Interpretation*, 318; André Feuillet, *Johannine Studies* (Staten Island, N.Y.: Alba House, 1964) 44–51; G. Beasley-Murray, *John* (WBC 36; Waco, Tex.: Word, 1987) 67.

29. See C. H. Dodd, "A Hidden Parable in the Fourth Gospel," *More New Testament Studies* (Grand Rapids, Mich.: Eerdmans, 1968) 30–40; Paul Gaechter, "Zur Form von Joh 5:19-30," *Neutestamentliche Aufsätze. Festschrift für Prof. Josef Schmid zum 70. Geburtstag* (ed. J. Blinzler, O. Kuss, F. Mussner; Regensburg: Pustet, 1963) 65–68.

30. Philo, *Allegorical Interpretation* 1.5. For discussion of God's activity on the Sabbath, see Dodd, *Interpretation*, 321–23; Brown, *Gospel*, 1.216–17; Jerome Neyrey, *An Ideology of Revolt: John's Christology in Social Science Perspective* (Philadelphia: Fortress, 1988) 9–36; Peder Borgen, "Creation, Logos and the Son: Observations on John 1:1-18 and 5:17-18," *Ex Auditu* 3 (1987) 88–97, esp. 88–92.

was God's intent that the dead should rise (*egeirein*, 5:21), Jesus commanded the invalid at Bethzatha to rise (*egeirein*, 5:8) after thirty-eight years of illness.[31] Jesus' actions did not violate God's purposes, but actually carried them out. Moreover, at Bethzatha Jesus sought out and healed a man who gave no indication of faith before or after his encounter with Jesus, showing that the Son indeed "gives life to whom he will" (5:21).

The other aspect of Jesus' work was judgment. Jewish people understood that God was the judge as well as the Creator, but Jesus insisted that in claiming to exercise judgment he was not usurping God's prerogatives. Instead, he said that responsibility for judgment had been entrusted to him by God: "The Father judges no one, but has *given* all judgment to the Son" (5:22). Therefore, by exercising judgment, Jesus was acting in obedience rather than in defiance of the divine will. In positive terms, Jesus promised that anyone "who hears my word and believes him who sent me has eternal life; he does not come into judgment, but has passed from death to life" (5:24). The official was an exemplary recipient of this promise, for he believed Jesus' word, and the physical life given to his son foreshadowed the eternal life given to all who believe. In negative terms, those who do not believe in him remain under divine judgment. Jesus said the hour was coming when all the dead would hear the voice of the Son of man and come forth, some to the resurrection of life, but others to the resurrection of judgment (5:27-29). Like the dead, the invalid by the pool heard Jesus' voice and arose but showed no evidence of faith; and Jesus warned that by persisting in the sin of unbelief he faced the prospect of final condemnation (5:14).

The discourse elaborates the christological significance of the signs by countering Jewish objections and seeking to make it possible for "all" to honor the Son (5:23). The form of the speech is consistent with the universal scope of its message. It addresses a number of Jewish concerns and introduces the two witnesses required by Jewish law (Deut. 19:15) while following established patterns of Greco-Roman judicial rhetoric. A central task of a judicial speech was to identify the crux or *stasis* of the issue: The disagreement might center on the facts of the case, on defining the kind of action that was performed, on justification for the act, or on matters of jurisdiction over the case. Having identified the *stasis,* the speaker would formulate a thesis, support it with arguments, and refute his opponent's position.[32] In John 5:17-47, Jesus defended himself against

31. Nichol, *The Sēmeia in the Fourth Gospel,* 107; Ernst Haenchen, *John 1* (Hermeneia; Philadelphia: Fortress, 1984) 251.

32. On *stasis* see Ray Nadean, "Hermogenes' *On Stases:* A Translation with an Introduction and Notes," *Speech Monographs* 31 (1964) 361–424, esp. 369, 376, 393; cf. George A. Kennedy, *New Testament Interpretation through Rhetorical Criticism* (Chapel Hill: University of

the charge that he had violated the Mosaic law by healing on the Sabbath. There was no dispute about the facts of the case or the definition of the action: Jesus and his opponents agreed that the action had been done and that it was an act usually defined as "work" under Jewish law. The crux of the issue was that Jesus claimed that it was right for him to work on the Sabbath because God worked on the Sabbath, a notion the Jewish authorities considered blasphemous (5:17-18).

The outline of the speech is conventional. The first part offered arguments for Jesus' unity with God based on a premise his opponents would accept, namely, that God gave life and judged even on the Sabbath. Alluding to the way sons throughout the ancient world learned trades from their fathers, Jesus contended that he too was carrying out the responsibilities given him by his Father (John 5:19-30; Quintilian, *Institutio Oratoria* 5.10.12). In the second part Jesus introduced witnesses to support his claims. These included the works themselves, which were consistent with God's life-giving purposes, and the Scriptures, which bore witness to him (John 5:31-40; *Institutio Oratoria* 5.7.3). In the third section of the speech, Jesus refuted his opponents by discrediting their character, charging that they were preoccupied with their own prestige rather than with God, and by warning that they faced the threat of divine condemnation for refusing to heed the witnesses God had put forward (John 5:41-47; *Institutio Oratoria* 5.13.39).

The speech presents Jesus as divine life-giver and judge with an eye to Jewish concerns and Greco-Roman conventions, but its message must finally be understood in terms of Jesus' death. The speech is given precisely at the moment Jesus' adversaries first designed to kill him (5:18). The signs and the discourse bore eloquent witness to Jesus' unity with the Father and provoked the persecution that would lead to his execution. Both aspects must be taken together. If the signs provide visible evidence that Jesus is one with God, this oneness will be expressed in an obedience so complete that Jesus will die carrying it out. And it is precisely by dying that Jesus will judge and give life to the world.

THE BREAD OF LIFE

The feeding of the five thousand and walking on the sea are the fourth and fifth signs recounted in the Gospel (John 6). These signs, like the two

---

North Carolina Press, 1984) 18. In addition to the thesis, proofs, and refutation, a full judicial speech might include opening remarks (*proem* or *exordium*), a narration of the facts of the case (*narratio*), and summary remarks (*epilogue* or *peroration*). Unlike the proofs, however, these elements are not necessary (Quintilian, *Institutio Oratoria* 4.1.72; 4.2.4–5; and 5.Preface.5; cf. *Ad Herennium*, ascribed to Cicero, 2.19.30).

previous miracles, are juxtaposed in the text and relate how Jesus' actions were perceived from different points of view. As in the previous chapter, a discourse follows the signs, addressing certain misconceptions and conveying the truth about Jesus' identity as the bread of life. The episode opens with a multitude following Jesus beside the Sea of Galilee. When Jesus asks how they are to buy enough bread for everyone to eat, the disciples notice a boy who has five barley loaves and two fish but realize that the food will do nothing for such a large crowd. Nevertheless, Jesus makes the people recline on the grass, and after giving thanks over the bread, he gives it to them and does the same with the fish, so that everyone is filled. Jesus then commands the disciples to gather up the remainder of the food, and twelve baskets are filled with the fragments.

Feeding the Five Thousand; the Prophet-King

From the crowd's point of view, the miracle proved that Jesus was "the prophet who is to come into the world" (6:14). Their response reflects the common expectation of a prophet like Moses, which was foretold in Deut. 18:18, where God told Moses, "I will raise up for them a prophet like you from among their brethren; and I will put my words in his mouth, and he shall speak to them all that I command him." The timing of the miracle seemed to invite such a response, since Jesus performed it during the Jewish Passover (John 6:4), which commemorated Israel's deliverance from bondage in Egypt under Moses' leadership. The connection between the crowd's response and traditions about Moses is made explicit later in the chapter (6:32).

Moses was the most important miracle-working prophet in Israel's history. There had been no one like him "for all the signs and the wonders which the Lord sent him to do in the land of Egypt" (Deut. 34:11). Moses' "signs" included miraculous demonstrations of divine authority (Exod. 4:8-9, 28-31) and the plagues inflicted on the Egyptians (7:3; 8:23; 10:1-2). The last and greatest of these "signs" (11:9-10 LXX) was the slaying of the firstborn of every household in Egypt, which was commemorated each year at Passover, when unleavened bread was eaten (12:17). Moses also worked wonders in the wilderness. When the people murmured because they had nothing to eat, God told Moses, "Behold, I will rain bread from heaven for you" (16:4). In the morning the people discovered something on the ground that was white and tasted like wafers made with honey; they called it manna (16:14, 31). This "bread from heaven" continued to appear throughout the forty years Israel wandered in the desert. After entering the promised land, they celebrated the Passover on the plains of Jericho. The next day the manna ceased, "and the people of Israel had manna no more, but ate the fruit of the land of Canaan that year" (Josh. 5:12).

Popular expectations for the appearance of a miracle-working prophet were also shaped by traditions about Elisha and especially Elijah, who was supposed to appear before the great and terrible day of the Lord (Mal. 4:5-6; John 1:21, 25). Like Moses, these two prophets miraculously fed people with bread: Elijah fed himself, a widow, and her son for many days with a handful of meal and a bit of oil (1 Kings 17:8-16); Elisha fed a hundred men with twenty barley loaves and some fresh ears of grain 2 Kings 4:42-44). If Moses had once parted the waters of the sea, Elijah and Elisha parted the waters of the Jordan River (2 Kings 2:8, 14). They also performed healing miracles similar to those that captured the attention of the people thronging to Jesus, such as bringing a boy back from the threshold of death (1 Kings 17:17-24; 2 Kings 4:32-37; John 4:46-54; 6:2).

After acclaiming Jesus as prophet, the crowd wanted "to seize him and make him king," but Jesus quickly slipped away from them (John 6:25). The assumption that a prophet should be king is surprising in some ways, since the roles of prophet and king were usually distinguished.[33] People expected miracles from prophets, but not from a king or the Messiah. A number of factors, however, suggest that the connection between prophet and king would have been a plausible one. Miracle-working prophets like Moses, Elijah, and Elisha played important roles in Israel's political and military affairs, and Moses was sometimes given royal functions in Jewish and Samaritan tradition.[34] Prophets in the first century sought to advance their political aspirations by replicating the feats of earlier prophets, like parting the Jordan or making the walls of a city collapse. The political implications were clear enough for the Romans to take military action against these movements.[35]

The Messiah was not specifically identified as a miracle-worker, but there were expectations that the messianic age would be accompanied by signs like those of the Mosaic period. The Scriptures said that in a future time of salvation God would perform wonders like those with which he brought Israel out of Egypt (Mic. 7:15; Isa. 48:20-21). One tradition maintained that the coming of the Messiah would be marked by the descent of manna again. A Jewish text roughly contemporary with the Fourth Gospel

33. On the distinction between the Messiah and Mosaic prophet see John 1:20-21; 1QS ix 11; 4QTestamonia. Cf. Bittner, *Jesu Zeichen im Johannesevangelium*, 38–40.

34. Meeks, *Prophet-King.*

35. On Theudas see Josephus, *Ant.* 20.5.1 §97. On similarities to Elijah and Elisha, see Martyn, *Gospel of John*, 20–27; Raymond E. Brown, "Jesus and Elisha," *Perspective* 12 (1971) 85–104; Nichol, *The Sēmeia in the Fourth Gospel*, 53–60. For a figure like Joshua see *Ant.* 20.8.6 §§ 169–72.

said that at the Messiah's coming, "the treasury of manna will come down again from on high, and they will eat of it in those years because these are they who will have arrived at the consummation of time."[36] Readers unfamiliar with Jewish tradition would have missed many of the messianic connotations of the sign, but they may have recognized in the crowd's reaction the typical readiness of people to acclaim anyone king as long as he provided them with a sure meal-ticket (see pp. 55–57).

The crowd's perception was correct in a limited sense, since Jesus fulfilled the promises concerning the Mosaic prophet found in Deuteronomy 18.[37] The Gospel alluded to Jesus' prophetic identity in the verses immediately preceding the feeding of the five thousand, where Jesus insisted that Moses had written of him (John 5:46; Deut. 18:18), that he had come in his Father's name (John 5:43; Deut. 18:19), and that those who refused to believe him were condemned by Moses himself (John 5:45; Deut. 18:19c).[38] Elsewhere Jesus is identified as "the prophet" by a crowd in Jerusalem (John 7:40), as "he who is coming into the world" by Martha (11:27), and as "a prophet" by the Samaritan woman and the man born blind, who are positive exemplars of faith (4:19; 9:17). The crowd in Galilee was also correct in perceiving Jesus as a king, just as Nathanael and a crowd in Jerusalem rightly called him King of Israel (1:49; 12:13). The problem was that the crowd could not *make* Jesus their king any more than Jesus would *make* himself equal with God (6:15; 5:18). They failed to recognize the difference between the power that comes from God above and the power that relies on the favor of the masses below—something that will be made clear in Jesus' remarks to Pilate about kingship (18:36-37).

Walking on the Sea
and the "I Am"

Jesus' encounter with his disciples on the sea discloses another facet of his identity. This incident should be understood as a sign, although the miraculous elements in the story are remarkably muted. The text says they had rowed for three or four miles but does not indicate whether this put them in the middle of the lake or near their destination (6:19a). The disciples saw Jesus walking on the sea and were frightened, but the text does not say Jesus looked like a ghost (6:19bc). Unlike the other Gospels, John does not say that Jesus stilled the storm or even that he got into the boat, but

36. *2 Bar.* 29:8. Cf. *Sib. Or.* frag. 3.46-49; *Eccl. Rab.* 1:8; *Mekilta* "Vayassa" 5.63-65 (Lauterbach ed., vol. 2, p. 119); Rev. 2:17.

37. Cf. Meeks, *Prophet-King*, 99. Jesus' identity as the prophet like Moses is rejected by de Jonge, *Jesus: Stranger*, 51; Bittner, *Jesu Zeichen im Johannesevangelium*, 163.

38. The transition between John 5 and 6 is abrupt, and it is sometimes suggested that the chapters were accidentally transposed. There are, however, important thematic connections between the sections.

only that the disciples quickly reached the shore after seeing Jesus (6:21). Some interpreters think this means that the boat was magically whisked the remaining miles across the lake, but others that the text is saying the disciples had nearly reached land when they saw Jesus.[39]

The focal point of the episode, however, is not the act of walking but the act of speaking. It was when Jesus told the disciples "I Am [*egō eimi*]; do not be afraid" (6:20) that their fear was transformed into a desire to receive him. Although the "I Am" was probably a traditional element in the story (cf. Matt. 14:27; Mark 6:50), John's subdued treatment of the miraculous aspects helped to place this expression at the center of his account. The "I Am" appears in several different forms in John's Gospel, all of which can have divine significance.[40] The divine overtones in the "I Am" are scarcely audible when Jesus speaks to the Samaritan woman (John 4:26), but they crescendo in his words to the disciples on the sea (6:20) and in statements like "I Am the bread of life" (6:35, 48) and "I Am the light of the world" (8:12). By the end of chapter 8, the divine connotations are so pronounced that a violent confrontation erupts when Jesus says flatly, "before Abraham was, I Am" (8:58).

Readers familiar with the Jewish Scriptures would probably have recognized that "I Am" (*egō eimi*) was a form of God's name. When God appeared to Moses in the burning bush, he said "I Am who I Am. . . . Say to the people of Israel, I Am has sent me to you" (Exod. 3:14). The words *egō eimi* do not appear in the Greek translation of this passage but are used in texts like the Song of Moses: "Behold, behold that I Am, and that there is no god beside me" (Deut. 32:39). The expression is especially prominent in Isaiah, a book quoted a number of times in John's Gospel.[41] According to Isaiah, God said, "I Am and there is no other" (Isa. 45:18); "I Am, I Am the one who comforts you" (51:12); and God called Israel to "know and believe and understand that I Am" (43:10).[42] The focus on the "I Am"

39. Those who see the landing as a miraculous journey across the lake include Bultmann, *Gospel*, 216; Haenchen, *John 1*, 280; and Fortna, *The Fourth Gospel and Its Predecessor*, 82. The nonmiraculous interpretation has been advocated by J. H. Bernard, *A Critical and Exegetical Commentary on the Gospel according to St. John* (ICC; Edinburgh, T. & T. Clark, 1929) 1.185; J. N. Sanders, *A Commentary on the Gospel according to St. John* (ed. B. Mastin; HNTC; New York: Harper, 1969) 183; Charles H. Talbert, *Reading John: A Literary and Theological Commentary on the Fourth Gospel and the Johannine Epistles* (New York: Crossroad, 1992) 133. The obscure points are noted by Brown, *Gospel*, 1.252; Barrett, *Gospel*, 280–81, and Barnabas Lindars, *The Gospel of John* (NCB; Grand Rapids, Mich.: Eerdmans, 1972) 245–46.

40. On the forms of the "I Am" sayings, see esp. Brown, *Gospel*, 1.533–38.

41. John 1:23 = Isa. 40:3; John 6:45 = Isa. 54:13; John 12:38 = Isa. 53:1; John 12:40 = Isa. 6:9-10.

42. There are a number of important studies of the "I Am" expression in John's Gospel and Jewish tradition. See Dodd, *Interpretation*, 93–96; Ethelbert Stauffer, *Jesus and His Story* (New York: Alfred A. Knopf, 1960) 174–95; Brown, *Gospel*, 1.533–38; Philip B. Harner, *The "I Am" of the Fourth Gospel: A Study in Johannine Usage and Thought* (Philadelphia: Fortress, 1971); Neyrey, *An Ideology of Revolt*, 213–20.

gives the incident the character of a theophany, showing that Jesus was the one in whom God's name and identity were revealed. The words "do not be afraid," which accompanied the "I Am," are consistent with the theophanic tone of the scene, since God and his heavenly emissaries frequently greeted people in this way.[43] Echoes of passages referring to God parting or traversing the waters, while not developed here, would enhance the theophanic aspects of the scene.[44]

By focusing attention on the I Am, the evangelist may have helped make the theophanic character of the sign apparent even to readers who were not well versed in the Scriptures. An incident that took place on the next Passover in the Gospel suggests that the numinous quality of the I Am expression would have been evident to Gentiles as well as Jews. Both Roman and Jewish soldiers were sent to arrest Jesus, and when Jesus told them, "I Am" (*egō eimi*), they all drew back and fell to the ground as people do at a theophany (18:6). Although John's account of the arrest is highly stylized, evidence from outside the text indicates that Greeks and Romans would have been able to hear overtones of divinity in the words *I Am*. Inscriptions to the goddess Isis, who was invoked throughout the Mediterranean world, typically began with the solemn and repeated use of *egō eimi*, such as "I am Isis, queen of every land" or "I am Isis, the mistress of every land." Magical texts and revelatory discourses in second-century gnostic sources also made use of the "I am" formula, suggesting that its numinous aspects would have been apparent to a broad spectrum of readers.[45] The discourse that follows makes this evocative language a vehicle for a distinctive message.

The Bread of Life Discourse

The disciples who wanted to "receive" Jesus after hearing him speak his Father's name (cf. 5:43) responded appropriately to his signs; the crowd that tried to make Jesus a king did not. The conversations and discourse in the remainder of the chapter will elaborate the meaning of signs in order that the readers—like the disciples—may respond positively to Jesus. Although some episodes affirm that Jesus is a prophet, Messiah or king,

43 On the use of "Do not fear" see Gen. 15:1; 26:24; Judg. 6:23. Noted by Nichol, *The Sēmeia in the Fourth Gospel*, 58.

44. Ps. 77:19; Job 9:8. See the discussion in Schnackenburg, *Gospel*, 2.29–30.

45. On the widespread worship of Isis, see Tran Tam Tinh, "Sarapis and Isis," *Jewish and Christian Self-Definition* (ed. Ben F. Meyer and E. P. Sanders; Philadelphia: Fortress, 1982) 3.101–17, esp. 102–3. For the inscriptions see Adolf Deissmann, *Light from the Ancient East* (London: Hodder & Stoughten, 1910) 138–40. On the significance of these texts and the "I Am" see Bernard, *St. John*, 1.cxvii–cxxi; Schnackenburg, *Gospel*, 2.86; Barrett, *Gospel*, 292; Bultmann, *Gospel*, 225–26 n. 3; Brown, *Community*, 57; George W. MacRae, "The Ego Proclamation in Gnostic Sources," *Studies in the New Testament and Gnosticism* (Good News Studies 26; Wilmington, Del.: Michael Glazier, 1987) 203–17.

and divine Son of man (e.g., 9:17, 22, 35-38), the crowd in Galilee fundamentally misunderstood what it meant to call Jesus prophet and king. Therefore, the bread of life discourse dissociated Jesus from their interpretation of the Moses tradition, emphasizing his unique relationship to God.

In the discourse, Jesus sharply distinguished two kinds of bread. He said, "Do not labor for the food which perishes, but for the food which endures to eternal life, which the Son of Man will give you" (6:27). On a literary level, the word *perish* (*apollynai*) echoes the enigmatic remark Jesus made to the disciples when he had finished feeding the multitude: "Gather up the fragments left over, that nothing may perish" (*apollynai*, 6:12). The bread they received could sustain them physically, but it pointed to a gift that would sustain them eternally. In the discourse, Jesus repeatedly contrasted the bread he provided with the manna eaten by Israel in the time of Moses. Those familiar with the manna tradition knew it was food that perished. People could gather only enough manna to last for one day, and those who tried to store it overnight found that it bred worms and became foul. They gathered it each morning, but when the sun grew hot it melted (Exod. 16:20-21). The sign Jesus performed could not be understood as a simple repetition of the bread they ate in the wilderness. It conveyed something of another order.

The crowd failed to grasp what Jesus meant and pressed him to give them bread as Moses had done, invoking the Scriptures in their demand. They said, "Our fathers ate manna in the wilderness; as it is written, 'He gave them bread from heaven to eat'" (John 6:30-31). Their words are not an exact quotation of any one biblical text but are similar to Ps. 78:24, Exod. 16:4 and 15, and other passages recalling the gift of manna. This reference to the Scriptures provides the basis for a kind of expository sermon, set in the synagogue at Capernaum (John 6:59), which successively explicates each portion of the biblical text and, in so doing, elaborates the meaning of the signs.[46]

The first part of the sermon (6:32-34) deals with the words "He gave them." The crowd apparently thought that the biblical passage referred to what Moses had done in the past, but Jesus argued that they understood the subject of the verb and the verb tense incorrectly. He contended that the subject of the verb was God not Moses, and that the verb was present tense not past tense. Following the pattern of a rabbinic disputation, Jesus gave his opponents' interpretation before countering it with his own. He said, "It was not *Moses* who *gave* you the bread from heaven; my

46. This pattern of biblical exposition in John 6 has been helpfully treated by Peder Borgen, *Bread from Heaven: An Exegetical Study of the Concept of Manna in the Gospel of John and the Writings of Philo* (NovTSup 10; Leiden: Brill, 1965) 59–98.

Father gives you the true bread from heaven" (6:32). This interpretive move changes the plane of the discussion from what Moses did in the past to what God is doing in the present. The shift in perspective is similar to that of the previous discourse, where Jesus insists that his actions paralleled God's actions (5:17). Jesus also redefined the meaning of the word *them* in the quotation by saying that the true bread from heaven gives life not just to Israel but to "the world" (6:33). This first section of the discourse places readers in a position to discern both the transcendent and universal dimensions of the miracle of the bread.

The second part of the sermon (6:35-48) deals with the next part of the biblical text cited earlier: "bread from heaven." The crowd associated Jesus with Moses, but Jesus identified himself with the gift of bread rather than the prophet, saying, "I Am the bread of life" (6:35, 48). His words effectively break the parallel between himself and Moses and demand that he be understood in other terms. His statement also brings together the central element in each of the signs recounted at the beginning of the chapter—the bread and the I Am—forming a metaphor that is incongruous when taken literally. Jesus was not claiming to be a baked mixture of flour and water in a physical sense, and this incongruity forces people to understand the meaning in another way, asking in what sense Jesus *is* claiming to be bread.

This metaphorical use of bread is evocative, and its significance can be discerned at several levels. At the level of the literary context, bread is explicitly connected with life. Jesus is the bread that gives people a life that is not merely physical and doomed to perish. As elsewhere in John's Gospel, "life" has an important theological dimension and indicates life in relationship with God. Here "life" is used interchangeably with "eternal life" (6:40, 47). Death is no longer an abiding threat for those who believe, because Jesus has promised that he will raise them up at the last day. The eternal life Jesus offers is a relationship with God that begins in faith and continues beyond the grave into eternity.

Readers familiar with Jewish tradition would probably have connected the bread metaphor with God's word, wisdom, and law. The Scriptures said that the manna Israel received pointed to the central place of God's word in human life. Moses told Israel, "God fed you with manna which you did not know nor did your fathers know; that he might make you know that man does not live by bread alone, but that man lives by everything that proceeds out of the mouth of the Lord" (Deut, 8:3; cf. Wisd. of Sol. 16:20, 26). Isaiah compared God's word to the rain and snow that come down from heaven, giving seed to the sower and bread to the eater (Isa. 55:10-11); and Amos warned that a famine would come, not of bread, but of hearing the word of the Lord (Amos 8:11). Similarly, Philo said that the manna eaten by Israel was the divine Word from which instruction and wisdom flow,[47] and Sir. 15:3 said that wisdom feeds people with "the bread of understanding."

Bread imagery was also extended to the Law of Moses in which God's word and wisdom were to be found. When God first gave Israel the manna, he said, "I will rain bread from heaven for you; and the people shall go out and gather a day's portion every day, that I may prove them, whether they will walk in my law or not" (Exod. 16:4). In other words, the way they received the manna revealed their readiness to obey the rest of God's instructions which are found in the law. Jesus seemed to suggest a connection between his role as "bread" and divine instruction when he announced that all who came to him would be "taught by God," as the Scriptures had said (John 6:45; Isa. 54:13). Jewish exegetes regularly took this passage as a reference to instruction in the law.[48] The words *bread of life* seem to echo the expression *law of life*, which was used for the Mosaic law,[49] and Jewish interpreters took the call of wisdom to "Come, eat of my bread" (Prov. 9:5) as an invitation to study the law (*Genesis Rabbah* 70:5). The bread of life discourse is set in a Jewish synagogue, where comments on the nourishment provided by the law would be appropriate. But John's Gospel effectively refocuses the imagery, so that the Scriptures themselves are not "bread" but witnesses to Jesus, who is the true bread. The Scriptures promised eternal life (John 5:39), but the gift of life is actually given in Jesus the Christ.[50]

Still other connotations appear when the passage is read in its wider cultural setting. Literary warrant for this approach is found at the beginning of the discourse, where Jesus referred to the bread that was given to "the world" (6:33). He maintains the same broad scope throughout this section by speaking of "he who comes to me" and "he who believes in me" (6:35); of "all that the Father gives me" (6:37, 39); and of "everyone" who sees and believes, hears and learns (6:40, 45). The discourse draws a number of elements from Jewish tradition but formulates a message for all humanity, and the basic imagery in the passage is consistent with this movement. Manna was unique to Israel, but "bread" was the staff of life for everyone. Readers unfamiliar with Jewish tradition would miss many of the subtleties in this passage, but the repeated references to Jesus as bread fix attention on this image and depict his life-giving power in terms that

47. Philo, *On Flight and Finding* 137; *Who Is the Heir* 191; *On the Change of Names* 259–60; cf. *Allegorical Interpretation* 3.161.
48. Borgen, *Bread from Heaven*, 150.
49. Sir. 17:11; 45:5; 4 Ezra 14:30; cf. *Pss. Sol.* 14:2.
50. On the transference of the bread image from the law to Jesus, see Severino Pancaro, *The Law in the Fourth Gospel: The Torah and the Gospel, Moses and Jesus, Judaism and Christianity according to John* (NovTSup 42; Leiden: Brill, 1975) 454–72.

would have been engaging and meaningful on a basic level to almost any reader in the ancient Mediterranean world.

Some of the broad cultural overtones of this text were noted in our last chapter, where we observed the similarities between the crowd in John 6 and the masses in many Greco-Roman cities who craved nothing so much as "bread and circuses." Such preoccupations arose from a real and widespread dependence on wheat, barley, and other grains, which provided over two-thirds of the food eaten by most people.[51] A well-known verse by Euripides put it simply: "What do mortals need except for two things: the grain of [the goddess] Demeter and a drink of water; they are there and were made to nourish us."[52] Where there was bread there could be life, but where bread was lacking, death would soon result. It was even said that as the philosopher Democritus lay dying, he was kept alive for several days by the smell of fresh bread wafting into his nostrils.[53] Many understood bread to be the gift of Demeter, the goddess of grain, although the philosopher Epictetus was astonished at the impiety of those "who eat bread every day, and yet have the audacity to say, 'We do not know if there is a Demeter.'"[54] His comment suggests that those who receive bread should acknowledge its divine giver. When read in this cultural context, Jesus' claim to be the bread of life presents him as the absolutely essential means of sustenance, the divine gift that is the basis for all life—though the next section distinguishes his claims from all others.

The third part of the sermon (6:49-58) picks up the words *to eat* from the biblical passage cited in 6:31, promising that all who ate of Jesus' bread would live forever. Then the text makes the startling disclosure that what was said about bread in this passage must be understood in terms of Jesus' crucifixion. He said, "The bread I shall give for the life of the world is my flesh" (6:51). The passage echoes what was said earlier about God giving the Son up to death so that those who believe would have eternal life (3:16). The use of the future tense "I shall give" points to the act of self-giving that Jesus would perform on the cross. The comment that this gift would be given "for" (*hyper*) the life of the world alludes to its sacrificial character, as do later references to the good shepherd laying down his life "for" the sheep and Jesus dying "for" the people (10:11, 15; 11:50).

The idea that Jesus gives people his flesh to eat is grotesque if taken literally, for it conveys an image of people devouring the flesh of a dead man; but when his hearers demanded further explanation, he heightened

---

51. K. T. White in *Civilization of the Ancient Mediterranean: Greece and Rome* (ed. M. Grant and R. Kitzinger; New York: Charles Scribner's Sons, 1988) 1.236–43.

52. For the Euripides fragment see J. Hausleiter et al., "Brot," *RAC* 2.611–20; quotation col. 613.

53. Diogenes Laertius, *Lives of Eminent Philosophers* 9.43.

54. Epictetus, *Discourses* 2.20.32.

the offense by insisting that they also drink his blood: "Unless you eat the flesh of the Son of Man and drink his blood, you have no life in you" (6:53). This text effectively underscores the allusion to the crucifixion, because for blood to be consumed it must be shed, which would happen when Jesus died (19:34). Jesus' statement ran counter to Jewish proscriptions against consuming blood, and it would have been repugnant even to non-Jews, yet the imagery was suitable for crucifixion, which was deemed abhorrent under Jewish law and considered repulsive by Greeks and Romans.

People partake of the crucified Jesus through faith. In this passage, "to eat" means "to believe." The centrality of faith was introduced at the beginning of the discourse when the crowd asked what was necessary for them to be doing the works of God, and Jesus replied that the work of God was that they *believe* in him whom he had sent (6:28-29). When Jesus identified himself as the bread of life, he said that those who came to him and believed in him would not hunger or thirst (6:35). He promised that "he who *believes* has eternal life" and will be raised at the last day (6:40, 47) and repeated the same idea by saying, "He who *eats* my flesh and drinks my blood has eternal life, and I will raise him up at the last day" (6:54). Jesus warned that those who do not eat and drink of him do not have life, as elsewhere he cautioned that those who do not believe face the prospect of death (3:18, 36; 8:24). To partake of Jesus as the bread of life is to believe that the crucified Messiah is the source of eternal life with God.

Readers familiar with the Christian celebration of the Lord's Supper probably would have heard echoes of its language in this passage from John. The other Gospels and Paul say that on the night Jesus was betrayed, he took bread, gave thanks, and gave it to his disciples saying, "This is my body given for you." He also gave them a cup of wine, saying, "This is my blood." Those who read John 6 with these other passages in mind might see connections between the Lord's Supper and John's account of the feeding of the five thousand, as Jesus took bread, gave thanks, and gave it to the crowd. They may also have connected the references to eating Jesus' flesh and drinking his blood with the words spoken elsewhere over the bread and cup. John 6 is not about the Lord's Supper, but its language might suggest to readers who knew the tradition from other sources that the gift of life provided through Jesus' crucifixion continued to be offered to them through the observance of the Lord's Supper in the Christian community.

It is difficult to determine how well known the celebration of the Lord's Supper was to the fourth evangelist and his earliest readers, and, if they knew about it, how they viewed it. Some have concluded that the evangelist is appreciative of the Lord's Supper, and others think he is critical.

Since these questions have implications for interpreting the whole of the Gospel's symbolism, they can best be addressed in the postscript after chapter 7. Here we observe that when interpreted in their present context, the signs and the discourse in John 6 point to Jesus, whose role as prophet, king, and divine Son of man culminates in his crucifixion, through which the gift of eternal life is given to those who believe.

BLINDNESS AND SIGHT

The sixth sign is the healing of a blind beggar, which is set within a lengthy series of debates that took place during the feast of Booths (7:1— 10:21). The encounter occurred in the vicinity of Jerusalem when Jesus happened upon the man after having fled from the temple following a confrontation with the crowd. The disciples asked questions about the reasons for the blind man's condition, and after a brief response, Jesus spat on the ground, made clay with the spittle, and placed it on the man's eyes, telling him to wash in the pool of Siloam. The man went to the pool as Jesus had instructed, and after washing the clay out of his eyes he was suddenly able to see (9:1-7).

Sinner or Sent by God?

The interchange between Jesus and the disciples at the beginning of the episode helps to disclose the symbolic significance of the healing. The disciples observed the man's physical condition and inferred that the blindness must have been the result of a sin committed by either the man or his parents. Their comments reflect the principle that where there is suffering there must be guilt. There was some biblical warrant for assuming that someone could suffer because of the sins of his parents, since God warned that he would visit "the iniquities of the fathers upon the children to the third and fourth generation" of those who hated him (Exod. 20:5). Other passages insisted that God would not make a son suffer for the sins of his father, but would punish each one for his own sin (Ezek. 18:20). Eventually Jewish scholars concluded that it was possible for a child to sin even in the womb,[55] although in some cases, like that of Job, the connection between individual sin and individual suffering remained elusive.

Jesus abruptly shifted the plane of discussion from questions about the cause of the blindness to what God could do with the blindness. Jesus rejected the idea that this man's blindness was the result of his sin or that of his parents, but he offered no alternative explanation of the cause. He accepted the blindness as a given and indicated that whatever the cause,

---

55. *Lev. Rab.* 27; Str-B 2.527-529.

the blindness would become a means of revelation.[56] Further comments help to focus the symbolism of the healing. (a) Jesus identified himself as "the light of the world" in 9:5 as he had done previously in 8:12. The main action in this episode involved opening or "enlightening" the eyes of a blind man, which demonstrated the truth of this claim. (b) The evangelist's commentary on the meaning of the word *Siloam* points to the location of the healing as a supporting symbol. Jesus was the one whom God had "sent" (9:4) and the evangelist explained that *Siloam* meant "one who has been sent" (9:7), creating a suggestive connection between Jesus and the pool.[57]

The neighbors of the beggar were the first ones to meet him after the healing had taken place, and they discuss the healing at the level of sense perception. Because of their previous acquaintance with the man, they knew he was blind, yet they now met someone who looked the same but could see. Therefore, either the man had undergone a change or they were dealing with two different individuals. After being assured that they were dealing with the same man, they asked how the healing had taken place. The beggar responded on the level of sense perception, describing how "the man called Jesus" put mud on his eyes and told him to go to Siloam, where he washed the mud from his eyes and received his sight. At this point, the physical aspect of the healing is clear but its significance is not.

The Jewish authorities posed the interpretive issue more sharply by pointing out that the healing had taken place on the Sabbath. As before, their frame of reference was shaped by their understanding of Jewish Sabbath regulations. There were provisions against healing on the Sabbath unless a person's life was in danger, which was not the case with congenital blindness. Jesus could have waited a day. As part of the cure, Jesus had spat on the ground and made mud from the spittle, but kneading was one of the thirty-nine forms of work forbidden on the Sabbath. Some later traditions also forbade the use of spittle and other forms of anointing the eyes on the Sabbath.[58]

As they debated the case, the Jewish authorities changed the focus of discussion from the details of the healing to the identity of the healer. Some concluded that Jesus must be a sinner, since his actions contravened

56. The NRSV renders John 9:3, "Neither this man nor his parents sinned; *he was born blind* so that God's works might be revealed in him." The words in italics are not in the Greek text and might suggest that God caused the blindness to reveal his glory. Jesus does not, however, resolve the issue of causality. Cf. Carson, *John* 361–62.

57. The two words for *send* (*pempein* in 9:4 and *apostellein* in 9:7) are used interchangeably in John. Cf. 5:36-38.

58. On kneading on the Sabbath see *m. Shabb.* 7:2. On anointing the eyes see *b. Abod. Zar.* 28d; *y. Shabb.* 14d, 17f. See also Brown, *Gospel,* 1.373; Barrett, *Gospel,* 358–60.

established Sabbath regulations, but others countered that a sinner would not have the ability to perform such a miracle. Their debate points out the difficulty in comprehending the sign within their frame of reference; the incongruity of the whole affair made them doubt that a healing had actually taken place. They called in the man's parents, who verified that he had been born blind and could now see, and this testimony forced the issue. The Pharisees most firmly entrenched in the legal tradition prevailed, and they ruled that the miraculous healing, which violated the law, proved that Jesus was a sinner (9:24).

Prophet—Messiah—Son of Man

The man born blind is the one who leads readers through the levels of meaning conveyed by the sign. His perspective was shaped by Jesus' command to go and wash in the pool of Siloam, which evoked a response of trusting obedience from the man. The physical sight he received confirmed that his trust in Jesus had been rightly placed and established this incipient faith as the context in which to interpret the sign. In this respect he is like the disciples and the Galilean official earlier in the Gospel. Initially the beggar described what had happened in purely physical terms, but the questions directed at him by the Pharisees made him reflect more deeply on the significance of his healing.

When the Jewish authorities pressed the man to say something about the identity of his healer, he replied, "He is a prophet" (9:17). The text does not say how this statement is related to the healing, but readers familiar with Jewish tradition would have found it plausible. We have already seen that miracles were commonly associated with prophets, who performed signs to show they had been sent by God. Moreover, the way Jesus commanded the man to "go and wash in the pool of Siloam" was reminiscent of the way Elisha spoke to Naaman, a Syrian military official who suffered from leprosy. The prophet told him, "Go and wash in the river Jordan seven times and your flesh will be restored" (2 Kings 5:10). When Naaman went and washed, he was healed, like the blind man in John's Gospel. Readers who knew about the pool of Siloam independently of John's Gospel might have heard that it had gotten its name because God had once "sent" water into it to quench the thirst of the prophet Isaiah. According to tradition, God continued sending water into Siloam as a "sign" he worked for the sake of the prophet.[59]

The next scene suggests a connection between the sign and Jesus' identity as Messiah. The man born blind had simply called Jesus a prophet, but

59. "The Life of Isaiah," in *The Lives of the Prophets* 1:2. Some think that the etymology of the name *Siloam* is a Christian interpolation based on John 9:7, but D. R. A. Hare has rightly challenged this, since the etymologies function quite differently in the two works (*OTP* 2.385 g).

the man's parents apparently realized that to say anything more would be tantamount to calling Jesus the Messiah, and they were afraid of being expelled from the synagogue for making such a confession (9:22). Pressure from the authorities only emboldened their son, however, who was adamant that Jesus was "from God," since God would not have granted such healing power to a sinner (9:31, 33). The beggar pointed out that "never since the world began has it been heard that any one opened the eyes of a man born blind" (9:32), and from a biblical perspective this was true; the Old Testament contains no accounts of someone being healed of congenital blindness. Yet the Scriptures did say that the "servant" of God— whom many took to be the Messiah—would be "a light to the nations" and "open the eyes that are blind" (Isa. 42:6-7).[60] The references to Jesus as "the light of the world" in the messianic debates in John 8 and again in 9:4 echo this Isaiah passage and make the opening of a blind man's eyes a sign that Jesus was God's messianic servant.

The name of the pool where the healing took place provides secondary support for the messianic interpretation of the sign. The word *Siloam,* or *Shiloah* as it was sometimes written (Isa. 8:6; cf. Neh. 3:15), was similar to the word *Shiloh,* which many Jews understood to be a name for the Messiah. One of the most important messianic passages in the Old Testament literally said, "The scepter shall not depart from Judah, nor the ruler's staff from between his feet, until Shiloh comes, and to him shall be the obedience of the peoples" (Gen. 49:10). By the first century, Jewish interpreters took Shiloh as a reference to the Messiah, and this view is widely attested in later sources.[61] By explaining that Siloam was the pool of the "one who has been sent," the fourth evangelist apparently alludes to this common Jewish tradition, suggesting that Siloam was in fact the pool of the Messiah whom God had sent.

The story culminates with the beggar's recognition that Jesus was the divine Son of man. The beggar's tenacious insistence that Jesus had come "from God" prompted the Pharisees to put him out of the synagogue. There he was met by Jesus himself, who asked him, "Do you believe in the Son of man?" (9:36). Readers of the Gospel learned earlier that the Son of man was the human being in whom God was revealed,[62] and when Jesus announced that he was the Son of man, the man born blind worshiped him—the response of someone in the presence of deity (9:38). Jesus was a

---

60. Also *1 Enoch* 48:4, 10; *2 Bar.* 70:10; cf. the references to the "light of the nations" in Luke 1:79; 2:32; Acts 26:18, 23; *Barn.* 14:7-8.

61. See esp. 4QPBless, which provides an early messianic commentary on Gen. 49:10. The Targums on Gen. 49:10 consistently refer to "Shiloh" as the Messiah. Cf. *Gen. Rab.* 98:8-9. On the use of these materials for interpreting John 9, see Schnackenburg, *Gospel,* 2.243.

62. The Son of man is the link between heaven and earth (1:51), ascends into heaven (3:13-14; 6:62), exercises divine judgment (5:27), gives life (6:27, 53), is the "I Am" (8:28).

man, a prophet, and Messiah; but he was also the one in whom people encounter God.

The beggar did not infer Jesus' divinity from the sign; he recognized it only when Jesus made it known to him. Yet the beggar's reaction suggests that at least in retrospect the sign does point to the divine aspect of Jesus. The Scriptures identified God as the true "light" (see pp. 140–41) and said God is the one who "opens the eyes of the blind" (Ps. 146:8), and that God would "lead the blind in a way that they know not" and "turn the darkness before them into light" (Isa. 42:16; cf. 35:4-5). Yet the episode also forces readers to move outside a strict Jewish frame of reference, since Jews found it unconscionable to ascribe the traits of deity to a man and to worship him (cf. John 8:59; 10:33). Significantly, the beggar's recognition of Jesus' divinity took place outside the synagogue, and non-Jews who were familiar with reports about various deities opening the eyes of the blind may have found the beggar's willingness to worship his healer quite plausible (cf. Acts 14:8-18).[63] Yet the healer in John 9 is not one more deity in the pantheon but a figure with a distinctive and exclusive role.

The good shepherd discourse concludes the episode by reinforcing the connections between Jesus' messianic and divine claims and stressing his uniqueness. The discourse follows the story of the beggar without pause, and its conclusion refers back to the beggar's healing (10:21). Although the transition seems abrupt, links between the section's main themes— light, water, and shepherding—may have been traditional.[64] After speaking in generally realistic terms about a sheepfold and shepherd, Jesus first identifies himself as "the door." He is the sole legitimate means of access, and "all" who came before him are thieves and robbers (10:7-9). The claim contrasts Jesus with the Jewish authorities who monitored access to the synagogue, but Jesus also distinguishes himself from the stranger, the wolf, and the hireling who flees. The effect is kaleidoscopic, making it

63. On this aspect of paganism see Robin Lane Fox, *Pagans and Christians* (San Francisco: Harper & Row, 1986); Acts 14:8-18 is treated on pp. 99–101. Earlier we noted how Vespasian was said to have healed a blind man by the power of Serapis. One report said that a god, perhaps Asclepius, told a blind man to go (cf. John 9:7a) and take the blood of a white cock, together with honey, and rub them into an eye salve (cf. 9:6a) and anoint his eyes (cf. 9:6b) for three days. The man received his sight (cf 9:7b), then came and gave thanks publicly to the god. Noted by Deissmann, *Light from the Ancient East*, 135; cf. Barrett, *Gospel*, 353. For other reports of Asclepius healing the blind, see Aelius Aristides, *Orations* 39.15, and the material from Epidaurus found in Frederick C. Grant, *Hellenistic Religions: The Age of Syncretism* (Indianapolis: Bobbs-Merrill, 1953) 57–58.

64. A passage in *2 Bar.* (77:13-17) laments that "the shepherds of Israel have perished, and the lamps which gave light are extinguished, and the fountains . . . have withheld their streams." But since "shepherds and lamps and fountains came from the Law," there is hope that "the lamp will not be wanting and the shepherd will not give way and the fountain will not dry up." These words were spoken between the feasts of Booths and Dedication (cf. 77:18), the same time as the Johannine shepherd discourse.

difficult to confine the meaning of the imagery to the conflict with the synagogue. By claiming to be "the door," Jesus sets himself against any and all who claim membership in God's flock apart from him, which counters the claims of the Pharisees and indirectly addresses prevailing attitudes in the wider Greco-Roman world, which easily accommodated veneration of a number of divine figures.[65] The man born blind did not leave the synagogue only to fall into paganism by worshiping his healer. He came to faith in the one source of life with God.

Jesus next identifies himself as the good shepherd, an image that encompasses all the facets of Jesus' identity mentioned in the story of the beggar's healing and defines them in terms of the cross and resurrection. We have already noted that a prophet, the Messiah, and God could all be called shepherd (pp. 16, 27–28); this image therefore integrates what was said about Jesus in the previous chapter into a consonant whole. Yet the premier trait of this shepherd is that he lays down his life for the sheep (10:11, 15, 17-18). To confess that the man Jesus is prophet, Messiah, and divine Son of man is also to confess that he is the shepherd who died for the flock. The healing of the blind man was a sign drawing together several aspects of Jesus' identity, conveying them in a way that would have been engaging to a wide spectrum of readers. The discourse reiterates the same facets of Jesus' identity in familiar images taken from shepherding but stressing his singular status and the centrality of his death.

THE RESURRECTION AND THE LIFE

The seventh sign, and the last one Jesus performed during his public ministry, was raising Lazarus from the dead. The miracle itself is recounted in just two verses (11:43-44), but the narrative framework that discloses its symbolic significance encompasses most of chapters 11–12. The story began after Jesus had fled to Transjordan because of mounting hostility in Jerusalem. Jesus' friend Lazarus, who lived in the village of Bethany near Jerusalem, became seriously ill and his sisters sent word to Jesus. When he heard about the illness, he delayed departing and arrived in Bethany after Lazarus had already been in the tomb for four days. Jesus was met at the outskirts of the village by Lazarus's sister Martha and then by his sister Mary, who took him to the tomb, where he wept. After demanding that the stone be removed from the tomb, Jesus prayed and cried with a loud voice, "Lazarus, come out!" (11:43), and Lazarus emerged

---

65. The adversaries have been variously identified with the Pharisees, pseudomessiahs, and Greco-Roman savior figures. The christological focus of the discourse and the way it excludes all rivals have been noted by Schnackenburg, *Gospel*, 2.291.

still wrapped in the grave cloths. Jesus told them to unbind the man and
let him go.

Glorification and Death

The comments Jesus made at the beginning of the episode help prepare
readers to discern its significance. He said, "This illness is not unto death;
it is for the glory of God, so that the Son of God might be glorified by
means of it" (11:4). The statement points to two interrelated facets of
meaning. (a) The sign discloses the glory of God by manifesting the power
of God to give life to the dead. Since Jesus, the Son of God, is the one
through whom God's power is exercised, he shares in the divine glory
revealed by the sign. (b) The raising of Lazarus also presages Jesus' final
glorification through his own death and resurrection. The sign solidified
the resolve of Jesus' opponents to kill him. Yet through his death, Jesus
would reveal the glory of the love of God that gives life to the world, and
by rising he would triumph over death to resume the glory he had with
God before the foundation of the world (see pp. 209–14). The meaning of
Jesus' actions is not apparent to those with whom he speaks in this episode, yet their reactions help the Gospel's readers discern the significance
of the seventh sign.

The perspective of the disciples is given in the next part of the episode.
They were baffled by Jesus' decision to go to Lazarus after delaying his
departure for two days, because this action did not conform to ordinary
patterns of human behavior. It might have been understandable for Jesus
not to go at all, since he had narrowly escaped arrest and death by stoning
during his last visit. It might also have been understandable for Jesus to go
immediately, since he loved Martha, Mary, and Lazarus (11:5) and might
therefore have risked hostility in Judea in order to aid his friend. But
when Jesus delayed for two days and only then announced that he was
returning to Judea, the disciples were incredulous—by that time Lazarus
was presumably either dead or recovering. Jesus' actions could not be
understood in terms of the usual concerns for personal safety or the
conventional bonds of friendship. Their significance lies on another plane.

The disciples' reaction to the peculiar timing of Jesus' decision reinforces the connection between this sign and the passion. When Jesus announced his intentions, the disciples immediately asked, "Rabbi, the Jews
were but now seeking to stone you, and are you going there again?"
(11:5). The answer to their question was yes, he would give life to others
precisely by facing death himself.[66] Jesus assured his disciples that those
who walk in "the light of this world" do not stumble (see pp. 145–47) and

66. Dodd, *Interpretation*, 367.

that he was going to "awaken" Lazarus from the sleep of death, but Thomas responded, "Let us also go that we may die with him" (11:16). This final rejoinder—whether spoken in courage or exasperation—reminds readers that the glory manifested by the sign would come only through Jesus' real and certain encounter with death.

The Resurrection and the Life

The next part of the episode focuses on the conversation between Jesus and Martha, which further discloses the christological significance of the sign. Martha and Mary were mourning the loss of their brother, who had been in the tomb for four days when Jesus came (11:17). The reference to the number of days that had elapsed gives a sense of finality to Lazarus's death; he was not merely sleeping but dead, and his tomb was filled with the stench of bodily decay (11:39). Many had come to console the two women, but when Martha heard that Jesus was coming, she went to meet him on the road. She said, "Lord, if you had been here my brother would not have died. And even now I know that whatever you ask from God, God will give you" (11:22). Although the first part of her statement could be understood as a reproach for not having come sooner, the second part expresses a continuing—if uncomprehending—trust in Jesus. As before, this basic trust or faith in Jesus provides a context within which the significance of the sign can be discerned.

Martha's conversation with Jesus culminated in her confession, "I believe that you are the Christ, the Son of God, he who is coming into the world" (11:27). This statement of faith was evoked by the words of Jesus prior to the actual raising of Lazarus. On one level it identified Jesus as the fulfillment of various Jewish messianic expectations. The expression "he who is coming into the world" was used earlier in the Gospel for the prophet God had promised to send (6:14). We have seen that hopes for this prophet were shaped to some extent by traditions about Elijah and Elisha. Both of these prophets were reported to have resuscitated dead individuals, and there is evidence to suggest that some people anticipated that Elijah's return would be accompanied by the general resurrection of the dead.[67] Martha explicitly called Jesus "the Christ." There is little indication that Jewish people expected the Messiah to raise the dead, but since the advent of the Messiah and the resurrection were both associated with the age to come, a close connection between them would be plausible from a Jewish perspective.[68]

---

67. See 1 Kings 17:17-24; 2 Kings 4:32-37; cf. *m. Sota* 9:15. See also the discussion in Martyn, *Gospel of John*, 18–19 n. 25.

68. E.g., 4 Ezra 7:28-32. Cf. Schürer, *History*, 2.539–44, and esp. Gerard Rochais, *Les recits de resurrection des morts dans le Nouveau Testament* (SNTSMS 40; Cambridge: Cambridge University Press, 1981) 166–76.

The wider narrative context enables readers to discern the divine implications of the conversation. Martha, like Nathanael in 1:49, apparently used the title "Son of God" in a traditional messianic sense without understanding its full import, and she therefore tried to prevent Jesus from opening the tomb. But Jesus told her what readers have known since the beginning of the episode: Those who believe will see the glory of God (11:4, 39-40). Earlier portions of the Gospel have indicated that Jesus was the only begotten "Son of God" who had come into the world "from above," and the "I Am" in the statement "I Am the resurrection and the life" has the numinous overtones apparent in other passages. It was understood that God alone had the power to give life to the dead, and by exercising that same power, Jesus revealed his unity with the God who had sent him (5:21).

The universal significance of Jesus is conveyed by his paradoxical claim to be both the resurrection and the life. This statement combines two rather different forms of eschatological expectation. Jesus explained that "resurrection" meant that "he who believes in me, though he die, yet shall he live" (11:25b), echoing what he said earlier about those in the tombs being enlivened physically when they heard the voice of the Son of man (5:28). Then Jesus explained that "life" meant that "he who lives and believes in me shall never die" (11:26a). Here he has shifted from a physical to a theological understanding of life and death, again recalling what was said earlier: "he who hears my word and believes him who sent me has eternal life; he does not come into judgment, but has passed from death to life" (5:24).[69]

A belief in future resurrection, like that voiced by Martha, would have been familiar to many readers, although forms of this hope remained fluid. The book of Daniel said that "many" of the dead would be raised at the end of the age, some to everlasting life and some to everlasting shame (Dan. 12:2). Other sources said that the righteous would be raised to life and that the wicked would remain dead forever (2 Macc. 7:14),[70] and still others expected all to be raised and judged according to their deeds (cf. John 5:28-29). Some texts stressed that resurrection would transform the body into glory (Dan. 12:3) and others that bodies would be restored physically (2 Macc. 7:10-11). Everlasting life was understood to be reserved for the righteous who kept the Law of Moses. The Maccabean martyrs said that "the King of the Universe will raise us up to an everlasting renewal of life, because we have died for his laws" (2 Macc. 7:9). Similarly, Jesus' contemporary Rabbi Hillel said that if a man has obtained a good reputa-

69. See Dodd, *Interpretation*, 364–66; MacRae, "The Fourth Gospel and *Religionsgeschichte*," 18–19; Carson, *John*, 413.
70. Cf. *Pss. Sol.* 2:31; 3:12; 13:11; 14:9-10.

tion, he has something of value, but "if he has gained for himself the words of the Law he has gained for himself life in the world to come" (*m. ʾAbot* 2:7).

Other readers would have heard echoes of the idea that in some sense people "never die." Understandings of the afterlife in the ancient world ranged widely, from skepticism about any existence after death to the idea that life dissolved into the elements, but many believed that a person's soul was released from the body at death to live on in some form.[71] The Wisdom of Solomon (3:1-4) said that the righteous only seemed to die, since their souls enjoyed immortality with God—a notion that has affinities with Platonism, which connected a blessed immortality to the practice of virtue in this life. Philo, a Jewish scholar of the early first century, seemed to think of immortality as the natural destiny of the soul rather than a reward for righteous living.[72] Similarly, his contemporary the philosopher Seneca remarked that in time "I shall leave the body here where I found it, and shall of my own volition betake myself to the gods. I am not apart from them now, but am merely detained in a heavy and earthly prison."[73] Some sought to assure their immortality through initiation into a mystery religion, although it is not clear how common this was; and in time various gnostic movements offered redemption by helping people come to knowledge of their soul's divine origin.

Jesus' claim to be both the resurrection and the life means that all hope for life with God, both in the present and the future, must be viewed christologically.[74] Whether people are looking for future resurrection or a continuance of life beyond death, hope of afterlife must be focused on Jesus. The coupling of two somewhat different perspectives means that neither is simply affirmed and that both are reconceived. The hope of resurrection does not mean that people are separated from God until the end of the age, since the relationship established through faith continues despite physical death; and resurrection is not the outcome of fidelity to the Law of Moses but is received through faith in Jesus. Yet the hope of unending life with God is not attained by escaping the body, since everlasting life entails bodily resurrection; and life beyond the grave is not the

71. On the range of beliefs concerning afterlife see Fox, *Pagans and Christians,* 95–98; Emily Vermeule, "The Afterlife: Greece," and John A. North, "The Afterlife: Rome," both in *The Civilization of the Ancient Mediterranean: Greece and Rome* (ed. M. Grant and R. Kitzinger; New York: Charles Scribner's Sons, 1988) 2.987–96, 997–1007; Ramsey MacMullen, *Paganism in the Roman Empire* (New Haven, Conn.: Yale University Press, 1981) 53–57. See the critique of MacMullen by Wayne A. Meeks, *The First Urban Christians* (New Haven, Conn.: Yale University Press, 1983) 241 n. 44.

72. Samuel Sandmel, *Philo of Alexandria: An Introduction* (Oxford: Oxford University Press, 1979) 116–17.

73. *Moral Epistles* 102.22.

74. See MacRae, "The Fourth Gospel and *Religionsgeschichte*," 18–19.

soul's natural destiny but an extension of the relationship with God given in faith.

Lazarus's emergence from the tomb at the end of the episode (John 11:43-44) was not actually the resurrection Jesus promised to those who believe, because Lazarus would die again; but it visibly demonstrated that Jesus was the guarantor of the final resurrection. The raising of Lazarus also brought the hope of the future resurrection into the present, so that the sign pointed physically to the present reality of the life he gives to those who believe. Lazarus was one follower of Jesus who died, but this particular incident foreshadows what Jesus means for those who believe.

The King of Israel

The aftershocks of the raising of Lazarus continue to be felt in the scenes that follow. The Pharisees and chief priests understood the sign in political terms. They said, "What are we to do? For this man performs many signs. If we let him go on thus, everyone will believe in him, and the Romans will come and destroy both our holy place and our nation" (11:47-48). Their comments seem to reflect experience with prophets like those mentioned earlier, who fueled anti-Roman sentiment by promising to work signs and wonders. The Romans violently suppressed these prophetic movements, and one could assume that if a movement became sufficiently large, they would finally destroy the temple and the Jewish people. The plausibility of this would have been apparent to readers in the late first century, who knew that the Romans in fact had quelled Jewish unrest in Palestine by destroying the temple in A.D. 70—though Jesus was not one of the insurrectionists.

Caiaphas, the high priest, told the others on the council that it would be "expedient for you that one man should die for the people, and that the whole nation should not perish" (11:50). That is, by executing Jesus they would eliminate the threat of Roman military action against the popular revolt the miracle-worker seemed to be fomenting. With a kind of sardonic humor, the evangelist added that the chief priests also planned to execute Lazarus, whom Jesus had raised from the dead, because on account of him many of the Jews were going away and believing in Jesus (12:9-11). Their desire to murder the one who was the resurrection and the life and to put Lazarus back into the tomb would seem to reveal a stunning incapacity to comprehend what the sign conveyed. Yet the evangelist observed the ironic truth reflected in their scheme: Jesus would keep people from perishing precisely by dying himself. He would give life to those who believe not by avoiding death but by overcoming it; and the cross would be the unifying symbol of all the scattered children of God who confess that Jesus is the resurrection and the life (11:51-52).

The last perspective on the raising of Lazarus is that of the crowd, who interpreted the sign in light of their own messianic expectations. Enthralled by the miraculous, people flocked to Bethany not just to see Jesus but to catch a glimpse of Lazarus, who had become something of a celebrity in their eyes (12:9). Like the chief priests and Pharisees, the crowds perceived the outcome of the sign in nationalistic terms, but they viewed Jesus' chances for success more favorably. When Jesus approached Jerusalem before Passover, people went out to meet him along the road, which was the way visiting dignitaries were welcomed by cities throughout the Greco-Roman world. They greeted him by waving palm branches, which were regularly used to celebrate victory, and shouted the words of Ps. 118:26, "Hosanna! Blessed is he who comes in the name of the Lord," adding to it, "even the King of Israel" (John 12:13).[75] Their nationalistic display was a response to the raising of Lazarus (12:17-18).

Jesus symbolically affirmed this messianic acclaim by finding a donkey and sitting on it. There was apparently some expectation that the Messiah, as the successor of David, would ride on a donkey when he arrived (cf. 1 Kings 1:38). The evangelist accents the royal character of Jesus' act by connecting it with the Scriptures, which said, "Fear not, daughter of Zion; behold your king is coming, sitting on a donkey's colt!" (John 12:15; Zech. 9:9).[76] The ensuing discourse makes clear that Jesus was in fact a warrior king, who had come to cast out "the ruler of this world" (John 12:31). Such kingship has both transcendent and universal dimensions. The power Jesus wielded was not that of a militia seeking to do battle with Rome but the power of God preparing for conflict with Satan. He was the king of Israel, foretold in the Jewish Scriptures, but his reign was to encompass the world. The crowd assumed that someone with the power to raise the dead would avoid death himself, especially since the Scriptures said the messianic "seed" of David would endure forever (12:34; Ps. 89:36). Yet Jesus, as "the resurrection," would conquer death by laying down his life and taking it up again; and he would give "life" to the world precisely at the expense of his own (see pp. 206–209).

ANOINTING AND WASHING FEET

The end of Jesus' public ministry and the beginning of his passion are marked by two symbolic actions set in the context of the meals Jesus ate

75. On crowds going out of the city to meet a visiting dignitary see, e.g., Josephus, *J.W.* 3.9.8 §459; 4.2.5 §§112–13; 7.4.1 §§70–71; 7.5.2–3 §§100–103, 119. For the use of palms as a victory symbol see 1 Macc. 13:51; 2 Macc. 10:7; cf. 2 Esd. 2:45-46; Rev. 7:9.

76. The quotation apparently combines Zech. 9:9 with Zeph. 3:15. On the messianic character of this text see *Gen. Rab.* 75 and 98; cf. Str-B 1.842-844.

with his followers during the week before Passover (12:1-2; 13:1-2). During a supper at Bethany, Lazarus's sister Mary anointed Jesus' feet with expensive ointment and dried them with her hair. During Jesus' last supper before his arrest, he washed the feet of his disciples and dried them with the towel with which he had girded himself. These actions, which are similar in form, appear together in the center of the narrative and direct the way readers reflect on the meaning of Jesus' work and death.

Mary Anoints Jesus' Feet

Mary's reasons for anointing Jesus' feet are not stated, but one level of significance is suggested by the proximity of the episode to the raising of Lazarus. When the evangelist first told of Lazarus's illness, he identified his sister Mary as the one who "anointed the Lord with ointment and wiped his feet with her hair" (11:2). Before relating the story of the anointing itself, he recalled how Jesus had raised Lazarus from the dead and noted that Lazarus was present at the supper (12:1-2). In this context it would appear that Mary's action was a gesture of gratitude for bringing her brother back to life.

Most readers would have been able to understand the anointing in this way. People generally washed and anointed their own feet. Foot washing was a routine matter of cleanliness, and the use of oil or ointment on one's feet was soothing for those shod in sandals. When guests arrived at someone's home, especially after a journey, the host usually provided a basin and water for the guests to wash their own feet before sharing the meal. In the Scriptures, for example, Abraham welcomed visitors to his tent by saying, "Let a little water be brought, and wash your feet, and rest yourselves under the tree" (Gen. 18:4). The same practice is attested in other biblical texts and Greco-Roman sources.[77] In some cases, a host might also provide oil for his guests, although they would ordinarily rub it onto their feet themselves.[78]

A slave was virtually the only one who could be expected to wash and anoint the feet of another person. Probably the most celebrated instance was in Homer's *Odyssey* when Odysseus returned home in disguise. He was recognized when his old nurse, a slave woman, washed his feet, rubbed them with oil, and finally noticed the distinctive scar on his leg (19.504-

---

77. Gen. 19:2; 24:32; 43:24; Judg. 19:21; 2 Sam. 11:8. On foot washing in the Greco-Roman world see B. Kötting, "Fusswaschung," *RAC* 8.743–77, esp. 744–45; John Christopher Thomas, *Footwashing in John 13 and the Johannine Community* (JSNTSup 61; Sheffield: JSOT, 1991) 44–46.

78. See the fanciful story in *b. Menah.* 85b, where a servant girl brings water and oil for a guest. In the version found in *Sifre Deut.* 355, the servant girl actually bathes the guest's feet in oil. A number of texts are found in J. F. Coakley, "The Anointing at Bethany and the Priority of John," *JBL* 107 (1988) 241–56, esp. 247–48.

505). Later sources confirm that anointing and washing someone else's feet was "such ministry and service as slaves give their masters."[79] Rabbinic rulings allowed children to perform these tasks for their parents but did not expect them to do so. Aristophanes parodied this in one of his plays, where a daughter was willing to wash, anoint, and kiss the feet of her father only because she was angling for a small coin in return.[80] This practice seems to have been exceptional, however, and washing or anointing the feet of another person remained identified with slavery.[81]

Because of these connotations, those who voluntarily washed someone else's feet showed they were devoted enough to act as that person's slave. According to the Scriptures, David sent messengers to bring Abigail to be his wife. When she arrived, she "bowed with her face to the ground, and said, 'Behold your handmaid is a servant to wash the feet of the servants of my lord'" (1 Sam. 25:41). An apocryphal Jewish romance told how Joseph the Israelite was once scorned by an Egyptian woman named Asenath, but she later repented when she realized that Joseph was favored by God. She prayed, "Lord, commit me to him for a maidservant and a slave. I will make his bed and wash his feet and wait on him and be a slave for him and serve him for ever and ever." Similarly, the Roman poet Catullus spoke of a woman who would have preferred to be a slave washing the feet of her beloved than endure separation from him.[82]

The act of anointing Jesus' feet, when taken in its literary and cultural context, displays Mary's utter devotion to Jesus following the resuscitation of her brother. Other elements of the action are consistent with this. The ointment she used was very expensive. It was made from pure nard, an imported aromatic herb, and the value of the pound Mary used up was estimated at three hundred denarii, a sum it would take a common laborer ten months to earn (John 12:3, 5). Since there is no indication that Mary belonged to one of the wealthier classes—the meal was served by Martha rather than a servant—the ointment was apparently a major expenditure. It was also significant that Mary wiped Jesus' feet with her hair, since well-kept hair contributed to a person's dignity in the ancient world. Women took pride in long hair, which was considered attractive, and damage to one's hair was considered degrading.[83] By using her hair to wipe the feet

79. Plutarch, *Pompey* 73.7.
80. The rabbinic ruling is in the *Mekilta*, "Nezikin" 1.56-63 (Lauterbach ed., vol. 3, pp. 5–6). The play of Aristophanes is *Wasps* 608.
81. Having one's feet washed by those conquered in war reflected the servitude of the victims (Herodotus, *Histories* 6.19). Cf. the discussion of Pss. 58:10; 60:8; and 108:9 in Thomas, *Footwashing in John 13 and the Johannine Community*, 40–41.
82. *Joseph and Asenath* 13:13-15; Catullus 64.158-63.
83. See 1 Cor. 11:15; Achilles Tatius 8.6; Dio Chrysostom's *Encomium on Hair; t. Sota* 5:9; *Jewish Encyclopedia* 6.158.

of Jesus, Mary heightened the sense of self-effacement already reflected in
her willingness to serve him as a slave.

Judas's perspective was quite different. He immediately objected, arguing that the unguent should have been sold for three hundred denarii
and given to the poor (12:5). Many readers may have understood this
negative reaction. The use of expensive perfume on one's feet was considered a wasteful luxury. The Greek comics often created burlesque scenes
featuring debauched and self-indulgent characters who delighted in having their feet swabbed with scented ointments. The playwrights lampooned
those who were so devoted to luxury that they sent servants scurrying to
find expensive perfumes for their feet and revelled in having them applied by a young woman, exclaiming that "to have my feet rubbed with
fair, soft hands, isn't it magnificent?"[84] But if Judas's reaction to the extravagance was understandable, the evangelist quickly discredited it by noting
that Judas was actually a thief who cared nothing for the poor and used to
embezzle from the funds entrusted to him (12:6).

A comment of Jesus shifts the frame of reference so readers can understand the anointing in terms of his death. He told Judas to leave Mary
alone, for it was intended "that she should save this perfume for the day of
my burial. You will always have the poor among you, but you will not
always have me" (12:7 NIV).[85] In one sense, the gift of ointment was an
appropriate response to the gift of life that Jesus had already given by
raising Lazarus from the dead; but in a more profound sense, the outpouring of the perfume was a proleptic response to the consummate gift
Jesus was about to give: his own life. The self-giving extravagance of Mary's
actions points to the way Jesus would expend himself completely through
his crucifixion.

Because Mary's action took place shortly before the crowds hailed Jesus
as the "King of Israel," the anointing also may help to convey the significance of Jesus' kingship. Traditionally, Israelite kings were anointed at the
time they acceded to the throne, but the oil was poured upon the head,
not the feet (1 Sam. 10:1). Jesus was indeed a king, who would be robed,
crowned, and presented to the people—during the process of his execution (John 19:1-6). He would be "lifted up" by the people of Jerusalem,
but this would take place on the cross; and he would glorified, but through
his suffering and death. Anointing Jesus with expensive perfume before
his approach to Jerusalem simultaneously prepared him for enthronement and burial. The regal amount of ointment cannot be understood

84. See the collection of comic texts in Athenaeus, *Deipnosophists* 553a–e, and Petronius,
Satyricon 70.8 (cf. 31).
85. The text is difficult to translate. It literally says, "Let her save it for the day of my
burial"; yet Mary could not save the perfume any longer because she had used it up. What is
clear is the connection between the action and burial.

apart from his death, and yet his death cannot be understood apart from the anointing, for through his crucifixion Jesus reigned as king.

Jesus Washes
the Disciples' Feet

The power and the death of Jesus continue to be juxtaposed in the story of the foot washing, which introduces the passion. The evangelist reveals that Jesus acted from a position of strength. Jesus knew "that the Father had given all things into his hands, and that he had come from God and was going to God" (13:3). Yet the way he expressed this power was by getting up from the supper, laying down his robe, and girding himself with a towel. Then he poured water into a washbasin and began to wash his disciples' feet and to dry them with the towel he had wrapped around his waist. Despite objections, Jesus persisted until he had washed the feet of each one of them. Then he took up his robe and resumed his place at the table.

Peter perceived this action as an astonishing breach of social convention. When Jesus came to him, he exclaimed, "Lord, do you wash my feet?" then added adamantly, "You shall never wash my feet" (13:6, 8). Many readers would have found Peter's reaction understandable, since someone who washed the feet of another person was assuming the position of a slave, as we have seen. There were instances in which a pupil might wash the feet of his teacher, apparently as an extraordinary show of devotion, but the reverse was not done.[86]

Peter's reaction to the foot washing is mirrored in other ancient sources. In the story of Joseph and Asenath noted earlier, Joseph vigorously protested when Asenath brought water to wash his feet, and he relented only when she insisted on doing it to show her devotion to him (*Joseph and Asenath* 20:2-4). One of the humorous stories about Aesop, the teller of fables, shows how obtuse someone would have to be *not* to object when someone of a higher social status performed foot washing. Aesop was a slave whose master, Xanthus, was looking for a pretext to beat him, so he demanded that Aesop bring him a dinner guest who would not try to correct his social behavior under any circumstances. When Aesop brought a boorish peasant to the table, his master tried to shock the fellow by telling his wife, "Get up and take a basin over to the stranger as though you intended to wash his feet. From your appearance he'll know that you're the lady of the house and won't let you do it, but will say, 'Lady, don't you have any slave to wash my feet?'" In so doing, the man would prove to be a meddler, and Aesop would get a beating. Xanthus's wife

---

86. On the possibility of a student washing his teacher's feet see the *Mekilta*, "Nezikin" 1.56-63 (Lauterbach ed., vol. 3, pp. 5–6).

hated Aesop so much that she tied a towel around herself, threw another one over her arm, and took a basin of water over to the peasant, but the dull-witted man failed to stop her. Aesop's master then had the cook beaten for improperly seasoning the soup and the baker burned alive for failing to put honey in the cake, but the peasant was so dense that even these actions failed to arouse his indignation, and Aesop thus avoided getting beaten.[87]

The evangelist's description of the foot washing reveals that it was a symbolic enactment of what Jesus would do for his followers through his death.[88] References and allusions to his death occur throughout the scene. The action took place when "the hour had come for Jesus to depart out of this world to the Father" (13:1), and the mention of Judas's scheme to betray Jesus makes clear that this departure would include his death (13:2). Instead of saying that Jesus "took off" and "put on" his robe, the text says that Jesus "laid down" (*tithenai*) and "took up" (*lambanein*) his garments, using the verbs that formerly referred to the laying down and taking up of his life (10:17-18; 13:4, 12). The meaning of these actions would become apparent only "afterward," however, after Jesus' death and resurrection (13:7).

The foot washing reveals that the crucifixion was Jesus' consummate act of complete self-giving love. The text says that Jesus, "having loved his own who were in the world," "loved them to the end" (*eis telos*, 13:1). In some sense "to the end" points to the cross, the *telos*, when Jesus could say "it is completed" (*tetelestai*, 19:30); and the foot washing presages the love of Jesus that would culminate in his death. "To the end" can also be rendered "to the utmost," and the foot washing, like the crucifixion, demonstrates how Jesus loved his followers, since voluntarily assuming the posture of a slave showed complete devotion to those whose feet were washed. By removing his clothing, Jesus heightens the sense of scandalous self-giving. Clothing gives people dignity, and laying down his garments anticipates the way he would lay down his life in a degrading execution. His clothing would be removed again only at the cross, where the soldiers would cast lots for it (19:23). When Peter asked Jesus to wash him more thoroughly, Jesus indicated that these actions could not be quantified. In the foot washing, as in his death, he gave himself completely.

A remark made to Peter indicates that the self-sacrificing love of Jesus would bring his followers into an abiding relationship with him. He said,

---

87. *Life of Aesop* 61–64. An English translation is available in Lloyd W. Daly, ed., *Aesop without Morals* (New York: Thomas Yseloff, 1961).

88. The centrality of Jesus' death in 13:1-11 has been widely noted. See, e.g., Brown, *Gospel*, 2.566; Schnackenburg, *Gospel*, 3.19; Georg Richter, *Die Fusswaschung im Johannesevangelium* (BU 1; Regensburg: Pustet, 1967) 287–300.

"If I do not wash you, you have no share with me," which we can para-phrase, "If I do not die for you, you have no share with me" (*met² emou*, 13:8). To have a share "with Jesus" is to be in relationship with him and thus in relationship with God. This relationship begins in faith and issues into life everlasting, so that at the end of the discourses Jesus will pray, "Father, I desire that they also, whom thou hast given me, may be with me [*met² emou*] where I am, to behold my glory which thou hast given me in thy love for me before the foundation of the world" (17:24).

The foot washing also presents Jesus' death as a means of cleansing. In his response to Peter's request to have his hands and head washed, Jesus said, "The one who has bathed does not need to wash, except for his feet, but is clean all over. And you people are clean, but not every one of you" (13:10). The details of this complex verse are difficult to interpret,[89] but they seem to connect the theme of purification with the death of Jesus that is signified by the foot washing. Purification must be understood in terms of the Johannine understanding of sin, which is fundamentally a hostile estrangement from God. The sinful actions people commit are expressions of this basic antipathy. Jesus cleanses people from sin by purging them of this hatred for God, through the transforming revelation of divine love that comes through the cross (see pp. 196–200).

The second part of the passage elaborates the significance of the foot washing as an example for the disciples to follow. The disciples would have understood that "a slave is not greater than his master" (13:16), taking it to mean that a respected teacher like Jesus should not wash feet, since foot washing was a demeaning task. Jesus affirmed the common-place view that "a slave is not greater than his master" but transformed it, so that it no longer meant that Jesus should not wash feet but that his disciples should wash feet, following their master's example (13:14-15).

If Jesus washed the feet of his disciples in order to reveal his love for them, they were to wash feet in order to manifest the love of Jesus through their love for other Christians. This is made explicit in the new command-ment to "love one another even as I have loved you" given later in the chapter (13:34). The charge to wash feet may have entailed physically washing the feet of others within the Christian community as a gesture of devoted service, but it was not limited to that practice. Jesus washed feet in anticipation of his death, which was his greatest act of love. Similarly, the command that his disciples should wash each other's feet is another way of calling upon them to show their love for each other in various

---

89. On 13:10 see, in addition to the commentaries by Barrett, Brown, and Schnacken-burg, Fernando F. Segovia, "John 13 1-20, The Footwashing in the Johannine Tradition," *ZNW* 73 (1982) 31–51; Thomas, *Footwashing in John 13*, 97–106.

forms of service, even laying down their lives for each other when necessary (15:12-13; 1 John 3:16).

Christian interpreters have often associated the foot washing with baptism, which was mentioned along with the death of Jesus and purification in John 3 and was called a "washing" in other early Christian writings.[90] Accordingly, the foot washing could suggest that the benefits of Jesus' death are received through Christian baptism. The baptismal connections are not developed in the text, however, and the focus remains on the love Jesus revealed through his crucifixion. Jesus is the subject of the verb *wash* in the first part of the passage. His statement "If I do not wash you, you have no part in me" (13:8) can be paraphrased to say, "If I do not love and die for you, you have no part in me"; it seems less plausible to paraphrase it "If I do not baptize you, you have no part in me," especially since the Gospel is ambivalent about saying that Jesus actually performed baptism (4:2). The disciples become the subject of the verb *wash* in the second part of the passage, and the washing they were to perform was a reciprocal action within the Christian community; love and self-sacrifice were reciprocal actions, but baptism was not. Together Mary's anointing of Jesus' feet and Jesus' washing of the disciples' feet prepare for his death, connect it with his kingship and servanthood, and model the kind of self-giving love that is to characterize Christian life. The function of this symbolism in Christian community will be explored in chapter 7.

THE GREAT CATCH OF FISH

The last of Jesus' symbolic actions takes place in chapter 21, which forms a kind of epilogue to the Gospel. Like the other Johannine symbols, the first part focuses on Christology (21:1-14), the second on discipleship (21:15-24). The peculiar details in this story have spawned various symbolic interpretations, making it especially important to distinguish between core and supporting symbols. The main actions Jesus performed were providing the disciples with a miraculous catch of fish and giving them a rather ordinary breakfast.

We begin with the significance of the breakfast. Jesus had a meal of bread and fish ready for the disciples by the time they landed. Although fish were already roasting on the coals, Jesus asked Peter to bring him the fish from the great catch (21:10). Peter did so and counted the fish in the net, but Jesus apparently did not cook any of them. Instead, he invited the disciples to eat the breakfast he had already prepared (21:12). The meal was his gift to them.

90. See 1 Cor. 6:11; Acts 22:16; Eph. 5:26; Heb. 10:22; Titus 3:5.

When read in connection with the rest of the Gospel, this gesture reveals the identity of the risen Lord with the earthly Jesus. Only two incidents in John's Gospel take place beside the Sea of Tiberius: the feeding of the five thousand and this appearance of the risen Jesus to the disciples. On both occasions Jesus "took bread and gave it to them, and likewise with the fish" (21:13; 6:11). Jesus, the host, is the primary actor, and the similarity of his actions on these two occasions shows that he continues to provide for people after the resurrection just as he did before his passion. If other portions of the Gospel speak of the way Jesus' relationship to the disciples changed after Easter from physical presence to the abiding presence of the Spirit, the appearance beside the sea stresses the continuity in the relationship.[91]

The other core action in the story is the disciples' "drawing" the nets full of fish at Jesus' bidding. The language used in the text is significant. The disciples had caught nothing all night, but when Jesus told them to cast their nets on the right side of the boat, they "were not able to draw [*helkyein*] it because of the quantity of fish" (21:6). After Peter plunged into the sea, the others continued dragging the nets in the boat (21:8). Then Jesus told them to bring some of the fish they had caught, and Peter "drew [*helkyein*] the net to the land full of large fish" (21:11).

The significance of the catch, like that of the meal, emerges when it is read in connection with the feeding of the five thousand and its aftermath. Jesus had told the multitude he had fed that "no one can come to me unless the Father who sent me draws him" (*helkyein*, 6:44). The statement recognizes that coming to Jesus is a human impossibility, but it also promises that people can and will be "drawn" to him by the power of God. At the end of his public ministry, Jesus used the same word to identify himself as the one who did the drawing. He said, "I, when I am lifted up from the earth, will draw [*helkyein*] all people to myself" (12:32). In this passage as in the previous one, the impossibility of faith (12:39) is offset by the promise that the crucified and risen Jesus would draw people to himself. The story of the great catch goes a step farther, showing that Jesus would accomplish this "drawing" through his disciples. The risen Jesus remains the source of the action. Without Jesus the disciples were no more able to catch fish than people can produce faith in themselves or anyone else. But in response to Jesus' directives, the disciples were able to bring an enormous catch of fish to Jesus, anticipating that through them Jesus would make good his word to draw people to himself.[92]

91. Schnackenburg, *Gospel*, 3.359.
92. The importance of "drawing" has been emphasized by Brown, *Gospel*, 2.1097. Okure has rightly stressed that from a Johannine perspective, the missionary is Jesus; the disciples are the means through which he carries out his work (*The Johannine Approach to Mission*, 219–26).

The fish and the net are supporting symbols in this scene. The text twice mentions the large quantity of the fish caught (21:6, 11). Counting out the specific number of fish—153—demonstrates the size of the catch, much as the mention of a thirty-eight year illness helped to show the seriousness of the invalid's condition in 5:5 and comments about five loaves and two fish feeding five thousand men helped show the scope of Jesus' power in 6:10. Attempts to discover some symbolic value in the number 153 will be considered on pp. 265–68; here we note that it plays only a secondary role in the text, helping to presage the broad scope of Christian missionary activity. The observation that the net was not torn by the great catch (21:11) may suggest that the community of faith would not be torn apart by the numbers of people coming into it. The connection between the word *tear* (*schizein*) used in this passage and the word for *schism* (*schisma*) used elsewhere in the Gospel would support this (7:43; 9:16; 10:19), although this interpretation is at most an interesting possibility.

Fishing as a way of ingathering would have been familiar to readers living in most parts of the ancient Mediterranean world, and those conversant with the Old Testament might have known of fishing as a metaphor for catching people for God, although there it often had connotations of judgment that are not apparent in John (Jer. 16:16; Amos 4:2). The way the story is told in John 21 helps screen out some of these negative associations, however, since the fish the disciples netted were simply brought to Jesus and counted but not eaten. Rabbis and philosophers sometimes spoke of fishing for disciples, seeking to capture them by their teaching. The connection between fishing and missionary activity is almost proverbial in the other Gospels, which suggests that it was widely known to early Christians. In Matthew and Mark, Jesus tells his disciples that they will become "fishers of men" without further explanation, and Luke's account connects this commission with a miraculous catch of fish like that in John 21 (Mark 1:17; Matt. 5:19; Luke 5:1-11).[93]

The second part of the passage discloses the character of the mission of Jesus by dealing with the respective roles of the two disciples who were specially mentioned in the miracle story: Peter and the Beloved Disciple. Peter's leadership role was clear in the first part of the passage. He was the one who decided to go fishing and who brought the net to shore, which suggests that he would play a leading role in Jesus' missionary work. The story of the great catch also showed that Peter's role cannot be understood apart from that of Jesus. Given only Peter's initiative, the work of the disciples proved fruitless; the fish were caught and brought to shore

93. On fishing as a metaphor see W. H. Wuellner, *The Meaning of "Fishers of Men"* (Philadelphia: Westminster, 1967).

in response to Jesus' directives. When the imagery shifts to shepherding in the latter part of the chapter, Peter's leadership position is reaffirmed. He was commissioned to tend the flock, but as its keeper rather than its owner. Jesus told him to feed "my lambs" and to tend "my sheep."

The passage connects Peter's leadership role to the death of Jesus and his own death. The allusions to Jesus' death are subtle at first. Beside the charcoal fire on the beach, Jesus asked three times, "Simon, son of John, do you love me?" and Peter confessed three times that he did, suggesting a contrast with the three times he denied Jesus beside the charcoal fire in the high priest's courtyard (18:17, 25-27; 21:15-17). The threefold commission to tend the flock also recalls what was said earlier about the relationship of Jesus to the flock. Jesus had said that the good shepherd lays down his life for the sheep, and the final chapter of the Gospel indicates that Peter would die in a manner fitting for a shepherd in the service of Jesus. The author explains that when Jesus spoke cryptically about Peter having his hands stretched out and being taken where he did not wish to go, he was speaking of the death by which Peter would glorify God. The implication is that Peter, like Jesus, would have his hands "stretched out" on a cross (21:18-19).

The other actions Peter performed may contribute indirectly to the symbolism of the passage. Peter's peculiar act of girding himself after he realized that Jesus was on the shore adds to the highly christological character of the first part of the episode. Peter was "naked," which probably meant that he was wearing only his light undergarment for work. Although people would ordinarily remove extra clothing before going into the water, Peter wrapped clothing around his waist, which would have left his legs free to swim while wearing a flowing garment. Jewish people understood that matters like praying, reading Scripture, and extending the greeting of peace were not to be done in places where people were indecently clothed, as in a public bath. Peter's care to remain clothed in the presence of Jesus suggests that meeting him was a religious act.[94] Hurling himself into the water also seems to be an act of devotion, and it may foreshadow Peter's answer to Jesus' question, "Simon, son of John, do you love me more than these?" since by plunging into the water Peter was able to reach Jesus ahead of the others.

The allusion to Peter's crucifixion later in the chapter suggests that Peter's actions on the sea might presage his own death. Peter had girded himself in the boat, but on shore Jesus told him, "When you were young, you girded yourself and went where you wished; but when you are old, another will gird you and take you where you do not wish to go," namely,

94. Barrett, *Gospel*, 580–81.

to die. Peter had "girded" himself in the boat before going to Jesus, and
Jesus' words suggest that his would eventually mean being "girded" before
being taken to his execution.[95] It is also striking that the text does not
actually say that Peter swam to Jesus, but that he "cast himself into the
sea"; and elsewhere in Scripture, that which is "cast into the sea" is usually
marked for destruction—something that was also true of Peter.[96]

The text finally gives attention to the Beloved Disciple, whose significance will be considered more fully at the end of chapter 6. In this context
the main action performed by the Beloved Disciple is witness: As soon as
they made the great catch, he told Peter, "It is the Lord" (21:7). The last
part of the chapter relates the Beloved Disciple's witness to Jesus' death
and his own death. The epilogue reminds readers that this disciple's
importance as a witness emerged during the last supper, when he learned
the identity of the betrayer (21:20). The text also counters the idea that
the Beloved Disciple would not die before Jesus returned; the Beloved
Disciple was not exempted from death any more than Jesus was (21:23).
The conclusion of the chapter affirms that despite the reality of his death,
this disciple would continue to witness through the testimony preserved in
the Gospel, and that his witness would remain vital to the church's mission
(21:24).

The evangelist wrote for those living after Jesus' ministry had ended,
when the opportunity to see his signs and other actions had passed, yet
symbolic actions constitute an integral part of his testimony: The Gospel
transforms the works into words. The symbolic actions it recounts are
evocative enough to engage a broad spectrum of readers, and their polyvalence enables them to encompass several different and potentially conflicting meanings: a single action can disclose both messiahship and
divinity. In themselves the actions are ambiguous, but the responses of
people in the story guide the readers' reflections, and the narrative con-
strains them to see each symbolic action in relationship to Jesus' consummate action, his crucifixion, where his humanity and unity with the Father
are singularly manifest.

---

95. Herold Weiss pointed out that, when Jesus girded himself at the last supper (13:4-5),
it portended his death ("Footwashing in the Johannine Community," *NovT* 21 [1979] 321).

96. On being "thrown into the sea" for destruction see Exod. 10:19; 15:1, 19; Jonah
1:5, 12, 15; Mark 9:42; Luke 17:2; Acts 27:38; Rev. 8:8; 18:21. Cf. Mark 11:23; Matt. 8:32;
21:21.

4

Light and Darkness

Images of light and darkness pervade the Fourth Gospel, creating what is probably its most striking motif. The prologue depicts God's Word as a source of life and light shining in the darkness (1:5). Later Jesus concludes his nocturnal encounter with Nicodemus with unsettling remarks about those who love darkness rather than light (3:19-21). Then the motif fades away until Jesus suddenly declares that he is "the light of the world" (8:12) and demonstrates the truth of his claim by enlightening the eyes of a man born blind (9:4-7). The healing of the blind man and its aftermath intensify hostility toward Jesus by many in Jerusalem, and shadows begin to fall over the period of daylight allotted for his ministry (11:9-10). With a final plea to believe in the light, Jesus vanishes from public view before plunging into the dark night of death (12:25-36, 46; 13:30). Afterward the motif is reduced to a glimmer, with but passing references to the glow of lanterns, a charcoal fire, and the predawn darkness of Easter morning.

These images are engaging for readers because the interplay between light and darkness is a fundamental feature of human existence. Day and night, brightness and shadow, establish the contours of the world we see with an evocative potency that has prompted people everywhere to ascribe religious significance to them; they are what Philip Wheelwright has called archetypal symbols.[1] Because these images are so much a part of human experience, they can be difficult to define, calling forth a host of varied and even contradictory associations on both the cognitive and affective levels. Light comes gently with the promise of dawn but glares down from the noonday sun; it gives the assurance of vision yet threatens exposure. Darkness may fall quietly around two lovers while cloaking the movements

1. Philip Wheelwright, *Metaphor and Reality* (Bloomington: Indiana University Press, 1962) 111.

of the thief; it can lull the weary to sleep but also awaken terror of the unknown.

Although light and darkness may signify many things, the Gospel creates a literary framework that focuses their meaning without completely delimiting it. The text establishes basic configurations of meanings by connecting light with God, life, and knowledge, and by associating darkness with their opposites. This network of associations recurs in the narrative with considerable consistency, making the cumulative effect of the light and darkness motif greater than any single occurrence of these images. The text also suggests other meanings by alluding to the Old Testament and Jewish traditions and by connecting the images with common life experiences and broader cultural perspectives. The network of associations established by the text acts as a filter that screens out some of the inappropriate meanings readers might connect with an image, while permitting more appropriate meanings to shine through. This process gives the symbols a "bright focussed center of meaning" without eradicating the connotations that create the "penumbra of vagueness" that is intrinsic to the symbols' power.[2]

THE TRUE LIGHT
THAT ENLIGHTENS EVERYONE

The light and darkness motif is introduced in the first part of the prologue to the Gospel. The scope of this part of the prologue is universal, relating God's Word to all humanity (1:1-13). The imagery is consistent with this message: The evocative references to light and darkness would have been engaging to many different kinds of people. In the latter part of the prologue (1:14-18), attention shifts to the significance of the incarnate Word for those who believe. Instead of speaking of "all things" and "the world," the text says that "the Word became flesh and dwelt among *us*" and that "*we* beheld his glory," voicing the confession of the community of faith (1:14). The imagery changes to reflect this focus. Instead of cosmic images like light and darkness, the text alludes to Israel's particular history by speaking of the glory that filled the tabernacle, of the "grace

2. The expressions quoted are from Philip Wheelwright, "The Archetypal Symbol," 220. Important studies of light and darkness imagery include Sverre Aalen, *Die Begriffe "Licht" und "Finsternis" im alten Testament, im Spätjudentum und im Rabbinismus* (Oslo: Jacob Dybwad, 1951); Hans H. Malmede, *Die Lichtsymbolik im neuen Testament* (Studies in Oriental Religions 15; Wiesbaden: Otto Harrassowitz, 1986); Hans Conzelmann, "*skotos, ktl.,*" *TDNT* 7.423–45; idem, "*phōs, ktl.,*" *TDNT* 9.310–58; Friedrich Nötscher, *Zur theologischen Terminologie der Qumran-texte* (BBB 10; Bonn: Peter Hanstein, 1956) 92–148; Günter Stemberger, *La symbolique du bien et du mal selon Saint Jean* (Paris: Seuil, 1970) 25–49; Otto Schwankl, "Die Metaphorik von Licht und Finsternis im johanneischen Schrifttum," *Metaphorik und Mythos im neuen Testament* (ed. Karl Kertelge; Freiburg: Herder, 1990) 135–67.

and truth" that God announced at Mount Sinai, and of the law given through Moses.[3] The location of light and darkness in the cosmic portion of the prologue suggests that after identifying the characteristics of light and darkness that are set forth in the text, we should ask how a broad spectrum of readers would have responded to the images.

The Light Shines in the Darkness
(1:1-5)

The prologue says that in God's Word was life, "and the life was the light of men. The light shines in the darkness, and the darkness has not overcome it." (a) According to this text, light manifests the power and presence of God. It emanates from the *logos,* a term that could designate the creative and sustaining power of God and the presence of God himself. (b) Light manifests the "life" given to people through God's Word. In John's Gospel, "life" has a physical dimension, since the Word was the power through which "all things" came into being and nothing was created without the Word, but the text emphasizes the theological dimension of life, which is God's relationship to human beings. The Gospel shows that many who are alive in body do not have "life" because they reject Christ and so reject God, yet those who receive Christ enter into a relationship with God that endures beyond the death of the physical body, so that "life" is often synonymous with "eternal life" (5:24). (c) Light means knowing God through faith in Christ. This aspect of the image is implicit in the prologue and becomes more prominent later in the Gospel, where it is connected with "seeing." According to John's Gospel, to believe in Jesus is to believe in God; to see Jesus is to see God; to know Jesus is to know God (12:44-46; 14:7). And those who come to know God in Jesus receive the light of eternal life (17:3).

Darkness is depicted as light's adversary. As the light shines, the darkness threatens to "overcome" or "overtake" (*katalambanein*) it—language that evokes a sense of the coming of nightfall and the lengthening of shadows that engulf the earth as the daylight fades (cf. 12:35). (a) Since light manifests the power and presence of God, the darkness refers to the powers that oppose God: sin and evil. In John's Gospel, sin is human rebellion against God, which is manifested in hostility toward Jesus, the

---

3. The word *dwell* (*skēnoun*) in 1:14 recalls the tent "dwelling" (*skēnē*) erected by Israel in the wilderness and identifies the locus of God's glory (e.g., Exod. 40:34-38). The phrase "full of grace and truth" recalls the expression used of God at Mount Sinai, namely, that he was "full of steadfast love and faithfulness" (Exod. 34:6). The prologue says that no one has ever seen God (John 1:18), and according to Exod. 33:17-23 that was true even of Moses. The giving of the law through Moses (John 1:17) is related in Exodus 20 and 34. See further my discussion in *The Dwelling of God: The Tabernacle in the Old Testament, Intertestamental Jewish Literature, and the New Testament* (CBQMS 22; Washington, D.C.: Catholic Biblical Association, 1989) 100—15.

Son of God. Evil is the suprahuman power that seeks to thwart God's will. It is sometimes identified with the devil, Satan, the ruler of this world, and the evil one, although none of these figures is fully personified. The powers of evil skulk in the background, seeking to extend their tentacles through the activities of Jesus' human adversaries.[4] Sin and evil are formidable foes, but the light of God's Word holds darkness at bay. (b) Since light means life, darkness connotes death in both a physical and a theological sense. Images of darkness—especially night—are used in the Gospel for the end of a person's physical life. But in a theological sense, darkness is the lethal estrangement from God that begins while a person is still breathing and eventually leads to a termination of the relationship. (c) Darkness means ignorance and unbelief. The Greek word *katalambanein,* which we translated "to overcome," can also mean to grasp or comprehend something with the mind. When the light came into the world, the benighted world "knew him not" and therefore "received him not" (1:10). The remainder of the narrative will demonstrate that those who do not know Jesus do not know God or have the light of life in them.

The characteristics of light and darkness noted here would have evoked familiar associations in the minds of readers from various backgrounds, transforming these associations to bear a distinctive witness to Jesus. The opening line, "In the beginning was the Word," would have transported many readers back to the dawn of time, when God, "in the beginning," created the heavens and the earth by uttering his word (Gen 1:1-3). The Genesis text was well known among Jews, Samaritans, and even some Greeks; in synagogues it was often recited from memory like a corporate confession of faith.[5] The first thing to appear in response to God's summons was light, which was the harbinger of all life that "came into being" (*egeneto,* Gen. 1:3, 6, 9, etc.; John 1:3). The primordial light manifested God's creative power, and God pronounced it "good." He also gave it preeminence by positioning lights in heaven to rule over both the night and the day (Gen. 1:15, 17). Darkness retained a proper place in the created order,[6] and the refrain "there was evening and there was morning" each day of creation undergirded the Jewish and Samaritan method of reckoning time, where the new day began with the onset of darkness.

Readers unfamiliar with the biblical tradition may have heard echoes of other cosmological teachings in the opening lines of the Gospel. The

---

4. The devil is mentioned in 8:44, where Jesus' hearers are identified as his children. Judas is called a devil in 6:70 and is the instrument of the devil in 13:2. Satan is mentioned in 13:27, where he is said to have entered into Judas. The ruler of this world is mentioned in 12:31; 14:30; and 16:11; and the evil one is mentioned in 17:15.

5. For a reference to Gen. 1:3 in a non-Jewish source, see Longinus, *On the Sublime* 9.9. On the recitation of the creation account in synagogues, see *m. Taʿan.* 4:2-3; *t. Taʿan.* 3:3-4.

6. See 1QH xii 1-9; *Jub.* 2:2, 8; 4 Ezra 6:38-59; Josephus, *Ant.* 1.1.1 §27.

prologue refers to God's *logos*, which is often translated "word" but in popular philosophy was understood to be the power that shaped the world. The logos animated all living things and established order within the universe, as was evident in the alternation of day and night. Some philosophical texts said that the logos was from God and others that the logos was God—a tension similar to that found in John 1:1.[7] Nevertheless, the light of John 1:5 cannot be comprehended as part of the natural cycle described in biblical and philosophical tradition. Unlike daylight, this light shines and will not give way to darkness. Because of the incongruity, readers must search for its significance at another level.

There was precedent for connecting the lingering primeval darkness with human sin. In *2 Baruch*, a Jewish source, Adam's transgression was depicted as black waters from which "black again were born and very deep darkness originated," because subsequent generations "took from the darkness of Adam" and continued to rebel against the will of God (18:2; 56:5-10). The Dead Sea text the *Community Rule* included an account of the creation that said that the children of falsehood spring from "a source of darkness" and "walk in the ways of darkness," which are the ways of sin (iii 13-21), and it ascribed dominion over the realm of falsehood to an Angel of Darkness. According to later rabbinic sources, the darkness persisted after the appearance of the primeval light in anticipation of the wicked generations to come.[8] Similarly, Samaritan sources lamented that "we are possessed of darkness, witness the many sinful actions we do."[9]

Jewish and Samaritan sources understood that sin led to death, and they used images of darkness for both. When Adam transgressed "untimely death came into being" and "the realm of death began to be renewed with blood" (*2 Bar.* 56:6). The place of the dead was called Sheol or Hades, which was the region of deep darkness where people were separated from God (Ps. 88:3-6, 10-12; Sir. 22:11). Although death was a threat for all people, its shadow hung especially over sinners, since those who rebelled against God embarked on a course of self-destruction. Some sources warned that sin would lead to premature death, which was depicted as a dark specter (Prov. 2:13, 18). Other texts said that the consequences would extend beyond the grave, that "the inheritance of sinners is destruction and darkness, and their lawless actions shall pursue them below into Hades."[10]

---

7. According to Cleanthes' *Hymn to Zeus*, the logos comes from Zeus, pervades all things, and is mingled with lights great and small (lines 7–10). Diogenes Laertius said that the logos was identical with Zeus himself in *Lives of Eminent Philosophers* 7.88. On the alternation of day and night as parts of the natural cycle, see Dio Chrysostom, *Discourses* 3.81; 40.38.

8. See *1 Enoch* 92:5; *b. Ḥag.* 12a; *Gen. Rab.* 2:3-5; 3:6.

9. *Memar Marqah* 6.2.

10. *Pss. Sol.* 15:10, 13; cf. 1QS ii 4-8; iii 11-14. Cf. the Samaritan *Memar Marqah* 4.11.

Readers unfamiliar with the biblical tradition would also have been acquainted with the connection between darkness and death. The epics of Homer, which were a mainstay of Greek education throughout the New Testament period, said of one who was dying that "darkness enfolded his eyes" or that "hateful darkness got hold of him."[11] In Greek tragedy the same images were used. For Euripides, the arrival of death meant that "Hades is near, and the night is darkening down on my sight." Aeschylus envisioned the realm of the dead as a place of shadows, "the evil darkness" beneath the earth. Although these texts do not evince the notion of sin in the biblical sense, Euripides thought that the gloom of death was a fitting destiny for the wicked, so that one could say, "Oh let me in black darkness pall my head; for I take shame for the evils wrought of me."[12] The classical tradition also associated light with life. For Homer, to live was to see the light of the sun, and Euripides said that someone about to cross the threshold of death would wish that those left behind might live and long continue "to look upon the light." Similarly, Aeschylus said that the message that a loved one "lives and beholds the light" would be received as "a great light of joy into my house, and bright day after night wrapped in gloom."[13]

Jewish and Samaritan sources went further, identifying the light that held back the shadow of sin and death with the wisdom of God. A tradition that circulated widely said that wisdom had been present with God at the dawn of time and shared in God's creative work.[14] Like a spoken word, wisdom came forth from the mouth of God and covered the earth like the mist that appeared when Adam was first formed (Sir. 24:3). Since wisdom reflects eternal light and God's own goodness, she does not give way before darkness; daylight "is succeeded by night, but against wisdom evil does not prevail" (Wisd. of Sol. 7:26-30). Those who found wisdom were said to have found life and favor from God, while those who spurned wisdom embraced death (Prov. 8:35-36). According to some sources, wisdom brought long life in peace and health, but others extended this to life in unending light beyond the grave.[15]

Many Jews and Samaritans understood that the wisdom of God was localized in the Law of Moses, which was often identified as a source of

11. *Iliad* 4.461; 5.47; 13.672.
12. Euripides on Hades, *Alcestis* 266; on death as punishment see his *Madness of Hercules* 1159. Aeschylus, *Eumenides* 72. On this and other texts see Rudolf Bultmann, "Zur Geschichte der Lichtsymbolik im Altertum," *Beiträge zum Verständnis der Jenseitigkeit Gottes im neuen Testament* (Darmstadt: Wissenschaftliche Buchgesellschaft, 1965) 7–42, esp. 10–16; Conzelmann, "*skotos, ktl.,*" *TDNT* 7.424–25.
13. Homer, *Iliad* 18.61; *Odyssey* 4.540; Euripides, *Alcestis* 272; Aeschylus, *Persians* 299–301.
14. Prov. 8:22-31; Wisd. of Sol. 9:9; cf. *2 Bar.* 56:4; the *Odes Sol.* 18:6 reflect the same wisdom tradition.
15. On wisdom bringing long life and health see Prov. 8:35-36; Bar. 3:14, 28; 1QS iv 6-7b. On life in light beyond the grave see Dan. 12:2-3; 1QS ii 1-3; iv 7; cf. Wisd. of Sol. 8:17. On light and wisdom among the Samaritans see *Memar Marqah* 4.9; 6.11.

light.[16] First-century texts said that the law was everlasting, shining with an imperishable light that would illumine all who sit in darkness (*2 Bar.* 59:2), and later writings would identify the law's radiance with the primordial light of creation itself.[17] Abraham and others in his generation lived by an unwritten code, but Moses kindled the lamp of the law to drive back the darkness of sin and death unleashed by Adam's transgression (*2 Bar.* 17:4—18:2; 57:1—59:2). The law was given especially to Israel, but its radiance was intended for all nations. Its statutes addressed the problem of human sin by making known what was pleasing to God, enabling them to live according to the divine will. By curbing human sin, the law also eased the threat of death under the judgment of God. The righteous had hope of resurrection to unending life "in the Lord's light," and the wicked could expect punishment and death.[18]

Many readers would have discerned echoes of these common uses of light and darkness imagery in the prologue of John's Gospel. The Johannine logos, like wisdom in other sources, was present at creation and brought life into being; it shines in the darkness of sin and death, bringing people into harmony with the will of God and granting them divine favor. But where Jewish and Samaritan texts would say that this reality is found in the Law of Moses, the Fourth Gospel declares that it became flesh in the person of Jesus. The prologue does not evince opposition to the law, and it utilizes imagery from the Old Testament and Jewish traditions to convey something about Jesus. At the same time, the imagery is transformed in a way that shows Jesus is not subordinated to the law; if the law was given through Moses, grace and truth *happened* in Jesus Christ (1:17). Therefore, respect for the Mosaic law means acceptance of Jesus, in whom the wisdom of God was enfleshed.[19]

True Light and Enlightenment
(1:6-9)

The next section of the prologue moves from the cosmic plane to the realm of human affairs, where the light comes to designate the incarnate logos in contrast to John the Baptist. John "came for testimony, to bear witness to the light, that all might believe through him. He was not the light, but came to bear witness to the light" (1:8). The emphasis on the difference between Jesus and John suggests that some people had not

16. *T. Levi* 14:4; *2 Bar.* 54:13-14; Bar. 4:1-2; cf. Sir. 24:23; *Memar Marqah* 3.5; 4.2.

17. *Gen. Rab.* 3:1-3.

18. On the radiance of the law as intended for all nations, see *Bib. Ant.* 11:1. On resurrection to life and light vs. punishment and death, see *Pss. Sol.* 3:12; *2 Bar.* 54:13-16; Bar. 4:1-2.

19. John 1:14, 17; Exod. 34:6. See also Severino Pancaro, *The Law in the Fourth Gospel: The Torah and the Gospel, Moses and Jesus, Judaism and Christianity according to John* (NovTSup 42; Leiden: Brill, 1975) 538.

adequately distinguished them. The potential for confusion is apparent elsewhere in the Gospel: Both men were from God, both apparently practiced baptism, and each had a circle of disciples who called him rabbi (3:22-30; 4:1-2, 31).[20] Traditionally, the people of Israel called their prophets, priests, and teachers "lights" or "lamps," because they possessed the wisdom needed to illumine people by their teaching. Moses kindled the light of the law, and Aaron and Deborah enlightened people by instructing them in God's ordinances, as did Samuel, whom some called the "light to the peoples."[21] After Jerusalem was destroyed by the Babylonians, scribes like Baruch and Ezra preserved the true teaching of the law, serving as lamps in the dark night of destruction, and priests and sages enlightened subsequent generations by their teaching.[22] When Jerusalem was destroyed again by the Romans, Rabbi Johanan ben Zakkai founded an academy for the teaching of the law at a place called Jamnia, and he was remembered as the "lamp of Israel" and the "lamp of the world."[23]

The fourth evangelist could grant that John the Baptist was "a burning and shining lamp" (5:35) in the traditional sense, because John faithfully bore witness to the truth. Jesus, however, not only spoke the truth, he was the truth; he not only imparted wisdom, he embodied wisdom. Jesus was singularly "the true light" (John 1:9). By calling Jesus "true" (*alēthinos*) the Gospel does not mean that John the Baptist was false but that he was of a different order. Later, for example, Jesus would contrast the manna eaten by Israel in the wilderness with the "true" bread that God gives in Jesus (6:32). Manna was indeed bread, but it nourished people only for a short time, unlike the bread offered in Jesus, which could sustain people in a relationship with God that would endure forever. Similarly, people could rejoice in the light of John the Baptist's testimony "for a while" (5:35), but his witness was intended to draw them to the true source of light in Jesus.

The prologue said that the light that entered the world in Jesus "enlightened everyone" (1:9). Enlightenment, according to Jewish sources,

20. That the Gospel engages in apologetic against claims being made about John the Baptist has long been acknowledged. This was formulated by Wilhelm Baldensperger (*Der Prolog des vierten Evangeliums. Sein polemisch-apologetischer Zweck* [Tübingen: Mohr/Siebeck, 1898]) and adopted in modified form by many others.

21. On Moses see *2 Bar.* 18:1-2; *Memar Marqah* 1.2; 5.3-4; 6.2; on Aaron see Sir. 45:17. See *Bib. Ant.* 33:1, 3 on Deborah; 51:3 on Samuel and 51:6, where he is called the "light to the peoples." See also Marc Philonenko, "Essénisme et gnose chez le Pseudo-Philon: Le symbolism de la lumière dans le *Liber Antiquitatum Biblicarum*," *The Origins of Gnosticism: Colloquium of Messina 13–18 April 1966* (ed. U. Bianchi; Studies in the History of Religions [Supplements to *Numen*] 12; Leiden: Brill, 1967) 401–10.

22. On Baruch see *2 Bar.* 46:1-3; on Ezra see 4 Ezra 12:42; on priests and sages see *Bib. Ant.* 23:7; Sir. 24:32; 1QSb iv 27; 1QH iv 27; Rom. 2:19.

23. *b. Ber.* 28b; *'Abot R. Nathan* 25.

sometimes referred to physical health,[24] but more often it meant that a person's understanding and manner of life were shaped by the wisdom of God, which was found in the Law of Moses. Knowledge was considered inseparable from one's manner of life. Those who genuinely possessed wisdom were those who lived in accordance with wisdom, and those who truly comprehended the law were those who followed its precepts—God was understood to have "enlightened those who conduct themselves with understanding" (2 Bar. 38:1).[25] Enlightenment, therefore, was said to overcome the darkness of sin by bringing people into conformity with the will of God, and it made death's shadow less ominous, since the righteous had the hope of a future life in God's endless light.

Enlightenment would have had similar connotations for non-Jewish readers. Many Greeks spoke of the movement from ignorance to knowledge as a process of illumination corresponding to the movement from darkness to "the true light." The idea appeared in various sources but was developed most extensively in Platonic philosophy, which envisioned the transcendent realm of God as pure light, which was reflected in the light perceived by the senses. According to this tradition, human beings are generally unaware of divine reality, just as the inhabitants of a dark cave are unconscious of the bright world outside. When light draws a person's gaze upward, it stimulates the mind to contemplate heavenly things and gradually to apprehend ultimate reality, the true light that is the absolute good.[26]

In philosophy, as in Judaism, enlightenment of the mind meant transformation of one's manner of life. The darkness of the human condition did not have the same menacing character in philosophical sources as it did in some Jewish writings, but it was associated with evil and vice. Plutarch, a younger contemporary of the fourth evangelist, said that there are degrees of evil in the soul and "degrees of progress produced by the abatement of baseness like a receding shadow, as reason [logos] gradually illuminates and purifies the soul," aided by the light of philosophy.[27] Those sunk in vice were considered dead,[28] but those who turned to a manner of life that accorded with reason (logos) discovered life itself. One convert to philosophy declared that "my whole life until now has been death rather than life. All was shadow: The beautiful, the holy, the good was evil; such was the earlier darkness of my understanding." Yet through philosophy, "I

24. Ps. 13:3; Job 33:30; Sir. 34:17; Bar. 1:12.
25. Cf. Ps 19:8; 119:130; Bib. Ant. 11:2; 19:6; Sir. 45:17; 1QS iv 2; 1QH iv 5-6.
26. Plato, Timaeus 47; Republic 7.517–18, 540; Plutarch, Moralia 563F–566C; cf. Seneca, Moral Epistles 102.28.
27. Moralia 76B, 77D, 81E.
28. See Epictetus, Discourses 1.3.3; 1.5.7; 1.9.19; 1.13.5; 3.23.28.

have come back to life" and have been "cured for the rest of my life," seeing anew "the clear light of today."[29]

The way Jewish understandings of light and enlightenment could be translated into philosophical categories is evident in the work of Philo, who connected biblical statements about the creative "word" of God with philosophical teachings about the logos. Philo said that the light that appeared on the first day of creation was an image of the divine logos, and that by contemplating the brightness of the logos the mind is drawn ever closer to God's own pure blinding light.[30] This process of enlightenment brings a person into harmony with true virtue, which is reflected in the Law of Moses. Similar fusions of philosophical and biblical imagery appear in other sources.[31] The analogies with John's Gospel suggest that the prologue's imagery would have been engaging to people of various backgrounds.

The opening lines of John's prologue deal with the relationship of the Word of God to all humanity, using images that would have had wide appeal—the medium is consistent with the message. The images are focused enough to be meaningful yet broad and evocative enough to engage a broad spectrum of readers. People familiar with any number of Jewish or philosophical teachings would have found something familiar in the Johannine notions of light and enlightenment. Like other sources, the Fourth Gospel speaks of enlightenment as a knowledge of God that transforms people, bringing them into the harmony with the Word, or logos, of God that is true life.

Yet readers also would have heard something new and perhaps disturbing, for enlightenment does not come through instruction in the Mosaic law or training in philosophy but through faith in Jesus, the one in whom God's Word is embodied. The startling Johannine particularity was noted by Augustine, who observed that the prologue's statements about the Word, light, and darkness were paralleled in philosophical writings, but "that the Word was made flesh and dwelt among us I did not read there," and that it was the incarnate Word who gave believers power to become children of God "I did not read there" (*Confessions* 7.9). Although the prologue says that the Word of God "enlightened everyone," the narrative will show that many were scandalized by Jesus' claims. They did not come to know God through him and were not enlightened in that sense. The term *enlighten,* however, can mean bringing someone's true character to

29. Taken from Stanley K. Stowers, *Letter Writing in Greco-Roman Antiquity* (Philadelphia: Westminster, 1986) 37.

30. *Creation* 30–31, 54–55, 71; *Dreams* 1.75.

31. *Allegorical Interpretation* 3.167; *Preliminary Studies* 106; *Flight and Finding* 139; *Change of Names* 81–82; *Dreams* 1.115–19; *Decalogue* 49; *Rewards and Punishments* 36–40. Cf. the work of Aristobulus, frag. 5 (*OTP* 2.841–42). Also note the Hermetic treatise *Poimandres.*

light (cf. 1 Cor. 4:5). Not all who encounter Jesus are brought to the light of faith, but all who encounter him will be exposed under the searching light of truth.

ONE WHO CAME BY NIGHT

The figure of Nicodemus emerges from the shadowed streets of Jerusalem to meet Jesus in the third chapter of the Gospel. At the end of their conversation Jesus declared that "the light has come into the world and men loved darkness rather than light because their deeds were evil. For everyone who does evil hates the light and does not come to the light, lest his deeds should be exposed. But he who does what is true comes to the light, that it may be clearly seen that his deeds have been wrought in God" (John 3:19-21). This passage presents a series of contrasts similar to those in the prologue. (a) There are those who understand Jesus and those who do not, those who accept testimony and those who reject it, believers and unbelievers. As before, knowing and believing are inseparable dimensions of a person's relationship with God in Jesus Christ. (b) There are those who have eternal life and those who are perishing, those who are saved and those who are condemned. As before, the theological dimensions of life and death are stressed. (c) The contrast between God and evil here becomes the distinction between those whose deeds are done in God and those who do evil, those who do the truth and those who practice wickedness.

Despite the sharp dualistic character of these verses, the encounter between Christ and the world remains complex. The whole world lies in darkness, but not all who are in darkness are the same. The night blankets both the godly and the wicked, and it is the coming of the light that reveals the true character of each. The light will expose (*elegxein*) the identity of the wicked, who flee as the dawn removes their concealment, while it reveals (*phanerein*) the true character of the righteous, who gratefully emerge from the shadows of night to conduct their affairs openly in the broad light of day.

The idea that the wicked shunned the light and took refuge in darkness was commonplace in the ancient world. Greek authors understood the difficulty in detecting evildoers, because it is "in some dark and secret retreat that the wretched culprits commit their heinous deeds all unobserved."[32] Jewish sources referred to "those who rebel against the light," such as the murderer, "who rises in the dark that he may kill the poor and needy," the thief who emerges at night, and the adulterer who "waits for

---

32. Dio Chrysostom *Discourses* 33.52. Cf. Libanius *Orations* 15.82–83 and the texts noted by Hans Conzelmann, "*skotia, ktl.*," *TDNT* 425 n. 18.

the twilight, saying, 'No eye will see me.'" None of these know the light, but are "friends with the terrors of deep darkness" (Job 24:13-17).[33] It was understood that those who work mischief would look for "profound darkness," there "to lie hid and keep the multitude of their iniquities veiled and out of the sight of all."[34]

At the same time, others found darkness oppressive and looked for the salvation that light would bring.[35] Those who came under God's judgment were said to "sit in darkness," which might be experienced in a very tangible way, like suffering defeat and imprisonment at the hands of one's enemies. "Some sat in darkness and gloom, prisoners in affliction and in irons, for they had rebelled against the words of God and spurned the counsel of the Most High" (Ps. 107:10-12). Nevertheless, experiencing the night of divine judgment sometimes moved people to turn to God for deliverance. To those held captive by darkness, light would be welcomed as a manifestation of divine salvation rather than divine judgment.[36] Only those entrenched in evil would shun the light. The association of light with deliverance from danger and oppression also appears in non-Jewish sources.[37]

Nicodemus came to Jesus "by night" (John 3:2), and the text leaves readers to ponder whether the incredulity reflected in his responses to Jesus (3:9-12) meant that he remained in darkness or that he was coming out of the darkness to light by coming to Jesus. In either case, the implications of the passage are unsettling. Nicodemus was a Pharisee and a ruler of the Jews, and we must assume that he lived a moral life according to the standards of the Mosaic law; there is no reason to think he was guilty of murder, theft, adultery, or any of the other actions commonly associated with darkness. The Torah was understood to be the light God had given to the benighted world (4 Ezra 14:20-21), and good and evil deeds could be measured according to its statutes. Those who persistently disobeyed the Torah would be condemned, and those who adhered to it would receive life in the world to come (14:22, 35; cf. John 5:29, 39). The text calls that perception into question, however. Whether we think Nicodemus came to the light or remained in the dark, his condition was revealed by his response to Jesus and not by some other standard. Nicodemus was a Jewish man, but he was also "every man"; what is true for him is true for the world he represents. If his condition before God was revealed by his

33. Cf. Ps. 139:11-12; Sir. 23:18; Isa. 29:15.
34. Philo *Special Laws* 1.321. Cf. Cicero, *In Catilinam* 1.3 §6.
35. See Isa. 13:9-10; Joel 2:1-2; Amos 5:18-20; Zeph. 1:15.
36. On the darkness of divine judgment see also Mic. 7:8-9; Isa. 47:5. On light as deliverance see Isa. 42:7; 49:9; Ps. 18:27-28; cf. Ps. 107:13-14.
37. On deliverance as light see Homer, *Iliad* 6.6; 8.282; 11.797; 16.39, 95; 18.102; 21.537–38. See Bultmann, "Lichtsymbolik im Altertum," 12–19; Conzelmann, "*phōs, ktl.*," *TDNT* 9.313.

response to Jesus rather than by some other source of illumination, then the same is true for all people.

After the Nicodemus episode, the light and darkness motif fades away for several chapters. The evangelist notes that the Samaritan woman, who is Nicodemus's counterpart, encounters Jesus in the full glare of noonday rather than at night (4:6), perhaps anticipating the way her life story is brought to light as she moves toward a more illumined understanding of Jesus; but the light imagery is not made explicit or developed in the episode. Later there is a passing reference to John the Baptist, who is called "a burning and shining lamp" (5:35), as we have already noted. And after Jesus had fed the five thousand, the disciples embarked onto the sea, where they were caught in a storm after dark (6:17), which might suggest something about the dangers of separation from Jesus; but again, the darkness is not connected with light nor is its significance elaborated in the narrative. The motif fully reappears only when Nicodemus does, during the feast of Booths.

THE LIGHT OF THE WORLD

The Gospel recounts at some length Jesus' return to Jerusalem for the feast of Booths. During the festival, pilgrims thronged through the streets of Jerusalem to the temple plaza, and the Gospel enables readers to eavesdrop on their conversations: Some in the crowd insisted that Jesus was a good man, but others argued that he was a charlatan who was deceiving the people (7:12). The Jewish authorities deliberated the matter and finally sent some officers to have Jesus arrested, but Nicodemus, who had not been heard from for several chapters, wondered if it was legal for them to condemn Jesus without a hearing. After a curt response from the other Jewish leaders, Jesus announced, "I am the light of the world; he who follows me will not walk in darkness, but will have the light of life" (7:52; 8:12). The intervening verses were not originally a part of the story.[38]

Jesus as a Teacher
(7:14-24)

The debates over Jesus' identity found in John 7–8 form the literary framework that discloses several facets of the light's meaning. The first issue concerned Jesus' identity as a teacher and the status of his teaching in relation to the Law of Moses. From a Jewish perspective, an accredited teacher was one who had studied with a recognized master and who

---

38. For a summary of the evidence against including John 7:53—8:11, see Barrett, *Gospel*, 589–90.

accurately passed on the tradition he had received. Since Jesus was not known to have studied at the feet of one of the sages, his claims to be a teacher were suspect. Moreover, his teaching lacked credibility since he had flagrantly disregarded the Mosaic law by healing on the Sabbath (7:15, 23). Jesus replied that he *had* studied with a recognized master—he had received his teachings from God and was transmitting them faithfully (7:16-17). Regarding the substance of his teaching, Jesus retorted that his opponents were in no position to condemn him for violating the Sabbath, since they themselves were trying to break one of the law's chief commandments by murdering him (7:19). Then he utilized the rabbinic form of argument from a lesser principle to a greater one to show that if they sought to keep the law by performing circumcision on the Sabbath— which involved minor surgery on a part of the body—then Jesus could do the same by making a man's whole body well on the Sabbath (7:23). Later Jesus acknowledged the law's stipulation that two witnesses be brought to verify a claim, calling upon himself and his Father to testify concerning the truth of his words (8:17-18).

The debates attempt to show that Jesus' teaching was consistent with the law but was not derived from the law, and the light imagery conveys the same message. The closest biblical antecedent for "the light of the world" is "the light of the nations," an expression that sometimes referred to the law. According to Isa. 51:4, God said, "Law will go forth from me and my judgment for a light of the nations." Later Jewish writings also spoke of the law as the imperishable light God had given to the world, so that people could "walk" in the light of its statutes rather than in the darkness of sin.[39] We have also seen that prophets, priests, and sages could be called a "light" or "lamp" in a secondary sense, since the instruction they provided manifested the brightness of the law. Yet the boldness of Jesus' claim to be *the* light of the world sets him apart from the lesser lights. In the case of Jesus, both the teacher and the teaching come directly from God; their authority is not derived from any lesser source. Jesus does not reject the law and even shows that his claims are consistent with the law; but he tacitly displaces it as the central locus of divine revelation. God's will is revealed in the person of Jesus; and the law that was given through Moses, when rightly understood, bears witness to the truth found in him.[40]

39. Wisd. of Sol. 18:4; *Bib. Ant.* 11:1; *T. Levi* 14:4; *2 Bar.* 17:4; 59:2.
40. Dodd sees a contrast between the Torah and Jesus, who was the real light of the world (*Interpretation*, 85). Pancaro is more cautious, concluding that "Jesus did not deny the divine authority of the Law, but claimed that his authority was equally divine and that it stood above the authority of the Law" (*The Law in the Fourth Gospel*, 492; cf. 485–87).

Jesus as Prophet and Messiah
(7:25-52)

A second level of the debate and the light symbolism revolves around Jesus' identity as prophet and Messiah. Unraveling this portion of the debate is complicated because several distinguishable strands of Jewish messianic expectation are interwoven: Some thought the Messiah's origin would be unknown, others that the Messiah would come from Bethlehem, and still others were looking for "the prophet" like Moses. It would seem that Jesus fulfilled none of these expectations, since he came from Galilee; but the evangelist understood that Jesus fulfilled all of these expectations, and he tried to convey this insight through the narrative and its symbolism.

The people who thought the Messiah's origin should be unknown entertained the idea that Jesus might be the Christ, since he seemed to defy the Jewish authorities with impunity, but they quickly rejected the idea since they knew Jesus was a Galilean, "and when the Christ appears, no one will know where he comes from" (7:27). Jesus had warned them before about the dangers of judging people by appearances rather than with right judgment (7:24), and he now challenged their perceptions more sharply, telling them that his origin actually was unknown, since he had come from God and they did not know God (7:28). Therefore, instead of discrediting Jesus' claim to messiahship, their views helped to demonstrate his messiahship. The image of light reinforced the point. We noted earlier that in the book of Isaiah the "light of the nations" was the Mosaic law, but this expression more often designated "the servant of the Lord" (Isa. 42:6; 49:6). The identity of the servant has been disputed, but a number of ancient sources identified him as the Messiah. Significantly, one of the few extant Jewish sources to mention the Messiah's hidden origins said that this Messiah would be "the light of the nations" (*1 Enoch* 48:4).[41]

Others in the crowd held an apparently contradictory form of messianic expectation. Instead of insisting that the Messiah's origin be unknown, they maintained that his origin should be known: The Christ was to be a descendant of David and come from Bethlehem, as the Scripture said (Mic. 5:2; John 7:42). The Fourth Gospel as a whole assumes that biblical prophecies concerning a Davidic Messiah were fulfilled in Jesus (1:45);

---

41. Most scholars hold that this portion of *1 Enoch* is a first-century Jewish composition. E.g., M. A. Knibb, "The Date of the Parables of Enoch: A Critical Review," *NTS* 25 (1980) 344–59; Schürer, *History*, 3.256–59; E. Isaac, "1 (Ethiopic Apocalypse of) Enoch," *OTP* 1.6–7; G. Vermes, *The Dead Sea Scrolls: Qumran in Perspective* (rev. ed.; Philadelphia: Fortress, 1981) 223; G. W. E. Nickelsburg, *Jewish Literature between the Bible and the Mishnah* (Philadelphia: Fortress, 1981) 222–23. The exception is J. T. Milik, who argues that it is a late Christian composition in *The Books of Enoch* (Oxford: Clarendon, 1976) 91–98. On the "servant" as the Messiah see *2 Bar.* 70:10.

that would be clear to readers.[42] Given this general position, readers could be expected to infer that Jesus must fulfill any particular prophecy—like the one concerning Bethlehem. The ironic nature of the arguments in John 7 and elsewhere in the Gospel also suggest that this passage presupposes familiarity with the tradition about Jesus' birth in Bethlehem.[43] Those who thought that Jesus could not be the Messiah since he was a Galilean were judging by appearances rather than right judgment; he met the crowd's seemingly incompatible criteria for messiahship. Yet Jesus' connection with Galilee continued to pose a problem, since the Jewish authorities insisted that messiahship and Galilee were mutually exclusive according to the Scriptures. The light imagery in John 8:12 was, in part, a response to that objection.

In the Old Testament, Galilee is mentioned rarely and only in passing, except for one highly significant text, which promised that "Galilee of the nations" would be made glorious, for "the people who walked in darkness have seen a great light; those who dwelt in a land of deep darkness, on them has light shined" (Isa. 9:1-2). The coming of this light would mark the accession of a Davidic king whose throne would endure forever (9:6-7). Jewish sources interpreted this both messianically and nonmessianically,[44] but Christians regularly understood it as a prophecy concerning the Davidic messiah. They connected it with Isaiah's references to the messianic servant of the Lord who was to be the "light of the nations" (Isa. 42:6; 49:6) and apparently invoked it in disputes over Jesus' identity, like those reflected in John 7–8.[45] Readers who knew what the Scriptures said about Galilee would have understood that Jesus' claim to be a light for those who walked in darkness was consistent with his identity as the Messiah.

42. See the discussion of Jesus in chapter 2 for more on the Davidic claims involved in John 1:45-49. John 12:34 alludes to the messianic understanding of David's enduring "seed" in Ps. 89:35-36. Jesus fulfills this promise not by avoiding death but by overcoming it. Cf. chapter 3 on connections between the wine at Cana and Davidic texts like Gen. 49:10-11 and Amos 9:11-14, and chapter 5 on the Spirit in John 1:32 and the Davidic passage Isa. 11:2.

43. See Paul Duke's comments on the Bethlehem tradition in *Irony in the Fourth Gospel* (Atlanta: John Knox, 1985) 66-67. Some interpreters argue that the text does not presuppose the Bethlehem tradition but that Jesus has come "from above" (e.g., Bultmann, *Gospel*, 305–6 nn. 5–6; Meeks, *Prophet-King*, 37; de Jonge, *Jesus: Stranger*, 93–94). Yet this fails to account for the Gospel's insistence that Jesus fulfills the scriptural passages concerning the Messiah. For cautionary remarks see Schnackenburg, *Gospel*, 2.158–59; Raymond E. Brown, *The Birth of the Messiah* (Garden City, N.Y.: Doubleday, 1977) 513–16.

44. The Targum refers Isa. 9:6 to the Messiah; other Jewish interpreters applied Isaiah 9 to Hezekiah. See Antti Laato, *Who Is Immanuel? The Rise and the Foundering of Isaiah's Messianic Expectations* (Åbo: Åbo Academy, 1988) 313–26.

45. On Christian use of this imagery see esp. Matt. 4:16-17, where Isa. 9:1-2 is quoted in a messianic sense. On the context see W. D. Davies and Dale C. Allison, Jr., *A Critical and Exegetical Commentary on the Gospel according to St. Matthew* (ICC; Edinburgh: T. & T. Clark, 1988–) 1.379–80. See also the references to the "light of the nations" in Luke 1:79; 2:32; Acts 26:17, 23; *Barn.* 14:7-8. The Davidic King is called a "lamp" in 2 Sam. 21:17; 1 Kings 11:36; 15:4; 2 Kings 8:19.

Returning to the narrative, some in the crowd called Jesus "the prophet" (7:40), namely, the prophet like Moses whose coming was foretold in Deut. 18:15-18. We have seen that Jesus was this prophet (pp. 90–92), but the Jewish authorities contended that according to Scripture, "no prophet is to rise from Galilee" (John 7:52).[46] As before, Jesus' detractors are correct in the principles they affirm but wrong in the way they apply them to Jesus. It was true that the Christ's origin would be unknown and, paradoxically, that his origin would be Davidic, as the Scriptures had said. Similarly, the authorities were right in saying that the Scriptures said nothing about a future prophet coming from Galilee, although prophets had come from Galilee in the past,[47] but they were wrong in attempting to discredit Jesus by this principle. Jesus worked in Galilee but was not "from Galilee," that is, he was not Galilean in origin. Therefore, instead of undermining Jesus' claim to prophethood, the Pharisees' objection actually supported it.

According to John's Gospel, Jesus was simultaneously the Messiah and the prophet like Moses. There was some precedent for this in Jewish tradition, as we observed in the discussion of Jesus' signs. Some assumed that the prophet and the Messiah would be two distinct figures, but other Jewish and Samaritan sources suggest that both roles could be assumed by a single person. Moses was said to have performed the duties of a prophet by delivering the words of God and to have governed people in ways analogous to a king; the promised prophet like Moses presumably could do the same (cf. 6:14-15). The fourth evangelist sought to integrate these facets of Jesus' identity more thoroughly in the conviction that the biblical promises concerning both figures were fulfilled in Jesus, and the image of light helped do this. We have seen that the Messiah—whether of unknown or Davidic origin—was expected to be the light of the nations, and that Moses brought light to the world by giving the law to those who walked in darkness. Therefore, by claiming the title "light of the world," Jesus announced that he was indeed the Messiah and the prophet like Moses foretold in the Scriptures. Through Jesus the Messiah, the righteous rule of God would extend to the nations; and through Jesus the prophet, the peoples of the world would come to know God's will and walk in his ways.

---

46. Meeks (*Prophet-King*, 34) has observed that John 7:40-52 exhibits a kind of symmetry, beginning and ending with comments about Jesus' identity as a prophet (7:40, 52) and including debates about his messiahship in between (7:41-42).

47. Jonah was from Gath-hepher in Zebulun (2 Kings 14:25). Interestingly, Jonah's Galilean ancestry is mentioned in connection with the feast of Booths in *y. Sukk.* 55a, where this Galilean prophet is said to have come up to the feast and to have borne the Holy Spirit.

Jesus as Divine Son of Man
(8:12-30)

A third level of the debates and the light symbolism in John 7–8 concerns Jesus' divinity. This dimension is implicit in the way Jesus introduces the light imagery with "I Am" (*egō eimi*), which was the name of God. Although this expression did not necessarily connote deity, its divine overtones gradually emerged in previous chapters[48] and are unmistakable at the end of chapter 8. There Jesus says, "Before Abraham was, I Am," and his opponents attempt to stone him for arrogating God's name to himself. Important antecedents for the Johannine use of the expression are found in the book of Isaiah, where God's "I Am" punctuates the prophet's message. In one scene reminiscent of a courtroom, God called upon himself, upon his servant or son, and upon his hearers to act as his witnesses, in order that people may "know and believe me and understand that I Am" (Isa. 43:10). Similarly, Jesus called upon himself and upon God his Father to act as witnesses. Then, echoing Isaiah's language, he told his accusers, "You will die in your sins unless you believe that I Am" and that "When you have lifted up the Son of Man, then you will know that I Am" (John 8:24, 28). The use of the title Son of man—which has divine overtones throughout John's Gospel—confirms the numinous quality of the I Am expression in this context (cf. 1:51; 9:38).

The light imagery in chapter 8 reinforces this sense of Jesus' divinity. The connection between light and God's power and presence established in the opening verses of the Gospel would have been especially clear for readers familiar with the Old Testament material that undergirds John 7–8. Isaiah warned that darkness shall cover the earth but summoned God's people to "arise, shine, for your light has come, and the glory of the Lord has risen upon you" (60:1-2). The prophet repeatedly assured them that "the Lord will be your everlasting light" (60:19-20) and called on them to "walk in the light of the Lord" (2:5). The use of light imagery for God is also common in the Psalms, another of the fourth evangelist's primary Old Testament sources. Psalm 27:1, for example, says, "The Lord is my light and my salvation," and in Ps. 36:9 the psalmist says, "With you is the fountain of life; in your light we see light."

The festival context adds to the divine character of Jesus' claim. Jesus' announcement that he was the light of the world is set during the Jewish feast of Booths (John 7:2), a weeklong celebration commemorating the forty years Israel wandered in the desert during the time of Moses. People

---

48. In Jesus' statement to the Samaritan woman, "I am, the one speaking to you" (4:26), divine overtones are possible but not certain. The overtones are stronger when Jesus says to the disciples on the sea, "I am, do not be afraid" (6:20). These are further developed in the saying "I am the bread of life" (6:35, 48).

built booths roofed with leafy branches in their courtyards and alleyways, where they would eat and sleep during the festival, recalling how God made Israel dwell in simple shelters when he brought them out of the land of Egypt (Lev. 23:42-43). The Hebrew word for "booths" is *Succoth*, and after the Israelites left the land of Egypt, they encamped at a place that bore this name—Succoth. It was there that God began to accompany them by day in a pillar of cloud and by night in pillar of fire "to give them light" (Exod. 12:37; 13:20-22). Light indicated the divine presence in the phase of Israel's history that was commemorated by the festival.[49]

The fourth evangelist noted that Jesus' claim to be the light of the world was made in the vicinity of the temple treasury (8:20), which was apparently located in the part of the temple where one of the most spectacular rituals of the festival took place. Each evening worshipers crowded into the women's court, where four enormous lampstands were erected, each supporting four large bowls of oil with wicks made from the discarded undergarments of the priests. Throughout the night, young men from the priestly families clambered up ladders with additional oil to refill the lamps, so that the light shone incessantly in the darkness. Its rays gleamed from the temple's white stone walls and the bronze gate at the end of the courtyard, where the Levites played their harps, lyres, cymbals, and trumpets, as men noted for their piety and good works sang and danced to the Songs of Ascents (Psalms 120–134) with as many as eight flaming torches in their hands. The radiance emanating from the temple illumined courtyards throughout the city until the first shafts of daylight appeared over the Mount of Olives. Then two priests sounded the ram's horn, processed eastward through the temple court, and turned around with their backs to the rising sun in order to declare their faith in God. They recalled how their ancestors had mistakenly worshiped the sun itself, as if it were God, but they themselves worshiped the Lord (*m. Sukkah* 5:4; cf. Ezek. 8:16).

The thousands of pilgrims who went to Jerusalem each year returned with stories about the festival's light to towns throughout the Diaspora.[50] For many of them it conveyed a sense of the divine presence. An important biblical text that connects the presence of God with light and the feast of Booths is Zechariah 14, where the prophet envisioned the time when the Lord God would come to reign as king over all the earth. At

---

49. There is a reference to the pillar of fire lighting up the night in Exod. 14:19-20 (MT). See also Ps. 78:14; 105:39; 2 Esd. 1:14. The pillar of fire is mentioned in the celebration of the feast of Booths in Neh. 9:12, 19. On the connection between Israel's booths, the place named Succoth, and the fiery pillar, see *Sifra* 239:6 (Neusner ed., vol. 3, p. 270); *Mekilta* "Pisha" 14.11-22 (Lauterbach ed., vol. 1, p. 108).

50. Philo, who lived in Alexandria in Egypt, connected the light of the feast of Booths with the equinox (*Special Laws* 2.210).

that time there would be continuous day, "not day and not night, for at evening time there shall be light" (Zech. 14:7), and people from all over the earth would go up to Jerusalem, to worship God as king and celebrate the feast of Booths (14:16). The actual celebrations held at Jerusalem each year gave people from all over the world a sense of what it would be like to enjoy "continuous day" in the victorious presence of God.

Jewish Christians reading the Gospel in the late first century would have understood that events appeared to have shown that the prophet's vision was a sham. The Romans (John 11:48) carried away the temple's main lampstand and displayed it as a sign of their victory; the only light shining in the sanctuary came from coals smoldering in the rubble. It would seem that the world had triumphed over God, not that God had triumphed over the world. Yet according to John's Gospel, Jesus was the light of the world, the one in whom the hopes of the festival of Booths were realized. He was the light that manifested the presence of God, and he was the one in whom the nations of the world would come to know the power of God. The presence of non-Jews in the Christian community was evidence of this.

Jesus claimed to be the light of "the world," not just the light of Israel, and the imagery is consistent with the message. The use of light to con- note divinity was so widespread that the message of his divine origin would have been intelligible to readers outside the Jewish tradition. The intricate arguments about Jesus' status as rabbi, Messiah, and prophet, as well as the connection between light and the feast of Booths, presuppose a cer- tain familiarity with the Old Testament and Jewish traditions, but the divine character of light was recognized by people throughout the ancient world. In Greco-Roman sources, the god Serapis was lauded as the "light of all men," and the goddess Isis was "light of all mortals."[51] Zeus could be called "the light of men," and it was said of Jupiter that "the whole world was filled with the light of his glory."[52] In this broad cultural context even readers unfamiliar with Jewish traditions would have discerned the divine connotations in Jesus' claims. Yet Jesus is not one light among many; his position is singular. He is "the light," and the Gospel makes clear that apart from him people remain in darkness.

Light and Discipleship

Jesus' statement about light began at the level of Christology but moved to discipleship: "He who follows me will not walk in darkness, but will have the light of life" (8:12b). The word *walk* points to the ethical dimension of

51. References noted in BAGD *phōs* 2. Also Cicero *De Divinitatione* 17.
52. On Zeus see Lucian, *Alexander* 18; on Jupiter see Cicero, *De Divinatione* 1.10 §17. See further Barrett, *Gospel,* 335–37.

discipleship. It was widely understood that walking in darkness meant acting sinfully and that walking in the light meant living in accordance with the will of God. In Jewish sources the imagery was developed in the notion of two ways: "the path of the righteous is like the light of dawn," but "the way of the wicked is like deep darkness" (Prov 4:17-18; 1QS iii). For Jewish people, the Law of Moses distinguished righteousness from wickedness. The Scriptures said that the law was a lamp for their feet and a light for their pathways (Ps. 119:105), and the dancers who whirled in the dazzling splendor of the temple's lights were deemed exceptionally devout by the standards of the law.[53]

If Jesus is the light of the world, however, the relationship between sin and the Law of Moses is reconfigured. From a Johannine perspective, walking in darkness means persisting in unbelief, since antipathy toward God and Jesus is the sin at the root of all other sins. Conversely, walking in the light means living by faith in Jesus. The disciple's relationship to the Law is analogous to Jesus' relationship to the law. Jesus' teaching was not contrary to the law, rightly understood, but neither was it dependent on the law. Similarly, godly conduct was compatible with the law but not derived from it.

Another facet of the text is that those who walk in the light have "the light of life." As before, life is life in relationship with God; in John's Gospel it begins in faith and continues even beyond death. Those who walk in darkness face the prospect of death in sin. Jesus explicitly warns his hearers that they will die in their sins, which means that they will not go where Jesus is going—namely, to God—unless they turn from sin to faith and come to believe Jesus (John 8:21, 24). At first Jesus' hearers quarreled with the idea that he was the light of the world, but when it became clear that he was claiming divinity, they went a step farther and attempted to stone him for blasphemy. Their reaction raises the question about the truth of his claim, for if he was the light of the world, why did people fail to recognize him?

THE LIGHT IS WITH YOU
A LITTLE LONGER

The story of the healing of a man born blind offers a response to this question and further elaborates what it means for people to be in the darkness or the light. This text also marks a shift in the Gospel's light imagery, which manifested its midday brilliance at the feast of Booths in

---

53. One of the best-known dancers was Rabbi Simeon b. Gamaliel, a Pharisee known for his expertise in Jewish law, his intelligence, and his good judgment (Josephus, *Life* 191; *t. Sukk.* 4:4; *y. Sukk.* 55c [Neusner ed., p. 124]).

the announcement that Jesus was the light of the world. Subsequent episodes follow Jesus through the lingering afternoon of his public ministry, anticipating the conclusion of his work on earth with the onset of darkness. The stories of the blind beggar, the raising of Lazarus, and Jesus' triumphant approach to Jerusalem present different aspects of this theme.

We Must Work While It Is Day
(9:1-41)

After Jesus fled from the crowd in the temple, he repeated, "I am the light of the world" (9:5), and to demonstrate the truth of his statement he enlightened the eyes of a man who had been blind from birth. The debates during the feast of Booths had reflected at least three aspects of Jesus' identity as the light, and these are reaffirmed in the story of the man born blind: people again identify Jesus as a rabbi (9:2), prophet and Messiah (9:17, 22), and divine Son of man (9:35-38). The episode also reveals what it means for people to see the light or remain in darkness. Jesus healed a beggar who had been blind from birth. The man gained the ability to see on a physical level and gradually came to recognize Jesus through the eyes of faith. The Jewish leaders could see in a physical sense throughout the story but had no faith perception. Their increasing hostility to Jesus makes clear that sin is manifested not in physical blindness but in spiritual blindness, which may entail the delusion that one can actually see (9:39-41).

The light imagery would have helped this story ring true for readers on multiple levels. At the broad level of life experience, readers would know that there is a natural connection between light and vision, and since Jesus enabled someone to see, he could legitimately claim to be a source of light. They would also know that light could produce blindness as well as sight. When the sun rises, it makes it possible for those who have been in darkness to see, but those who are obstinate enough to stare at it and refuse to recognize its power will become blind. The beggar, who knew full well that he could not see, welcomed the light and became enlightened about Jesus as well, while the hubris of the Pharisees meant that they looked into the light of truth and saw only blackness, their darkened eyes displaying their ignorance of the truth.

On another level the text shows that Jesus was acting in a manner consistent with the Scriptures. The Jewish authorities argued that Jesus was violating the Law of Moses by healing on the Sabbath, but readers familiar with the Scriptures would know otherwise. There are no accounts of a blind person being healed in the Old Testament, and from this perspective the beggar was right when he declared, "Never since the world began has it been heard that anyone opened the eyes of a man born blind" (9:32). But the Scriptures did promise that God would send his prophetic or messianic "servant," who would be the "light of the nations, to open the eyes of the blind" (Isa. 42:6-7). Other texts suggested that God himself would make the blind to see (Isa. 29:18; 35:5; 42:16; Ps. 146:8). Therefore, although Jesus' act of healing appeared to violate the Law of Moses, it was consistent with what the Scriptures said God and his servant would do. As before, light is consistent with God's will, while darkness connotes sin.

What remains disturbing about this passage is that the man born blind received "the light of life" yet was persecuted for it. The more clearly he saw, the more intensely he was attacked. This theme of persecution will be an important element in subsequent chapters, and Jesus introduces it here with the comment "We must work the works of him who sent me while it is day; night comes when no one can work" (John 9:4). The statement is proverbial in character.[54] People throughout the ancient world knew that work had to be done during the daylight hours, since night made most kinds of labor impossible; statements to this effect appear in the Scriptures and other sources.[55] Jesus was saying that he had a certain period within which to do his work on earth. A span of time—a "day"— had been appointed for him to carry out his ministry before death came at nightfall. The same was true of the disciples, who were included in the statement "*we* must work while it is day." Like Jesus, they would have a limited period of time in which to carry out the work God had given them. Earlier passages of the Gospel affirmed that those who believe do have "life," but this text cautions that those who see the light are not exempted from the grave any more than Jesus himself was.

Walking in the Day
(11:9-10)

The shadow of death looms more ominously over subsequent episodes. Jesus apparently remained in Jerusalem for some time after healing the blind man, but after further debates, the people again attempted to stone him for blasphemy, and he fled across the Jordan River (10:31-42). Word reached him there that his friend Lazarus lay ill in the village of Bethany near Jerusalem. After delaying for two days, so that one would assume that Lazarus was either dead or recovering, Jesus inexplicably said that he was going to Jerusalem again. The disciples were incredulous. "Rabbi, the Jews

---

54. A proverb is a short expression based on common experience that can be generalized to apply to various situations. See the work ascribed to Cicero, *Ad Herennium* 4.17 §24. Cf. Roger D. Abrahams, "Proverbs and Proverbial Expressions," *Folklore and Folklife: An Introduction* (ed. R. M. Dorson; Chicago: University of Chicago Press, 1972) 117–27.

55. Ps. 104:23; *Bib. Ant.* 33:3; *m.* ʾAbot 2:15 (Str-B 2.529); Dio Chrysostom *Discourses* 3.81.

were just now seeking to stone you, and you're going there again?" But
Jesus replied, "Are there not twelve hours in the day?" (11:9a). His question expected a positive answer; everyone knew that there were twelve
hours in the day. The period between dawn and sunset was always divided
into twelve equal parts regardless of the season; the number of hours in a
day could not be lengthened or shortened. This reaffirmed what Jesus had
said before: He had a fixed period within which to do his ministry. The
"hour" of his death had been appointed, and as long as he "walked in
the day" set aside for him "he would not stumble" (11:9b), that is, he
would not be in physical danger. His freedom to carry out his mission in
the face of the threat of death came from knowing the divine purposes.

Something similar was true of Jesus' followers, who also would face
threats of persecution and death; only their confidence would come not
from knowing how long their lives would be but from knowing Jesus, "the
light of the world." Jesus said that a person who walks in the day does not
stumble, "because he sees the light of this world" (11:9c). This comment
signals a new level of meaning, since readers know from earlier passages
that Jesus himself is the light of the world. Jesus walked in the day by
acting within the span of time appointed for his ministry on earth, but his
disciples would walk in the day by living in the light of Christ through
faith. Thus the word *day* initially refers to a period of time but later
designates the person of Jesus, and *walking* comes to mean living in a
relationship with him. Physical injury or "stumbling" would become a real
danger for Jesus only at the end of the "day" set aside for his work; but for
the disciples, "stumbling" meant the loss of faith that would separate them
from the light of Christ and plunge them into the darkness of sin, divine
condemnation, and death (cf. Prov. 4:19; Jer. 13:16).

The connection between stumbling and loss of faith is reinforced by
the statement "if anyone walks in the night, he stumbles, because the light
is not in him" (John 11:10). According to this text, those who do not see
the light of the world have no source of inner illumination. On a physical
level, the imagery apparently reflects an understanding of vision that was
common among Jews and Greeks, who thought that the eye actively emitted light, instead of passively receiving it. The eye was thought to illumi-
nate a person as the sun illuminated the earth; it was not so much a
window through which light passed as a lamp from which light rays ema-
nated.[56] The ability or inability to see depended not only upon a person's
external circumstances but upon one's internal condition. The inability to

---

56. D. C. Allison, "The Eye Is the Lamp of the Body (Matthew 6.22-23 = Luke 11.34-36),"
NTS 33 (1987) 61–83; H. D. Betz, "Matthew vi.22f and Ancient Greek Theories of Vision,"
Text and Interpretation: Studies in the New Testament Presented to Matthew Black (ed. E. Best and R.
McL. Wilson; Cambridge: Cambridge University Press, 1979) 43–56.

see the light of the world corresponds to the darkness of sin within the person's own heart, and those who have the ability to see the light of the world also have a source of light within themselves, much as those who receive living water from Jesus find that it is a spring welling up inside them.[57]

Becoming Children of Light
(12:27-50)

Jesus traveled into Judea, summoned Lazarus from the tomb, and departed again without incident, but the specter of death grew as the chief priests and Pharisees formulated their plot to kill him. When Jesus returned to Jerusalem, the crowds poured out of the city to meet him, hailing him as the king of Israel, but Jesus announced that the hour had come for him to be "lifted up" from the earth, which the bystanders rightly understood to mean death. They demanded, "We have heard from the Law that the Christ remains forever. How can you say that the Son of man must be lifted up? Who is this Son of man?" (12:34). Their question is a haunting reminder of the debates over Jesus' identity at the feast of Booths, where the same three issues were raised: his status as a rabbi and relation to the law, his identity as the Christ, and his claims to be the Son of man.

When these questions were raised before, Jesus responded by calling himself the light of the world, which encompassed all three facets of his identity in a single image: Light indicates that his teaching was consistent with the law but not derived from it, that he was the messianic "light of the nations," and that he was the Son of man in whom the light of God's own presence was manifested. When the Palm Sunday crowd raised these same questions, Jesus responded with the same image—light—which recalled what he had already told them, accenting their inability to understand him. His response also fused what he had said about his identity as the light of the world with his warnings about the imminent onset of darkness. He said, "The light is with you for a little longer" (12:35). Jesus' ministry would not last indefinitely; he would be "lifted up" in death.

Jesus also told his hearers, "Walk while you have the light, lest the darkness overtake you." His words take a surprising turn. He did not tell them to walk while they had the light before the darkness overtook the light—in fact the prologue used identical language to say that "the light shines in the darkness and the darkness has not overtaken it" (1:5). Instead, Jesus warned his hearers that the darkness would overtake *them,* just as the sun continues to shine even while slipping over the horizon, leaving the traveler on the road prey to the night, unable to see. Initially it seemed

---

57. Schnackenburg, *Gospel,* 2.325; Barrett, *Gospel,* 392; Dodd, *Historical Tradition in the Fourth Gospel* (Cambridge: Cambridge University Press, 1963) 375.

that the light would be removed through Jesus' death, but this was true only in a limited sense. Jesus would not be present with people after his crucifixion as he had been before, but neither would he be completely absent from the world; he would remain present through the Spirit.[58] The evangelist wrote the Gospel decades after the death of Jesus but assumed that people could still come to Jesus as a living presence; his light continued to shine in the darkness. Nevertheless, belief remained urgent, because people in subsequent generations, like the crowds who first heard Jesus, would have a limited amount of time to come to faith. We have seen that in John's Gospel the image of darkness often referred to the power of sin and death, and this text warns that those who do not believe will be overcome by the darkness of sin and finally separated from the light—not through his death, but their own.

Those who walk in the light believe in the light and become "children of light" (12:36). Only here does John's Gospel use this suggestive expression, which also appears elsewhere in the New Testament and the Dead Sea Scrolls, but not in the Old Testament or other Jewish writings.[59] In ethical terms, the children of light were understood to be the righteous, who lived in accordance with the will of God. The Dead Sea community called their opposites "the children of darkness, the army of Satan," and identified them as greedy, deceitful and cruel, insolent, ill-tempered, and lewd.[60] In the New Testament, the counterparts to the "children of light" were variously called those who are "of the night or of darkness" (1 Thess. 5:5), the "children of disobedience," who were noted for impurity, idolatry, and fornication (Eph. 5:5-6), or the crafty "children of this age," who were adept at the use of unrighteous mammon (Luke 16:8). These sources cast the children of light as participants in a cosmic drama in which the power of God was in conflict with the forces of evil. Those who were on the side of light could anticipate deliverance and blessing in the age to come, when the kingdom of God dawned, but those who were of darkness would be requited for their sin by the vengeance of God and cursed without mercy because of the darkness of their deeds. They would face the wrath of God and have no place in his kingdom.[61] These sources also understood that people became children of light by divine election, by sharing in the "lot of light" established by God, or by being chosen or predestined for salvation rather than wrath.[62]

58. Rightly noted by Martyn, *History and Theology*, 29.
59. See Joseph A. Fitzmyer, *The Gospel according to Luke* (AB28–28A; Garden City, N.Y.: Doubleday, 1981–85) 2.1108.
60. See 1QM i 1; 1QS ii 13—iv 14.
61. See 1QS i 9-11; ii 5-8; 1 Thess. 5:5; Eph. 5:5.
62. Eph. 1:4-5; 5:8; 1 Thess. 5:9. On the "lot of light" and election in the Dead Sea Scrolls, see E. P. Sanders, *Paul and Palestinian Judaism* (Philadelphia: Fortress, 1977) 257–59.

In John's Gospel, as in these other texts, the expression "children of light" has ethical connotations, but these must be understood in terms of the light and darkness imagery used elsewhere in the Gospel. Those who walk in the light live in accordance with the will of God by acting out of faith in Jesus. Those who believe in Jesus believe in God (John 12:44), and this relationship is the basis for conduct congruent with God's will. Conversely, sinful actions emerge out of unbelief, which is the fundamental form of sin. Jesus' adversaries would appear to be morally upright by the standards of the Mosaic law, but their animosity toward Jesus revealed the hostility toward God that would lead them to commit the ultimate sin: murdering the Son of God.

The sense of impending conflict often connected with the expression "children of light" is also apparent in John's Gospel when Jesus announces that the time has come for the "ruler of the world" to be cast out (12:31). The summons to become children of light comes against the backdrop of this crisis. According to John's Gospel, those who reject the light are not destroyed by God but are allowed to remain in the darkness, and like travelers groping along a path at night, they bring about their own demise. Jesus warned that "he who walks in darkness does not know where he goes" (12:35), which suggests the seriousness of the situation. In earlier portions of the narrative, Jesus often declared that he knew where he was going—he was going to God. By implication, those who do not know where they are going must be headed elsewhere, while those who believe in the light and become "children of light" know where they are going and are saved from the destructive powers of darkness for life with God. Jesus does not need to judge those who "remain in darkness"; their own rejection of the light condemns them (12:44-48).

As the curtain draws over Jesus' public ministry, the evangelist grapples with the question as to why so many lingered in the darkness instead of coming to the light, and he concludes that people become children of light only by the power of God (12:37-43). The evangelist surveys the whole of Jesus' public ministry and finds that "though he had done so many signs before them, yet they did not believe in him." Such a reaction meant not that people were simply unwilling to believe but that they could not believe, just as the prophet Isaiah had said: "He has *blinded* their eyes and hardened their heart, lest they should see with their eyes and perceive with their heart, and turn for me to heal them" (12:39-40; cf. Isa. 6:9-10). The wrenching irony was that people became blind because God had sent them the light. Their persistent inability to see the power of God in the person of Jesus manifested the depths of human resistance to God.

The crowd's response to Jesus demonstrated that faith is a human impossibility. But if faith is impossible for human beings, it is not impossible for God. The story does not end in John 12. There would be children of light who would come to faith because Jesus, after being lifted up, would draw them to himself (12:32). The text contains a profound tension that remains unresolved. People are responsible for unbelief, and God is responsible for faith. Both are true. Unbelief reveals the power of sin, faith reveals the power of God. And the problem becomes more acute in the figure of Judas in the next section.

THE LIGHT SHINES IN
THE DARKNESS

As the day of Jesus' ministry waned, the powers of darkness prepared to mount a final attack upon him. Jesus gathered with his disciples for a last meal, washed their feet, and warned that one of them would betray him. Readers are told that by this time the devil had put it in the heart of Judas Iscariot to betray Jesus (13:2). No specific motive, such as greed, is given for Judas's action; attention is focused on Judas's role as the agent of Satan, who arranged to have Jesus murdered. Thus the powers of darkness—sin, death, and evil—are fused in the figure of Judas. Jesus revealed the identity of the betrayer to the Beloved Disciple by dipping a piece of food into a dish and giving it to Judas. The gesture was a common way of showing affection toward someone at a meal, but when Judas received the morsel, Satan recoiled within him (13:27). So as soon as he was able, he went out "and it was night" (13:30). Judas plunged into the darkness of which he had become a part, plotting to destroy Jesus but in reality destroying himself (17:12).

It was precisely against this black backdrop of betrayal and death that Jesus announced, "Now the Son of man is glorified, and in him God is glorified" (13:31). Here for the first time in the Gospel darkness is coupled with "glory" rather than light. The connection is an apt one, because in the Old Testament "glory" frequently referred to a manifestation of God's presence and power, which could readily be connected with the radiance of light. The book of Isaiah, for example, told Israel, "Arise, shine; for your light has come, and the glory of the Lord has risen upon you," and promised that "the Lord will be your everlasting light and your God will be your glory" (Isa. 60:1, 19). This connection between light and glory is introduced implicitly in the prologue to John's Gospel, which tells how "the true light" entered the world in the person of Jesus, and those who believed "beheld his glory, glory as of the only Son from the Father" (John 1:9, 14). Although light is not explicitly identified with glory in subsequent passages, we have noted how often the image of light has divine connotations in the Gospel.

During Jesus' public ministry, his followers could see the glory of God in the miraculous signs he performed (2:11; 11:40), but whenever the Gospel speaks of Jesus' glorification, it alludes to his crucifixion. C. H. Dodd rightly observed that "if in the incarnate life of Christ the eternal, archetypal light is manifested, its final manifestation is in His death."[63] On Palm Sunday Jesus announced that the time had come for him to be glorified, but in the manner of a seed falling into the earth and dying (12:23-24). At the conclusion of the last supper Jesus prayed that God would glorify him (17:1) but then departed to a garden outside Jerusalem to meet the soldiers who would soon escort him to the cross. Glorification of Jesus takes place through conflict with the powers of evil, sin, and death. But light shines in the darkness, and the darkness has not overcome it.

The departure of Judas is like a stone cast into a moonlit pool—it dissipates the patterns of darkness and light that pervaded the Gospel up to this point. Images of light and darkness are not explicitly conjoined in the remainder of the Gospel, and the motif never regains its former prominence. Jesus remained with his disciples at the supper for some time before going to the garden, and when Judas met him there he was accompanied by armed guards who brought the light in the form of lanterns and torches. These sources of artificial light in the hands of Jesus' adversaries could, perhaps, be understood as pathetic substitutes for the true light,[64] yet making Jesus' adversaries into bearers of light would be a twist not found elsewhere in the Gospel. When Peter entered the courtyard of the high priest, he denied knowing Jesus in the glow of a charcoal fire (18:18), and Jesus was led to the praetorium when "it was early" (18:28). In neither case, however, is light coupled with darkness or is the imagery developed in the text. The comment on Nicodemus is more significant, for when Nicodemus brought the spices for Jesus' burial, the evangelist recalled that he had first come to Jesus "by night." But because of the complexity of Nicodemus's character, we must reserve discussion of this scene for the chapter on the crucifixion (see pp. 204–6).

Mary Magdalene came to the tomb on Easter morning "early," "while it was still dark" (20:1), and the darkness might suggest her incomprehension. Similarly, the disciples gathered behind closed doors when it was "evening" (20:19), and the darkness could correspond to their fear. In these instances, however, darkness does not convey a sense of sin or evil as it did elsewhere in the Gospel, and the imagery is not developed within the episode: Neither Mary's nor the disciples' recognition of Jesus is connected with light. The use of darkness and light in John 21 is perhaps

63. *Interpretation*, 208.
64. Culpepper, *Anatomy*, 192.

more promising, since Jesus reveals himself to the disciples by the Sea of Tiberius at daybreak after they had spent a futile night fishing (21:3-4). The night may suggest separation from Jesus, though it does not carry the sense of sin or evil found elsewhere in John. And daybreak would be an appropriate time for the light of the world to manifest himself to the disciples, though the image is not developed and its symbolic import is not integral to our understanding of this text as it is of other texts.

Symbolic references to light and darkness span "the day" of Jesus' public ministry in John 1–12, then give way to the idea of glorification at the beginning of the passion (13:30-32). Images of light bind together facets of Jesus' identity as a teacher, prophet and messiah, and divine Son of man, helping to convey what it means to believe and have life in him. The implications for discipleship or "walking in the light" are construed primarily in terms of living in faith. Darkness conveys the ominous reality of unbelief and its relationship to sin, evil, and death. The message conveyed by this motif is universal in its scope; it concerns a light for the world, a radiance that enlightens everyone. The medium of light and darkness is consistent with this message: The familiar imagery would have communicated with a broad spectrum of readers. Yet the way the Gospel focuses light on the person of Jesus tacitly displaces the claims of other sources of illumination. Jesus remains *the* light, the true light, whose radiance must be seen in and through the cross.

LIGHT AND DARKNESS IN 1 JOHN

Light and darkness continue to play important roles in the First Epistle of John, a text that was probably written within the community in which the Gospel was composed. The epistle offers glimpses into the way images like those found in the Gospel were developed after the Gospel was completed.[65] Although the epistle's language closely resembles that of the Gospel, the imagery functions somewhat differently, and some brief comparisons may be useful. Instead of characterizing the conflict between those who do and those who do not believe in Jesus, the epistolary author used light and darkness to characterize two factions within the Christian community: those for whom the author spoke and those who had broken away from the group (1 John 2:19). Both sides shared a common heritage, like that preserved in John's Gospel, and the epistolary author interpreted the tradition in the context of this schism.

The author of 1 John focused the image of light on God rather than on Jesus. The opening lines of the epistle culminate in the statement "This is

---

65. See esp. Brown, *Epistles*, 69–71, 92–93.

the message we have heard from him and proclaim to you, that God is light and in him is no darkness at all" (1:5). This statement is surprising in some ways, since the Gospel connects light with divinity but consistently uses "light" for the preexistent Word (John 1:3-5, 9) and for Jesus (8:12; 9:5) rather than for God. Despite the shift, the epistolary author presents the claim that God is light not as a religious commonplace but as an interpretation of the message received from Jesus.[66] Later the author connects "the true light" with what is true in Christ and in the community, a light that "is already shining" (1 John 2:8). The light that continues to be manifested within the community of faith includes the proclamation of the message of Jesus and obedience to Jesus' command, which serves as testimony to the truth of the message.

Discipleship, or "walking in the light," is an expression of fellowship, or *koinōnia*, with God who is light (1:6). In John's Gospel, what distinguished walking in light from walking in darkness was faith in Jesus; the author of 1 John gives the idea a sharper moral focus by connecting it with Jesus' command to love one another. This development helps bring light and darkness to bear on the schism within the community, in which those on both sides would presumably claim to be believers and to be living out their faith. The author of 1 John understood that faith issues in godly life but insisted that the reverse was also true: One's manner of life discloses the true character of one's faith. Therefore, if "we say we have fellowship with him while we walk in darkness, we lie and do not live according to the truth" (1:6). Walking in darkness is particularly identified with violation of the love command, so that he "who says he is in the light and hates his brother is in the darkness still" (2:9). Walking in the light is reflected in "fellowship with one another," for it is the person who loves his brother who truly abides in the light (1:7; 2:10). The author of 1 John does not equate walking in the light with moral perfection; he recognizes that Christians do sin and places forgiveness of sins in the context of one's relationship with God and with other Christians.

Those who walk in darkness face the ominous prospect of "stumbling," which in the Gospel of John meant a loss of faith in Jesus and divine condemnation (John 11:9-10; *proskoptein*). The author of 1 John interprets stumbling in terms of the love command. He assures his readers that those who love their fellow Christians are not in danger of stumbling (1 John 2:10; *skandalon*), unlike the hateful one who walks in darkness and does not know where he is going, "because the darkness has blinded his eyes" (2:11).

---

66. See Günther Klein, "'Das wahre Licht scheint schon': Beobachtungen zur Zeit- und Geschichtserfahrung einer urchristlichen Schule," *ZTK* 68 (1971) 261–326, esp. 285–91.

The power of darkness to produce blindness is given special prominence in 1 John, while in the Gospel both blindness and sight were occa-
sioned by the coming of the light in Jesus. This was shown most vividly in
the Gospel's account of the blind beggar, who eventually saw who Jesus
was, and the Jewish authorities, who became blind by staring into the light
of truth and refusing to recognize its power (John 9:39). The Gospel
writer recalled how Isaiah said that God would blind people's eyes and
harden their heart so that they could not see, and he understood that this
prophecy was fulfilled in the ministry of Jesus (12:40; Isa. 6:9-10). Nevertheless, the Gospel did not make Jesus or God into the ultimate author of
sin but held people accountable for the delusion that they could see and
for seeking their own glory (9:41; 12:43).[67] The Gospel also warned against
being overtaken by darkness, like a traveler who gropes along a pathway
without knowing where he goes (12:35). The imagery found in
1 John 2:11 is akin to this strand of the Gospel, which gives the darkness of
sin a more active role.

The conflict between light and darkness in 1 John appears in a temporal framework somewhat different from that of the Gospel. According to 1
John 2:8, "the darkness is passing away and the true light is already shining." The light that shines and drives back the darkness includes both the
message of Jesus, which continued to be proclaimed by the community,
and the love within the community, which bore witness to the truth of the
message. The Gospel often depicted light and darkness in punctiliar terms,
focusing on the divine light manifested in Jesus that the darkness did not
overcome, or on light and darkness as the two alternatives confronting
human beings. The Gospel warned that night would fall without actually
saying that the darkness would pass away. The author of the epistle, however, looks for the final eradication of darkness, identifying the light within
the Christian community as an anticipation of its demise.

---

67. See esp. J. M. Lieu, "Blindness in the Johannine Tradition," *NTS* 34 (1988) 83–95.
She takes 1 John 2:11 to be an interpretation of Isa. 6:9-10 but overlooks possible connections with the language of being "overtaken" by darkness in John's Gospel. See Schnackenburg, *Gospel*, 2.271.

5

Water

Images of water, like those of light and darkness, create another rich and variegated motif. John baptized with water in order to reveal the one God sent to baptize with the Holy Spirit (1:24-25), and Jesus transformed water into wine, manifesting his glory (2:6). Nicodemus was told that a person had to be born of water and the Spirit to enter the kingdom of God (3:5), and John's disciples learned that people went to Jesus for baptism because it had been granted from heaven (3:22-27). Jesus offered "living water" to a woman of Samaria, who left her water jar to bring her townspeople to meet him (4:10, 28), and with a word he healed an invalid who sought help from the troubled waters of the pool at Bethzatha (5:7-8). At the feast of Booths, Jesus invited all who thirsted to come and drink of "living water" (7:37-39), and he gave sight to a blind man who washed in the pool of Siloam (9:7). On the eve of his death, Jesus poured water into a basin and washed his disciples' feet in the manner of a slave (13:5). He was crucified the next day; and when a soldier poked a spear into his side, blood and water poured out (19:34).

These references to water convey meaning through one of the most common elements of human life; drinking and washing are part of a daily routine for people everywhere. Because no one can live without water, it is widely used in religious symbolism. Common experience enables water to call forth a range of different and even contradictory associations on both the cognitive and affective levels. A glass of cool water is refreshing on the tongue, but waves surging over one's head bring the threat of drowning. The gentle rains that spatter on parched earth awaken the seeds within it to life, but the torrents that wash down the hillsides wreak destruction. Paradoxically, water brings both life and death.[1]

1. Günther Stemberger, *La symbolique du bien et du mal selon Saint Jean* (Paris: Seuil, 1970) 149–51.

The water motif in the Fourth Gospel is less consistent than that of light and darkness. Like a stream on a hillside, it maintains a general direction of movement while readily conforming to the contours of the narrative through which it flows. The significance of water is almost always connected with washing or drinking. There is an easy movement from one type of action to the other, and both may have the same meaning. The jars at Cana contained water normally used for ritual washing, but Jesus transformed it into wine that was drunk, and the account of Jesus in Samaria begins with references to baptism, then shifts to the living water that quenches thirst. At the feast of Booths the movement is the reverse: Jesus invited the thirsty to drink from his living water, then healed a blind man by having him wash in the pool of Siloam. The sea stories in John's Gospel do not mention washing or drinking, and these episodes are only distantly related to the other components of the water motif. Since the symbolic actions in the texts mentioning the sea were discussed earlier, they will not be treated again here (see pp. 92–94, 118–22).

Like the other images in the Gospel, water must be understood christologically. Although Jesus is not identified with water in the way he is called the light of the world or the bread of life, some passages present him as the source of living water, and others use water to help reveal who he is. The christological significance of the imagery is multifaceted and its levels of meaning can be correlated with the different aspects of Jesus' identity noted in the surrounding narrative. The water Jesus provides is both revelation and the Spirit. The constant interplay between revelation and Spirit occurs in part because the water imagery must span two periods of time: the period of Jesus' ministry and that of the later church. If living water is the revelation Jesus offered people during his ministry, this revelation is extended through the Spirit to readers living after Jesus' departure to the Father.[2]

BAPTISM WITH WATER AND
THE SPIRIT

The theme of water interlaces the first three chapters of the Gospel. Water is mentioned in relation to John's baptism and the Holy Spirit in chapter 1 and in connection with Jewish purification rites in chapter 2. These two subthemes flow together in chapter 3, when a dispute over purification roils up between John's disciples and a Jew. As the debate subsides, the

---

2. See Felix Porsch, *Pneuma und Wort: Ein exegetischer Beitrag zur Pneumatologie des Johannesevangeliums* (FTS 16; Frankfurt am Main: Josef Knecht, 1974) 65–72, 128, 144; Gary M. Burge, *The Anointed Community: The Holy Spirit in the Johannine Tradition* (Grand Rapids, Mich.: Eerdmans, 1987) 99–100.

significance of the water becomes clearer through a connection with the baptism practiced by Jesus' followers and the activity of the Holy Spirit.

John Baptized with Water
(1:19-34)

The narrative portion of the Gospel begins when a Jewish delegation from Jerusalem asked John who he was and why he was baptizing. John firmly denied that he was one of the eschatological figures they expected to appear: He was neither the Christ nor Elijah nor the prophet like Moses, but "the voice of one crying in the wilderness, 'Make straight the way of the Lord,' as the prophet Isaiah said" (John 1:23). John had come in order that someone greater than himself might be revealed. He said, "I baptize with water; but among you stands one whom you do not know," someone of such stature that John was not worthy to untie his sandal (1:27). Not even John would have recognized this figure apart from revelation, but "came baptizing with water that he might be revealed to Israel" (1:31, 33). The use of the passive voice in this statement is significant. John was not a revealer, but the water he used for baptism did provide the context within which divine revelation took place.

The agent of revelation was the Spirit. John said, "He who sent me to baptize with water said to me, 'He on whom you see the Spirit descend and remain, this is he who baptizes with the Holy Spirit'" (1:33). A relationship between water and the Spirit is suggested but not delineated in this passage. Although John's baptismal activity was the setting in which the Spirit descended on Jesus, the text does not actually say that Jesus was baptized by John. Readers would have to know accounts of Jesus' baptism like those found in the other Gospels to ascertain that it was the specific occasion for revelation. As the text stands, it says only that John's baptismal ministry was the context within which revelation through the Spirit took place.

The significance of the water can be discerned by relating it to the facets of Jesus' identity mentioned in the passage. First, John introduced Jesus as "the Lamb of God," balancing the disclaimers about himself with the proclamation that Jesus is the one who "takes away the sin of the world" (1:29). The repeated reference to Jesus as the Lamb of God (1:36) indicates that comprehending the significance of Jesus' sacrificial death is basic to understanding his identity. At the same time, the focus on Jesus' role seems to exclude the idea that sin could be removed in other ways, including baptism by John.

The Gospel was written in a way that suggests that at least some readers may already have known something about John. The prologue's careful distinction between Jesus and John (1:6-8) suggests that some may have failed to appreciate the difference between the two figures, and the questions raised by the delegation from Jerusalem indicate that John had attained public recognition well before Jesus. According to 3:26, the disciples of John resented that Jesus had become so popular even though he was a relative latecomer. John's emphatic denial that he was the Christ and repeated insistence on the priority of Jesus seem designed to counter the idea that he should have precedence over Jesus (1:15, 30; 3:27-30). Accounts of John's ministry circulated in both Jewish and early Christian sources, and groups of John's disciples continued to exist well after his death. The Fourth Gospel seems to correct certain exaggerated claims made about John while incorporating him firmly into the narrative as a witness to Jesus.[3]

John's baptism differed from Jewish proselyte baptism in that John baptized those who were already Jews as well as, perhaps, some Gentiles. Extant sources offer varying explanations of John's baptism, but several aspects seem prominent. (a) The water was understood by some to purify the body from defilement. It differed from ordinary Jewish lustrations, which people performed for themselves whenever they became unclean, in that John apparently performed the act of baptism for people and baptized the person only once. (b) Participation in John's baptism expressed repentance from sin, which meant turning away from sin back to God and manifesting the fruit of repentance by righteous conduct. John's preaching included warnings about the judgment that would befall those who did not turn from wickedness. (c) The baptism John administered apparently included receipt of forgiveness for sins, although it is not clear whether forgiveness was thought to be mediated through the use of water or to accompany the baptism in some other way.[4]

Readers familiar with the idea that John's baptism cleansed people from sin would find this notion tacitly displaced by the emphasis on Jesus'

3. According to Acts 18:25 and 19:1-7, there were followers of John the Baptist at Ephesus during Paul's ministry there. See Hermann Lichtenberger, "Täufergemeinde und frühchristliche Täuferpolemik im letzten Drittel des 1. Jahrhunderts," *ZTK* 84 (1987) 36–57. For surveys of texts on John and his ministry, see Robert L. Webb, *John the Baptizer and Prophet: A Socio-Historical Study* (JSNTSup 62; Sheffield: JSOT, 1991); Josef Ernst, *Johannes der Täufer: Interpretation—Geschichte—Wirkungsgeschichte* (BZNW 53; Berlin: de Gruyter, 1989). The likelihood that the Gospel reflects debates over the relative status of Jesus and John was argued by W. Baldensperger at the end of the nineteenth century and has been adopted in modified form by many others. For nuanced assessments of the evangelist's stance toward John the Baptist, see Walter Wink, *John the Baptist in the Gospel Tradition* (SNTSMS 7; Cambridge: Cambridge University Press, 1968) 106; Brown, *Community*, 69–71; Ernst, *Johannes der Täufer*, 215–16; Webb, *John the Baptizer and Prophet*, 76–77.

4. The other Gospels say John preached "a baptism of repentance for the forgiveness of sins" (Mark 1:4; Luke 3:3) or simply a baptism "for repentance" (Matt. 3:11). Josephus said that the baptism was not used "to gain pardon for whatever sins they committed, but as a consecration of the body, implying that the soul was already cleansed by right behavior" (*Ant.* 18.5.1 §117). See the discussion in Webb, *John the Baptizer and Prophet*, 163–216.

singular role as "the Lamb of God who takes away the sin of the world" (1:29). Neither the water nor John's baptismal practice is significant in itself, but both are meaningful insofar as they direct attention to Jesus, whose death purifies people from sin. Throughout this episode the term *baptize* refers to something John did by means of water; but it finally designates something Jesus would do by means of the Spirit (1:33). This text does not say whether baptism with the Spirit would or would not include water, but it does suggest that the cleansing effect of Jesus' death would be extended to people through the Spirit's work.

On a second level the water helps disclose that Jesus was the fulfillment of Jewish messianic expectations. These expectations were listed twice and included questions about the Christ, Elijah, and the prophet like Moses (1:20-21, 25). John flatly denied that he was "the Christ," a title readers would know belonged to Jesus (cf. 1:17), testifying that he "saw the Spirit descend and remain" on Jesus (1:32-33). The descent of the Spirit marked Jesus as God's anointed. Israel's first king, Saul, bore the Spirit for a time before it was given to David, his successor (1 Sam. 10:10; 16:13-14), and the messianic heir to David's throne was also expected to bear the Spirit. One of the most important messianic passages in Isaiah—the book mentioned in John 1:23—said that a shoot would come forth from the stump of Jesse and that "the Spirit of the Lord shall rest upon him" (Isa. 11:2). A similar idea appears later in Isaiah, where God promises to put his Spirit upon his anointed one (61:1), and it is also found in other Jewish sources of the period.[5]

After the Spirit descended, John testified that Jesus was "the Son of God" (John 1:34). This title is, in an important sense, messianic; it is used in this way by Nathanael in 1:49, who couples it with "King of Israel" (see pp. 40–41). Passages like 2 Sam. 7:14 and Ps. 2:7 speak of the anointed heir to David's throne as God's "son," and Jewish sources use the language of sonship for the Messiah, though in an adoptive rather than a metaphysical sense.[6] The expression "Son of God" was exceptionally useful for the evangelist because it could present Jesus as the fulfillment of Jewish messianic expectations while allowing for an expanded understanding of messiahship that would include Jesus' heavenly origin. The messianic character of the scene is also reflected in the title "Chosen One," which some manuscripts have instead of "Son of God" in 1:34. This title echoes

5. See esp. *T. Judah* 24:1-6; *Pss. Sol.* 17:37. Cf. Brown, *Gospel*, 1.66; Porsch, *Pneuma und Wort*, 23–26; Burge, *The Anointed Community*, 55–59; Wolfgang J. Bittner, *Jesu Zeichen im Johannesevangelium: Die Messias-Erkenntnis im Johannesevangelium vor ihrem jüdischen Hintergrund* (WUNT 26; Tübingen: Mohr/Siebeck, 1987) 139–43.

6. E.g., 4QFlor i 11-13; 4 Ezra 7:28. See Ashton, *Understanding*, 260–62, and the cautionary remarks by Sigmund Mowinkel, *He That Cometh: The Messiah Concept in the Old Testament and Later Judaism* (Nashville: Abingdon, 1954) 293–94.

Isa. 42:1: "Behold my servant, whom I uphold, my chosen one, in whom my soul delights; I have put my Spirit upon him." Although Jewish sources referred to various figures as God's chosen, the strong affinity between John's text and Isa. 42:1 suggests that it should be understood in a messianic sense.[7]

The Johannine presentation of Jesus' messiahship combines Davidic traits with those of Elijah and the prophet like Moses, the other two figures mentioned by the Jews who questioned John (see pp. 90–92). The Scriptures said that Elijah was to return before the great and terrible day of the Lord (Mal. 4:5-6) and that God would raise up for Israel another prophet like Moses (Deut. 18:15-18). The water John used for baptizing was located at a place that would have been appropriate for either of these figures to appear. The location would have enhanced the significance of the water for readers familiar with the topography of the area. The Fourth Gospel said that John was baptizing at a place called Bethany, east of the Jordan (John 1:28), which was apparently on the plains opposite Jericho. It was in that area that Elijah was swept up into heaven by a whirlwind and that his successor Elisha received a share of the prophet's spirit and parted the waters of the Jordan on his return.[8] Moses too was endowed with a special spirit from God in order to lead Israel until he died and was buried on Mount Nebo overlooking the area around Bethany, and his role was assumed by his spirit-filled successor, Joshua, who parted the waters of the Jordan when he crossed.[9] The symbolic value of these local traditions is attested by the attempt of the prophet Theudas to part the waters of the Jordan in the first century and by later traditions associated with the area around Bethany.[10]

John refused to claim the role of the Christ, Elijah, or the prophet like Moses, pointing instead to Jesus, who appeared at Bethany and fulfilled all these roles. Although Jesus is not called Elijah or the prophet, he per-

---

7. See *1 Enoch* 48:5, 10, which connects the titles Chosen One and Messiah, and 49:1-3, which connects the Chosen One with Isa. 11:2; cf. *Apoc. Abr.* 31:1-2. See G. W. E. Nickelsburg, *Jewish Literature between the Bible and the Mishnah* (Philadelphia: Fortress, 1981) 217–18; Ashton, *Understanding*, 257–58. It is a messianic title in Luke 23:35; cf. 9:35. On the various uses of "chosen" see G. Schrenk, "*eklektos*," *TDNT* 4.182–83.

8. Second Kings 2:9-15; cf. "the spirit and power of Elijah" in Luke 1:17.

9. Deut. 34:1, 9; Josh. 3:7-13. For eschatological traditions surrounding the burial place of Moses, see *The Lives of the Prophets* 2:14-19.

10. On Theudas see Josephus, *Ant.* 20.5.1 §§97–98. On Theudas's use of past associations, see Richard A. Horsley and John S. Hanson, *Prophets, Bandits, and Messiahs: Popular Movements in the Time of Jesus* (Minneapolis: Winston, 1985) 164–67. On the association of Elijah and Moses with Bethany, see Clemens Kopp, *The Holy Places of the Gospels* (New York: Herder, 1963) 113–29; Gustav Dalman, *Sacred Sites and Ways: Studies in the Topography of the Gospels* (London: SPCK, 1935) 87–93. For further discussion on the location of Bethany see my "Topography and Theology in the Gospel of John," in *Fortunate the Eyes That See: Essays in Honor of David Noel Freedman* (ed. Andrew H. Bartelt, Astrid B. Beck, Chris A. Franke, Paul R. Raabe; Grand Rapids: Eerdmans, 1994).

formed works reminiscent of the miracles of these prophets during his ministry, and the evangelist gives readers no reason to think that an Elijah or Moses *redivivus* would appear alongside Jesus. Like these earlier figures, Jesus bore the Spirit of God; but unlike them, he bore it permanently. The Spirit was not a temporary possession but an abiding presence. The Spirit "remained" (*menein*) on Jesus, a word that regularly indicates a continuing relationship elsewhere in the Gospel (e.g., 8:31; 15:4-10). Jesus would eventually give the Spirit to believers, but that did not mean he would give it away. No other prophet or Messiah would succeed Jesus.[11]

At a third level, John's baptismal ministry provided a context in which Jesus' divinity was made known. John bore witness that Jesus ranked before him since he was before him (1:30). This recalls for readers what the prologue said about the Word of God becoming flesh in the person of Jesus, God's only begotten Son (1:14-15). John's allusion to Jesus' preexistence shows that the title Son of God conveys a sense of divinity as well as messiahship. John announced that Jesus would baptize with the Holy Spirit (1:33), which meant that Jesus was the agent of God's own power. The Spirit was God's own gift, which was given to Jesus and through Jesus, the one who had come from above and made it possible for people to be born from above (3:3-5, 31, 35). When Jesus finally gave the Spirit to his disciples after Easter, he breathed it into them, just as God breathed the breath or "spirit" of life into Adam at the dawn of creation (20:22).[12]

A number of biblical texts used images of water to speak of the day when God would send his Spirit to enliven the people of Israel. According to the prophet Joel, for example, God said, "I will pour out my spirit on all flesh . . . even upon the menservants and maidservants in those days, I will pour out my spirit" (Joel 2:28-29). The expression "baptize with the Holy Spirit" suggests that Jesus would provide a divine washing or cleansing through the Spirit, as God told Ezekiel, "I will sprinkle clean water upon you, and you shall be clean from all your uncleannesses . . . and I will put my Spirit within you" (Ezek. 36:25-27). The idea of God purifying his people through the Spirit is reflected in a number of Jewish writings. One text, echoing Ezekiel's prophecy, said that God would cleanse humankind of "all wicked deeds with a spirit of holiness; like purifying waters he will shed upon him the spirit of truth" (1QS iv 20-21). According to another, God said, "I shall create for them a holy spirit, and I shall purify them so that they will not turn away from following me from that day and forever" (*Jub.* 1:23). By baptizing with the Spirit, Jesus would carry out the cleansing action God himself had promised to perform.

---

11. On succession in Johannine Christianity see pp. 228–29 below.
12. See Schnackenburg, *Gospel*, 1.305.

In this opening section of the narrative, water is associated with the Spirit and the revelation of several interrelated facets of Jesus' identity. The water John used for baptism did not cleanse people from sin but provided the context in which the Spirit revealed the Lamb of God, whose death would take away the sin of the world. The Spirit's descent marked Jesus as Israel's Messiah, who fulfilled the eschatological hopes rooted in the Scriptures. And the promise that Jesus, the Son of God, would baptize with the Spirit identified him as the one who wielded God's own power to purify and enliven people.

Water for Jewish Rites of Purification
(John 2:1-11)

Water continues to be associated with revelation at the wedding at Cana, where there were six stone jars ordinarily used for the Jewish rites of purification (2:6). Jesus had the jars filled with water which he turned into wine. We have seen (pp. 77–82) that the sign confirmed that Jesus was the Messiah foretold in the Law and the Prophets, and that it revealed his divine glory to those who believed in him. This sign also anticipated the "hour" of his death and resurrection, which would be the completion of his messianic work and glorification. By transforming the water in the stone water jars, Jesus also transformed the way purification was to be understood.

The use of water for purification was a widely known Jewish practice. Unlike John's baptism, which was apparently administered only once, most Jewish ablutions were performed whenever someone became unclean. Uncleanness could be contracted in various ways, by contact with the carcass of an unclean creature such as a pig, a raven, or a lizard, for instance, or by touching a human corpse. It was also connected with skin diseases, with eating or lying down in a house with rot in its walls, and with emissions from the sexual organs. Uncleanness meant that a person was excluded from the place of worship and from close contact with other members of the community. It could usually be remedied by washing with water and waiting for a period of time. Stone vessels were especially important for purification, since stone was not subject to contagion as were vessels made of other materials.[13] Although most devout Jews performed ablutions before praying,[14] the Pharisees went further, applying the strin-

---

13. On unclean creatures see Lev. 11:25, 28, 40; on corpses see Num. 19:11-13; on skin diseases see Lev. 13:6, 34; 14:8; on rot in houses see Lev. 14:47; and on emissions from sexual organs see Lev. 15:5-33. Cf. Jacob Neusner, *The Idea of Purity in Ancient Judaism* (SJLA 1; Leiden: Brill, 1973) 7–71; Webb, *John the Baptizer and Prophet*, 95–132. On vessels of stone see *m. Beṣa* 2:2-3; Str-B 2.406–7.

14. Jth. 12:6-8; *Epistle of Aristeas* 305–6; *Sib. Or.* 3.591–93. See Webb, *John the Baptizer and Prophet*, 109 n. 47.

gent purity demanded of priests in the temple to life in their own homes, which involved elaborate washing of cooking utensils and personal purification (cf. Mark 7:3-4). The Dead Sea sect developed even more extensive systems of lustration, as did certain Jewish ascetics.[15]

The transformation of the water at Cana indicates that purification would now be accomplished through revelation. Ritual ablutions were an integral part of the processes by which Jewish people cleansed themselves from physical and moral defilement. In John's Gospel, sin is conceived radically as the deep-seated human antipathy toward God, which is expressed in one's manner of life. God purges away the hatred at the root of sin by revealing the glory of his love for the world in the death of his Son. Through that revelation, God "cleanses" by transforming sin into faith, and in so doing replaces the system of Jewish ritual purification.[16]

Birth from Water and the Spirit
(3:1-36)

The theme of water developed in the first two chapters reaches a confluence in chapter 3. The images in this passage are developed gradually. We have already seen (pp. 133–35) how the evangelist initially made the suggestive observation that Nicodemus came to Jesus "by night" (3:2) but did not disclose the significance of the darkness until later (3:19-21). Similarly, water is mentioned only briefly at the beginning of the chapter in connection with new birth (3:5), but its import is made clearer in the subsequent discussion of baptism (3:22-26). The conclusion of the chapter reiterates many of the themes mentioned earlier—belief and unbelief, above and below, testimony, the Spirit, and eternal life—helping to integrate the parts of this chapter into a whole (3:31-36).[17]

Jesus told Nicodemus, "Truly, truly, I say to you, unless one is born of water and the Spirit, he cannot enter the kingdom of God" (3:5). The sudden reference to water in this conversation is peculiar, and some have suggested that it refers to natural conception through seminal fluid or to physical birth out of the water in the womb. The wider literary context, however, shows that the water connotes ritual washing. Earlier in the Gospel, water was associated with John's baptismal practices and with Jewish purification rites. Both would have been appropriate in a conversation

15. E.g., Bannus in Josephus, *Life* 2 §§11–12 and the Essenes in his *J.W.* 2.8.2 §§119–61. See Webb, *John the Baptizer and Prophet*, 112–16.

16. Cf. Dodd, *Interpretation*, 299–303; Brown, *Gospel*, 1.104; Barrett, *Gospel*, 192.

17. Chapters 3 and 4 have the same structure: an initial encounter (3:1-21; 4:1-30), an interlude (3:22-30; 4:31-38), and a conclusion (3:31-36; 4:39-42). See my "Hearing, Seeing, and Believing in the Gospel of John," *Bib* 70 (1989) 332–35. In chapter 4 the idea of food is introduced in the first scene but not developed until the interlude (4:8, 31-34). The use of water in chapter 3 follows an identical pattern (3:5, 22-26).

with Nicodemus since he was one of "the Jews," who presumably would have been familiar with "the purifications of the Jews" mentioned in 2:6, and he was a Pharisee and a leader of the Jews in Jerusalem, the group that had sent a delegation to question John about his identity and baptismal practices (1:19, 24; 3:1).[18]

In this initial encounter, Jesus gave washing with water a place in the process of new birth, closely connecting it with the work of the Spirit; but the emphasis falls on the Spirit rather than the water. Jesus' preceding remark to Nicodemus said that one must be "born from above" but said nothing about water (3:3). His subsequent comments sharply distinguish between birth from the flesh and birth from the Spirit and repeatedly stress the need to be born "from above" and "of the Spirit," but he does not mention water again (3:6-8). The use of water is assumed; the action of the Spirit is emphasized.[19]

The meaning of birth through water and the Spirit should be understood in terms of faith. Being born from above means coming to faith in Jesus, who came from above. Faith is new birth because through it people enter into the relationship with God that issues in eternal life. The visible anchor point for faith is the cross (3:14-16).[20] Those who believe discern in Jesus' crucifixion the consummate expression of God's love for the world. They also come to know that Jesus resumed his heavenly glory through his physical elevation on a gibbet (see pp. 209–14). Those who do not believe cannot recognize the transcendent reality that Jesus and his followers conveyed through earthly speech. Their purview is bounded by what is below, and they face the prospect of perishing under divine condemnation (3:18).

The significance of water in this process is made clearer in an interlude that explicitly mentions baptism (3:22-30). The episode refers to disputes involving the three different persons or groups that have been prominent in the first three chapters. (a) Jesus and his disciples were in Judea, baptizing (3:22). A later comment explains that only the disciples performed baptisms (4:2), but the text clearly associates the practice of baptism using water with Jesus and his followers. (b) John was baptizing at a place called Aenon, near the village of Salim, where there was much water (3:23). Many people came to him for baptism, and some of John's disciples eventu-

18. For a summary and discussion of views on water in 3:5 see Burge, *The Anointed Community*, 161–65.
19. Some have suggested that 3:5 argues for the need to make public entry into the community of faith through water. See Rensberger, *Johannine Faith*, 57–59; C. H. Cosgrove, "The Place Where Jesus Is: Allusions to Baptism and the Eucharist in the Fourth Gospel," *NTS* 35 (1989) 522–39, esp. 530–34. Yet the emphasis is not that baptism is necessary but that baptism without the Spirit is defective (Culpepper, *Anatomy*, 193; cf. Schnackenburg, *Gospel*, 1.369–70).
20. Burge, *The Anointed Community*, 169–70.

ally joined him. (c) There is a brief but significant mention of a Jew or possibly a group of Jews who were engaged in a controversy with John's disciples over issues of purification (*katharismos*), which was done with water (3:25; cf. 2:6).[21]

The disputes in this passage show how difficult it could be to distinguish between the ritual washings used by Jews, by John's disciples, and by the followers of Jesus. The differences were not readily apparent at the level of practice and could be understood only in terms of the contrast between the heavenly and the earthly. The text places John's disciples and their Jewish interlocutor in the same category: Despite their disagreements, both seemed to approach questions of purification on the same earthly plane. Like other "Jews," the followers of John belonged to the earth and spoke from an earthly perspective, and both groups resented the popularity of the baptism administered by Jesus and his followers (3:26; 4:1-2). Jesus, however, had come from above, and people received his baptism because it had been granted from heaven (3:27, 31). What made Jesus unique was not the rite that he and his followers performed but his own divine origin—a truth that could be grasped only by faith in the testimony borne to Jesus (3:33).

The Gospel intimates that the water used by Jesus and his followers should be connected with the baptismal practices of the early church. The temporal perspective of John 3 fuses the periods before and after Jesus' death and resurrection. There is no clear distinction between the words of the earthly Jesus and those of the Son of man who already "has ascended into heaven" (3:13). The shift from singular to plural forms of speech enables Jesus and Nicodemus to speak not only for themselves but for groups of Christians and Jews in later periods, as we have seen in our second chapter. Baptism with water was widely practiced by early Christians. It is reflected in the letters of Paul, the risen Christ's commission to baptize when making disciples of all nations (Matt. 28:19), the missionary activity of the disciples described in the book of Acts, and other sources. The Spirit was regularly associated with baptism, but the mode of connection varied. In some cases people were touched by the Spirit before becoming baptized (Acts 10:44-48); in other cases the Spirit came through the laying on of hands after baptism (19:5-6); and in still others the Spirit was said to work in and through the baptism (1 Cor. 12:12-13).

The Fourth Gospel closely connects baptism and the activity of the Spirit without fully elaborating the relationship.[22] A vital tension marks

21. Some early manuscripts say that John's disciples disputed with "Jews" rather than "a Jew" over purification.

22. For a survey of positions relating water and Spirit, see M. Vellanickal, *The Divine Sonship of Christians in the Johannine Writings* (Rome: Biblical Institute, 1977) 181–86; Burge, *The Anointed Community*, 165–69.

the two parts of the chapter. In the first part (3:5), water and the Spirit together are the agents of new birth. The text does not say whether water is the physical element in and through which the Spirit works or whether the application of water provides the occasion for the Spirit's activity, but both play a role in engendering the faith that is new birth. The next part of the chapter, however, says that the willingness to come to Jesus for baptism showed that God had already been at work; they came because it had been granted "from heaven" (3:26-27; cf. 6:44, 65). Here baptism does not initiate God's activity but is the fruit of God's activity; baptism is the consequence of a faith engendered through witness borne to Jesus (cf. 3:28-29, 32-34). In either case, baptism is the material sign of the Spirit's work.

John's Gospel maintains important connections and critical distinctions between water and Spirit and between baptism and discipleship. After joining water and Spirit in the process of new birth, the text immediately stresses the Spirit's freedom to "blow where it wills"; the Spirit's activity is connected with baptism but cannot be confined to baptism (3:5-8). The narrative context indicates that Jesus and his disciples practiced baptism with water, while recognizing that there were forms of lustration that do not convey the Spirit. The emphasis "is not that baptism is necessary but that any baptism which does not involve cleansing by the Spirit is defective."[23] Similarly, baptism is associated but not equated with discipleship. The text said that Jesus "was making and baptizing" disciples (4:1). This means that a disciple of Jesus would be baptized, but not that the reverse was true; we cannot assume that everyone who came for baptism automatically became a true disciple. The next verse adds that "Jesus himself did not baptize, but his disciples did" (4:2). This qualification maintains the vital tension between baptism and discipleship. Jesus' followers may have performed baptisms (4:2), but Jesus alone could make disciples (4:1); the two actions were not identical.[24]

The water in this episode helps integrate the Gospel's first three chapters while introducing chapter 4. There is an explicit reminder of the testimony John had borne to Jesus when he had baptized across the Jordan (3:26-28; cf. 1:28). Jesus is also called "the bridegroom" (*nymphios*), which seems to recall the sign he performed at the wedding at Cana, turning the water into wine and thereby providing the guests with drink, which was the task of the bridegroom (*nymphios*, 3:39; cf. 2:9-10). The next episode relates how Jesus met a woman beside a well and offered to give her living water—an incident reminiscent of biblical courtship scenes (see

23. Culpepper, *Anatomy*, 193.
24. See the perceptive treatment by Teresa Okure, *The Johannine Approach to Mission: A Contextual Study of John 4:1-42* (Wunt 31; Tübingen: Mohr/Siebeck, 1988) 81–83.

pp. 48–49). Their encounter culminated not with a wedding but with the woman's testimony to Jesus, which brought her townspeople to meet him for themselves.

The location of the water at Aenon contributes to its significance in a secondary way. The word *Aenon* means "springs" in Aramaic, and the evangelist explained that "there were many waters there" (3:22-23). He described the location of Aenon by relating it to the village of Salim, which suggests that he expected at least some readers to know where Salim was. Readers familiar with the Greek translation of the Scriptures and other Jewish writings may have heard that there was a village named Salem or Salim in the vicinity of Shechem, in the region of Samaria.[25] It was best known from the story of Jacob, who stopped there when he bought the piece of land mentioned in John 4:5 and used it as a place of worship (cf. 4:20). Those who knew these stories may have seen in John's movement to Aenon a foreshadowing of Jesus' ministry in Samaria, where he would offer Jacob's descendants living water and a new way of worship.[26]

LIVING WATER

When Jesus arrived at Jacob's well, he offered a Samaritan woman "living water," an expression that introduces another phase of the water motif. The woman's response to Jesus' offer prompted a spirited interchange about the nature of the living water and true worship. Then the motif recedes for several chapters. The invalid at Bethzatha mentions the troubled water in the pool, but Jesus ignores it, commanding the man to rise and walk. The motif returns with full force only in chapter 7, when Jesus calls out to the people in the temple, inviting anyone who is thirsty to come and drink, promising that out of his heart "living water" will flow. The invitation echoes what was said to the Samaritan woman, indicating that these texts should be taken together.

Jacob's Well and the Spring
of Living Water
(4:1-42)

Jacob's well near the village of Sychar is the setting for Jesus' encounter with the Samaritan woman. Their conversation about water is complex and multilayered; meanings are often suggested rather than stated. One of Jesus' initial remarks, however, focuses the discussion. He told the woman, "If you knew the gift of God and who it is who is saying to you

25. Gen. 33:18; Jer. 41:5 [48:5 LXX]; *Jub.* 30:1.
26. On the location of Aenon and its significance for John 3–4, see M.-E. Boismard, "Aenon, près de Salem," *RB* 80 (1973) 218–29.

'Give me a drink,' you would have asked him and he would have given you living water" (4:10). According to this comment, there were two things the woman should know about: the identity of Jesus and the meaning of "living water," which was the "gift" he mentioned. The giver and the gift must be understood together. The text discloses the identity of Jesus in several stages with different aspects of the water apparent at each stage. Although water is most prominent in the first part of the conversation (4:7-15), the intriguing comment about the water jar at the conclusion of their encounter (4:28) indicates that the imagery must be understood in the context of the whole passage.

The first level of the conversation about water deals with disputes stemming from national identity. The Samaritan woman recognized that Jesus was a Jew, a perception that was accurate as far as it went, and when he asked her for a drink she was surprised, since "Jews have no dealings with Samaritans" (4:9). Jesus responded by telling the woman about the living water he had to give. Although Jesus was Jewish, he crossed the line separating Jews from Samaritans by offering the woman living water. At this level the water is a gift that can erode the barrier between the two peoples.

Some of the reasons Jews had "no dealings with Samaritans" had to do with purity, which was associated with water earlier in John's Gospel. Jewish people often considered Samaritans to be unclean, and a Jewish council adopted a ruling in A.D. 65–66 deeming Samaritan women "menstruants from the cradle." This meant that they were to be treated as if they were in a constant state of impurity.[27] Samaritan worship on Mount Gerizim also raised the specter of defilement (4:20-24). Jews often charged that Samaritans were idolaters who worshiped what they did not know, contending that it was nothing but "filth" that Samaritans revered on their holy mountain.[28]

Jews and Samaritans sometimes used the expression "living water" for flowing water, like that bubbling up from a stream or spring, in contrast to the water entombed in a cistern. Significantly, the Scriptures used by both groups said that "living water" was to be used when purifying people from defilement incurred by skin diseases, touching a corpse, and bodily discharges like menstruation.[29] Jewish sources also envisioned the time when God would wash people from the uncleanness incurred through idolatry (Ezek. 36:25). In the context of acknowledged national differences, the living water imagery helps convey the idea that Jesus offered a gift that would remove the taint from the Samaritans and lead to their inclusion in the worshiping community.

27. *m. Nid.* 4:1; *b. Shabb.* 16b; *y. Shabb.* 3c.
28. *Gen. Rab.* 81:3.
29. "Living water" was used to purify from skin disease (Lev. 14:5-6, 50-52), bodily discharges (15:13), and corpse defilement (Num. 19:17). Cf. *m. Miqw.* 1:8.

A second level of meaning emerges in connection with the disclosure that Jesus was a prophet and Messiah. The woman realized that it was incongruous for Jesus to offer her ordinary water since the roadside well was deep and he had nothing with which to draw. She exclaimed, "Are you greater than our father Jacob who gave us the well, and drank from it himself, and his sons, and his cattle?" (4:12). Despite the woman's incredulity, readers would know that Jesus was indeed greater than Jacob. The woman realized this too after Jesus demonstrated his knowledge about her marital history, and she called him a prophet (4:19). Later she spoke about the Messiah, a prophetic figure similar to Moses (see pp. 42–44) who would tell them "all things" (4:25). Jesus declared that he was this Messiah, and since he had told the woman "all things" about herself, she wondered if this might be true (4:26, 29).

Like the living water that springs up at this point in the text, the imagination of the Gospel's readers must also leap up to a new level in order to catch the meaning of the symbolism. Jesus said, "Whoever drinks of this water will thirst again, but whoever drinks of the water that I shall give him will never thirst; the water that I shall give him will become in him a spring of water welling up to eternal life" (4:13-14). The water in Jacob's well was bound to a place; it needed to be hauled out by hand, and it quenched thirst only for a short time. But the water Jesus promised was not bound to one place; it would spring up within a person so that he or she would never thirst again. The water from Jacob's well could extend life for a while, but living water from Jesus would issue into life everlasting, which in John's Gospel refers to life lived in relationship with God. The gift is more than ordinary water because it issues in eternal life, and the giver is greater than Jacob because he is the prophet-Messiah.

Jesus' comments are reminiscent of the way the prophet Moses miraculously provided water for Israel in the desert, which would be appropriate for the one who fulfilled the Samaritan hope for a Moses-like messiah.[30] According to tradition, the water Moses miraculously gave Israel was not bound to one place. He threw a tree into the bitter water at Marah and it became sweet (Exod. 15:3) and later struck a rock that released a stream of water for the people to drink (Exod. 17:3, 6; Num. 20:4, 10-11). Eventually God commanded Moses, "Gather the people together and I will give them water" (Num. 21:16). When the people assembled, they sang, "Spring up, O well—Sing to it!" (21:17). According to tradition, the water that

---

30. Some Jewish sources say that Jacob actually did make water spring up in a well. See Birger Olsson, *Structure and Meaning in the Fourth Gospel: A Text-Linguistic Analysis of John 2:1-11 and 4:1-42* (CB 6; Lund: Gleerup, 1974) 169–70. Nevertheless, John 4 stresses that Jesus is different from Jacob yet the fulfillment of Samaritan expectations, which were informed by traditions about Moses. Samaritan sources focus attention on the water Moses gave (*Memar Marqah* 4.4; 4.8; 5.3; 6.3).

sprang up at different times and places in the desert actually came from a single miraculous well. Like the water Jesus promised, it accompanied the people as they traveled. The tradition also pointed out that God gave them the water at a place called Mattanah, which means "gift" (Num. 21:18; cf. John 4:10a).[31]

Besides water, Moses had given people the law, which was understood to be the gift of God and a source of life in relationship to God. Both Jews and Samaritans likened the law to water. Extant Samaritan sources speak of the law as "a well of living water dug by a prophet whose like has not arisen from mankind. The water in it is from the mouth of the Divine One." Therefore, those who "are thirsty for the waters of life" should know that "mighty rivers are before us," for God "gave a perfect law to His servants to provide life and length of days."[32] Although these passages are late, Jewish sources attest to similar views in the first century. The Damascus Document identified the well mentioned in Num. 21:17 with the Law of Moses, which was a well of "living water,"[33] and Philo said that the water that sprang up in Moses' well was divine wisdom, for which the law was a channel.[34]

The traditional use of water imagery for divine wisdom and the Mosaic law made it well suited to describe the revelation given by the prophet-Messiah who declares "all things" (4:25, 29). A connection between water and revelation is analogous to the use of light and bread for wisdom and revelation elsewhere in the Gospel.[35] The woman's response to Jesus also suggests the revelatory quality of water. The evangelist observed that the woman "left her water jar" before inviting her townspeople to meet the one who had told her "all things" about herself (4:28). Elsewhere the evangelist uses the word *leave* (*aphienai*) when someone abandons something or leaves it behind.[36] The woman came to the well to draw the kind of water that quenches physical thirst but went away without her jar, pondering what Jesus had revealed to her (4:7, 28-29). The shift suggests that

31. On traditions concerning the well see Olsson, *Structure and Meaning*, 162–73. Cf. Germain Bienaimé, *Moïse et le don de l'eau dans la tradition juive ancienne: targum et midrash* (AnBib 98; Rome: Biblical Institute, 1984).

32. *Memar Marqah* 6.3 and 2.1. Cf. the Samaritan liturgy: "I seek to drink now a little water from wisdom's fount, a well whose waters bubble up from the depth of righteousness. All who drink there are filled with living water." Quoted by J. MacDonald, *The Theology of the Samaritans* (London: SCM, 1964) 276.

33. CD vi 2-5; cf. iii 12-17a; xix 32-35.

34. Philo, *Drunkenness* 112–13; *Dreams* 2.271.

35. On "living water" as revelation see Bultmann, *Gospel*, 180–87; Pancaro, *The Law in the Fourth Gospel*, 473–85.

36. *Aphienai* is used for "abandonment" in 8:29; 10:12; 14:18; 16:32; for "cessation" in 4:52; 12:7; for "release" in 11:44; 18:8; cf. 20:23; for "permission" in 11:48; for "departure" in 4:3; 16:28; and for the peace Jesus left for his followers in 14:27.

the water she needed was the revelation that Jesus was the Messiah for whom her people had been waiting.[37]

Yet neither Jesus nor his revelation could be contained in the vessel of Samaritan tradition; he transcended Samaritan hopes even as he fulfilled them. Like other Samaritans, the woman expected the prophet to establish a form of worship that was congruent with the Law of Moses. Jesus did so, but in an unexpected way. The law mandated that there be a central locus for worship (Deut. 12:5), but Samaritans and Jews disputed whether the place was to be Jerusalem or Mount Gerizim. Jesus said that the locus of true worship was God's Spirit and truth rather than a geographical location. Like the law, Jesus' revelation provided for true worship; yet its form was not derived from the law, and it actually transcended disputes involving the law. The woman's source of drinking water and the Samaritan form of worship were bound to a place, but neither the living water nor the worship Jesus foretold were confined to one location; they were of another order.

The expanding scope of the discussion culminates in a third level of meaning, which concerns the divine and universal significance of Jesus and the living water. Initially the Samaritan woman did not "know" Jesus and her people did not "know" what they worshiped (John 4:10, 22). At the end of the episode they came to "know" that Jesus was truly the Savior of the world (4:42), and in knowing Jesus they also came to the knowledge of God from which true worship flows. The title "Savior" points to this divine dimension of Jesus' identity, since in the Fourth Gospel people are "saved" by coming to know God through faith in Jesus (cf. 12:44-45). Salvation came *from* the Jews but it was *for* the world (4:22, 42). As the world's Savior, Jesus transcended the disputes that divided Jews from Samaritans and offered water that would quench the thirst of "whoever" drank from it.

If Jesus is both Messiah and Savior of the world, the living water is both revelation and the Spirit.[38] The Old Testament often identified the Spirit as God's gift and used water imagery when speaking about the outpouring of the Spirit upon Israel, as we noted in connection with John 1:19-34. Moreover, when Jesus said that the water would "well up" or

37. Cf. Brown, *Gospel*, 1.173. Some argue that she left the water pot so that Jesus could drink from it (Barrett, *Gospel*, 240), or that it was unnecessary to take it with her since she would return anyway (Gail R. O'Day, *Revelation in the Fourth Gospel: Narrative Mode and Theological Claim* [Philadelphia: Fortress, 1986] 75; Schnackenburg, *Gospel*, 1.443). The detail functions much like the reference to "night" in 3:2. It does not have independent significance, but must be associated with similar images elsewhere in the episode.

38. Some interpreters insist that the water is mainly either revelation (cf. Pancaro, *The Law in the Fourth Gospel*, 473–85) or the Spirit (cf. Burge, *The Anointed Community*, 96–99), but many acknowledge that both aspects are included. For this position and a survey of the debate, see Brown, *Gospel*, 1.178–80; Olsson, *Structure and Meaning*, 212–18.

"spring up" (*hallomai*) to eternal life within a person (4:14), he used an expression that sometimes referred to the effect of God's Spirit on figures in the Old Testament.[39] Other early Christian writings made a similar connection between water and the Spirit.[40]

The interplay between revelation and the Spirit that was apparent earlier in the Gospel is further developed here by the dual temporal perspective reflected in the passage: The narrative speaks simultaneously about the future and the present, about what "is coming and now is" (4:23), about a gift that was given to Jesus' followers after his return to the Father yet presaged in what he offered people while on earth. The living water is the Spirit that would be given after Jesus was glorified (7:39), yet this was anticipated by Jesus' offer of living water to the Samaritan woman, who left her water jar to tell others about him. During his ministry Jesus could "declare" to the Samaritan woman "all things" (4:25), yet after his departure it would be the Spirit that would remind the disciples of "all things" Jesus had said (14:26) and "declare" to them what was to come (16:13). Living water encompasses both aspects of meaning in a single image.

Troubled Waters at Bethzatha

Water often helps to convey Jesus' identity, but it does not always do so. This is demonstrated by Jesus' encounter with the invalid at Bethzatha, whose attention centered on the healing properties of the water in the pool. Instead of using or transforming this water, Jesus bypassed it entirely. An important term in this story is *hygiēs,* which means "healthy" or "well." The evangelist uses the term repeatedly in this passage (5:6, 9, 11, 14, 15) and when recalling this incident later (7:23) but nowhere else in the Gospel. The invalid perceived the connection between water and health in an almost magical way (see pp. 85–86), apparently thinking that a well-timed entry into the pool would virtually guarantee healing. Jesus gave the man his health without using the water at all. He simply commanded the man to rise, and healing occurred immediately. There was no connection between Jesus' power to restore someone's health and the mysterious water of the pool.

Although the invalid was Jewish, many in the ancient world shared his attitude toward water sources. Establishments like Bethzatha were found in various places, and their water was typically thought to promote health, often because it was associated with supernatural power. Vitruvius Pollio, a leading builder of the Augustan age, said that the "healthiest regions and suitable springs of water therein be chosen first of all for all temples

---

39. Judg. 14:6, 19; 15:14; 1 Sam. 10:10.
40. Cf. Acts 2:38; 8:20; 10:45; 11:17; Heb. 6:4.

and particularly for Asclepius" and other gods of healing, for when the sick "are treated with water from wholesome fountains, they will recover more quickly."[41] The orator Aelius Aristides extolled the virtues of the water at one of these sanctuaries by saying that "the water is brought from a spot that is healthful and promotes health, inasmuch as it comes forth from the shrine and the feet of the savior," Asclepius. "For when bathed with it many recovered their eyesight, while many were cured of ailments of the chest and regained their necessary breath by drinking from it. In some cases it cured the feet, in others something else."[42]

The troubled water of Bethzatha had taken on a life of its own in the mind of the invalid, but it was not the kind of "living water" Jesus promised the Samaritan woman. The encounter by the pool cautions against thinking that water is inherently revelatory. The water at Bethzatha is not connected with the Spirit's work, as in John 1 and 3; it is not transformed as it was at Cana; Jesus does not even talk about it, as he did in Samaria. Significantly, the water was not instrumental in healing, as it will be in the case of the blind beggar in John 9. At Bethzatha, Jesus' life-giving word did not work through the water but was an alternative to it.

The Feast of Booths:
Rivers of Living Water

The theme of living water resurfaces when Jesus returns to Jerusalem for the feast of Booths. Like the image of light, which we discussed in the previous chapter, the water imagery is set in the context of debates about Jesus' identity: Some in the crowd thought Jesus was a good man, and others argued that he was deceiving people, yet everyone was afraid to speak openly about Jesus because the Jews sought to kill him (7:12-13). Jesus went into the temple and taught, and on the last day of the festival he stood up and cried out, "If anyone thirst let him come to me, and let him who believes in me drink. As the scripture has said, 'Out of his heart shall flow rivers of living water.'" The evangelist explained that "he said this about the Spirit, which those who believed in him were about to receive; for as yet there was no Spirit, for Jesus had not yet been glorified" (7:37-39).

We have seen that this complex passage must be understood in terms of primary and secondary levels of meaning: The primary level concerns Jesus and the secondary level concerns discipleship (pp. 12–14). Living water is explicitly identified with the Spirit, although its revelatory aspects also play a role in the text, and the significance of the imagery is associated

41. Vitruvius, *On Architecture* 1.2.7.
42. Aelius Aristides, *Orations* 39.6 and 15. On other waters purported to heal see Pausanias, *Description of Greece* 4.31.4; 5.5.11; 6.22.7; 8.19.2.

with the different facets of Jesus' identity. The reference to rivers of living water flowing from someone's heart, or literally "belly" (*koilia*), is not a quotation of any one biblical text but a statement that draws together themes found in a number of Old Testament passages. The difficulty in firmly identifying the quotation with a single biblical source actually enables readers to relate various Old Testament passages to facets of Jesus' identity noted in the surrounding context.[43]

The debates first consider the question of Jesus' identity as a teacher and his relationship to the Law of Moses (7:14-24). We saw in the last chapter how Jesus argued that his teaching was consistent with the law but not derived from it; his claim to be the source of living water conveys the same message through its imagery. In Jewish tradition, water was often used for wisdom and the law. It was said that the "teaching of the wise is a fountain of life" (Prov. 13:14), that "the fountain of wisdom is a flowing stream" (18:4), and that those who delight in the law of the Lord are "planted by streams of water" (Ps. 1:3). For Philo, the divine word, or *logos,* was "full of the stream of wisdom" flowing "from that perennial fountain"; the logos was a river pouring forth a "constant stream of words and doctrines ever sweet and fresh."[44] Ben Sira taught that those who feared the Lord would be given "the water of wisdom to drink," although once tasting it, they would "thirst for more" (Sir. 15:3; 24:21); and all who desired such a refreshing draught were invited to drink their fill from the Law of Moses, which poured forth rivers of divine wisdom (24:23-26).

Jesus' invitation to come and drink is set in the context of the feast of Booths. Two biblical texts associated with the festival contained similar invitations, which the Targums connected with the law. Isaiah 12:3 said, "With joy you will draw water from the wells of salvation," and the Targum paraphrased it to say, "you will receive a new teaching with joy." Similarly, Zech. 13:1 said, "There shall be a fountain opened for the house of David and the inhabitants of Jerusalem to cleanse them from sin and uncleanness," and the Targum rendered it, "At that time the teaching of the law shall be revealed like a spring of water to the house of David and the inhabitants of Jerusalem." Similar references appear in other sources.[45]

Those who shared their learning with others were considered channels of wisdom's waters. The Scriptures said that "the teaching of the wise is a fountain of life" (Prov. 13:14) and expressed delight in someone who had the law within his heart, or literally "belly" (*koilia,* Ps. 40:8). Ben Sira

43. For discussion of the interpretive problems see Brown, *Gospel,* 1.320–24; Burge, *The Anointed Community,* 88–92; Anthony Tyrrel Hanson, *The Prophetic Gospel: A Study of John and the Old Testament* (Edinburgh: T. &. T. Clark, 1991) 99–115.

44. *Dreams* 2.245; *Flight and Finding* 97; *Posterity* 129; *Allegorical Interpretation* 2.87.

45. *Tg. Isa.* 55:1; *Mekilta* "Vayassa" 1.64-81 (Lauterbach ed., vol. 2, pp. 89–90); 4 Ezra 14:47; Bar. 3:12. Cf. Str-B 2.435-36.

compared his role as a teacher to a canal going forth from the river of wisdom flowing from the law (Sir. 24:30-31; 51:24). A hymn writer at Qumran gave thanks that he had been placed near the streams of God's wisdom and could serve as a source of instruction for others, saying that God had put into his mouth "a fount of living waters which shall not fail" (1QH viii 4, 16). In the wake of Jerusalem's destruction, people lamented the loss of leadership, saying that "the fountains from which we used to drink have withheld their streams." But they were assured that such "fountains came from the Law" and that "the Law will abide"; therefore if they "look upon the law and are intent upon wisdom . . . the fountain will not dry up" (*2 Bar.* 77:13-16). Rabbinic sources also say that one who occupies himself with the study of the law for its own sake "is made like to a never-failing spring and like to a river that flows ever more mightily" (*m. ʾAbot* 6:1).

If the interchange earlier in the chapter identified Jesus as one whose teaching is consistent with the law, the invitation to drink the living water flowing from his heart is, at that level, an invitation to partake of divine wisdom. Yet this was not wisdom derived from the law or learned through rabbinic channels. Jesus brought revelation that came directly from God, and his insistence that the thirsty come to him and drink tacitly displaces other sources of water. The Scriptures themselves are not the sources of water but witnesses to Jesus, the true fountain of water, a figure who "cries out" to people as divine wisdom personified (John 7:37; Prov. 1:20; 8:1-2).

A second level of the water symbolism corresponds to the disputes over Jesus' identity as prophet and Messiah (John 7:25-52). We saw in the last chapter that there is a confluence of several streams of Jewish messianic expectations in this section: Some people were looking for "the prophet" like Moses, others for a Messiah whose origin was unknown, and still others for the Davidic Messiah who would come from Bethlehem. Jesus' adversaries tried to discredit him because he was a Galilean who met none of these expectations, but through the disputes and water symbolism the evangelist helps readers to see that Jesus actually fulfilled all of these expectations.

As soon as Jesus invited people to drink of the living water he offered, some people said, "This is really the prophet." Their conclusion was plausible since Moses was the prophet who had given Israel water to drink when they sojourned in the wilderness. The explicit connection between Jesus' words and the last day of the feast of Booths reinforces this idea (7:37) since the festival commemorated the forty years the people of Israel were encamped in the desert. The celebration took place in September or October, toward the end of the long dry season when the worshipers were concerned about the availability of water. Stories of Moses providing water for their ancestors in the wilderness were a part of the festival context

(Exod. 17:1-7; Num. 20:2-13). Jesus' reference to what the Scripture said seems to echo some of the poetic accounts of these incidents: "He opened the rock, and water gushed forth; it flowed through the desert like a river" (Ps. 105:41) and "He made streams to come out of the rock, and caused waters to flow down like rivers" (78:16). Since Moses had formerly made rivers of water flow for thirsty people, the prophet like Moses would presumably do the same when he appeared.[46]

Others in the crowd declared that Jesus must be the Messiah (John 7:41). This possibility was debated just before he issued his invitation to come and drink. Some objected that the Messiah's origin was to be unknown, and everyone knew that Jesus was from Galilee (7:27). Jesus, however, indicated that his origin actually was unknown since his hearers did not know the God who had sent him (7:28). Therefore he met the criterion for messiahship. The invitation to come and drink seems to be consistent with that claim. Extant texts rarely mention the Messiah's hidden origin, but one of the few that does associated the Messiah with "an inexhaustible spring of righteousness, and many springs of wisdom surrounded it, and all the thirsty drank from them and were filled with wisdom" (*1 Enoch* 48:1, 10; 49:1).

Still others in the crowd voiced what was an apparently contradictory view. Rather than expecting the Messiah's origin to be unknown, they argued that it must be known: The Messiah was to be a descendant of David and come from Bethlehem, as the Scripture said (John 7:42; Mic. 5:2). The evangelist assumed that readers would know that Jesus was the Davidic Messiah foretold in Scripture (pp. 137–38). The invitation to "come and drink" can be related to the Davidic claim at two levels: the water itself and the Spirit signified by the water. A correlation between Davidic messiahship and water is indirect at best but can be made by connecting John's text with three verses from the final chapters of Zechariah. At the feast of Booths Jesus said he would provide the "living water" promised in the Scriptures, seeming to recall Zech. 14:8, which said that "living water" would flow out of the temple. Later, water flowed from the side of the crucified Jesus, and the evangelist connected it with the piercing mentioned in Zech. 12:10. The other pertinent passage is Zech. 13:1, which said that one day there would be "a fountain opened for the house of David"; this may have suggested connections between flowing water and the Davidic Messiah. Connections between the Spirit and Davidic messiahship are stronger. In John 1:32-33 Jesus was identified as the one on

46. A late Jewish text made the connection explicit. "As the first redeemer was, so shall the latter redeemer be." "As the former redeemer made a well to rise, so will the latter Redeemer bring up water, as it is stated, 'And a fountain shall come forth from the house of the Lord, and shall water the valley of Shittim'" (*Eccl. Rab.* 1:8; cf. Joel 3:18).

whom God's Spirit descended and remained, which was an identifying mark of the Davidic Messiah according to Isa. 11:3 and other passages. The disputes at the feast of Booths reveal that Jesus fulfills the roles of both prophet and Messiah, and his invitation to partake of living water helps integrate these facets of his identity.

The third phase of the debates concerns Jesus' divinity (John 8:12-30), helping in retrospect to disclose the divine level of the water imagery. In this section the divine connotations of the "I Am" expression are made increasingly clear. Jesus told his hearers, "You will die in your sins unless you believe that I Am" (8:24), and said that "when you have lifted up the Son of man, then you will know that I Am" (8:28). These passages echo portions of Isaiah in which God is the speaker (Isa. 43:10) and couple the "I Am" with the title "Son of man," which has divine connotations in John's Gospel (1:51; 3:13-14; 9:38). The reference to Jesus' adversaries "lifting up" the Son of man presages Jesus' elevation on the cross, which in John's Gospel is a revelatory event that discloses Jesus' unity with the Father.

The call to come and drink from the living water is congruent with the divine aspect of Jesus' identity. According to the Scriptures, Moses struck the rock in the wilderness, but it was God who made the water pour forth. The section of Isaiah in which the "I Am" frequently appears uses images reminiscent of the exodus to envision Israel's future deliverance, and there too God is the one who provides rivers of water for those who thirst (Isa. 41:18; 43:20; 48:21; 49:10). Readers familiar with Isaiah might also have heard in Jesus' invitation to come and drink an echo of God's invitation to let "every one who thirsts come to the waters" (55:1). The prophet Jeremiah called God himself "the fountain of living waters" (Jer. 2:13; 17:13), and later Jewish writings continued to speak of God in this way.[47] The divine connotations of the water source are reinforced by the mention of the Spirit in John 7:39, for God is the one who pours out water on the thirsty ground and gives the Spirit to the children of Israel (Isa. 44:3).

The festival context reinforces the divine aspect of Jesus' words. He spoke of the living water while teaching in the temple, which was where one of the most important rituals of the festival took place. Each morning the pilgrims gathered in the temple carrying festal plumes called *lulabs,* which were made of branches from palm, myrtle, and willow—trees typically associated with water. They also brought citrons, suggesting fruitfulness (Lev. 23:40). A priest would appear with a golden pitcher in his hand and process out of the temple through the streets of the city to the pool of Siloam. There he would scoop up a pitcher full of water and return to the temple. When the procession reached the Water Gate, which led into

---

47. Philo, *Flight and Finding* 197–98. God is connected with "living water" in 4QDibHam v 2-3 and with the Spirit in v 15.

the sanctuary, the ram's horn was blown three times. The priest bearing the pitcher climbed the ramp leading to the top of the altar, where he held his hand high and poured out the water into a small bowl with a spout that drained it onto the altar. The ram's horn was sounded again, the priests processed around the altar, and all the worshipers shook their lulabs, shouting, "Save us, O Lord, we beseech you; O Lord we beseech you, give us prosperity!" (Ps. 118:25). The outpouring of the water and the words of the crowd were a prayer that God would send the life-giving rains again and grant prosperity to his people during the coming year (*m. Sukk.* 4:1-10).

The rituals in the temple recalled the water God gave Israel in the wilderness and anticipated the time when God would be present with them in triumph. The prophet Ezekiel envisioned the time when God's glory would return to the house of the Lord and rivers of water would flow out from it, making the desert bloom (Ezek. 47:1). The book of Joel said that "a fountain shall come forth from the house of the Lord" when God came to dwell in Zion (Joel 3:17-18). Most significantly, the book of Zechariah ends with a vision of the day when God would come to reign as king over all the earth. When that happened, "living waters shall flow out from Jerusalem, half of them to the eastern sea and half of them to the western sea; it shall continue in summer as in winter" (Zech. 14:8). In other words, the cycles of rain and drought would end, and streams of water would flow year round, ensuring life and prosperity. On that day all the nations of the earth would go up to Jerusalem to worship God and celebrate the feast of Booths (14:16).[48] Jesus' invitation to come and drink from him shows that the hopes of the festival are fulfilled in him. People would not discern God's gift of life by scrutinizing changes in the weather but through the Spirit given by the crucified and risen Jesus.

Jesus' words have the kind of universal scope Zechariah envisioned. He invited "anyone" (*tis*) who was thirsty to come and drink the living water that would flow from him after his death. This does not mean that everyone would be receptive to Jesus' invitation—the preceding verses warned that Jesus' detractors would seek without finding him (John 7:28-36)—but the literary context suggests that Jesus was extending his invitation beyond the traditional confines of Israel. Immediately before Jesus offered living water to anyone who was thirsty, the crowd wondered if they would have trouble finding him because he was going into the Diaspora to teach the Greeks (7:35-36). Jesus had been speaking of his return to God through his death and resurrection, but the text intimates that his teaching would indeed be taken to the Greeks through his disciples (see pp. 21–22). The promise of living water anticipated the coming of the Spirit, which the

---

48. On these texts and the festival see *t. Sukk.* 3:1-18.

crucified and risen Jesus would give his disciples when he sent them into the world (7:39; 20:21-22).

The image of living water was consistent with the broad scope of the passage. Readers of Greek or Roman background who came into the Johannine circle may not readily have discerned the significance of the reference to Scripture or the allusions to Jewish tradition. Yet they would have understood that water was essential for life and that the best kind of drinking water was the "living" water flowing from a spring or stream.[49] There was widespread precedent for taking thirst as a metaphor for desire or longing, and the numinous connotations of living water would have been familiar to many Greek readers. Fresh flowing water was frequently associated with divine powers, and shrines to the Muses who inspired art, music, and poetry were often situated beside water sources. More important, the spirit of prophecy was associated with flowing water, and the shrines where oracles were delivered were often located by streams or springs. Delphi is the best-known example, but there were others as well. Plutarch explained that the "stream and spirit of prophecy is most divine and holy, whether it issue by itself through the air or come in the company of running waters."[50] The frequent connection between water and prophetic inspiration made it easy to use flowing water as a metaphor for inspired utterances. Lamenting the decline in prophecy in the late first century, Plutarch said it was as if the oracles "were streams of flowing water and a great drought of prophecy has spread over the land."[51]

The image of living water is taken *from* the biblical tradition, but is presented in a form that would be accessible *to* a wide audience. The familiar yet evocative connection between water and the Spirit would have been engaging to a broad spectrum of readers, encompassing in a single image the various dimensions of Jesus' identity debated in John 7–8: Jesus is the source of divine wisdom, God's prophet and Messiah, and the giver of God's own Spirit. Yet all the associations readers would have brought to the text are redefined in terms of Jesus' crucifixion. Jesus would be "glorified" (7:39) in death; water would flow from his side as he hung on the cross; the disciples would receive the Spirit from the one who displayed

---

49. In Latin as in Hebrew, "living water" (*aqua viva*) in springs and streams was distinguished from water in cisterns and ponds (Cato and Varro, *On Agriculture* 1.11.2). See Walter Bauer, *Das Johannesevangelium* (HNT 6; Tübingen: Mohr/Siebeck, 1933) 67; Martin Ninck, *Die Bedeutung des Wassers im Kult und Leben der Alten: Eine symbolgeschichtliche Untersuchung* (Philologus, Supp. 14/2; Leipzig: Dieterich, 1921) 1–46.

50. Plutarch, *Moralia* 432D; cf. 412B. Plutarch mentions shrines of Muses near springs in 402CD, quoting the poet Simonides to the same effect. On the connection between oracles and springs, see Pausanias, *Description of Greece* 7.21.11–13, and on sacred springs 3.23.2; 3.24.7; 9.34.4. Shrines were built near water sources in and around Palestine as well as in Greece; the most famous was Paneas at the northern edge of Galilee. Cf. Ninck, *Die Bedeutung des Wassers im Kult und Leben der Alten*, 47–99; Hans Dieter Betz, *Plutarch's Theological Writings and Early Christian Literature* (SCHNT 3; Leiden: Brill, 1975) 171–72.

51. *Moralia* 411F; cf. 414C. Cf Acts 16:13, 16.

the scars from his execution (19:34; 20:20-22). It would be the Spirit's task to bring people to know the wisdom of God revealed through the death of the Messiah, his Son.

The meaning of the passage is primarily christological, but on a second-ary level the water imagery issues in discipleship. We have seen (p.14) that the punctuation in the passage is ambiguous, allowing the words "Out of his heart shall flow rivers of living water" to apply to believers as well as to Jesus. Believers cannot give others revelation and the Spirit in the way that Jesus does; everyone must come to Jesus to drink. But those who receive the gift Jesus offers find it springing up within them to eternal life, as Jesus promised the Samaritan woman (4:14), and their witness to Jesus is a channel for the activity of the Spirit (15:26-27; 20:22-23).[52]

The christological significance of water and its implications for disciple-ship are developed in the story of the man born blind. Both symbols used in the debates at the feast of Booths—water and light—are incorporated into this dramatic sequence. The blind beggar was told to wash in the pool of Siloam, the place from which the water was drawn during the festival. The evangelist explained that the word *Siloam* meant "one who has been sent," enabling readers to connect the pool with Jesus, the prophet and Messiah "sent" from God (see pp. 101–3). After he washed in the pool of the "one who has been sent," the man's eyes were opened physically, and in the ensuing scenes he came to recognize who Jesus was. Some have detected baptismal overtones in the passage, because water was associated with baptism earlier in the Gospel and a number of early Christian sources occasionally identify baptism with "enlightenment," which would corre-spond to the beggar's receiving his sight. Nevertheless, baptism is not identified with enlightenment elsewhere in the Gospel, and the beggar's self-washing seems to run counter to the usual practice in which someone else did the baptizing. The primary symbolism in the chapter is christolog-ical, and issues of discipleship center on public profession of faith in Jesus, as Rudolf Schnackenburg has pointed out.[53] A baptismal interpretation of the blind man's washing lends itself to pastoral application but goes be-yond the Johannine context.

After the story of the blind beggar, the water motif subsides until the beginning of the last supper, when Jesus fills a basin and washes the feet of his disciples. We have already seen (pp. 115–18) that in the first part of the episode, washing foreshadows the cleansing effect of Jesus' death in love for his disciples, and that in the second part, washing connotes the kind of service Jesus' followers are to perform out of love for each other.

---

52. See E. C. Hoskyns, *The Fourth Gospel* (ed. F. N. Davey; 2d ed.; London: Faber, 1947) 322; Barrett, *Gospel*, 326–27.

53. See his summary and critique of baptismal interpretations in *Gospel*, 2.257–58.

We can therefore turn to the passage in which the water motif culminates: the crucifixion of Jesus.

THE FLOW OF BLOOD AND WATER

The Johannine account of the crucifixion says that Jesus was condemned to death shortly after midday. Suspended upon the cross, the one who had invited others to come and drink from him uttered the words, "I thirst" (19:28). When he died later that afternoon, "one of the soldiers pierced his side with a spear, and at once there came out blood and water. He who saw it has borne witness—his testimony is true, and he knows that he tells the truth—that you also may believe" (19:34-35). Throughout the Gospel, Jesus' adversaries persistently argued that he was merely a human being (5:18; 10:33; 19:7), and the blood oozing from the wound in his side confirmed that he was indeed a man. The appearance of water is more remarkable, although we will see in the next chapter that this too could be explained as a natural occurrence according to the canons of ancient physiology. The physical reality of death was clear; the evangelist's task was to disclose what the death meant. We will explore the symbolic aspects of John's passion narrative more fully in our next chapter, attempting here only to connect the effusion from Jesus' side to the other components of the water motif.

In the crucifixion scene, as earlier in the Gospel, water is associated with revelation and the Spirit. The revelatory significance of the water is reflected in the evangelist's emphatic declaration that he spoke the truth when he said that Jesus' wound emitted water as well as blood and that he testified in order that readers might believe (19:35). The text also intimates that water should be connected, although not equated, with the Spirit. Earlier in the Gospel Jesus promised that the "living water," which signified the Spirit, would flow "out of his heart" or "belly" (7:37-39), and the water issuing from his wound confirms this promise, identifying the crucified Jesus as the source of the Spirit. Yet the wider literary context shows that the water cannot fully be identified with the Spirit. The Gospel says that Jesus actually breathed the Spirit into the disciples on Easter evening after displaying the wounds in his hands and side to show that the giver of the Spirit was precisely the Jesus who was crucified (20:20-22). The symbolism of the water from Jesus' side is proleptic, as Raymond Brown has suggested, showing that the Spirit given by the risen Jesus "flows from the whole process of glorification in 'the hour' of the passion, death, resurrection, and ascension."[54]

54. Brown, *Gospel*, 2.951. The comment that Jesus "handed over the spirit" at the moment of death also may be a proleptic reference to the gift of the Holy Spirit.

Christologically, several facets of meaning can be identified in the evocative comment about the flow of water. On one level the water helps to convey the cleansing effect of Jesus' death. Connections between water, purification, and Jesus' death were established early in the Gospel. John's practice of baptizing with water directed people to the Lamb of God who would take away the sin of the world and cleanse people through baptism with the Holy Spirit (1:29-34). The sign Jesus performed at Cana foreshadowed the "hour" of his passion and resurrection, when purification would be accomplished through the revelation of his glory, which would replace Jewish ablutions (2:1-11). At the beginning of the passion narrative, the foot washing anticipated the way Jesus' death would make his followers clean (13:1-11). The water from Jesus' side is not primarily a baptismal symbol, and its role is not to explain the meaning of the Christian rite.[55] But if connected with baptism, it shows that baptism must be understood in light of the crucifixion. The disputes over purification in chapter 3 showed that a ritual washing like baptism is significant only through association with the Spirit that engenders faith in Jesus, who was "lifted up" in death.

On a second level the water confirms that Jesus is prophet and Messiah. Earlier in the narrative Jesus met a woman beside Jacob's well at the sixth hour—perhaps dimly foreshadowing the hour of his death (4:6; 19:14). In language reminiscent of the well the prophet Moses provided for Israel, Jesus offered the woman the water that would "spring up" to life everlasting. As a prophet, Jesus foretold the coming of worship in Spirit and truth, and the woman gradually realized that he was telling her "all things," something she expected the Messiah to do (4:26, 29). At the feast of Booths Jesus echoed traditions about Moses producing water from the rock, prophesying that "living water" would flow from his own body, which the crowd took to be a mark of the prophet and Messiah. The Scriptures said that people would recognize a true prophet when the words he had spoken came to pass (Deut. 18:22), and the water flowing from Jesus' side fulfilled his word, showing that he was the prophet God had sent.[56] Water itself was not widely associated with the Messiah, but the Messiah was expected to bear the Spirit (Isa. 11:2; John 1:31-34). The use of water as a symbol for the Spirit, together with the references to messiahship in conversations about living water, helps readers perceive the water from Jesus' side as additional confirmation that he was the Christ.

On a third level water helps disclose the divinity of Jesus. John announced that Jesus would baptize with the Holy Spirit, an act the Scrip-

55. On possible baptismal connotations see Brown, *Gospel*, 2.951–52.
56. A later Jewish tradition says that both blood and water came from the rock Moses struck in the wilderness (*Exod. Rab.* 3:13). Readers familiar with this tradition could connect it with the blood and water from Jesus' side.

tures and Jewish tradition expected God himself to perform. The repeated invitations to receive living water echoed biblical passages that invited people to come to God and drink, identifying God himself or the city and temple where God was present as the source of living water (Isa. 55:1; Jer. 2:13; Zech. 14:8; Ezek. 47:1; John 7:37-39). The crucified and risen body of Jesus was the temple of God (2:21), and he would "breathe" the Spirit into his disciples as God had once "breathed" spirit or breath into the first human being (20:22; Gen. 2:7). The water streaming from Jesus' side brings a sign of the postresurrection gift of the Spirit into the heart of the crucifixion, revealing the power and presence of God in the death of his Son. Taken alone, the water could have been perceived as the *ichōr*, the colorless liquid said to flow "from the wounds of the blessed immortals";[57] but it is conjoined with the blood issuing from a human corpse.

Earlier in the gospel Jesus invited those who were thirsty—the woman at the well, the crowds in Galilee, and the worshipers in Jerusalem (4:13; 6:35; 7:37)—to come and drink from him. At the cross it was he who said, "*I* thirst"; and with these words he put himself in the place of those he came to aid. The ministry of King Jesus began with a lavish gift of wine at a banquet, and it ended when an anonymous bystander served as courtier, offering the thorn-crowned monarch a taste of sour wine. The earlier episodes and the crucifixion must be taken together. It was the Jesus who thirsted who was the fountain of living water. His gift was not given without cost; he gave life to others precisely at the expense of his own. The spear that pierced Jesus' side demonstrated that he actually was dead; yet the water that came forth revealed that in death he was the source of life.[58]

WATER IN 1 JOHN

The Johannine epistles mention water only once, in a passage that seems to echo the crucifixion account. The author of 1 John wrote, "This is he who came by water and blood, Jesus Christ, not with the water only but with the water and the blood. And the Spirit is the witness, because the

57. On this saying see Plutarch, *Moralia* 180E and 341B; *Life of Alexander* 28; cf. Diogenes Laertius, *Lives of Eminent Philosophers* 9.60.
58. See Duke, *Irony in the Fourth Gospel*, 113. Stephen Moore has said that the paradoxical coupling of Jesus' thirst with the water from his side marks the failure of Johannine irony since irony depends upon the clear separation of the physical and spiritual levels, as in the conversation with the Samaritan woman (*Literary Criticism and the Gospels: The Theoretical Challenge* [New Haven, Conn.: Yale University Press, 1989] 159–63, and "Are There Impurities in the Living Water that the Johannine Jesus Dispenses? Deconstruction, Feminism, and the Samaritan Woman," *Biblical Interpretation* 1 (1993) 207-27. Yet Moore fails to note that paradox is fundamental to the Gospel's message and that it functions along with irony. Moreover, understanding Johannine symbolism demands attention to both the contrasts and the connections between levels of meaning. See my first chapter (pp. 27–31).

Spirit is the truth" (1 John 5:6). The language of the passage is obscure, although the direction of the argument seems clear. The emphasis is the reverse of that in the Gospel. If the fourth evangelist stressed that "blood *and water*" flowed from Jesus' side in death, the author of the epistle emphasizes that Jesus came "not with water only" but with "the water *and the blood*." This is consistent with their respective christological emphases: The gospel argues for Jesus' messiahship and divinity while assuming his humanity was genuine (John 10:30, 33; 20:31), and the epistle emphasizes Jesus' humanity against those who focused one-sidedly on his divinity (1 John 4:2-3).

The epistolary author apparently wanted to counter those who taught that Jesus "came" with "water only" (5:6). This seems to recall John's baptism "with water," which was the context in which the Spirit descended and Jesus "came" into public view (John 1:29a). The author did not deny the importance of this but insisted that what happened through the water must be coupled with "the blood," which the Johannine writings consistently identify with the blood Jesus shed at the time of his death (1 John 1:7; John 19:34; cf. 6:53-56). The water motif in the Gospel began with John's baptism, when Jesus was presented as the suffering Lamb of God as well as the Spirit-bearing Son of God, and the motif culminated with the piercing of Jesus' side, when water and blood flowed out together. The first epistle maintains a similar connection, insisting that neither Jesus' baptism nor the witness of the Holy Spirit can be understood apart from Jesus' death.

After recalling how Jesus "came" with water and blood in the past, the author of the epistle shifts to the present, saying that "there are three that testify: the Spirit and the water and the blood, and these three agree" (1 John 5:8). If the previous verse connected the Spirit and water with the blood Jesus shed, this verse points to the ongoing significance of Jesus' death for the life of the community. The use of the present tense suggests to some that "water" now refers to the Christian practice of baptism, which is possible, although the Johannine writings give little reason to think that "blood" by itself alludes to the Lord's Supper (see pp. 257–62). If the "water" is understood baptismally, the passage interprets baptism as a form of "testimony" to the abiding significance of Jesus' death. The focus remains christological.[59] As in the Gospel, the text binds the work of the Spirit to the crucified Jesus; and it is to the significance of his death we now must turn.

59. For a survey and discussion of the various interpretations of this passage, see Brown, *Epistles*, 575–85.

6

The Crucifixion

The glory of God was revealed most fully in the suffering and death of Jesus the Christ. The marks of his scourging, the dull thumping of the mallet upon the nails driven through his wrists, and the trickle of blood from his side are palpable ways that crucifixion brings the transcendent glory of God into the realm of human experience. During his ministry, Jesus manifested divine glory in acts of power like turning water into wine and raising the dead (2:11; 11:40), yet these signs were only a prelude to his final glorification in death. Jesus was welcomed to Jerusalem at the end of his ministry by a crowd bearing palm branches and acclaiming him king of Israel, but he told them the Son of man would be glorified in the manner of a grain of wheat, which must fall into the earth and die (12:23-24). Troubled by the menacing shadow of death, Jesus prayed that God's name would be glorified in the hour of his death, and a voice from heaven replied, "I have glorified it, and I will glorify it again" (12:27-28).

The crowds failed to comprehend the heavenly voice, and Jesus uttered the cryptic remark that "I, when I am lifted up from the earth, will draw all people to myself" (12:32). The bystanders rightly understood that this foreshadowed his death but immediately objected, "We have heard from the law that the Christ remains forever. How can you say that the Son of man must be lifted up? Who is this Son of man?" (12:34). And with their incredulous question, Jesus' public ministry drew to a close. The crowd's understanding of messiahship was apparently based upon the biblical promises concerning the everlasting rule of David's "seed" (Ps. 89:36), and from their perspective crucifixion would mean that Jesus could not be the Messiah, since by dying he would not remain forever. The Gospel writer faced the formidable challenge of showing that it was precisely by dying that Jesus would reveal the power of God and reign forever as the Christ.

The difficulty of grasping that the power of God was manifested in the death of Jesus is apparent throughout the Gospel.[1] The bystanders who demanded that Jesus perform a sign after he had driven the merchants out of the temple were baffled when he spoke of the destruction and raising up of the temple, which readers learn referred to the crucifixion and resurrection of his body (2:19-21). The crowd in the synagogue at Capernaum was delighted to hear of the "bread from heaven" that God would give them, but they were appalled to hear that they would receive it in the flesh of Jesus and the shedding of his blood (6:33, 51-52, 60). Questions about Jesus' departure to the Father, which would be accomplished through his death, reveal the people's incomprehension (7:32-36; 8:21-22), and his remarks about the good shepherd, who lays down his life for the sheep, led many to think him mad (10:11-21).

The Fourth Gospel was written for believers, but it was forged in a context of disputes with the non-Christian world. Crucifixion remained a public and brutal part of life in the ancient Mediterranean region, and the Christian proclamation of a crucified Messiah continued to arouse contempt long after the ministry of Jesus had ended. Justin's *Dialogue with Trypho,* which was composed in the second century, still grappled with Jewish objections to the idea of a crucified Messiah. Trypho, the Jewish interlocutor in the piece, argued that the Scriptures foretold the coming of the Son of man who would establish an everlasting kingdom, "but this so-called Christ of yours was dishonorable and inglorious, so much that the last curse contained in the law of God fell on him, for he was crucified."[2] Pagan protests appear in Justin's *Apology,* which relates that many said that "our madness consists in the fact that we put a crucified man in second place after the unchangeable and eternal God, the Creator of the world."[3] The Latin author Minucius Felix concurred, concluding that only "abandoned wretches" could possibly center their worship on "a man put to death for his crime and on the fatal wood of the cross."[4]

Against such objections, the Gospel of John seeks to create a frame of reference that can disclose the transcendent significance of Jesus' death. The crucifixion itself functions as a core symbol in the narrative. The specter of the cross is present throughout John's account of Jesus' public ministry, from the moment Jesus is introduced as the sacrificial Lamb of God (1:29) to his final remark about being "lifted up" in death (12:32); the departure of the betrayer in chapter 13 sets in motion the final events

---

1. Cf. Culpepper, *Anatomy,* 163.
2. *Dialogue* 32.1.
3. *Apology* 1.13.4.
4. *Octavius* 9.4. On these and other texts see Martin Hengel, *Crucifixion* (Philadelphia: Fortress, 1977) 1–3.

of the passion. Supporting symbols that help convey the meaning of the crucifixion include many of the images and actions we have already considered: the motifs of light and water, the seed falling to the earth and dying; signs like the first miracle at Cana and the feeding of the five thousand; and symbolic actions like the cleansing of the temple and foot washing. We will draw on these and other materials but will give greatest attention to the supporting symbols within the passion narrative itself, including the discourses in the trial narrative, the scourging, and the incidents that take place at the cross.

The Johannine passion narrative is complex and conveys several levels of meaning simultaneously. The primary level of meaning is christological, and it will be useful to order our discussion of the Christology according to the aspects found frequently in earlier sections of the Gospel: (1) the meaning of his death at the simple human level, (2) its relationship to the Jewish Scriptures, (3) the crucifixion of Jesus the prophet and Messiah, and (4) the cross as glorification of Jesus and God. All of these dimensions are interrelated, and no one dimension can be divorced from the others. The secondary level of meaning deals with discipleship, and we will reserve that for the end, since, from a Johannine perspective, discipleship is rooted in the person and work of Jesus.

BEHOLD THE MAN

The crucifixion of Jesus is, in a fundamental sense, the account of one man's death. The human reality is made explicit in Jesus' encounter with Pilate, the Roman governor. During the interrogation, Pilate had Jesus scourged and crowned, then displayed him to the crowd with the words "Behold the man!" (19:5). Interpreters have often sensed the inadequacy of simply calling Jesus "the man" in this pivotal scene and have suggested that readers should find in this title an ironic intimation of Jesus' identity as "the Son of man" or perhaps the Messiah (cf. Zech. 6:12). Yet what the Roman governor said was true: Jesus was a man. The figure who wore the crown upon his brow had also bled under Pilate's lash. Jesus would be called king of the Jews and Son of God later in the narrative—titles that reveal important facets of his identity—but these epithets do not negate the plain truth of Pilate's statement, "Behold the man!" Here "the abject humanity of the Word made flesh is starkly affirmed." Whether Pilate intended to evoke pity or scorn, his remark was profoundly correct.[5]

5. On interpreting "man" as a messianic title see esp. Meeks, *Prophet-King*, 69–72, and F. J. Maloney, *The Johannine Son of Man* (Rome: Las, 1976) 202–7. On the humanity reflected in the term see Bultmann, *Gospel*, 659; G. Sevenster, "Remarks on the Humanity of Jesus in the Gospel and Letters of John," *Studies in John Presented to Professor Dr. J. N. Sevenster on the*

"Crucify him, crucify him"

Jesus' crucifixion, according to John's Gospel, followed procedures that were commonly used for public executions. Scourging prisoners and forcing them to carry their crosses to the place of death, shattering victims' leg bones, and gouging the body of a corpse with a spear were all part of what was a very human affair. The evangelist did not heighten the sense of horror that most people in the Roman Empire associated with crucifixion by dwelling on its details, but neither did he omit any of the steps in the ghastly process. Crucifixion was practiced throughout the Roman Empire in full public view, so that its procedures would have been widely familiar. Most people who read the Gospel today, however, know of crucifixion almost solely as it has been portrayed in the New Testament. Therefore it may be useful carefully to consider the incidents that John describes, quoting the specific passages from his account of the passion and asking what kinds of associations early readers of the Gospel would have brought to this text from their cultural context.

On the night of his arrest, the Jewish authorities interrogated Jesus at the house of the high priest and then took him to the praetorium. The Roman governor also questioned Jesus, but upon learning that Jesus' kingship was not of this world, he declared that Jesus was innocent and offered to release him. The Jewish authorities demanded that a prisoner named Barabbas be released instead. "Then Pilate took Jesus and scourged him" (19:1). The term used for the scourging (*mastigoun*) refers to a severe form of chastisement in which a prisoner was stripped and often bound to an upright post. The beating was administered using a short whip that had several single or braided leather thongs fixed into a wooden handle. Metal balls or fragments of bone were attached to the leather thongs. With each blow, the metal balls and bone fragments tore through the victim's skin and muscles, shredding his back, buttocks, and legs. The flogging could continue until parts of the backbone or inner organs were exposed.[6]

Occasion of His Seventieth Birthday (NovTSup 24; Leiden: Brill, 1970) 185–93; Paul Duke, *Irony in the Fourth Gospel* (Atlanta: John Knox, 1985) 107; Marianne M. Thompson, *The Humanity of Jesus in the Fourth Gospel* (Philadelphia: Fortress, 1988) 108; Rosel Baum-Bodenbender, *Hoheit in Niedrigkeit: Johanneische Christologie im Prozess Jesu vor Pilatus (Joh 18,28-19,16a)* (FB 49; Würzburg: Echter, 1984) 267–70, 285–86; Charles Panackel, *Idou ho Anthropos (Jn 19,5b): An Exegetico-Theological Study of the Text in the Light of the Term "anthropos" Depicting Jesus in the Fourth Gospel* (Analecta Gregoriana 251; Rome: Pontifica Universita Gregoriana, 1988). For a summary of disputes concerning the relative emphasis on Jesus' humanity and glory in John's Gospel, see Robert Kysar, *The Fourth Evangelist and His Gospel: An Examination of Contemporary Scholarship* (Minneapolis: Augsburg, 1975) 185–99.

6. For descriptions of scourging see Josephus, *J.W.* 2.14.9 §§306–8; 2.21.5 §§612–13; William D. Edwards, Wesley J. Gabel, Floyd E. Hosmer, "On the Physical Death of Jesus Christ," *Journal of the American Medical Association* 255 (1986) 1455–63, esp. 1457–58.

After the scourging, "the soldiers plaited a crown of thorns, and put it on his head, and arrayed him in a purple robe; they came up to him saying, 'Hail, King of the Jews!' and they struck him with their hands" (19:2-3). Similar displays of mockery occurred elsewhere in the ancient world. The Jewish writer Philo told how crowds in Alexandria seized a lunatic, adorned him with a papyrus crown, a rug, and a scepter made from a reed, and saluted him as their "lord."[7] The occasion for this incident was a visit from Herod Agrippa, whom the emperor had appointed tetrarch over southern Syria, and the mock coronation displayed the crowd's contempt for the arriving Jewish king. The philosopher Dio Chrysostom knew of a similar practice among the Persians, in which a prisoner who had been sentenced to death was given a royal cloak and allowed to give orders, drink, and carouse before being scourged and executed.[8]

After Jesus was handed over to the executioners, "he went out, bearing his own cross, to the place called the place of a skull, which is called in Hebrew Golgotha" (19:17). The usual procedure was to force the condemned person to carry the horizontal beam of the cross to the place of execution, where the vertical portion of the gibbet was already fixed in the ground. Plutarch commented that indeed "every criminal who goes to execution must carry his own cross on his back."[9] The Greek author Chariton explained that cross bearing was done for its exemplary effect. After relating how a group of prisoners were forced to carry their own crosses, he commented that "their persecutors added this external display of gruesomeness" to the crucifixion itself "to serve as a fearful example to any other such people."[10]

When they arrived at the place of execution, "they crucified him" (19:18). The condemned man was laid upon the ground, and square iron spikes, about five to seven inches long, were driven through his wrists, fastening him to the crossbar, which was then hoisted onto the upright post that had been sunk in the ground. A block of wood was often attached to the middle of the cross to form a crude seat. The lower portion of the man's body was twisted to one side, with his knees bent and together; then a third spike was driven in through the side of his feet. The weight of the body, suspended by the nails, produced searing pain in the hands and

7. *Flaccus* 36–40.

8. *Discourses* 4.66–68.

9. *Moralia* 554B. Cf. Artemidorus, "If a wrongdoer dreams that he is carrying one of the demons of the lower world, Pluto himself or Cerberus or some other one of those in Hades, it signifies that he will carry a cross. For the cross is like death and the man who is to be nailed to it carries it beforehand" (*Oneirocritica* 2.56). Quoted from *The Interpretation of Dreams* (trans. Robert J. White; Park Ridge, N.J.: Noyes, 1975).

10. *Chaereas and Callirhoe* 4.2.7. Cf. the references to the practice of "bearing the cross" in Matt. 10:38; 16:24; Mark 8:34; Luke 9:23; 14:27. Hengel notes a wordplay on cross bearing in Plautus (*Crucifixion*, 52).

feet. The agony increased each time the victim moved, gasping for breath in this contorted position. The Stoic philosopher Seneca captured the horror of crucifixion as it was known throughout the Roman Empire to show that there were situations in which life was far worse than death.

> Is it worth while to weigh down on one's own wound and hang impaled on a gibbet in order to postpone . . . the end of punishment? . . . Can anyone be found who would prefer wasting away in pain, dying limb by limb, or letting out his life drop by drop, rather than expiring once for all? Can any man be found willing to be fastened to the accursed tree, long sickly, already deformed, swelling with ugly weals on shoulders and chest, and drawing the breath of life amid long-drawn-out agony? He would have many excuses for dying even before mounting the cross! (*Moral Epistles* 101.11–14)

Social degradation added to the physical agony inflicted by crucifixion. Certain forms of execution allowed the victim to retain some measure of dignity, but crucifixion did not. The process was viewed with disgust as well as horror. To crucify someone was to "hang him on the tree of shame."[11]

A placard was placed above Jesus' head identifying him as "the King of the Jews." Many read the title, "for the place where Jesus was crucified was near the city" (19:20). Crucifixion was a public event, and its open display of brutality made it useful as a deterrent to lawbreakers. A text attributed to Quintilian explains, "Whenever we crucify the guilty, the most crowded roads are chosen, where the most people can be seen and moved by this fear. For penalties relate not so much to retribution as to their exemplary effect."[12] This form of execution was regularly inflicted upon slaves and outlaws who threatened the prevailing social order, but it could also be used for Roman citizens convicted of serious crime and especially high treason.[13] The horror evoked by crucifixion made it useful for bringing the general populace into submission in wartime or periods of unrest. During the Roman siege of Jerusalem, Titus commanded that a Jewish prisoner be crucified before the walls "in the hope that the spectacle might lead the rest to surrender in dismay." Later he resorted to mass crucifixions before the city walls, hoping to pressure its defenders into surrender.[14]

As the prisoners crucified along with Jesus writhed in the afternoon sun, "the Jews asked Pilate that their legs might be broken and that they might be taken away. So the soldiers came and broke the legs of the first and of the other who had been crucified with him; but when they came to

11. Cicero, *In Defence of Rabirius* 4 §13, quoted by Hengel, *Crucifixion*, 44.
12. *Minor Declamations* 274; noted by Hengel, *Crucifixion*, 50. On placing a placard above the cross see *Minor Declamations* 380.
13. Hengel, *Crucifixion*, 39.
14. *J.W.* 5.6.5 §289; 5.11.1 §§449–51.

Jesus and saw that he was already dead, they did not break his legs" (John 19:31b-33). Those who had been crucified were brought to the threshold of death by blood loss from the scourging, shock, and other factors. Death itself came when the victim finally gave up struggling to breathe against the pressure of the suspended body weighing down upon the chest cavity. The process could be shortened by smashing the leg bones below the knee with a mallet or club, so that the pressure of the body weight would be borne by the arm and shoulder muscles alone, further impairing the victim's ability to breathe and quickly leading to asphyxia.[15]

Seeing that Jesus was dead, "one of the soldiers pierced his side with a spear, and at once there came out blood and water" (19:34). The soldier apparently pushed the metal tip of his spear into Jesus' corpse to ensure that he was really dead. The blood trickling from the wound in the limp figure on the cross demonstrated the human reality of death. From the perspective of ancient physiology, the appearance of the water could be perceived in the same way. It was understood that the body contained a measure of water as well as blood, and that wounds would emit a colorless fluid called *ichōr*, or sometimes *hydor* (water), along with the blood.[16] From scourging to death, the passion narrative recounts the execution of "the man" Jesus according to a process that was notorious for its brutality; but in so doing, the text also places these incidents in a frame of reference that helps to disclose their significance (cf. pp. 181–83).

"I find no crime in him"

Pilate's statement "Behold the man" is framed by declarations that Jesus was innocent. Before and after he presented "the man" to the crowds, he announced his verdict: "I find no crime in him" (19:4, 6). On a simple human level, the passion narrative makes clear that what Pilate said was true: Jesus died as an innocent man. Two charges were leveled against him. First, the Jewish authorities considered him a rebel against God: "We have a law, and by that law he ought to die, because he has made himself the Son of God" (19:7). The law they referred to was Lev. 24:16, which prescribed the death penalty for those who blasphemed the name of God. From their perspective, Jesus' references to God as his Father and the use of the divine name for himself constituted blasphemy. Second, they presented Jesus to Pilate as a rebel against Rome, telling him, "If you release this man, you are not Caesar's friend; every one who makes himself a king sets himself against Caesar" (19:12).[17]

15. See Edwards et al., "On the Physical Death of Jesus Christ," 1461.

16. See the texts collected by Eduard Schweizer, "Das johanneische Zeugnis vom Herren-mahl," *Neotestamentica* (Stuttgart: Zwingli, 1963) 371–96, esp. 382–83.

17. See Anton Dauer, *Die Passionsgeschichte im Johannesevangelium: Eine traditionsgeschicht-liche und theologische Untersuchung zu Joh 18,1-19,30* (SANT 30; Munich: Kösel, 1972) 232.

The trial narrative exonerates Jesus and reveals that his accusers were guilty of precisely the charges they had made against him. The Gospel shows that Jesus was not a rebel against Rome. At the time of his arrest, Jesus willingly went along with the soldiers, and when Peter made an abortive attempt to resist, Jesus immediately intervened to prevent further outbursts (18:10-11). When questioned by Pilate, Jesus replied that his kingship was not of this world, and, in sharp contrast to the brigands that harried the Romans, Jesus did not allow his servants to resort to violence (18:36). Hearing this, Pilate announced, "I find no crime in him" and offered to release Jesus (18:38-39). The Jewish authorities immediately responded with a demand that placed the burden of guilt onto themselves. They cried out, "Not this man, but Barabbas!" and the evangelist commented, "Now Barabbas was a terrorist" (*lēstēs*, 18:40). The accusers, not Jesus, were guilty of fomenting rebellion against Rome, since it was they who demanded the release of a notorious insurrectionist.[18]

Pilate twice more repeated the verdict, "I find no crime in him," over the objections of Jesus' accusers (19:4, 6), but they remained adamant and charged that Jesus deserved death under Jewish law for making himself into the Son of God. When Pilate heard this, he became afraid, apparently at the prospect of confrontation with the supernatural,[19] and he demanded to know where Jesus was from. Jesus did not reply to Pilate's inquiry, but readers learned in previous episodes that Jesus was not trying to usurp divine prerogatives; he was an obedient Son carrying out the responsibilities his Father had given him (5:19-30). Again the charge returns to condemn Jesus' accusers, who planned to partake of the Passover that evening. The paschal meal celebrated God's victory over the tyrant who enslaved Israel in Egypt, and during the meal God's sole sovereignty was praised with words like, "From everlasting thou art God. . . . We have no king but thee."[20] But when Pilate asked the Jews who gathered at the judgment seat, "Shall I crucify your king?" they told him, "We have no king but Caesar" (19:15). And the Caesars were the men who had been made into gods, the human beings who had usurped God's prerogatives. By claiming "no king but Caesar," the Jewish authorities revealed that they were the ones guilty of rebellion against the sole lordship of God. The charges raised against Jesus in the trial narrative provide a basis for ascertaining that he died as an innocent man, and they also point to other dimensions of the cross's meaning.

18. On the connotations of this word see K. H. Rengstorf, "*lēstēs, ktl.*," *TDNT* 4.257–62. Cf. the political comments in Mark 15:7 and Luke 23:19.

19. On Pilate's fear see Rensberger, *Johannine Faith*, 94.

20. The text from the Passover liturgy is provided by Meeks, *Prophet-King*, 77, and Duke, *Irony in the Fourth Gospel*, 135.

BEHOLD THE LAMB OF GOD

The Jewish authorities said, "We have a law, and by that law he ought to die, because he has made himself the Son of God" (19:7). This charge had loomed over Jesus' ministry ever since he had healed a man at the pool of Bethzatha. The healing appeared to violate Jewish regulations concerning the Sabbath, and hostility against Jesus intensified when he called God his own Father, which they interpreted as a blasphemous attempt to make himself equal with God (5:16-18). The same accusation was repeated later, when the Jews attempted to stone Jesus for saying "I and the Father are one" (10:30). Finally, during the hearing before Pilate, they pressed Pilate to issue the death sentence prescribed by the law for blasphemy: "He who blasphemes the name of the Lord shall be put to death; all the congregation shall stone him; the sojourner as well as the native, when he blasphemes the Name, shall be put to death" (Lev. 24:16). Pilate acceded to their demand and handed Jesus over to be crucified.

Crucifixion was widely regarded as a degrading form of execution, but according to Jewish law was especially abhorrent since a crucified person came under a divine curse. Deuteronomy 21:22-23 said, "And if a man has committed a crime punishable by death and he is put to death, and you hang him on a tree, his body shall not remain all night upon the tree, but you shall bury him the same day, for a hanged man is accursed by God; you shall not defile your land which the Lord your God gives you for an inheritance." The actions of the Jewish authorities later in the passion account seem to reflect this understanding of crucifixion. They went to Pilate late in the day and asked that the legs of those who had been crucified be broken and the bodies taken away. They did so "in order to prevent the bodies from remaining on the cross on the sabbath," which would begin at sundown (John 19:31). Jesus appeared to be a lawbreaker accursed by God, whose corpse suspended upon the cross threatened to defile the people.

That the Scripture Might Be Fulfilled

The Johannine portrayal of the crucifixion attempts to reverse this judgment by showing that Jesus died in complete obedience to the will of God, not in violation of it.[21] Before his death, Jesus identified himself as the

---

21. On the significance of Jesus' obedience and the fulfillment of the Old Testament, see Dauer, *Die Passionsgeschichte im Johannesevangelium*, 231–32, 278–306; Jürgen Becker, *Das Evangelium nach Johannes* (Gütersloh: Mohn, 1979–81) 2.403–6; Georg Richter, *Studien zum Johannesevangelium* (ed. J. Hainz; Regensburg: Pustet, 1977) 58–62. Robert T. Fortna relates the use of Scripture more to the Gospel's source than its present text (*The Fourth Gospel and Its Predecessor: From Narrative Source to Present Gospel* [Philadelphia: Fortress, 1988] 266–73).

good shepherd who would lay down his life for the sheep, insisting, "No one takes it from me, but I lay it down of my own accord," for "this charge I have received from my Father" (10:18). When the hour of death drew near, Jesus was troubled and asked, "What shall I say? Father, save me from this hour? No, for this purpose I have come to this hour"; and he prayed that God's name would be glorified (12:27-28). After giving Judas the opportunity to arrange for the arrest, Jesus went to meet his captors, declaring, "I do what the Father has commanded me, so that the world may know that I love the Father" (14:30-31). Although Peter made an abortive attempt to stave off Jesus' captors, it was Jesus who told him to put his sword back into its sheath, saying, "Shall I not drink the cup which the Father has given me?" (18:11).

Earlier in the Gospel, the Scriptures were cited as witnesses to the truth of Jesus' claims. The Johannine passion account also correlates events in Jesus' passion with passages from the Old Testament to show that Jesus' death revealed his obedience to the will of God. The first incident took place at the last supper, when Jesus informed his disciples that one of them would betray him. The betrayal threatened to undermine the possibility of faith in Jesus, since even one of his most intimate followers turned against him and helped secure his arrest. Yet the passion narrative discloses the connection between the betrayal and God's will. Jesus included Judas among his disciples knowing that he was a devil who would betray him, yet even this treachery could be turned toward the accomplishment of God's purposes. This is shown by the citation of a passage of Scripture in connection with the supper. Long beforehand the psalmist had written of betrayal, saying, "He who ate of my bread has lifted his heel against me" (Ps. 41:9; John 13:18).

When Jesus had been arrested, tried, and nailed to the cross, the soldiers divided his clothing into four parts, one for each of them. Jesus' tunic, however, was an undergarment made from a single piece of cloth, so they decided to cast lots for it rather than tear it (19:23-24). The clothing of a criminal was the perquisite of the executioners, and one would ordinarily assume that their actions reflected their desire to gain what they could from this chore.[22] But the meaning of the scene is completely transformed when it is read in connection with the Scriptures. The two actions of the soldiers correspond to the two parts of Ps. 22:19: "They parted my clothing among them" and again "for my garment they cast lots." By coupling this scene with Psalm 22, it becomes clear that contrary to appearances, the purposes of God are being carried out even here in Jesus' crucifixion. Some have detected a kind of sacerdotal symbolism

22. The clothes of an executed criminal were a perquisite of the executioners according to Justinian's *Digest* 48.20.6, noted by Barrett, *Gospel*, 550.

in this scene, since the high priest's tunic was without seam, but seamless garments were apparently not unique to priests, and the literary context does not attribute a priestly role to Jesus.[23]

Just before he died, Jesus said, "I thirst." Nearby there was a bowl full of sour wine (*oxos*), so someone soaked a sponge in the sour wine, placed it on a stalk of hyssop, and held it up to Jesus' mouth (19:28-29). The use of hyssop in this scene is odd, since the stalk of the hyssop plant is too flimsy to support a wet sponge, but otherwise there is little in the actions themselves that seems extraordinary. It would have been natural for a dying man to be thirsty, and sour wine was often drunk by soldiers and laborers. The Scriptures, however, reveal the deeper significance of the action. The evangelist understood that Jesus said he was thirsty "to fulfil the scripture" (19:28). No passage of Scripture is quoted, but the evangelist was almost certainly referring to Ps. 69:21, "For my thirst they gave me sour wine to drink." Thus Jesus' thirst and the response of the bystanders were consistent with what had been written of a righteous sufferer in the Psalms.

The evangelist observed that the soldiers did not break Jesus' legs, although they did break the legs of the two men crucified with him. Shattering the legs was a typical way of terminating the slow movement toward death, and the significance of the fact that Jesus' legs were *not* broken emerges when it is understood in light of the Scriptures: "Not a bone of him shall be broken" (19:36). This quotation could direct readers to several passages of the Old Testament. It can be connected with Ps. 34:21, which describes a righteous sufferer, of whom it is said, "The Lord keeps all his bones, not one of them shall be broken." The episode can also be connected with prescriptions regarding the sacrifice of a Passover lamb: "You shall not break a bone of it" (Exod. 12:46; Num. 9:12). In either case, the fact that Jesus' legs were not broken sets him apart from the others who were crucified and shows that he alone died in a manner consistent with what had been written in the Scriptures concerning the righteous sufferer or paschal lamb.[24]

When the soldiers saw that Jesus was already dead, they did not break his legs. "But one of the soldiers pierced his side with a spear, and at once there came out blood and water" (19:34). By piercing Jesus' side, the soldier was apparently attempting to ensure that he was dead, but the evangelist correlated this act with a passage of Scripture, indicating

23. Especially helpful on this is Schnackenburg, *Gospel,* 3.274. Cf. Brown, *Gospel,* 2.920–22.
24. For discussion of the Old Testament texts involved see Edwin D. Freed, *Old Testament Quotations in the Gospel of John* (NovTSup 11; Leiden: Brill, 1965) 108–14. J. Terence Forestell, in his generally excellent study, has argued that John refers only to the psalm, not to the Passover lamb, but his reasons for desiring to exclude the sacrificial connection are not convincing (*The Word of the Cross: Salvation as Revelation in the Fourth Gospel* [AnBib 57; Rome: Biblical Institute, 1974] 90–92).

that it contributed to the fulfillment of God's purposes. The passage was Zech. 12:10, "They shall look on him whom they have pierced." To the eyes of many observers, the events of Jesus' passion would have appeared to be an ordinary sequence of events, but by coupling them with passages of the Scriptures, the evangelist indicated that all of these actions worked together to accomplish God's will.

The Cross and Sacrifice

The Scripture citations suggest a connection between the death of Jesus and the practice of sacrifice, especially the Passover sacrifice, that is elaborated in the surrounding narrative.[25] The Scriptures said that a paschal lamb was to be "without blemish" and stipulated that none of its bones were to be broken, which was a regulation peculiar to the Passover sacrifice (Exod. 12:5, 46). The lambs were to be sacrificed between noon and sundown on the fourteenth day of the month of Nisan, which was known as the Day of Preparation for the Passover. During the early first century, worshipers crowded into the court of the temple in Jerusalem, each bringing a lamb. The gates were shut, a ram's horn sounded, and participants began slaughtering their lambs. Priests stood in rows, holding basins to catch the blood. When a basin was filled, it was passed along a row of priests and finally thrown against the base of the altar. Later that afternoon, a second and then a third group of worshipers entered the sanctuary and followed the same procedure. The carcasses of the lambs were taken to the homes of the worshipers, roasted, and consumed that evening.[26]

The fourth evangelist carefully observed that Jesus was slaughtered at the right time and in the appropriate manner for a Passover sacrifice. According to John's Gospel, Jesus ate his last meal with the disciples on the night before the Passover, rather than on Passover evening as in the other Gospels (13:1). On morning before Jesus' execution, the Jewish authorities scrupulously avoided entering the praetorium in order to keep themselves undefiled for the Passover meal that evening (18:28). Jesus was

25. On the sacrificial character of Jesus' death in John see Theophil Müller, *Das Heilsgeschenen im Johannesevangelium* (Zurich: Gotthelf, 1961) 38–75; F.-M. Braun, *Jean le théologian. Sa theologie, I. Le mystère de Jésus Christ* (EB; Paris: Gabalda, 1966) 153–72; Barnabas Lindars, "The Passion in the Fourth Gospel," *God's Christ and His People: Studies in Honor of Nils Alstrup Dahl* (ed. J. Jervell and W. A. Meeks; Oslo: Universitetsforlaget, 1977) 71–86, esp. 72–74. The sacrificial interpretation is disputed by Forestell, but see the review by Raymond E. Brown in *Bib* 56 (1975) 276–78; Max Turner, "Atonement and the Death of Jesus in John: Some Questions to Bultmann and Forestell," *EvQ* 62 (1990) 99–122.

26. On the importance of not breaking the lamb's legs see also Num. 9:12 and Exod. 12:10 (LXX). The lamb was to be sacrificed "between the two evenings" (Exod. 12:6), which was interpreted as the time between noon and sundown. On this sacrifice see *m. Pesaḥ.* 5:1-10.

sentenced to death and taken away to be crucified on the Day of Prepara-tion of the Passover at noon, or "the sixth hour," which was the time the Passover sacrificing began (19:14), and his sacrifice was completed on the afternoon of the Day of Preparation, before evening came (19:31). Shat-tering the bones of a paschal lamb made it unacceptable as a sacrifice. The soldiers did break the legs of the two others who were crucified with Jesus, but they did not break Jesus' bones. By correlating the death of Jesus with regulations for the slaughter of a paschal lamb, the evangelist showed that Jesus' death was consistent with the scriptural requirements for a perfect Passover sacrifice.

The Passover sacrifice, unlike other sacrifices, was not ordinarily consid-ered to be an offering for sin but a sign of deliverance from death. When Pharaoh had refused to release the people of Israel from bondage, God warned that he would kill the firstborn children and animals of every Egyptian household, but God also promised that when he saw lamb's blood on the doorposts of the Israelites, the destroyer would pass over them and let them live. Therefore the Israelites who first celebrated the Passover in Egypt smeared some of the lamb's blood on their doorposts with leafy branches of hyssop—the plant that seems to play a symbolic rather than a practical role in John's crucifixion account (19:29). Future generations of Israel were commanded to remember that this is "the sacri-fice of the Lord's passover, for he passed over the houses of the people of Israel in Egypt, when he slew the Egyptians, but spared our houses" (Exod. 12:27).

John's Gospel appropriated and modified this understanding of the Passover sacrifice, insisting that the death of Jesus spared people from death *precisely by* delivering them from sin. Jesus was introduced at the beginning of the Gospel as "the Lamb of God who takes away the sin of the world" (1:29), accomplishing this through his own sacrificial death. The Fourth Gospel usually speaks of "sin" in the singular, as human rebel-lion against God. Individual sins are particular manifestations of this fun-damental antipathy toward God and the one whom he sent. Sin is endemic to those who are "of this world," and it works death for those who persist in it (8:23-24). It constitutes a condition of bondage from which people need to be liberated (8:34-36). God addressed sin through the crucifixion of Jesus. He gave his only Son to suffer and die in order to reveal the fullness of his love, that by its transforming power he might wrest the world from sin's death grip and bring all who believe to everlasting life (3:16). Sin is lethal estrangement from God, but through the cross the self-sacrificing love of God is revealed, overcoming the hostility by trans-forming it into faith. This reconciliation is atonement, or better, "at-one-ment" in a Johannine sense.

Although in Jewish circles a paschal lamb was not ordinarily understood to take away sin, such a portrayal of the crucifixion would have been especially compelling to readers who connected the death of Jesus with the sufferings of the servant of God depicted in Isa. 52:13—53:12. This servant was like "a lamb that is led to the slaughter," who was "wounded for our transgressions and bruised for our iniquities," and in his sufferings "he bore the sin of many" (53:4, 5, 7, 12). This portion of Isaiah was known to the evangelist, who explicitly quoted Isa. 53:1 in John 12:38, and was applied to Jesus by other early Christians (Matt. 8:17; Acts 8:32; cf. Heb. 9:28). The servant in this text was said to have been "lifted up" (*hypsoun*, Isa. 52:13), as was Jesus in his sufferings (John 3:14). According to the Isaiah text, the servant took the consequences of the sins of others upon himself, but this view does not suggest that this is how the Fourth Gospel depicts the sufferings of Jesus. The word *airein* (take) in the Johannine writings usually means to take something away rather than to take something upon oneself (cf. 1 John 3:5).[27]

For other early readers, the image of the Lamb of God may have evoked memories of the binding of Isaac upon the altar.[28] Isaac was the child of promise, who, according to tradition, had been preserved from the threat posed to him by the slave's son Ishmael (Gen. 21:8-10). Jesus too was a Son promised by God, who was preserved through menacing encounters with the descendants of Abraham still enslaved by sin (John 8:33-38). Eventually, however, God commanded Abraham, "Take your son, your only son Isaac" and offer him as a burnt offering (Gen. 22:2), and eventually God himself gave up "his only Son" to die (John 3:16). Abraham and Isaac traveled together to the place of sacrifice, and Isaac asked where they would get the lamb for the burnt offering. Abraham replied that God would provide the lamb (Gen. 22:7-8), and according to John 1:29, Jesus was the Lamb that God provided. Isaac trudged along, bearing the wood for the sacrifice on his back (Gen. 22:6) in a manner that later Jewish and Christian interpreters would compare to carrying a cross. Jesus too went to the place of execution carrying his cross upon his shoulders (John 19:17). Although the biblical account focused on Abraham's faithfulness in a time of testing, Jewish tradition transformed it into the story of Isaac's willing

27. Forestell, *The Word of the Cross,* 160–65.
28. On possible allusions to Isaac see Geza Vermes, *Scripture and Tradition in Judaism: Haggadic Studies* (Studia Post-Biblica 4; Leiden: Brill, 1961) 193–227; F.-M. Braun, *Jean le théologien,* 3.157–65; Robert J. Daly, "The Soteriological Significance of the Sacrifice of Isaac," *CBQ* 39 (1977) 45–75, esp. 68, 72–74; Wayne A. Meeks, "The Man from Heaven in Johannine Sectarianism," 63; Raymond E. Brown, *The Death of the Messiah: From Gethsemane to the Grave* (New York: Doubleday, 1994) 2.1434-44. On allusions to Isaac in John 8:33-38 see Bruce E. Schein, "Our Father Abraham" (Ph.D. diss.: Yale University, 1972) 136–91.

obedience to God's commands, even to the point of giving his life, as Jesus died in obedience to God's will.[29]

Isaac's deed was sometimes understood as an act of obedience that satisfied God's demands and became a source of merit that could be extended to others. Although the biblical account said that Abraham stayed the knife before harming his son, some Jewish traditions concluded that a portion of Isaac's blood was shed and that "on account of his blood" Abraham and Isaac merited election.[30] The redemptive power of the binding of Isaac was associated with the Passover sacrifice in a number of Jewish texts, and according to later tradition, the Israelites smeared the lamb's blood on their doorposts because God had promised that "when I see the blood, I will pass over you—I see the blood of the binding of Isaac."[31] Nevertheless, this understanding of sacrifice does not conform to the Johannine portrayal of Jesus' death. There is little to suggest that Jesus' death vicariously satisfied the demands of God's justice or placated God's anger.

A more promising way to understand the sacrificial character of Jesus' death according to John's Gospel is by considering what it means for Jesus to die "for" or "on behalf of" (*hyper*) others.[32] Caiaphas the high priest foreshadowed the sacrificial character of Jesus' death when he said that "it is expedient for you that one man should die for the people, and that the whole nation should not perish" (11:50; 18:14). This theme, when traced throughout the Gospel, points to the cross as the supreme manifestation of divine love. Jesus identified himself as the good shepherd who laid down his life for the sake of the sheep (10:11, 15). The shepherd would die in order that the sheep might be spared, but there is nothing to suggest that the shepherd took upon himself the consequences of the flock's sins. Instead, the action expressed the shepherd's complete devotion to the sheep, in contrast to the hireling, who cared nothing for them (10:13-14). Similarly, laying down one's life for one's friends was considered to be the consummate manifestation of love (15:13). By laying down his life, therefore, Jesus manifested his love—and thus the love of God.

The connection between purification and the crucifixion points in the same direction. Jesus began his ministry by transforming water used for

29. On carrying the wood as carrying a cross see *Gen. Rab.* 56:3, noted by Brown, *Gospel*, 2.917. On Isaac's obedience see Josephus *Ant.* 1.13.4 §232; 4 Macc. 13:12; 16:20; *Bib. Ant.* 32:3; 40:2.

30. *Bib. Ant.* 18:5.

31. On the connection between the binding of Isaac and the Passover see *Jub.* 17:15-16; 18:18-19; 49:1; noted by Vermes, *Scripture and Tradition in Judaism*, 215. The quotation is from the *Mekilta*, "Pisha" 7.81; cf. 11.95 (Lauterbach ed., vol. 1, p. 57).

32. Forestell, *The Word of the Cross*, 193–94.

the Jewish rites of purification (2:6) into a surfeit of wine, revealing in a preliminary way what would be completed in the "hour" of his passion. Purification involves an actual removal of sin; and at the last supper, Jesus anticipated the purifying effect of his death by washing his disciples' feet. The foot washing, like Jesus' death itself, was an act of love undertaken for the disciples (13:1). By revealing the love of God on the cross, Jesus would purge away the antipathy toward God that is the root of sin. During the passion itself, the priests remained outside the praetorium to avoid defilement (18:28) and apparently requested that Jesus' body be removed from the cross so that it would not create defilement (19:31; Deut. 21:22-23), but the flow of water from Jesus' side should prompt readers to reverse this judgment, by pointing to the cleansing power of his death. This would be especially clear to those who recalled the context from which the Zechariah quotation was taken, since after referring to the one who was pierced, the text says that "there shall be a fountain opened for the house of David and the inhabitants of Jerusalem to cleanse them from sin and uncleanness" (Zech. 13:1).

The Johannine Epistles convey a similar understanding of the sacrificial quality of Jesus' death, interpreting the cross in terms of cleansing and as a manifestation of divine love. According to 1 John 1:7, "the blood of Jesus his Son cleanses us from all sin"; and in 2:2, Jesus is called the "*hilasmos* for our sins, and not for ours only but also for the sins of the whole world." The term *hilasmos* was used in sacrificial worship for the means of atonement. It can be translated as "expiation," suggesting that it is the sacrifice by which sins are removed, or it may be better to render it "atonement," since its effect is to reconcile God and people, thus achieving an "at-one-ment." The author later said that God's love was made manifest by God sending his Son into the world, and that God "loved us and sent his Son to be the *hilasmos* for our sins" (1 John 4:9-10). The imagery is sacrificial, but it is used in a distinctive way to describe the effects of the death of Jesus as the supreme manifestation of the love of God, as something that transforms people from antipathy into faith, thereby effecting reconciliation.[33]

BEHOLD YOUR KING

Jesus' adversaries expected that his crucifixion would discredit the claim that he was Messiah and king. The crowds that gathered about him when he approached Jerusalem were incredulous when he said that "the Son of man must be lifted up," because if he was lifted up in crucifixion, he could not be the Christ, since by dying he would obviously not "remain forever" (12:34). The Jewish leaders brought Jesus before the Roman governor

33. See Brown, *Epistles*, 217–22.

demanding his execution and denouncing him as a man with royal pretensions, someone who threatened Caesar's authority (19:12). The fourth evangelist recounted Jesus' death in a way that showed that crucifixion did not negate his messiahship but actually demonstrated it and revealed its true character.

The Enthronement of the Prophet-King

Earlier in the Gospel, Jesus was often identified as a prophet before being called Messiah or king, and the same is true in the passion narrative itself (4:19, 29; 6:14-15; 7:40-41; 9:17, 22). The title "prophet" is not used in this section, but several incidents reveal Jesus' prophetic powers. First, a large group of heavily armed soldiers were sent to arrest Jesus, but before he allowed himself to be seized, he secured the release of his disciples. The evangelist noted that this "was to fulfil the word which he had spoken, 'Of those whom thou gavest me I lost not one'" (17:12; 18:9; cf. 6:39; 10:28). Next, the soldiers took Jesus to the house of the high priest, and an unnamed disciple followed along into the courtyard, securing access for Peter, who stood warming himself by the fire. The servants of the high priest questioned Peter about his relationship with Jesus, but Peter denied three times that he knew Jesus, thereby fulfilling another word of Jesus, "Truly, truly, I say to you, the cock will not crow, till you have denied me three times" (13:38; 18:27). Finally, the Jewish leaders brought Jesus to Pilate the Roman governor for judgment, but Pilate refused to hear the case until the Jews pressed him, reminding him that they were not permitted to put anyone to death. The evangelist observed that this happened "to fulfil the word which Jesus had spoken to show by what death he was to die" (18:32), recalling how Jesus had said that he would be "lifted up" in death, which would be accomplished by crucifixion—a Roman rather than a Jewish form of execution (3:14; 12:32).

Jesus' role as a prophet is fused with his identity as Messiah during his initial parrying with Pilate. The term *messiah* or *christ,* which appeared frequently in debates with Jews earlier in the Gospel, is here replaced by the title "King of the Jews," which reflects Pilate's perspective as an outsider to the Jewish tradition; but Pilate's questions about Jesus' kingly status draw the theme of messiahship toward its climax. On the previous Passover, the crowd acclaimed Jesus a prophet and tried to make him into their king, but Jesus slipped away from them (6:14-15). When Jesus arrived in Jerusalem for this Passover, they again hailed him as king, but he hid himself from them (12:13, 36). Was he or was he not then "the King of the Jews"? Jesus affirmed that he had kingly power, but not the kind that was based on his ability to curry favor with the populace; his power came "from above" and was expressed in bearing witness to the truth, not in the exercise of the sword (18:33-37). Pilate seemed satisfied that Jesus posed no threat to him and offered to release "the King of the Jews," but the Jews outside the praetorium retorted that if anyone was released, it should be the insurrectionist Barabbas, not Jesus.

Pilate's scourging and coronation of Jesus, which takes place amid this confrontation between the Roman governor and the Jewish leaders, was an incident subject to differing interpretations. Scourging was sometimes used as a punishment in its own right, and from a Roman point of view the scourging would demonstrate that Jesus' pretensions to kingship were ludicrous. Jesus was easily subjected to Pilate's lash, and the royal robes only heightened the pathetic character of his claims; therefore he could be released as Pilate had suggested. At the same time, the mock crown and kingly garb would manifest Roman contempt for Jewish nationalism, and the public display of a man who had been raked by the scourge could help dissuade other Jews from pursuing their national aspirations. Alternatively, scourging could be used as a prelude to crucifixion, and the Jewish leaders apparently seized upon this interpretation of the incident, demanding that since Pilate had already scourged Jesus, he should finish the process by having him crucified, which is now demanded explicitly for the first time in the narrative (19:6).[34]

Readers whose perspectives have been shaped by the earlier portion of the narrative will see the significance of this incident in yet a different way. The scourging and coronation of Jesus revealed that his death and his kingship were not mutually exclusive, as the crowds had thought, but actually belonged together. Regardless of Pilate's motives, the scourging brought Jesus to the threshold of death just as he received the crown upon his brow and the cloak upon his shoulders; and the blows of the soldiers rained down upon him as he was acclaimed "King of the Jews!" (19:1-3). Still wearing the royal robes, Jesus was presented to the public, who rightly proclaimed that the destiny of this king was crucifixion (19:5-6).[35]

Jesus was taken to the dais where the seat of judgment was located, and although Pilate was apparently the one who sat down,[36] Jesus was the one

34. On the uses of scourging see Josef Blinzler, *The Trial of Jesus* (Westminster, Md.: Newman, 1959) 222–29; Josephus, *J.W.* 2.14.9 §§306–8; 2.21.5 §§612–13; *Life* 147. On the views of Pilate and the Jewish authorities reflected in John's narrative, see Schnackenburg, *Gospel*, 3.256; Rensberger, *Johannine Faith*, 93–94.

35. On the fusion of kingship and death in the scourging scene see Josef Blank, "Die Verhandlung vor Pilatus Joh 18,28-19,16 im Lichte johanneischer Theologie," *BZ* 3 (1959) 60–81, esp. 61–63, 73–74.

36. Some interpreters have argued that Pilate seated Jesus upon the judgment seat. See I. de la Potterie, "Jésus roi et juge d'après Jn 19,13: *ekathisen epi bēmatos*," *Bib* 41 (1960) 217–47; the piece appeared in a less technical form as "Jesus King and Judge according to John 19:13," *Scripture* 13 (1961) 97–111. Cf. Meeks, *Prophet-King*, 73–76. For discussion and critique see Schnackenburg, *Gospel*, 3.263–64; Brown, *Death of the Messiah*, 2.1388-93.

who silently presided while Pilate and the Jews successively condemned themselves. The Jewish leaders had scrupulously observed the statutes regarding purity and had avoided defilement by refusing to enter the praetorium (18:28); they had clamored for the release of a Jewish freedom fighter and pressured Pilate to carry out the death sentence for blasphemy prescribed in the Jewish law (18:40; 19:7). But in the end, they betrayed their heritage by confessing that their only king was Caesar, the man who attempted to usurp the place of God. Pilate knew that Jesus was innocent and repeatedly said so publicly; he grandly offered to have Jesus released but proved to be incapable of acting in accordance with what he knew to be true (18:38-39; 19:5-6, 12). When all his ploys had failed and the Jews had betrayed their faith, Pilate betrayed the truth and handed Jesus over to the executioners.

Pilate placed a sign above the cross that read, "Jesus of Nazareth, the King of the Jews," and the message was inscribed in Hebrew, in Latin, and in Greek (19:19-20). Crucifixion was regularly used for its exemplary effect; the public display of its brutality served to deter others from committing the same crime. From a Roman perspective, the placard identified Jewish messianism as a capital offense and reminded the populace that threats to Roman rule would not be tolerated. From a Jewish perspective, the placard created a demeaning caricature of Jewish national sentiment; therefore they asked that it be changed to read, "*This man said* I am King of the Jews" (19:21) so that the onus would fall squarely upon Jesus himself. Readers whose perspectives have been shaped by the narrative, however, can see that whatever Pilate's motives for writing the sign and refusing to remove it, the placard above the cross proclaimed the truth about Jesus: He was the Messiah, "the King of the Jews," and in fulfilling the Jewish hopes, he reigned for all peoples of the world.[37]

The Death of the Prophet-King

Jesus breathed his last that afternoon, and a soldier pushed a spear into his side, apparently to ensure that he was dead, and when he did so, water flowed from the wound along with the blood. Ancient physiology may have been able to account for the trickle of water as a natural phenomenon, but the water assumes a profound christological significance when interpreted within the context of the Gospel narrative. Jesus had told the Samaritan woman that if she had asked, he would have given her the living water that would become in her a spring welling up to life eternal (4:10, 14). The woman soon recognized that the one offering her

---

37. When the Samaritans recognized that Jesus, the Jew, was "Savior of the World," they anticipated that his rule would extend to all peoples (4:42). See my article, "'The Savior of the World' (John 4:42)," *JBL* 109 (1990) 665–80.

living water was a prophet, and Jesus later identified himself as the Messiah (4:19, 25-26). The crowds that gathered in the temple to celebrate the feast of Booths heard Jesus announce that anyone who was thirsty should come to him and drink, for as the Scripture said, "Out of his heart shall flow rivers of living water" (7:37-38). Some of the bystanders rightly understood that Jesus was the prophet foretold by Moses in Deuteronomy 18, who would provide them with a kind of life-giving water as Moses had done (7:40). Others exclaimed that if Jesus was the source of the water, he must be the Christ (7:41), which was also true (see pp. 175–77). The flow of water from Jesus' wounded side points to the fulfillment of what he had promised earlier, and it also was consistent with Zech. 12:10, which even outside of John's Gospel was sometimes understood to be a messianic text.[38]

The living water that Jesus had promised to give his followers was the Spirit. After the Samaritan woman asked for the water, Jesus announced the advent of worship in Spirit and in truth (4:23-24), and after Jesus invited the thirsty pilgrims at the feast of Booths to come and drink, the narrator explained that the living water was "the Spirit, which those who believed in him were to receive" (7:39). The Spirit had once descended upon the anointed kings of Israel like Saul and David and upon prophets like Moses, Elijah, and Elisha. Since Jesus was both prophet and king, it was fitting that he too should bear the Spirit of God, but in contrast to Israel's ancient leaders, Jesus bore the Spirit permanently. John the Baptist testified that the Spirit both descended and "remained" on Jesus (1:32-33); Jesus would give the Spirit to his followers, but he would not give it away. The poke of the soldier's spear point was intended to show that Jesus was dead, but it actually revealed that through death Jesus was the fountainhead of the life-giving Spirit. When he breathed the Spirit into the disciples on Easter evening, he did so only after showing them the wounds in his hands and his side. The Spirit binds believers to the crucified prophet-king.

As the afternoon waned on the day of Jesus' execution, Joseph of Arimathea asked Pilate for permission to take away Jesus' body, and Pilate granted his request. Joseph was joined by Nicodemus, and together they gave Jesus a burial fit for a king. A week before, Mary had lavishly anointed Jesus with myrrh—an anointing that simultaneously prepared Jesus for burial and enthronement (12:7, 13-14). On the day of Jesus' death, Nicodemus brought still more myrrh—a hundred pounds of it—another gift so

---

38. Brown, *Gospel*, 953–56; Forestell, *The Word of the Cross*, 89; Rudolf Schnackenburg, *Das Johannesevangelium: Ergänzende Auslegungen und Exkurse* (HTKNT 4/4; Freiburg: Herder, 1984) 164–73. The Zechariah passage is connected with a figure known as the messiah ben Joseph in *b. Sukk.* 52a.

extravagant by comparison with other burials that it would have been suitable only for a king. They laid Jesus in a tomb that had never been used before, as was appropriate for someone with kingly status, and the tomb was located in a garden, which would have been suitable for a royal burial. The Old Testament often speaks of gardens as places created by kings (Esther 7:7-8; Eccl. 2:5) and used as sites for royal tombs (2 Kings 21:18, 26), including the tomb of David (Neh. 3:16 LXX). The character of the burial may not in itself demonstrate Jesus' regal status, but it was consistent with Jesus' identity as the king of the Jews, which was repeatedly proclaimed during his trial and on the sign above his cross.[39]

Nicodemus was a shadowy figure earlier in the Gospel, and his role here remains disputed. His first encounter with Jesus ended with ominous words about those who love darkness (3:19-21), and he was linked with Jesus' adversaries during his cameo appearance at the feast of Booths (7:50). The reminder that Nicodemus had come to Jesus "by night at first" (19:39) could suggest that he was still in the dark and that the horizon of his thinking ended at the grave, for the piles of spices he heaped upon the corpse would be useless for one being "lifted up."[40] Yet such a judgment is too harsh, for on Good Friday Nicodemus acted before nightfall, while it was still the Day of Preparation (19:42), and his extravagant outlay of myrrh surpassed even what Mary had expended upon Jesus the week before. If Nicodemus failed to comprehend that resurrection would make the spices superfluous, we must also note that even the Beloved Disciple needed time to grasp the significance of the resurrection (20:8-9). Joseph of Arimathea was a disciple, but he had avoided making a public profession of his faith "for fear of the Jews," like the secret believers whom the evangelist chided for coveting the glory bestowed on them by their peers more than the glory of God (12:42-43). Yet he did ask the Roman governor for Jesus' body, and on Easter evening it was the inner circle of disciples who huddled behind closed doors "for fear of the Jews" (20:19).

Perhaps the appearance of these two figures at the cross can best be understood in light of a promise Jesus made before his death rather than through attempted assessments of their character. The throngs of people who gathered around Jesus at the end of his public ministry were enamored with miracles; and Jesus hid himself from them. The evangelist remarked that although they had seen so many signs, they did not believe,

39. On the regal character of Jesus' burial see Brown, *Gospel*, 2.960; Dauer, *Die Passionsgeschichte im Johannesevangelium*, 277. For a recent attempt to connect the garden with Eden see Frédéric Manns, "Le symbolism du jardin dans le récit de la passion selon St Jean," *LA* 37 (1987) 53–80; idem, *L'evangile de Jean à la lumière du Judaïsm* (Studium Biblicum Franciscanum 33; Jerusalem: Franciscan, 1991) 401–29.
40. Meeks, "The Man from Heaven in Johannine Sectarianism," 55; de Jonge, *Jesus: Stranger*, 34; Dennis D. Sylva, "Nicodemus and His Spices (John 19.39)," *NTS* 34 (1988) 148–51.

and he chided the cowardice of the authorities who had faith but concealed it (12:18, 36-43). Yet in the face of such pervasive unbelief, Jesus promised that "I, when I am lifted up from the earth, will draw all people to myself" (12:32). Faith is a human impossibility, but it can be engendered by the power of God; Joseph and Nicodemus may be the first indication of what Jesus' death would accomplish.[41] Jesus perished, like a seed falling into the earth. And as he was buried in the garden, his death began to bear fruit.

WE BEHELD HIS GLORY

Those who condemned Jesus at the trial charged that he not only aspired to kingship but tried to make himself the Son of God (19:7). The issue was Jesus' claim to divinity. Jesus had called God his Father, used the "I Am" of himself, and claimed to be one with God; and mobs had twice before attempted to stone him, charging that he was a mere man trying to usurp the place of God. The cross would seem to mark the triumph of their view. Death upon the "tree of shame" would appear to demonstrate conclusively that Jesus was the adversary of God not the Son of God, and that his presumption was demonic (7:20; 8:48, 52; 10:20). The Gospel reverses this judgment to show that the crucifixion actually reveals Jesus' oneness with God, manifests his glory, and signals the triumph of the Son of God over the forces of Satan.

The Ruler of This World
Is Cast Out

The transcendent character of the conflict in which Jesus was engaged during the passion was foreshadowed in earlier confrontations with the crowds in Jerusalem. The debates were sparked by questions about the legitimacy of Jesus' teaching but flared up into a deadly struggle between the Son of God and the children of the devil (8:42-44). Unlike the other Gospels, John's Gospel does not mention any exorcisms among the miracles Jesus performed during his public ministry; but as the hour of his passion and glorification tolled, Jesus said, "Now is the judgment of this world, now shall the ruler of this world be cast out" (12:31). The one "exorcism" in John's Gospel is the crucifixion itself.[42]

41. See Brown, *Community*, 72 n. 128, and *Death of the Messiah*, 1268. For a helpful discussion of the different interpretations of Joseph of Arimathea and Nicodemus in this scene, see Jouette Bassler, "Mixed Signals: Nicodemus in the Fourth Gospel," *JBL* 108 (1989) 640–43.
42. On Jesus' death as a victory over Satan see Dauer, *Die Passionsgeschichte im Johannesevangelium*, 236–77; Josef Blank, *Krisis: Untersuchungen zur johanneischen Christologie und Eschatologie* (Freiburg: Lambertus, 1964) 281–94.

The shadow of the demonic emerges dramatically at the beginning of the passion narrative in the figure of the betrayer. Judas was first mentioned in the Gospel immediately after Simon Peter identified Jesus as "the Holy One of God," and Jesus foreshadowed his coming conflict with Satan by revealing that one of the Twelve he had chosen was "a devil," which referred to his betrayer (6:70-71). The introduction to the last supper discloses the transcendent nature of the powers that collide in Jesus' passion by explaining that it was "the devil" who had put the desire to betray Jesus into Judas's heart, but that it was God who had put "all things" into Jesus' hands (13:2-3). The interactions between Jesus and Judas at the supper constitute a preliminary skirmish in this cosmic battle, in which the power of God will rout the forces of Satan.

The encounter began with the foot washing, in which Jesus laid down his garments, girded himself with a towel like a slave, and stooped to wash the feet of his disciples. Jesus performed the action not out of weakness but out of the strength possessed by one who had come from God, who was going to God, and who had been invested with supreme authority by God to manifest his power in an act of devoted love (13:1, 3). The betrayer was among the recipients of this action, but he was not affected by it (13:11). Since he was included within the circle of those whose feet were washed, his perfidy cannot reflect a lack of love on Jesus' part but must display a hardened resistance to Jesus' graciousness.

Next, Jesus alluded to the betrayal in a way that indicated that the powers of evil could resist but not thwart the will of God. Treachery had been placed in Judas's heart by the devil, not by God, but Jesus was able to harness the evil to carry out God's redemptive purposes. Evidence that the betrayal came within the divine purview appears in the quotation of Ps. 41:9: "He who ate my bread has lifted his heel against me" (John 13:18). Jesus portended his betrayal ahead of time and connected it with the Old Testament Scriptures in this way so that his disciples would be able to discern the power and presence of God even in his arrest and death, that is, that they might "believe that I Am" (13:19). Finally, Jesus dipped a morsel of food into the dish at the supper and gave it to Judas. The gesture was a common way of showing affection toward someone, but it only evoked more intense demonic resistance, for when Judas received the morsel, "Satan entered into him" (13:27). Nevertheless, Judas did not depart from the table until Jesus gave him leave, saying, "What you are going to do, do quickly" (13:27). The Son of God was stronger than Satan's emissary, for Judas left the table only at Jesus' bidding.

Jesus told the disciples who remained with him, "I will no longer talk much with you, for the ruler of this world is coming. He has no power over me, but I do as the Father commanded me so that the world may know that I love the Father" (14:30-31).[43] When Jesus left the meal and went to a garden on the other side of the Kidron Valley, he was met by Judas and a group of Jewish and Roman troops. These representatives of "the world" and its murderous powers approached in the flickering torch-light, heavily armed, yet with no power over Jesus. Seizing the initiative, Jesus demanded to know whom they were seeking. When they replied, "Jesus of Nazareth," he said, "I Am," and Judas and the soldiers drew back and fell to the ground, kept at bay by the numinous "I Am" that passed from Jesus' lips (18:5-6). The soldiers were accompanied by a high-rank-ing military official working in cooperation with the leading Jewish author-ities, but Jesus was the one who gave the orders. He secured the release of his disciples in order to keep them safe from the evil one (17:12, 15; 18:9) and only then allowed himself to be taken away. In John's Gospel, the arrest did not mark the world's triumph over Jesus but was part of Jesus' victory over the world (16:33). His captors could not compel him to go with them; he went along willingly in order to reveal his obedient love for the Father.

Jesus was brought before the Jewish and Roman authorities for ques-tioning and judgment. The charges leveled against him were false, but Jesus responded with testimony that was true. He had come into the world "to bear witness to the truth" (18:37), and truth won out in the end. The trial exonerated Jesus, who was repeatedly pronounced innocent, and dem-onstrated the guilt of his accusers, as noted earlier. The transcendent significance of these encounters would become apparent to the disciples only later, when the Paraclete would reveal that Jesus' passion brought about "the judgment of this world" (12:31), for in it "the ruler of this world has been judged" (16:11). The Paraclete would prove that the world—not just Pilate or the Pharisees—was guilty of the sin of unbe-lief and would vindicate Jesus' claim to righteousness by revealing his unity with God over against the accusations of his detractors (16:7-11; 5:30; 7:24; 8:45-46).[44]

The ruler of the world extended his dominion through the power of hatred. The world hated Jesus because he testified that its works were evil (3:20; 7:7), and it would continue to hate his followers after he returned to the Father (15:18-19), but God responded to the world's hatred with

43. Many interpreters have argued plausibly that in an earlier version of the Gospel, 14:31 immediately preceded Jesus' movement to the garden. This would strengthen the connection between Jesus' comment regarding the ruler of the world and the appearance of Judas and the soldiers. On the possibility that chaps. 15–17 were added later, see the summary of research by Fernando F. Segovia, *The Farewell of the Word: The Johannine Call to Abide* (Minneapolis: Fortress, 1991) 29–31. On the way 14:30-31 anticipates the arrest and trial, see the same work, p. 114 n. 97.

44. Schnackenburg, *Gospel*, 3.131.

love and gave his Son to be crucified as the consummate manifestation of his love (3:16). The cross of Jesus was the weapon that God wielded in the battle with Satan, for through the cross the love of God engaged and defeated the forces of hatred arrayed against him.[45] The ruler of the world also relied on deceit to exert control, since falsehood was part of his nature. He was a liar and the father of lies, and those whom he influenced were unable to bear the truth (8:44-45); but God sent Jesus into the world to bear witness to the truth (8:40; 18:37). Jesus' trial and execution exposed the duplicity of his adversaries and unmasked the murderous tendencies they had tried to conceal (7:1, 20) while revealing Jesus' innocence and complete conformity to the will of God. Finally, the ruler of the world sought to conquer by inflicting death. He was a murderer from the beginning (8:44), and his accomplices tried to bring Jesus into submission by killing him and even by assassinating Lazarus, whom Jesus had called out of the tomb (12:9-11). But the weapons of Satan's henchmen did not prevail against Jesus in the garden where he was arrested, and the spear that pierced him only revealed the irrepressible quality of the life he embodied, for the waters flowing from his side showed that life, not death, was victorious and that the crucified one was the source of the life-giving Spirit. Jesus' opponents had lifted him up onto the cross to die, but the cross—like the serpent on the pole—became the source of vitality to all who gazed upon it in faith, the ensign marking life's victory over death.

The Johannine Epistles retain a vivid sense of conflict and victory over Satan but translate it into terms of Christian life. The author of the first epistle recognized that the world was under the power of the evil one (1 John 5:19) and that all who commit sin are of the devil, who sinned from the beginning (3:8a). The minions of the evil one hate and murder their brothers as Cain did and are blinded by the spirit of deceit (4:6). Yet he also reminded his readers that "the reason the Son of God appeared was to destroy the works of the devil" (3:8b), that those who are born of God triumph over the world through faith in Jesus the Son of God, and that this victory is manifested in the love within the community of faith (4:4; 5:4-5; cf. 2:13-14).[46]

Exaltation and Glorification

The victory of the Son of God over the forces of Satan glorified both God and Jesus. As Jesus rode to Jerusalem for the battle, he announced that

---

45. Hebert Kohler connects the casting out of the ruler of the world (John 12:31) with the perfect love that casts out fear (1 John 4:18). See *Kreuz und Menschwerdung: Ein exegetisch-hermeneutischer Versuch zur johanneischen Kreuzestheologie* (AThANT 72; Zurich: Theologischer, 1987) 238–39.

46. See Brown, *Epistles*, 304–5.

the hour had come for the Son of man to be glorified and prayed in that same hour that God's name would be glorified in the casting out of the ruler of this world (12:23, 27-28, 31). The initial engagement with Judas ended when the betrayer, animated by Satan, went out into the darkness and Jesus announced, "Now is the Son of man glorified, and in him God is glorified" (13:31). The term *glorify* (*doxazein*) can mean to honor or praise someone (5:41, 44; 7:18; 8:50, 54); but the term can also mean to manifest the power and presence or "glory" (*doxa*) of God (11:4, 40; 17:4, 6). In the Gospel of John, the crucifixion of Jesus is the locus of divine revelation, for through it the glory of God was brought within the realm of human experience.

The evangelist prepares readers to see the cross as the visible manifestation of divine power by referring three times to the crucifixion as the moment when Jesus was "lifted up" (*hypsoun*).[47] This term holds together the physical and transcendent dimensions of the crucifixion because it refers both to physical elevation and exaltation in glory. The expression was first used in 3:14-15: "And as Moses lifted up the serpent in the wilderness, so must the Son of man be lifted up, that whoever believes in him may not perish but have eternal life." The text alludes to an incident recorded in Num. 21:4-9 in which the people of Israel rebelled against God and Moses and were bitten by fiery serpents as punishment. When the people repented, God told Moses to fashion a serpent of bronze and place it on a pole, so that all who looked at it might live. Although the power of the bronze serpent was sometimes viewed in a magical or superstitious way (2 Kings 18:4), first-century interpreters understood that turning to the serpent on the pole was a visible way of turning to God, and it was God's power that healed.[48] Like the bronze serpent, Jesus was lifted up onto a gibbet—a physical action with two revelatory dimensions suggested by the context and developed elsewhere in the Gospel. The death of Jesus reveals the fullness of God's love for the world, the love that delivers people from death by bringing them into the relationship with God that is eternal life (3:16). Jesus' elevation on the cross was also part of his ascension to the Father (3:13), and those who view the cross with faith are able to see there the risen and ascended Lord.[49]

Later in the Gospel, Jesus was engaged in a heated debate with some of his Jewish detractors and told them, "When you have lifted up the Son

---

47. On the exaltation of Jesus see Wilhelm Thüsing, *Die Erhöhung und Verherrlichung Jesu im Johannesevangelium* (NTAbh 21; Münster: Aschendorff, 1960) 3–37; Forestell, *The Word of the Cross,* 61–65; Schnackenburg, *Gospel,* 2.399–401; Maloney, *The Johannine Son of Man,* 42–67, 124–41, 160–85.

48. Wisd. of Sol. 16:5-12; *m. Rosh Hash.* 3:8; Philo, *Allegorical Interpretation* 2.81; see also the Targums noted in Forestell, *The Word of the Cross,* 62.

49. Forestell, *The Word of the Cross,* 63, 74; Schnackenburg, *Gospel,* 2.400.

of man, then you will know that I Am [*egō eimi*] and that I do nothing on
my own authority but speak thus as the Father taught me" (8:28). The
saying again points to the physical elevation of Jesus on the cross, since it
anticipates that his adversaries will be the ones who lift him up. The
comment also intimates that the crucifixion will have revelatory significance. Jesus told his hearers that they were from below and he was from
above, warning that "you will die in your sins unless you believe that I Am"
(*egō eimi*, 8:24), the expression that recalls the name of God. Jesus could
identify himself with God because he had been sent from God to speak as
God had taught him, and he claimed no authority independent of God
(8:25, 28b). In his crucifixion, Jesus conformed so completely to the divine
will that his death revealed the depth of his unity with the Father and
became the visible sign of Jesus' return to God, who had sent him. Because of this revelatory power, the cross brings both salvation and condemnation. Some, by faith, recognize the divine dignity of the crucified Jesus
and are thereby delivered from sin and brought into life. But there is also
the ominous sense that some will come to know who Jesus is only when it
is too late and will thereby incur divine judgment.[50]

Jesus uttered the last of these sayings at the conclusion of his public
ministry, when he told the crowds, "I, when I am lifted up from the earth,
will draw all people to myself" (12:32). The physical dimension of the
lifting up is pointed out by the narrator, who explains that Jesus said this
"to show by what death he was to die," and is recognized by the crowds,
who take it as a foreshadowing of his death (12:33-34). The saying also
discloses that the cross is the physical manifestation of the power of the
risen and ascended Son of man. Following his exaltation through death,
Jesus would draw all people to himself—an action that earlier had been
ascribed to God (6:44). Prior to Jesus' death, unbelief prevailed. The
evangelist concluded his account of Jesus' public ministry with the sweeping observation, "He had done so many signs before them, yet they did
not believe in him"; moreover, "they could not believe in him" for God
had "blinded their eyes and hardened their heart" (12:37-40). Yet unbelief
would not be the final word, for after Jesus was lifted up, people would be
drawn into faith in the crucified Jesus, a faith that could be engendered
only by the power of God.

The term *glorify* is broader in scope than *lift up*. It includes the actions
that Jesus performed during his ministry on earth, culminating with the
crucifixion. It also refers to the work that would continue among Jesus'
followers, through the agency of the Spirit, after his return to the Father.

50. See Thüsing, *Die Erhöhung und Verherrlichung*, 16; Schnackenburg, *Gospel*, 2.202–3;
Maloney, *The Johannine Son of Man*, 135–41; Frank Matera, "'On Behalf of Others,' 'Cleansing,' and 'Return': Johannine Images for Jesus' Death," *LS* 13 (1988) 161–78, esp. 174.

To some extent, we can say that Jesus' activity unfolds in two phases—the work of the earthly Jesus and that of the ascended Lord; but in John's Gospel the two phases are part of a single movement. The term *glorify* comprehends in a single complex idea the whole of Jesus' saving work. The cross is the moment of glory that brings Jesus' ministry to its climax as well as the visible sign of the glory of the exalted Lord.[51]

One side of glorification was that God was glorified by Jesus through the crucifixion. First, Jesus glorified or honored God throughout his ministry by performing the works that God had given him to do, thereby demonstrating his own obedience to the divine will (17:4). The cross was the capstone of these works, for by his obedience even to death, Jesus revealed the fullness of his love for the Father (14:31). Second, through his work on earth, Jesus also manifested the "name"—that is, the reality or the presence of God to people—in order that they might come to know God and enter into the relationship with him that is eternal life (17:3, 6). The signs revealed God's glory by displaying the scope of divine power; the cross would reveal God's glory by displaying the depths of divine love. C. H. Dodd commented that if the signs are the means by which "the power and presence of God are brought within human experience," then Jesus' "self-devotion to death in love for mankind is the conclusive manifestation of the divine glory."[52]

The passion narrative began by stating that Jesus, "having loved his own who were in the world, loved them to the end," or perhaps it could be translated, "loved them completely" (*eis telos*, 13:1). Then he laid down his garments, assumed the posture of a slave, and washed the disciples' feet in an act that showed the kind of complete devotion that would lead him to lay down his life for them. As he prepared to leave the supper, he summed up the whole of his ministry by saying, Father, "I glorified you on earth by completing [*teleiōsas*] the work which you gave me to do" (17:4). The Gospel's portrayal of Jesus' death recalls the love and glory presaged in these earlier passages. As Jesus' life finally ebbed away on the cross, "all things were completed" (*tetelestai*, 19:28), and after receiving the sour wine

51. The distinction between the two phases was used by Thüsing in *Die Erhöhung und Verherrlichung*. See Blank, *Krisis*, 267–69; Ulrich Müller, "Die Bedeutung des Kreutzestodes Jesu im Johannesevangelium," *KD* 21 (1975) 49–71; Harald Hegermann, "Er kam in sein Eigentum: Zur Bedeutung des Erdenwirkens Jesu im vierten Evangelium," *Der Ruf Jesu und die Antwort der Gemeinde: Festschrift für Joachim Jeremias* (ed. E. Lohse et al.; Göttingen: Vandenhoeck & Ruprecht, 1970) 112–31; Schnackenburg, *Gospel*, 2.401–4, and *Das Johannesevangelium*, 4.173–83; Godfrey C. Nicholson, *Death as Departure: The Johannine Descent-Ascent Schema* (SBLDS 63; Chico, Calif.: Scholars, 1983) 75–160; Lindars, "The Passion of Jesus in the Fourth Gospel," 74–83. Ernst Käsemann argued that the glory of Jesus was so prominent that the Gospel conveyed a docetic impression of Jesus in which the cross seemed to be a postscript (*The Testament of Jesus according to John 17* [Philadelphia: Fortress, 1968] 4–26). See the critique by Thompson, *The Humanity of Jesus in the Fourth Gospel*, 87–115.

52. *Interpretation*, 207–8.

he said, "It is completed" (*tetelestai*, 19:30); then he bowed his head and gave up his spirit. The cross revealed the scope of divine glory by revealing the depths of divine love.

The other side of glorification was that through the cross Jesus himself was glorified. Through death Jesus passed over to God and resumed his preexistent glory. The Father had granted the Son a share in divine glory before the foundation of the world as an expression of his love (17:24). The signs Jesus performed during his time on earth revealed that even in "the flesh" he shared in divine glory (1:14; 2:11), but through death God "glorified" Jesus by restoring him, in divine love, to the fullness of heavenly glory. The departure of Jesus to the Father was not simply a continuation of his earthly glory; it marked what Wilhelm Thüsing has called the transition from the glory of obedience to the glory of sovereignty.[53] Jesus prayed for this transcendent glory before he died, asking, "And now Father, glorify me in your own presence with the glory which I had with you before the world was made" (17:5).

Jesus' prayer would be answered, but the answer would be apparent only after Easter. John's accounts of the resurrection appearances offer readers a glimpse of Jesus' return to the Father. Peter and the Beloved Disciple saw the empty tomb and the useless grave cloths that no longer bound the body of Jesus. Mary Magdalene encountered Jesus outside the tomb and was told that he was ascending to God (20:17). Yet throughout this exaltation to glory, Jesus remained the one who was crucified. He appeared to the disciples on Easter evening and breathed the Spirit into them, which was an act reminiscent of the way God had enlivened the first human being and one that showed Jesus had returned to the Father; but he did so only after showing the wounds in his hands and side (20:19-23; cf. 16:7; Gen. 2:7). And a week later Thomas called the risen Lord who still bore the scars of his execution "My Lord and my God" (John 20:27-28).

In John's Gospel, the crucifixion, resurrection, and ascension are aspects of a single event. It shows that in retrospect the radiance of divine glory can be perceived in the crucified body of Jesus through the agency of the Holy Spirit. The Gospel says that at first the disciples did not understand everything Jesus had said and done, but later "remembered" and comprehended it. The Fourth Gospel, which is the product of such reflection, shows that the moment of Jesus' glorification encompasses both crucifixion and resurrection, culminating with his return to the Father, which was signaled by the coming of the Spirit (2:22; 7:39; 12:16). The Spirit continued to glorify Jesus within the community of faith, by declaring the

---

53. *Die Erhöhung und Verherrlichung*, 291. Cf. Thompson, *The Humanity of Jesus in the Fourth Gospel*, 88, 95; Blank, *Krisis*, 267.

truth to his followers, enabling them to remember and comprehend what had happened (14:26; 16:14).

J. Terence Forestell has said that the Fourth Gospel presents "the cross as the visible sign of the exaltation and glorification of the Son of Man in the presence of God." The victory Jesus won over death and the world includes his resurrection and ascension to the Father, "but the elevation of Jesus on the cross is the visible sign of this triumph."[54] The cross is not only the beginning of Jesus' movement toward transcendent glory; faith sees the glory of the exalted Lord already present in the crucified body of Jesus. The Holy Spirit would be given only when Jesus had risen and ascended to the Father, but the water that signified the Spirit was already trickling from the wound in Jesus' side on the day of his death. "Those who view the cross with faith are able to see there the risen and ascended Lord who has manifested God's glory by revealing his love."[55]

BEHOLD YOUR SON,
BEHOLD YOUR MOTHER

The work through which Jesus glorified the Father and was himself glorified culminated in the crucifixion, but it did not end there. The Johannine portrayal of Jesus' death expands the horizon to include the continued glorification of the Father and the Son within the community of faith that had its inception at the cross. The community was the "fruit" of Jesus' glorification (12:23-24, 32), and the cross gave shape to its corporate life.[56] Jesus had glorified God by being obedient unto death and by abiding in God's love; the disciples would glorify God by expressing the love of Jesus through obedience to his commandment to love one another, even to the point of giving up their lives (15:8-13). God had glorified Jesus by restoring to him his preexistent glory; the disciples would glorify Jesus by recognizing his singular relationship with the Father (18:9-10) and by reflecting the glory of the mutual love shared by the Father and the Son in their own community (17:22-23).

Forming a Community
of Faith

The passion narrative binds the Christian community to the crucifixion of Jesus through an incident that is both simple and evocative. "Jesus, seeing

---

54. *The Word of the Cross,* 73. Cf. Blank, *Krisis,* 269 n. 12; Dauer, *Die Passionsgeschichte im Johannesevangelium,* 237; Becker, *Das Evangelium nach Johannes,* 2.406. On the fusion of temporal horizons in Jesus' claim to victory, see Gail R. O'Day, "'I Have Overcome the World' (John 16:33): Narrative Time in John 13–17," *Semeia* 53 (1991) 153–66.

55. Forestell, *The Word of the Cross,* 74.

56. Thüsing, *Die Erhöhung und Verherrlichung,* 141.

his mother and the disciple whom he loved standing there, said to his mother, 'Woman, behold, your son.' And to the disciple, 'Behold, your mother'" (19:26-27). This gentle scene forms an inclusio for Jesus' ministry. His mother appears only twice in the Gospel: at the wedding at Cana and at Golgotha. In both scenes Jesus addresses his mother in the same way, as "woman." At Cana Jesus' ministry had its beginning, and even though his "hour" had not yet come, he offered a preliminary manifestation of his glory by turning water into wine. At Golgotha Jesus' ministry reached its conclusion, and in that hour he offered the consummate manifestation of glory by laying down his life.

The ministry that began at a wedding in a Galilean village was completed by the formation of a new relationship between a woman and a man at the cross. Jesus' words effectively entrusted his mother to the care of the Beloved Disciple, an act consistent with Jewish practice in which a son was expected to provide for his mother who would otherwise remain alone.[57] Therefore it was appropriate that "from that hour the disciple took her to his own home" (19:27). Yet the gesture was not an ordinary display of filial devotion, since Jesus persistently addressed her as "woman," the same expression he used for other women in the Gospel (4:21; 20:15). Although he used the term without apparent disrespect for the other women, it was a startling way for a son to address his mother. Moreover, at Cana Jesus also said, "What have you to do with me?" (2:4), an expression that was generally used brusquely to establish distance between the one speaking and the one being addressed. This manner of speech indicates that Jesus' actions cannot be understood in terms of ordinary familial relations.[58]

The statement "Behold, your son" is also striking, since Jesus had brothers who were present alongside his mother at Cana (2:12), and they would ordinarily have been the ones to provide care for Jesus' mother. Yet the Gospel shows that although Jesus' brothers may have been his kindred in a human sense, they were not his brothers in faith. They were not included among his disciples but challenged Jesus to go to Judea "that your disciples may see the works you are doing"; and they said this because "even his brothers did not believe in him" (7:3, 5). Conversely, the Beloved Disciple is a model of faith throughout John's Gospel, although there is no suggestion that he was part of Jesus' kinship circle.[59] The words that Jesus spoke—"Behold, your son" and "Behold, your mother"—resemble to

57. See Heinz Schürmann, "Jesu Letzte Weisung: Jo 19,26-27a," *Ursprung und Gestalt: Erörterungen und Besinnungen zum Neuen Testament* (Düsseldorf: Patmos, 1970) 13–28, esp. 14–16.

58. For helpful discussion of Mary's role see Raymond E. Brown et al., *Mary in the New Testament* (New York/Mahwah: Paulist, 1978) 188–90, 206–18.

59. See Schnackenburg, *Gospel*, 3.277.

some extent the formulas used for rites of adoption in the ancient world. They are appropriate for a scene in which two people, who are connected by their common faith relationship with Jesus rather than by kinship ties, are brought together into relationship with each other, forming the nucleus of a new community.

Representative Figures

The significance of this scene becomes clearer when we consider the representative traits of the two figures involved, Jesus' mother and the Beloved Disciple. The mother of Jesus was, of course, a unique individual. Her name never appears in the Fourth Gospel; she is always identified in her singular role as "the mother of Jesus." Her distinctive maternal relationship to Jesus is acknowledged. Nevertheless, the Gospel portrays Jesus' mother in a way that suggests that she, like other individuals in the narrative, is a representative of believers generally,

The scene at the cross contains several indications of her representative role. First, Jesus' mother was not alone but was one of several women present for the crucifixion. These included his mother's sister, Mary the wife of Clopas, and Mary Magdalene (19:25).[60] Representative figures earlier in the Gospel were usually identified with groups of people either explicitly or implicitly.

Second, by calling his mother "woman," he placed her in the same category as other women in the Gospel. He had told the woman at the well, "Woman, believe me, the hour is coming when neither on this mountain nor in Jerusalem will you worship the Father" (4:21). And outside the empty tomb he would ask Mary Magdalene, "Woman, why are you weeping, whom do you seek?" (20:15). Each of these women initially responded to Jesus with incomprehension: His mother did not grasp the significance of his "hour," the Samaritan woman did not understand what he meant by the living water or the worship in Spirit and truth, and Mary Magdalene mistook him for the gardener. But each woman eventually moved toward a more complete recognition of who he was.

Third, the group of women beside the cross was introduced with a Greek construction (*men . . . de*) that contrasts them with the soldiers who gambled for Jesus' clothing in the previous scene: "Now [*men*] the soldiers did this. But [*de*] standing by the cross of Jesus were his mother" and the other women (19:25).[61] The soldiers appear negatively as those crucifying Jesus, but the women appear positively as those present in faith. Earlier in the Gospel, Jesus' mother appeared as a positive example at Cana

---

60. See Dauer, *Die Passionsgeschichte im Johannesevangelium*, 329; Schürmann, "Jesu letzte Weisung," 23. On the number of women beside the cross see Brown, *Gospel*, 2.904–6.
61. See Dauer, *Die Passionsgeschichte im Johannesevangelium*, 329.

in contrast to the negative example of the bystanders in the temple. In that pair of scenes, Jesus' mother displayed uncomprehending trust in Jesus, while the crowds reflected uncomprehending skepticism at Jesus' words and actions. At the cross the mother of Jesus continues to exemplify discipleship.[62]

The anonymous "disciple whom Jesus loved" also has both a singular and a representative role to play. In many respects he is unique. At the last supper he was the one who lay beside Jesus and learned the identity of the betrayer. He was apparently the "other disciple" who entered the courtyard of the high priest (18:15-16) and, unlike Peter, did not deny his relationship with Jesus but followed all the way to the cross. It was Mary Magdalene who discovered the open tomb, but the Beloved Disciple was the first to look into the tomb, the first to believe there, and the first to recognize Jesus when he later appeared in Galilee (20:4, 8; 21:7). Although the Beloved Disciple appears to be an idealized figure, the conclusion of the Gospel indicates that he was an actual person who was the mediator of the tradition on which the Gospel was based (21:24). The death of this disciple created a crisis within a circle of believers who believed that he would survive until Jesus' return (21:22-23), and such a crisis is comprehensible only if the disciple is understood to have actually lived.

Yet the Beloved Disciple also has a representative function. First, he is always identified as a "disciple," which was the same designation used for other followers of Jesus. He is not set apart as an apostle, an elder, or by any title that would distinguish him from other believers. The faithfulness he exhibited was exemplary, and it is precisely as a disciple that he provides a model for all disciples. He was especially loved by Jesus, but the Gospel also makes clear that Jesus' love extended to all those who believed in him. As a recipient of Jesus' love and a model of fidelity, the Beloved Disciple is the paradigm of discipleship generally.

Second, the primary task of the Beloved Disciple was to bear witness to Jesus. The Gospel preserves his testimony, and through it he continues to bear witness to what Jesus has said and done (21:24). It is apparently the voice of this disciple that speaks at the conclusion of the crucifixion, saying, "He who saw it has borne witness—his testimony is true and he knows that he tells the truth—that you also may believe" (19:35). At the same time, witnessing was the task given to all of Jesus' followers. John the Baptist (1:19, 32, 34) and the Samaritan woman (4:39) are explicitly said to have "witnessed" to Jesus, and at the last supper Jesus told those present that all of them were his witnesses (15:27). Apparently speaking for his disciples generally, Jesus said, "We speak of what we know and bear

62. On Jesus' mother as a representative disciple see Schürmann, "Jesu letzte Weisung," 20–23; Dauer, *Die Passionsgeschichte im Johannesevangelium,* 329.

witness to what we have seen; but you do not receive our testimony" (3:11). The testimony of the Beloved Disciple expresses the faith of a community of disciples.

Third, the Beloved Disciple was entrusted with the care of Jesus' mother, which suggests that he himself became a brother of Jesus at the foot of the cross. Earlier in the Gospel, the term *brother* was used for some who were apparently related to Jesus by blood but not by faith (2:12; 7:3, 5). After the resurrection, however, *brother* was used in the opposite way, for those who were related to Jesus by faith but not necessarily by kinship ties. Outside the empty tomb, Jesus told Mary Magdalene to "go to my brothers," which now referred to his disciples, and tell them, "I am ascending to my Father and your Father," which indicated that they now were part of the same family (20:17). *Brother* became the common designation within the circle of Christians who accepted the Beloved Disciple's testimony. If this disciple became Jesus' brother at the cross, he was the first of many brethren.[63]

Jesus' mother and the Beloved Disciple have sometimes been understood individually, with one figure or the other standing for the whole church, or each representing one facet of the church. But both are models for all disciples to follow, and it is in their relationship with each other that they represent the church.[64] The scene in which Jesus' mother is entrusted to the Beloved Disciple portrays the beginnings of a faith community that would extend into the future and would come to include "those who have not seen, yet believe" (20:29). The Gospel relates that Jesus took the initiative in creating this community and that it came into being in response to the words he spoke from the cross. The gathering of the first disciples began when John the Baptist pointed to Jesus, "the Lamb of God" (1:35-37), and the post-Easter community had its inception on Good Friday. Given only the signs and wonders, unbelief prevails; Jesus remains alone in the crowd. His ministry comes to its fruition through death, as Marianne Thompson has commented; for there is no fruit unless a seed falls into the earth and dies, "just as the 'other sheep' can be brought into the fold only if the shepherd lays down his life (10:15-17); and the scattered children of God are gathered only if Jesus dies (11:52)."[65]

The crucifixion of Jesus is the central symbolic action in the Fourth Gospel, fusing and conveying several levels of meaning simultaneously: It was the death of an innocent man who sacrificed his life in accordance

---

63. See Dauer, *Die Passionsgeschichte im Johannesevangelium*, 323. On the use of "brother" among Johannine Christians see John 21:23; 1 John 2:9–11; 3:10–17; 4:20–21; 5:16.

64. For discussion of the various symbolisms proposed for Mary and the Beloved Disciple see Dauer, *Die Passionsgeschichte im Johannesevangelium*, 324–33; Brown, *Gospel*, 2.923–27; Schnackenburg, *Gospel*, 3.279–82.

65. *The Humanity of Jesus in the Fourth Gospel*, 96.

with the will of God; it was the enthronement of Israel's Messiah, the glorification of the Son of man, and the inception of the community of faith. This symbolic presentation of Jesus' death finds its coherence in the divine love that each aspect discloses, yet the elusive element of transcendence remains. The tensions in the symbolism convey meaning that finally resists full explication.

7

Symbol and Community

John's Gospel was written in and for a community of faith. The text is expressive, voicing the convictions of the Christians who added their affidavit to its final page: "We know" that this testimony is true (21:24; cf. 1:14, 16). Yet the Gospel is also persuasive, making its case "in order that you might believe" (19:35; 20:31). As it bears a message from the "we" to the "you," the text serves as a means of interpersonal communication, shaping the way people see themselves in relation to God, to each other, and to the world in which they live. People almost certainly were drawn into the first Johannine communities through testimony delivered orally and invitations to "come and see" (1:39, 46; 4:29); but faith is not self-sustaining, and Johannine Christians had an ongoing need to hear and reaffirm the community's testimony. The text was an integral part of that process.

Much of the Gospel's witness is presented in symbolic form, and in Johannine terms an effective symbol must enable people to "remain" in Jesus and "continue" in his word together with other disciples (*menein*, 6:56; 8:31; 15:4). Interpreting the symbolism, therefore, involves asking about what it does as well as what it means, about its role in community life as well as its theological significance. The Gospel bears the marks of the social setting in which it was composed; like the hands of the risen Jesus, it displays transcendent realities through scars incurred in earthly conflict. The text conveys a "symbolic universe" that provides ways to conceive of life and death, community and contention; and by affecting the way readers perceive their situation, it influences the way they respond to it.[1]

1. On the way "symbolic universes" integrate provinces of meaning, affect actions, and are challenged and reaffirmed, see Peter L. Berger and Thomas Luckmann, *The Social Construction of Reality: A Treatise in the Sociology of Knowledge* (New York: Doubleday, 1966) 92–

Correlating the symbols in the narrative with the social experience of an early Christian community is a promising but complex task, the difficulties of which have been summarized by Bengt Holmberg.[2] One problem is that the symbols themselves provide little information about the social situation of the readers. When Jesus says, "I am the vine, you are the branches" (15:5), for example, the symbolism has both indicative and imperative force. The imagery describes a community of believers rooted in Jesus, yet it is accompanied by exhortations to be and become this kind of community by abiding in the vine. There is always a gap between norm and practice, and the symbol itself does not tell us how fully Johannine Christians realized the ideal. It is also difficult to glean much information about the social or economic background of the readers from these symbols. For example, believers are depicted as branches of a vine and the flock of the good shepherd. Yet we cannot assume that Johannine Christians were engaged primarily in agrarian occupations, especially since nearly all the encounters described in the Gospel take place in towns.

Another issue is that symbols often affect people in different and sometimes contradictory ways.[3] When Jesus declared that he was "the light of the world" in the context of heated debates over his identity, his opponents heard the claim as blasphemous self-aggrandizement (8:12-13). Later Jesus used similar symbolism to assure his disciples that they could follow him to Judea without fear of persecution, since those who walk by the light of this world do not stumble (11:9-10). In addition, Jesus told a querulous crowd that the light would be with them only a little longer, calling them to genuine faith (12:35-36). Light and darkness may alienate or assure, motivate or confuse, depending on the perspective of the listener.[4] Even among the faithful a symbol often functions in different ways. The cross, for example, symbolizes the victory of the Son of man

---

128. On the relationship of symbols to communities see esp. Clifford Geertz, "Religion as a Cultural System," *Anthropological Approaches to the Study of Religion* (ed. M. Banton; A.S.A. Monographs 3; London: Tavistock, 1966) 1–46; Victor Turner, *The Forest of Symbols: Aspects of Ndembu Ritual* (Ithaca, N.Y.: Cornell University Press, 1967) 19–58. For a sketch of studies on symbolism and social anthropology see F. W. Dillistone, *The Power of Symbols in Religion and Culture* (New York: Crossroad, 1986) 99–116.

2. *Sociology and the New Testament: An Appraisal* (Minneapolis: Fortress, 1990) 134–44. In Holmberg's terms, the first issue is "symmetry or asymmetry in correlation" between symbol and social reality. See also Gerd Theissen, *Studien zur Sociologie des Urchristentums* (3d ed.; Tübingen: Mohr/Siebeck, 1989) 40–51. Cf. John Elliott, *A Home for the Homeless: A Social-Scientific Criticism of 1 Peter, Its Situation and Strategy* (Minneapolis: Fortress, 1990) xxiv–xxvi, 1–20; idem, "Social-Scientific Criticism of the New Testament: More on Methods and Models," *Semeia* 35 (1986) 1–33; Carolyn Osiek, "The Social Sciences and the Second Testament: Problems and Challenges," *BTB* 22 (1992) 88–95.

3. Holmberg calls this "the multifunctionality of beliefs" (*Sociology and the New Testament*, 137–39).

4. See Jonathan Z. Smith, "The Influence of Symbols upon Social Change: A Place on Which to Stand," *Worship* 44 (1970) 457–74.

over the demonic ruler of the world (12:31-32), yet it also exemplifies the way of servanthood, which Jesus and his disciples must follow for their lives to bear fruit (12:23-26). The complexity is compounded when we consider the impact of an entire network of symbols on community life. In one passage Jesus' followers are a flock following the shepherd amid thieves and wolves (10:1-18), but elsewhere they are laborers ready to enter a field that is white for harvest (4:31-38). The image of the flock fosters an attitude of wariness about the world, but the image of the reapers contributes to a sense of openness.

Finally, we must contend with our own distance from the world in which the Fourth Gospel was composed. The first Johannine Christians died centuries ago and lie buried under the rubble of a culture quite different from our own. We have no way of observing their community life directly and must glean information from ancient texts to which we bring questions and assumptions informed by our own experiences. Interpretation can be disciplined by using models drawn from the social sciences, which help us test our assumptions about human behavior against those of others. These models, however, have been developed through observation of contemporary groups and cultures, all of which differ from the earliest Johannine communities and the Greco-Roman culture in which they existed.[5] The social sciences can stimulate ideas about what to look for in texts and offer ways to organize and interpret information, but they do not finally close a gap of two millennia.

Our approach will be to explore ways the Johannine writings themselves correlate symbols with their community's experience. (a) We will begin by listening to the way Johannine Christianity is characterized in the Fourth Gospel and Johannine Epistles, looking for the basic beliefs that Johannine Christians understood shaped community life. Instead of assuming that their professed beliefs mask the social dynamics actually governing community life, and that an outside observer must discount these beliefs when attempting to understand the group, we will give priority to the Johannine authors' own perceptions of their situation.[6] (b) We will explore social issues that seem to be especially prominent in these texts, including the unity of the group, patterns of discipleship, and the community's relationship to the world. Some of the factors affecting these issues will be inferred from the text. (c) We will note which symbols the Johan-

5. Holmberg calls this the problem of "intercultural commeasurability" (*Sociology and the New Testament*, 139–40).
6. Stressed by Stowers, "The Social Sciences and the Study of Early Christianity," 152–60; Richard L. Rohrbaugh, "'Social Location of Thought' as a Heuristic Construct in New Testament Study," *JSNT* 30 (1987) 103–19; Walter Rebell, *Gemeinde als Gegenwelt: Zur soziologischen und didaktischen Funktion des Johannesevangeliums* (BBET 20; Frankfurt am Main: Peter Lang, 1987) 18; Martyn, *History and Theology*, 18.

nine writings associate most closely with each issue, asking how these and other symbols fit the social situations reflected in the texts.

SYMBOL AND UNITY

Jesus' unity with the Father is a central theological affirmation in the Fourth Gospel and one that embroiled Johannine Christians in intense social controversy. In the face of accusations that Jesus was attempting to usurp God's place, the Gospel tries to show that Jesus spoke and acted in harmony with God's will, declaring to the world what he heard from God and performing deeds that gave life and brought judgment as God commissioned him to do (5:19-24; 8:28). In previous chapters we have seen that the text conveys this unity through symbols like light, water, and the good shepherd, which help to show that Jesus is at once a teacher or leader, a prophet, Messiah, and divine. A single image encompasses seemingly contradictory aspects of his identity. The depth of Jesus' unity with God is disclosed by the crucifixion, which was his consummate act of obedience to God's will on earth and the way he rejoined the Father in heaven (see pp. 212–14).

Unity among Jesus' followers expresses Jesus' own unity with God and is one of the Gospel's most important social issues. In the good shepherd discourse and its aftermath, Jesus declared, "I and the Father are one" and that there must be "one flock, one shepherd" (10:16, 30). Since the crucifixion manifested Jesus' unity with God, the evangelist expected Jesus' death to "gather into one the children of God who are scattered abroad" (11:52). Before the departure to the Father, which he accomplished through his passion, Jesus prayed that the followers he left behind might be one as he and the Father were one (17:11), and that those who came to believe through their witness might "become perfectly one, so that the world may know that you have sent me and have loved them, even as you have loved me" (17:21, 23).[7]

Unity and
the Johannine Context

The passages just quoted allow us to discern some of the issues affecting the unity of Johannine Christians during a formative period in their history. First, Jesus' farewell prayer treats the issue of unity against the backdrop of conflict with the nonbelieving world. After Jesus' departure, the

---

7. On the theme of unity see Mark L. Appold, *The Oneness Motif in the Fourth Gospel: Motif Analysis and Exegetical Probe into the Theology of John* (WUNT 1; Tübingen: Mohr/Siebeck, 1976); Rudolf Schnackenburg, *Das Johannesevangelium* (HTKNT 4; Freiburg: Herder, 1965–84) 4.173–83.

disciples remained in a world that hated them (17:14), and the threat of being expelled from the synagogue or killed placed pressure on Christians to leave the community of faith (16:1-2). The risk of expulsion and public dishonor prevented some Jewish Christians from publicly confessing their faith (12:42), but others openly identified themselves with Jesus and his followers and were put out of the Jewish community (9:34). After this separation had occurred, expulsion was no longer a threat for many of the Gospel's readers; some fear of persecution may have persisted, but the one reminiscence of actual violence against a disciple of Jesus is the allusion to Peter's martyrdom, which was apparently carried out by Roman rather than Jewish authorities (21:19).

By the time the Gospel was completed, conflict with the synagogue took the form of attempts to discredit Christian claims about Jesus. The fourth evangelist allows readers to eavesdrop on disputes that probably echo many of the charges leveled against Christian teachings in the later part of the first century.[8] Some opponents insisted that Jesus' miracles were the work of a charlatan, the product of demonic powers rather than genuine acts of God (7:12; 10:19-21). Others argued that Jesus' teaching lacked credibility and contended that anyone thinking that he was a prophet or the Messiah showed deplorable ignorance of Scripture (7:40-52). The idea that the Messiah should be crucified was deemed absurd (12:34), and the assertion of Jesus' unity with God was taken to be a blasphemous assault on the fundamental belief that God was one (5:18; 10:33; 19:7). Opponents who succeeded in undermining Christian teaching at these points would effectively erode the basis of Christian community.

The fourth evangelist, instead of attempting to avoid these issues, gave them a prominent place in the Gospel. Conflicts that threatened the community were portrayed vividly, and questions that were potentially devastating to the faith were posed and addressed with a combination of irony, humor, and symbolism. Such attention to the controversy with the synagogue may have had an important group-binding effect. John Elliott has noted that in many cases cooperation within a group is enhanced through conflict with outsiders. "Conflict presents an opportunity and a reason for the clarification and reaffirmation of those features of the group which make it distinctive, superior and motivated by a common 'cause.'"[9] The beggar who grew more tenacious in his loyalty to Jesus precisely in the face of escalating confrontation with synagogue officials exemplifies the ideal response to a threatening situation.[10] Jesus' deft replies to the repeated attempts to discredit his miracles and teachings give readers a

---

8. Martyn, *History and Theology*, 90–100.
9. *A Home for the Homeless*, 116.
10. Cf. Elliott, *A Home for the Homeless*, 115; Rebell, *Gemeinde als Gegenwelt*, 114.

perspective from which to withstand challenges from their own opponents. And symbolic language, which fuses several dimensions of meaning in a single image, provides a coherent way to conceive of the paradox that God was revealed in the person of Jesus and that "the light of the world" provoked the blindness of rejection as well as the illumination of faith (see pp. 27–28).

Second, Jesus' farewell prayer relates the concern for unity to the expansion of the Christian community through the evangelistic work of the disciples. The central part of the prayer asked God to protect and sanctify those whom Jesus was sending "into the world" (17:15-19), and the final section broadens the scope to include those who would come to faith through their witness, asking that both the earlier group of disciples and those who came to faith later might be one (17:20-21). The text does not indicate why the expansion of the community would raise questions about its ability to maintain its cohesiveness, but other passages in the Gospel suggest that ethnic diversification was a factor.

A changing ethnic composition is suggested by the evangelist's comment on Caiaphas's counsel that one man should die for the nation (11:51-52). The evangelist noted that Caiaphas was correct in saying that the Jewish nation would not "perish" since some would be saved by coming to faith in Jesus; yet he stressed that Jesus died not only for the Jewish nation but for "the children of God," an expression referring to believers of any background. From a Johannine perspective "the children of God" cannot be identified by physical descent but by birth "from above" through the Spirit (1:11-13; 3:3-8; 8:31-37). The Gospel narrative bears this out by showing that some Jews came to faith but many did not, and that some Samaritan and Greek outsiders responded favorably to Jesus.

Ethnic factors are also reflected in Jesus' promise to bring "other sheep, that are not of this fold" into his flock (10:16). The context of his remark is the good shepherd discourse, which follows the story of the beggar's expulsion from the synagogue and provides a kind of commentary on that incident. Jesus spoke to a group of Jewish listeners (9:40; 10:19) about the way a shepherd comes to the fold where sheep are kept, invoking a common pastoral image for God's relationship with Israel. Yet Jesus did not bring out all the sheep, only "his own sheep," those he actually called by name (10:3). He also had other sheep that were not from "this fold," that is, the Jewish fold, although the text does not say whether they would be of Samaritan, Greek, or some other background. They are called out of the fold and into a "flock," which is a broader term that encompasses all Jesus' followers. The future tense "they will heed my voice" indicates that they will be called at some later time, presumably through the activity of Jesus' disciples. Although the imagery echoes traditions about the ingathering of Israel, these are transformed to depict the ingathering of all who believe in Jesus. The Johannine Epistles suggest that the community eventually became mixed, since all the Christians identified in these letters bear Greco-Roman names: Gaius, Diotrephes, and Demetrius.[11]

The potentially complex effect of ethnic diversification on cohesiveness within Johannine communities can be inferred from the Gospel. One part of "the world" into which Jesus "sent" his disciples was Samaria, and the Gospel intimates that their work resulted in a number of Samaritan converts (4:38; cf. 17:18). Internally, a community composed of Jewish and Samaritan Christians would have had to deal with the animosities that formerly divided them (4:9). Externally, the inclusion of Samaritan Christians could have aggravated relationships with non-Christian Jews, who could charge that Johannine Christians had abandoned the tradition with their idolatrous regard for Jesus and showed their true character by affiliating with the Samaritans, who had apostatized long ago (4:22). Nevertheless, the Gospel suggests that a common faith in Jesus (4:42) and a sense of shared opposition from the synagogue (8:48) helped alleviate friction between Jewish and Samaritan Christians.

John's Gospel does not suggest that receiving Greeks into the community was a point of contention. Unlike the book of Acts and letters of Paul, the Fourth Gospel shows no trace of disputes over the need for gentile Christians to be circumcised or to observe other Jewish practices. Johannine Christians apparently bypassed this controversy because they had already separated from the synagogue over questions of Jesus' identity, and this rift made clear that "children of God" could not be identified along ethnic lines. Moreover, attempts to discredit Jesus on the basis of the Scriptures effectively undermined the credibility of the Pharisaic interpretation of Jewish law in the eyes of Johannine Christians (5:39; 7:19-24, 49-51). In the wake of these disputes, Johannine Christians would have been able to receive Samaritan and Greek converts on the basis of a common faith without the kind of rancor over Jewish observances evident in other sources.[12]

Yet as Johannine Christians endeavored to "teach the Greeks" (7:35), they had to make a message forged in conflict with the synagogue accessible to people who were not rooted in Jewish tradition without allowing it to be perceived as a new form of Greco-Roman religion. Johannine Christians argued that Jesus was the Messiah foretold in the Scriptures and the divine Son of man; but after claiming that Jesus had come "from above," that he could be worshiped, and that those who saw him saw God (8:23; 9:38; 12:45), they had to rebut charges that they had fallen into a kind of

11. Brown, *Epistles*, 34.
12. Brown, *Community*, 55–56.

polytheism (5:18; 8:41c; 10:33).[13] If the increasingly non-Jewish complexion of Johannine congregations reinforced their distinctiveness in relation to the synagogue, it also would have increased the need to maintain their unity and separate identity over against the wider Greco-Roman culture (cf. 1 John 5:21; 3 John 7).

A third factor affecting Johannine unity was geographical dispersion. The evangelist looked for Jesus' death to bring together the children of God "who are scattered abroad" (11:52). Although it is common to speak of "the Johannine community," it is probably more accurate to think of a number of Johannine communities located in different places. Even in the early phases of Johannine history, groups of Johannine Christians may have lived in different locations rather than in a single community whose members resided near each other. The Gospel itself says that there were groups of believers at places like Bethany in Transjordan (1:28; 10:40-42), Sychar in Samaria (4:5, 39), Bethany near Jerusalem (11:1-2), and perhaps Cana and Capernaum in Galilee (2:1, 12; 4:46, 53). The evangelist's detailed knowledge of topography and local traditions suggests that the earliest Johannine communities may actually have been located at sites in and around Palestine.[14] The population of Palestine was sufficiently diverse to account for the spectrum of readers envisioned by the Gospel. Jews and Samaritans were the dominant population in their respective areas, and there were significant numbers of Greeks and Romans in Caesarea, Sebaste, and the cities of the Decapolis, which were found on both sides of the Jordan.

Nevertheless, the concern for those "scattered abroad" suggests that Johannine communities were not confined to Palestine at the time the Gospel was completed. The final form of the text translates common expressions like "Messiah" and "rabbi," assuming that some readers would not have even the most rudimentary knowledge of the local languages of Palestine, Hebrew and Aramaic (1:38, 41; 20:16). Some Johannine Christians may have moved out of Palestine because of the conflict with the Jewish authorities—"scattering" in the Fourth Gospel usually does occur in response to a threat (10:12; 16:32)—although it is unlikely that the

13. Martyn notes the importance of the charge of "ditheism" but locates it firmly within a Jewish milieu (*History and Theology*, 64–81).

14. See the pioneering work of Karl Kundsin, *Topologische Überlieferungstoffe im Johannes-Evangelium: Eine Untersuchung* (FRLANT 22; Göttingen: Vandenhoeck & Ruprecht, 1925); cf. Meeks, *Prophet-King*, 314–16; idem, "Breaking Away: Three New Testament Pictures of Christianity's Separation from the Jewish Communities," *"To See Ourselves as Others See Us": Christians, Jews, "Others" in Late Antiquity* (ed. J. Neusner and E. S. Frerichs; Chico, Calif.: Scholars, 1985) 93–115, esp. 99–103; Charles H. H. Scobie, "Johannine Geography," *SR* 11 (1982) 77–84. Klaus Wenst argues for Batanaea, east of Galilee (*Bedrängte Gemeinde und verherrlichter Christus: Der historische Ort des Johannesevangeliums als Schlüssel zu seiner Interpretation* [2d ed.; Biblisch-theologische Studien 5; Neukirchen-Vluyn: Neukirchener, 1983]).

whole community did so. Those living in "dispersion among the Greeks" apparently instructed non-Jews in the faith (7:35), and Johannine congregations were probably established in a number of towns in the eastern Roman Empire. The exact locations of these house churches cannot be identified, and groups of Jews and Samaritans are known to have lived alongside Greeks in various places around the Mediterranean.[15] For our purposes the impact of geographical separation itself is more significant than the exact location of these congregations.

The Johannine Epistles provide glimpses into the difficulties confronting Christians who attempted to maintain ties between congregations geographically separated from each other. At least two of the letters were written because the author, who belonged to one congregation, was personally unable to visit the addressees in another congregation (2 John 12; 3 John 13). Problems arose because Johannine Christians, who did not always know each other personally, depended on their sister congregations for hospitality when they traveled. Inns were available but were considered disreputable, and travelers sought accommodations among their associates whenever possible. It was imperative that hospitality be extended to traveling visitors from other Johannine communities, especially the "strangers" who had set out as missionaries in God's service (3 John 3-5). Not every stranger who appeared at the door could be trusted, since the world was filled with charlatans (2 John 7), and Johannine Christians relied on shared professions of faith and letters of recommendation rather than personal acquaintance to identify the other members of their circle (2 John 10-11).[16]

A fourth factor affecting unity was the organizational pattern of Johannine congregations. Raymond Brown has observed that John's Gospel and epistles describe a group of people "personally attached to Jesus" and "guided by the Holy Spirit."[17] The principal authority for Johannine Christians was God. Jesus was God's emissary, whose words and actions were authoritative because they expressed God's will. In his farewell prayer, Jesus said that while he was in the world he had kept his followers in his Father's name but asked that after his departure they might continue to be one (17:11). His petition points to the problem of maintaining Christian unity when Jesus was no longer physically present with his followers. Johannine Christians understood that Jesus' teaching role was assumed by the Paraclete, who was also called the Spirit of Truth or Holy Spirit; it was through the Paraclete that the risen Jesus and the Father continued to be

15. Evidence of Samaritan as well as Jewish groups in diaspora has recently appeared. See Alan D. Crown, *The Samaritans* (Tübingen: Mohr/Siebeck, 1989) 195–217.

16. On issues pertaining to travel and hospitality see Abraham J. Malherbe, *Social Aspects of Early Christianity* (2d ed.; Philadelphia: Fortress, 1983) 60–70, 94–103.

17. *The Churches the Apostles Left Behind* (New York: Paulist, 1984) 84, 102.

present with the disciples (14:16-17, 23). The Paraclete reminded the disciples of what Jesus had said, disclosed the implications of Jesus' words and actions for their own time (14:25-26), and bore witness to Jesus and to the world's sinfulness in a manner consistent with the testimony of the disciples who were with Jesus from the beginning (15:26-27).

The person who most fully carried out the functions of the Paraclete was "the disciple whom Jesus loved," whom Johannine Christians considered to be the premier eyewitness to Jesus. This disciple had been with Jesus at the last supper and the crucifixion; he was the first to peer into the empty tomb, the first to believe on Easter morning, and the first to recognize the risen Jesus beside the Sea of Tiberius. In the period after the resurrection, the Beloved Disciple was a living link with Jesus, a special agent of the Paraclete, the guarantor of the community's traditions.[18] After his death, the Beloved Disciple's influence was extended through the legacy of his witness, which is preserved in the Fourth Gospel (21:24), and by the ongoing activity of the Paraclete rather than through a personal successor. Although this disciple's relationship with Jesus was unique in many ways, he was not the only recipient of the Paraclete. The Paraclete was given to all believers, so that even after their premier witness died, Johannine Christians could be sure that the work of teaching and witnessing would continue in their communities.

The Beloved Disciple occupied no established office; like other followers of Jesus, he was simply called a disciple. Although many early Christian texts distinguish Christians by rank or function, the Fourth Gospel does not refer to apostles, deacons, teachers, or other positions, and it indicates that Johannine Christians called each other friend and brother (11:11; 15:15; 20:17; 21:23). Similar modes of address were used when the epistles were written, but by that time certain members of the Johannine congregations were identified as "elders" (*presbyteroi*). Brown has shown that a Johannine elder was apparently "a second-generation figure who served as a transmitter of the tradition that came down from the first generation." His influence was "that of a prophetic witness rather than that flowing from jurisdiction or structure."[19] Since Johannine Christians believed that those who received the Spirit needed no one to teach them (1 John 2:27), elders had to lead by forming a consensus around commonly accepted standards of belief.

The importance of common confessional commitments for Johannine community life is reflected in a dispute in John 6. Some of Jesus' disciples

---

18. On the Beloved Disciple's role and relationship to the Paraclete see R. Alan Culpepper, *The Johannine School: An Evaluation of the Johannine School Hypothesis Based on an Investigation of the Nature of Ancient Schools* (SBLDS 26; Missoula: Scholars, 1975) 264–70.

19. *Epistles*, 650–51.

took offense at his insistence that they eat his flesh and drink his blood, and drew back, refusing to follow him any longer (6:60, 66). In contrast to them, the Twelve did not go away, and with Peter as their spokesperson they confessed that Jesus had the words of eternal life and that he was the Holy One of God (6:67-69). Although the references to eating and drinking could allude to a dispute over the Lord's Supper, the focus of the problem is christological. Fidelity is manifested by confessing faith in Jesus. The epistles also reflect disputes within the community. When divergent teachings claimed to be inspired, the community was to test them against its basic confession of faith (1 John 4:1-3). Elders apparently had little ability to enforce discipline by virtue of office. When a problem arose, the elder who wrote 3 John promised to "bring up" the problem for deliberation while reproving an individual like Diotrephes, who tried to prescribe church practice (3 John 9-10).[20] The cohesion of these congregations depended on their ability to formulate consensus around a common confession.

Symbol and Unity

The symbols in John's Gospel conveyed a confession of faith that distinguished Johannine Christians from the synagogue and helped to unite a network of house churches that was becoming ethnically more diverse and geographically diffused without an elaborate leadership structure. We can explore the role of symbols in this social setting by reflecting on some of the traits of Johannine symbols that we have identified in previous chapters, then focusing on the two symbols that the Gospel connects most closely with Christian unity: the good shepherd and the crucifixion.

The structure of Johannine symbolism is twofold: The primary level of meaning concerns Christ, and the secondary level concerns believers. The christological focus reinforces the centrality of Jesus for the Christian community, while the connection between Christology and discipleship means that the life of a believer must always be understood in relation to Jesus, the community's common center. Jesus is the bread—his disciples eat of him; Jesus is the light—his followers walk in his brightness; Jesus is the vine—his disciples are the branches. Through this constant interplay between Christology and discipleship, the Johannine symbols create a centripetal effect, bringing believers into relationship with each other by reinforcing their common relationship to Jesus.

The form of the Gospel's core symbols is succinct and memorable, so that they can function as unifying slogans. Although the discourses are complex, they are punctuated by sayings that vividly and repeatedly encapsulate the message: "I am the bread of life" (6:35, 48), "I am the light of

20. See Brown, *Epistles*, 738.

the world" (8:12; 9:5), "I am the door" (10:7, 9), "I am the good shepherd" (10:11, 14), and "I am the vine" (15:1, 5). James Dunn has noted
how essential it was for early Christians to make their basic claims in
simple, epigrammatic form. "To be able to sum up the distinctiveness of
one's faith in a single phrase; to be able to express one's worship in a
single word; to be able to unite around a single banner; to be able to cling
to simply stated conviction in the face of persecution and testing—that
is important."[21] The significance of a shared idiom for community life is
evident in the Johannine Epistles, which affirm ties between the author
and readers by invoking common expressions like "walking in the light" or
"the truth" (1 John 1:7; 2 John 4; 3 John 3-4; John 12:35; 14:6) and
"abiding" (1 John 4:12-16; 2 John 2, 9; cf. John 15:4-10).[22]

Repeated presentation of core symbols in easily remembered formulas
like the "I Am" sayings produced a vehicle for discourse that was distinctive yet accessible to newcomers and simple enough to be used throughout a network of house churches. The recurring symbolic summaries of
the Gospel's message would have been especially important since most
Johannine Christians would have had to appropriate its message by listening to it—the Fourth Gospel always addresses readers in the plural, and
evidence from other early Christian sources shows that texts were designed to be read aloud in a corporate setting.[23] Practiced speakers rely on
repetition to communicate with listeners, who are much less likely to
notice occasional breaks in logical and narrative sequence than those who
study the printed page.[24] During oral delivery words flow continually, and
listeners cannot stop to ponder how each sentence relates to the previous
one. A listener's memory seizes upon what is stated repeatedly and color-
fully, making symbols a primary vehicle for the Gospel's message.

The dynamics of Johannine symbolism foster bonds between the text
and its readers in ways that help maintain a sense of community. We noted
in chapter 1 that readers recognize and interpret symbols by identifying
an element of incongruity at the literal level and discerning coherence on
another level. Ted Cohen has elaborated the social implications of this
process. When using a metaphor "(1) the speaker issues a kind of concealed invitation; (2) the hearer expends a special effort to accept the

---

21. *Unity and Diversity in the New Testament: An Inquiry into the Character of Earliest Christianity* (2d ed.; London: SCM; Philadelphia: Trinity, 1990) 59.

22. Note also that which was "from the beginning" (1 John 1:1; 2 John 5-6; cf. John 1:1);
"joy made complete" (1 John 1:4; 2 John 12; cf. John 15:11); "testimony that is true" (3 John
12; cf. John 19:35; 21:24).

23. See 1 Thess. 5:27; Col. 4:16; Rev. 1:3.

24. Wayne Meeks identified the breaks in the logical narrative sequence as the Gospel's
principal means of communication, but this does not adequately consider the factor of oral
presentation ("The Man from Heaven in Johannine Sectarianism," *JBL* 91 [1972] 44–72).

invitation; (3) this transaction constitutes the acknowledgment of a community."[25] The principal speaker in John's Gospel is Jesus, and most of the major metaphors disclose something about his identity. As readers comprehend the meaning of these metaphors and relate them to the other symbols in the Gospel, they are drawn farther into the circle of Jesus' associates.

The speaker and listeners must share certain kinds of information and attitudes for symbols and metaphors to work; otherwise they remain incongruous, like a joke that no one gets. For Johannine symbols to be effective they have to be accessible enough to appeal to the spectrum of readers described earlier yet distinctive enough to create an identifiable community. Although some have argued that John's Gospel is a "closed system of metaphors" whose meaning is clear to insiders but opaque to the uninitiated,[26] we have tried to show the opposite. Those who read the Gospel for the first time often find its meaning to be rather obvious; the complexity and richness become increasingly apparent with rereading. John's Gospel can better be described as "a book in which a child can wade and an elephant can swim."[27] Its message is accessible at a basic level to less-informed readers yet sophisticated enough to engage those who are better informed, incorporating both into the same community.

The impact of symbols on the believers depicted in the Gospel allows us to glimpse the way symbols were designed to function among Johannine Christians. The initial effect of the symbols on the people in the story is to generate interest in Jesus rather than immediate understanding. When John the Baptist introduced Jesus as "the Lamb of God," two disciples became intrigued and followed him (1:35-37), although subsequent episodes do not suggest that they understood what the lamb symbolism meant at this point. Similarly, the woman at the well asked for living water, as Jesus said she should, without understanding what the water signified (4:15); the man born blind identified with his healer before learning that

---

25. "Metaphor and the Cultivation of Intimacy," *Critical Inquiry* 5 (1978) 3–12, esp. 8. Cf. Culpepper, *Anatomy*, 181–82.

26. Meeks, "The Man from Heaven in Johannine Sectarianism," 68; Leroy refers to the Gospel's "Sondersprache" (*Rätsel und Missverständnis: Ein Beitrag zur Formgeschichte des Johannesevangeliums* [BBB 30; Bonn: Peter Hanstein, 1968] 21–25); cf. Ashton, *Understanding*, 451, 530.

27. Robert Kysar, *The Fourth Evangelist and His Gospel: An Examination of Contemporary Scholarship* (Minneapolis: Augsburg, 1975) 6. He is quoting an anonymous source mentioned in Siegfried Schulz, *Die Stunde der Botschaft: Einführung in die Theologie der vier Evangelisten* (Hamburg: Furche, 1967) 297. I have since been able to trace the idea back to Gregory the Great: Scripture is "a kind of river . . . which is both shallow and deep, in which both the lamb may find a footing and the elephant float at large" (*Moralia*, "Epistle" 4.177-78 [CChr 143.6]. Persons teaching Bible in various institutions in North and South America, Asia, and Latin America have commented to me that their students often find that the symbolism in John's Gospel makes it the most accessible to students.

it was the Son of man who enlightened his eyes (9:25-28, 35-38); and Martha confessed her faith in Jesus, "the resurrection and the life," without comprehending what that meant (11:25-27, 39-40). Each figure is a positive exemplar of faith, and in each case the symbol generates interest or trust that leads to discovering more about Jesus.

At the cognitive level, the symbols would have been accessible to most people in the eastern Mediterranean world through association with life experience and common metaphorical usage. For example, we have seen that the importance of water for life was well known and that the connection between water, revelation, and Spirit had precedents in the Scriptures, Jewish and Samaritan traditions, and even the wider Greco-Roman environment. Light and seeing were widely associated with life and understanding, while darkness and blindness connoted death and ignorance. Views concerning life after death varied, but Jesus' claim to be "the resurrection and the life" echoes two common views of afterlife: one with distinctly Jewish antecedents and the other a more common Hellenistic view.

The conversations surrounding the symbols direct readers toward an adequate grasp of the symbolism through the positive and negative responses of the interlocutors. The objections raised by symbolic sayings and actions are of the most obvious sort, the kind that might occur to any reader: Jesus cannot provide living water because he has no bucket (4:11), and he should not open Lazarus's tomb because of the foul smell (11:39). Allowing interlocutors to voice basic objections is especially important when a symbol is potentially offensive, as in the violent expulsion of merchants from the temple (2:20), Mary's seemingly wasteful use of costly ointment (12:5), and Jesus' washing the feet of his disciples (13:8). Although some of the characters in the story persistently misunderstand Jesus' sayings and actions, the explanatory comments help prevent readers from doing so. They teach readers how to interpret the Gospel, remove misperceptions about key points in the Gospel's theology, and draw readers farther into the circle of insiders.[28]

A number of the Gospel's symbols are christological reinterpretations of common Jewish symbols. Socially this had several important functions. (a) It helped provide an element of continuity during a period of profound social change.[29] Some of the Gospel's early readers were familiar with bread and light as symbols for the law, which was central to Jewish life. When these Jewish Christians separated from the synagogue and were threatened with the loss of much of their heritage, they were able to

---

28. Culpepper, *Anatomy*, 164–65. Cf. François Vouga, *Le cadre historique et l'intention théologique de Jean* (Paris: Beauchesne, 1977) 15–36; Brown, *Community*, 61–62.

29. See further my *Dwelling of God: The Tabernacle in the Old Testament, Intertestamental Jewish Literature, and the New Testament* (CBQMS 22; Washington, D.C.: Catholic Biblical Association, 1989) 21–22, 73–75, 184–86.

retain some of their symbols by reinterpreting them. Bread and light continued to be central symbols for their community, but now as symbols of the Messiah to whom the Torah bore witness rather than of the Torah itself. (b) These symbols were presented in a way that contributed to the community's sense of its own legitimacy. Both sides in the controversy, for example, would have agreed that light is connected with God, life, and understanding, while darkness means evil, death, and ignorance. Similarly, both would have understood bread as God's gift and the vine as a symbol for God's people. Questions revolved around the application of these symbols. When Johannine Christians identified with "the true light," "the true bread," and "the true vine," they associated their community and its beliefs with venerable and well-known symbols. (c) Symbolism was integral to Johannine apologetics, as we have seen (pp. 27–28). Light's ability to produce blindness and sight helped account for the reality of unbelief, while images such as light, bread, and the shepherd showed how seemingly contradictory aspects of Jesus' identity—human, messianic, divine—could be conceived in a coherent whole.

The symbols in John's Gospel stand on the boundary between various Jewish and Hellenistic modes of speech, as Takashi Onuki has observed. They evoke associations from various quarters and transform them to convey a distinctive message.[30] The effect is that Johannine symbolism may be approached in various ways, but it can be comprehended only in Christian terms.[31] Individual symbols sometimes draw on the numinous qualities of an image that are known in many religious traditions, but these are given a specifically christological referent, so that they point in their own ways to Jesus, the Messiah and Son of God who came down from heaven to be crucified: He is *the* light, *the* bread, *the* vine. When combined in the narrative, the symbols create a distinctly christological configuration that no longer corresponds to those of other traditions. Images with strong roots in Judaism are expanded and universalized, enabling them to evoke a broad range of associations: Manna becomes bread for the world, and the light in the temple become the light of the world. Other elements, such as the anointing and washing of feet, which were familiar culturally but not prominent symbols for any group, are also integrated into the Johannine constellation. Finally, the various images, motifs, and actions direct attention to the cross, the distinctive lens through which all the symbols should be viewed.

30. *Gemeinde und Welt im Johannesevangelium: Ein Beitrag zur Frage nach der theologischen und pragmatischen Funktion des johanneischen "Dualismus"* (WMANT 26; Neukirchen-Vluyn: Neukirchener, 1984) 26–27.

31. George MacRae, "The Fourth Gospel and *Religionsgeschichte*," *CBQ* 32 (1970) 13–24; Rensberger, *Johannine Faith*, 149; Gail O'Day, *Revelation in the Fourth Gospel: Narrative Mode and Theological Claim* (Philadelphia: Fortress, 1986) 73.

An effective symbol can open up new perspectives by getting listeners to yoke, even for a moment, what they had not yoked before. This does not mean, however, that those who understand the symbol will assent to its truth.[32] Jesus' adversaries objected not that his claim to be the light of the world was unintelligible but that it was unacceptable (8:12-13), and while understanding his metaphorical use of "blindness," they rejected its application to them (9:39-40). From a Johannine perspective, assent to the truth as well as the meaning of a symbol or metaphor comes about through divine agency, not through the inherent properties of the symbols themselves.

Readers who accept the validity of the symbols find that they retain a limited polyvalence. The text excludes some meanings for symbols and embraces a number of other meanings, enabling the symbols to function as a unifying force among people who share certain basic commitments but have somewhat different points of view. For example, water may signify revelation and the Spirit, but not impurity; light may connote knowledge, prophethood, messiahship, and divinity, but not ignorance and evil; and Jesus' claim to be the resurrection and the life fuses two different views of afterlife but rules out the idea that death separates a believer from God. By excluding certain perspectives, symbols help maintain the boundaries of a community. By holding together a number of valid perspectives, symbols help hold together the community of people who have those perspectives.[33]

Polyvalence means that in some situations different members of a community may appeal to the same symbol to support conflicting points of view. No symbol can guarantee the unity of a group, and no symbol is self-interpreting, but as long as people within the group recognize the validity of a symbol, they have a common basis upon which to argue.[34] The author of 1 John, for example, wrote in the wake of a schism, seeking to strengthen the communal bonds (*koinōnia*, 1:3) between those he represented and readers who were at least potentially attracted to his opponents. He began his argument by invoking symbols that all sides could accept: "God is light and in him is no darkness at all" (1:5). Assuming that readers would grant this premise, he elaborated the symbolism in terms of truth and falsehood, righteousness and sin, eventually applying it to the issues that divided the group. Perspectives within the community may have differed, but by appealing to symbols he shared with his readers, the

32. See the survey and discussion of the problem by Richard Moran, "Seeing and Believing: Metaphor, Image, and Force," *Critical Inquiry* 16 (1989) 87–112.

33. See Klaus Berger, *Exegese des Neuen Testaments: Neue Wege vom Text zur Auslegung* (Heidelberg: Quelle & Meyer, 1977) 230–31. He develops his position in opposition to Meeks.

34. The rabbinic collections illustrate this on a wider scale. They convey a sense of community that is constituted by debates on a common corpus of tradition.

author showed that some level of *koinōnia* already existed and that issues confronting the group could be addressed on that basis.

With these general observations about symbolism in mind, we can consider the symbols most closely related to unity in the Fourth Gospel. In John 10:16, Jesus said there must be "one flock, one shepherd," using imagery well suited to foster the unity envisioned in this text. Formally the discourse is complex. In quick succession Jesus speaks of a sheepfold and sheep, a doorkeeper, shepherd, thieves, robbers, and strangers; and when bystanders fail to grasp his meaning, Jesus compounds the problem by adding a hireling, a wolf, and sheep from another fold. Nevertheless, by repeating "I am the door" (10:7, 9) and "I am the good shepherd" (10:11, 14), Jesus establishes himself as the center of this swirling array of images. Readers may not know the precise identity of the hireling or the wolf, but they do know that Jesus is the door and the shepherd and that they must focus their attention on him, since he is the sole legitimate means of access to the flock and the one who leads and cares for it.

The imagery is accessible enough to engage a spectrum of readers from different "folds," both Jewish and non-Jewish, yet it is transformed to convey a distinctly christological message. In our first chapter we noted that shepherd imagery could be approached at various levels. Shepherds were a common sight throughout the ancient Mediterranean world; both Jews and Greeks also used shepherding as a metaphor for leadership and expected gracious leaders, like good shepherds, to seek what was best for the sheep and perhaps even to risk their lives for the flock. Readers more familiar with the Scriptures and Jewish tradition would have been able to go further, discerning messianic and divine connotations in the imagery. When Jesus identified himself as the good shepherd, he appropriated these familiar associations but redefined them in terms of his crucifixion, insisting that *the* good shepherd is the one who lays down his life for the sheep.

The polyvalence of the symbolism helps to maintain the unity of the community by encompassing several valid perspectives while maintaining a boundary between believers and nonbelievers. Members of Jesus' flock who came from different "folds" would have perceived Jesus from somewhat differing vantage points. The evocative quality of the good shepherd image allows people to make a number of valid statements about Jesus: He is an ideal leader, the Messiah, and the one in whom God is present. All these claims are true, but alone no one of them is entirely true; Jesus' identity emerges from the tension between these perspectives. The images used for Jesus' opponents are also polyvalent. Because the passage follows the expulsion of the beggar from the synagogue, the "thieves and robbers" are presumably the Pharisees, but Jesus expands the scope of the imagery by saying that "all" who came before him were thieves and robbers (10:8) and by introducing the hireling and the wolf, who seem to present a different kind of threat to the community. Such kaleidoscopic shifts make it difficult to identify all these figures with any one set of opponents. The imagery distinguishes Jesus from all competitors in a manner that is supple enough to function in multiple life-settings.

The other symbol associated most closely with the unity of believers is the cross.[35] Both 10:15-16 and 11:51-52 connect the death of Jesus with the oneness of believers, and the sign above the cross, written in Hebrew, Latin, and Greek, shows that the significance of the crucifixion transcends the boundaries of language and ethnicity. The Johannine account of the crucifixion is multifaceted, but its overall symbolic structure is consistent with that found elsewhere. The primary level of meaning is christological, and Christians are brought into relationship with each other through their common bond to Jesus. The secondary level of the symbolism points in this direction: One of his final gestures was to entrust his mother to the Beloved Disciple, inaugurating a new community that was based not on family ties but on a shared relationship with Jesus.

Crucifixion was considered repulsive by people throughout the ancient world. Unlike shepherding, which had many positive connotations, the associations ordinarily evoked by a cross were negative. For crucifixion to function as a unifying symbol, its transcendent significance needed to be disclosed. The Gospel helps readers to see the cross as the symbol of God's love for the world by relating it to other symbols. The major motifs in the text—light and water—culminate in the betrayer's departure into the night and the water flowing from the wound in Jesus' side. Similarly, the signs and other actions anticipate a glorification that would take place through Jesus' death.

The polyvalence of the crucifixion operates within limits. Certain interpretations are ruled out: For example, Jesus did not die as a guilty man, and those who insist that he did are outsiders to the community. Yet the Johannine portrayal of Jesus' death also includes several valid perspectives. The trial shows that the crucifixion was the death of an innocent man; the Scripture quotations and paschal imagery disclose that it was a sacrifice that took place according to the will of God. The connections between the passion and Jesus' earlier words show that he died as a true prophet, while the trial reveals that he died as a king. Other comments depict the passion as a triumph over the demonic ruler of the world and the glorification of the Son of man. The cross is a tensive symbol that

35. Cf. Onuki, *Gemeinde und Welt,* 62; Rebell, *Gemeinde als Gegenwelt,* 15, 51, 212.

holds together a number of perspectives, and in so doing it helps hold together a community of people who have such perspectives.

SYMBOL AND PATTERNS OF
DISCIPLESHIP

Jesus' manner of life was characterized by obedience to the two commandments he received from God. One was the "commandment about what to say" (12:46). Jesus claimed no independent authority for his teaching but spoke as the Father had taught him, which was pleasing to God (7:17; 8:28). The second commandment was that he should lay down his life and take it up again (10:18). He had the power to perform this action and did so knowing that God loved him. The command for self-sacrifice gave direction to the actions Jesus performed during his ministry, from the gift of wine at Cana to the death and resurrection of Lazarus, and from the cleansing of the temple to the foot washing at the last supper. It was the final action presaged in all of Jesus' other actions.

The path of discipleship was, in turn, to be congruent with the two commands Jesus gave to his followers, as Urban von Wahlde has noted.[36] The first command was that they should keep Jesus' word, which meant holding fast to the message that Jesus had received from God and delivered to them. Keeping Jesus' word was a fundamental expression of a disciple's love for Jesus, the context in which Jesus' presence and the Father's love would be manifested (14:15, 21, 23-24; cf. 1 John 3:23a). The second commandment was that disciples should love one another as Jesus loved them. This "new commandment" was reciprocal in character, focusing on relationships within the community of faith and patterning the love the disciples had for each other after the love Jesus had for them. Jesus loved his followers by laying down his life for them in obedience to his Father's command; they were now to show the same kind of love, even laying down their lives for one another (13:34; 15:13; cf. 1 John 3:16, 23b).

Discipleship and the Johannine Context

The Johannine commandments make comprehensive claims upon the lives of Jesus' followers with an almost unparalleled simplicity. They give basic directives rather than detailed instructions, providing coordinates by which to navigate rather than a map of the entire route. A command like "Love one another as I have loved you" was brief and easy for listeners to remember and could therefore serve as a standard for behavior throughout a network of house churches scattered over some distance. Although

36. *The Johannine Commandments: 1 John and the Struggle for the Johannine Tradition* (New York: Paulist, 1990) 9–38.

it left many questions unanswered, its simplicity allowed it to function as a common point of appeal and deliberation within communities that relied on consensus, rather than a strong central administration, to maintain discipline.

Certain implications of the love command were fairly clear. If, for example, Jesus laid down his life for his followers and his followers were to lay down their lives for each other, they should also help each other in lesser ways, such as providing the poor in the community with the necessities of life (1 John 3:16-17). The experience of schism made application more difficult, since it was not clear that communities were obliged to offer such support to traveling missionaries who preached a message deemed contrary to the truth, thereby violating the command to hold fast to Jesus' word (2 John 5-7, 10). The Johannine commandments were not self-interpreting, but they did provide a basis upon which deliberation could take place.

Johannine Christians worked out the implications for discipleship in settings where other norms for behavior existed, many of which they neither fully embraced nor entirely rejected; Jesus' commands drew his followers into a dialectic encounter with competing norms. Here we will consider three: the commandments of the Torah, friendship, and honor.

Most Johannine Christians would have been somewhat familiar with the patterns of behavior based on interpretation of the Mosaic law, or Torah. The Pharisees and rabbis used the statutes contained in the Scriptures along with a body of tradition that came to be known as the oral Torah. Although the essence of the Torah was sometimes summarized as the dual command to love God and the neighbor, the corpus of written and oral material was complex, and the priests and scribes were its acknowledged interpreters until the temple was destroyed. Afterward a Jewish academy was established at Jamnia near the Mediterranean coast, and its leaders, who came to be called rabbis, gained prominence as teachers of the Torah. In the absence of a temple, Torah study was deemed the equivalent of sacrifice, and the Romans recognized the rabbis as the official representatives of Judaism.

Johannine Christians neither derived a pattern of discipleship from the Mosaic law and Jewish tradition nor accepted "lawlessness" (cf. 1 John 3:4); they followed alternative norms. In the eyes of these Christians, the Pharisaic interpretation of the law had been discredited: While condemning Jesus for healing on the Sabbath, the Pharisees performed circumcision—a form of minor surgery—on the Sabbath (7:19); while scrupulously observing standards for personal purity, they arranged for the murder of the Son of God (18:28; 19:6); and while condemning Jesus for blasphemy, they collaborated with the Romans, who deified their Caesars (19:7, 15).

Evidence that Johannine Christians did not observe Jewish practices appears in the need to explain that stone jars were used for purification (2:6) and that Passover and Booths were feasts of the Jews (6:4; 7:2), as well as the statement that Jesus' Jewish opponents were the ones who circumcised (7:22-23). Nevertheless, Johannine Christians considered the law to be an indispensable witness to Jesus (5:39); they understood that obedience to divine "commandments" had a central place in the life of faith; and the new commandment's emphasis on love was a christological recasting rather than a rejection of the traditional emphasis on love as the basis and essence of the Torah.[37]

A similar tension surrounds the Johannine perception of friendship, a value that governed many social relations in the ancient world. Older Jewish sources sometimes treated the subject of friendship, but the theme was most fully developed in Greco-Roman writings and Jewish texts familiar with these conventions.[38] The philosophical ideal of friendship was "nothing else than an accord in all things, human and divine, conjoined with mutual goodwill and affection."[39] Although cordial relations would be shared with many people, the highest form of friendship was possible only with a few, whose relationship was based on virtue, equality, and similarity of character and interests. True friends would be warm yet frank with each other, sharing all their joys and sorrows. These bonds of loyalty and affection mean that a friend is someone "for whom I may die, whom I may follow into exile, against whose death I may stake my own life, and pay the pledge."[40]

In practice, friendships provided the most important network of associations outside the family. A friendship was a relationship of some duration that involved mutual obligations and benefits.[41] People were counseled to choose friends carefully, and for most people reciprocity was integral to a friendship, but equality was not. People valued "friends in high places" who could help arrange for legal aid, administrative appointments, favor-

37. Norman Petersen speaks of a Johannine "inversion" of Jewish values, and he contends that Johannine language is "the anti-language of an anti- society" (*The Gospel of John and the Sociology of Light: Language and Characterization in the Fourth Gospel* [Valley Forge, Pa.: Trinity, 1993] 87, 89). His analysis minimizes and negates the elements of continuity, however.

38. On friendship in older Jewish texts see, e.g., Prov. 17:17; 22:24; 27:6, 10; Sir. 6:5-17; 9:10; 12:8-9; 13:21; 37:1-6. On the Greco-Roman discussion see the next note. Cf. Philo, *Virtues* 109; *Noah's Work as a Planter* 104, 106.

39. Cicero, *de Amicitia* 20. Many texts relating to this theme are collected and discussed with bibliography in Gustav Stählin, "*philos, ktl.*," *TDNT* 9.146–54; K. Treu, "Freundschaft," *RAC* 8.418–34; Hans Dieter Betz, *Galatians* (Hermeneia; Philadelphia: Fortress, 1979) 220–37.

40. Seneca, *Moral Epistles* 9.10. Cf. Aristotle, *Nicomachean Ethics* 9.9 1169a; Diogenes Laertius, *Lives of Eminent Philosophers* 10.121; Rom. 5:7; and the other examples in *TDNT* 9.153.

41. On the practice of friendship see Richard P. Saller, *Personal Patronage under the Early Empire* (Cambridge: Cambridge University Press, 1982) 11–15, 24–34; Halvor Moxnes, "Patron-Client Relations and the New Community in Luke-Acts," *The Social World of Luke-Acts: Models for Interpretation* (ed. J. H. Neyrey; Peabody, Mass.: Hendrickson, 1991) 241–68, esp. 244–46.

able business transactions, and other matters. Similarly, those in influential positions relied on the friendship of those to whom they entrusted their affairs. Working through a network of friends was considered appropriate and respectable in a society that lacked more impersonal ways to provide services and opportunities for social advancement. Loans, citizenship, and help for one's family in time of difficulty were sought through connections; there was no bureaucracy that could offer aid based on universally applicable standards. Those who had influence were expected to use it for friends and even for associates of friends; those who refused were disreputable.

People were often able to reconcile the idea of true friendship based on virtue with the understanding that friendship involved a mutual exchange of goods and services, but in some instances friendship forced people to compromise their integrity. Pilate is a most vivid example of this in the Fourth Gospel. Pilate was one of "Caesar's friends," an amorphous group of people who had access to the emperor.[42] Friendship with Caesar could be warm or purely formal; it provided the emperor with loyal support and his friends with prestige and the ability to secure benefits for themselves and others. Genuine friendship involved a commitment to truth, but during the trial of Jesus the crowd outside the praetorium forced Pilate to choose between friendship and truth. Pilate knew that Jesus was an innocent man and repeatedly said so publicly, yet the crowd reminded him that Jesus had made himself a king, and no friend of Caesar could let a rival king go free (19:12). Therefore Pilate abandoned the truth in order to maintain the friendship of the emperor, upon which his own career depended.

Johannine Christians neither rejected friendship in order to embrace an ideal of complete independence and self-sufficiency nor relied on the network system of friendships that had the emperor at its apex. Instead, they adopted a christological understanding of friendship through which Jesus' command to love one another could be brought to expression. Friendship with Jesus was not egalitarian—he retained a singular position—yet it brought Jesus' followers into a relationship of reciprocal love, creating a community in which people who addressed each other as "friends" could realize the ideal of mutual self-sacrifice (15:12-14).

Honor, which is the positive value ascribed to a person by others, was still another norm for conduct in the ancient world.[43] Honor is often

---

42. On Caesar's friends see Fergus Millar, *The Emperor in the Roman World* (Ithaca, N.Y.: Cornell University Press, 1977) 110–22; Saller, *Personal Patronage under the Early Empire*, 59–62.

43. For basic discussion of honor in antiquity see A. J. Vermeulen, "Gloria," *RAC* 11.196–226, esp. 197–203; Louis I. Rabinowitz, "Honor," *EncJud* 8.965–67. For treatment from an anthropological perspective see Bruce Malina and Jerome H. Neyrey, "Honor and Shame in Luke-Acts: Pivotal Values in the Mediterranean World," *The Social World of Luke-Acts* (ed. Neyrey) 25–65.

mentioned together with "glory" (*doxa*), which, in a basic sense, refers to what people think (*dokein*) of someone. Honor reflected someone's location in the social matrix, informing how people were to relate to peers, superiors, and subordinates. A person's family ties, status as a parent, occupation, and community responsibilities affected the degree of honor one received. Jewish sources stressed that honor was due to parents and older people, priests, teachers, physicians, and other leaders; similar views appear in Greek and Roman sources.[44] Honor could be enhanced by personal accomplishments such as a display of heroism, building projects, and other beneficent acts.[45] A person's "name" or reputation conveyed one's honor and affected everything from business dealings to marriage contracts and dinner invitations. The promise that one's name would be perpetuated after death offered hope for a kind of immortality.[46]

Giving and receiving honor helped create and maintain social cohesion while providing means for social advancement. Those who honored their parents brought honor to themselves, and those who disgraced their parents disgraced themselves (Sir. 3:10-11). Similarly, parents who brought shame upon themselves brought shame upon their children (41:6-7; 47:20). Throughout the ancient world, someone who faithfully honored and served a king could expect honors from the king, such as appointment to an administrative post, inclusion among the king's circle of friends, and favorable treatment from those who recognized the king's authority (1 Macc. 12:43). When dealing with peers, the rabbis enjoined people to let "the honor of your colleague be as dear to you as your own," for the person who receives honor is the person who gives honor to others.[47]

Although honor was a cherished possession, many distinguished true honor from the acclaim of the masses. Public opinion was fickle and an unreliable measure of a person's worth. Those who occupied prestigious positions sometimes acted in ways that would have been considered shameful for anyone else. Acclaim for personal achievements faded quickly, and those honor-seekers who tried to purchase favor with gifts and banquets, or by fawning over those in power, compromised their integrity.[48] According to Jewish sources, true honor belonged to those who honored God by following the law, whether the person was poor or an aristocrat.[49] Fidelity

---

44. Exod. 20:12; Lev. 19:32; Sir. 3:2-11; 7:29-31; 10:20; 38:1-3.

45. Honor is connected with heroism and courage in 1 Macc. 5:63-64; 9:10; 10:88; 11:51; 2 Macc. 6:19; with civic or national improvements in Sir. 40:19; 1 Macc. 14:4-5.

46. Sir. 37:25-26; 39:9; 41:11-13; Cicero, *De Doma Sua* 86.

47. *m. ʾAbot* 2:10; 4:1. In the late second century, Rabbi Judah said that the best path of life was that "which is an honor to him and gets honor from men" (*m. ʾAbot* 2:1).

48. See esp. Dio Chrysostom, *Orations* 66.

49. Sir. 10:19-25; Wisd. of Sol. 4:8; *b. Taʿan.* 21b.

to the law could bring people honor even in the face of public opposition. The Maccabees, for example, refused to abandon the law in order to receive honors from the king but later achieved renown for their loyalty to the tradition, the deaths of their martyrs, and successful military exploits.[50] Although the faithful could not be assured of such honors during their lifetime, there was hope that God would honor them in a life after death.[51] For Greek and Roman writers "honor is the prize of virtue, and it is to the good that it is rendered."[52] People were urged to hold on to virtue even if public opinion turned against them. Seneca insisted that those who publicized their virtue were seeking notoriety, not true glory, and he warned that truly virtuous people would often be disgraced.[53]

Johannine Christians understood that honor belonged to God and that since Jesus performed the works of God they were "to honor the Son as they honor the Father" (5:23). Yet Jesus was publicly dishonored by adversaries, who called him a Samaritan and a demoniac (8:48-49). Through these public displays of contempt, Jesus' adversaries gained greater prestige in the eyes of their compatriots. From a Johannine perspective, opposition to Jesus was fueled by the desire to gain glory from other people rather than from God (5:44; 8:50, 54), and a similar desire kept some Christians from openly professing their faith in Jesus (12:43). The Fourth Gospel grants that faith may lead to dishonor but does not, therefore, consider dishonor a virtue in itself. Honor remains a value—the honor that comes not from public opinion but from God. If Jesus' adversaries dishonored and executed him, God "glorified" Jesus through death. Similarly, faith in Jesus may bring dishonor, but those who faithfully serve him even to death receive genuine honor from God.

Symbolism and Patterns of Discipleship

Johannine Christians neither drifted along with the predominant cultural flow nor tried to navigate directly upstream but embarked on an independent course across the prevailing currents. The new commandment has Jesus as its source and norm, and the symbols in the Gospel help to convey and reinforce this distinctly christological focus while transforming contemporary understandings of the Torah, friendship, and honor.

We noted in earlier chapters that symbols for the Torah, including bread and water, were transferred to Jesus. The symbol with the most pronounced ethical connotations was light, which was used for divine

50. 1 Macc. 2:18, 64; 5:63-64; 2 Macc. 6:19.
51. Wisd. of Sol. 5:4, 16; 4 Macc. 17:20.
52. Aristotle, *Nicomachean Ethics* 7.3 1123b.
53. *Moral Epistles* 113.32; cf. 102.17.

wisdom and the Mosaic law in Jewish sources and for philosophy and virtue in Greco-Roman texts.[54] Enlightenment meant that one's understanding and manner of life were shaped by the light of wisdom through the study of the Mosaic law or training in philosophy. By presenting Jesus as the light of the world, the Gospel identifies him as the true source of wisdom and moral transformation, tacitly displacing other norms of conduct. The conclusion to the Nicodemus episode insists that the true character of one's deeds will be disclosed by a response to Jesus and not by conformity to some other standard (3:19-21), and the debates at the feast of Booths argue that "walking in the light" means following Jesus (8:12). But even though Jesus displaced the law and made claims that were not derived from the law, the debates show that his teaching was consistent with it, and that the law, when rightly understood, bore witness to him.

The specific pattern of discipleship conveyed by the new commandment is closely connected with the foot washing. Like the commandment itself, the foot washing is simple, arresting, and memorable, capable of appealing to people on the affective as well as the cognitive level. Structurally, the foot washing and the new commandment are identical: Both anticipate the love Jesus shows for his disciples through his death on their behalf and make it an example of the love his disciples should show to one another. The statement "If I then, your Lord and Teacher, have washed your feet, you also ought to wash one another's feet" is another way of saying "Love one another even as I have loved you" (13:14, 34).

Foot washing was known throughout the culture but was not a norm for behavior in the Torah or philosophy; Jesus' use of the action as a pattern for community life was "new," like the love commandment itself. Washing other people's feet was widely understood to be a task for slaves. Although people occasionally performed this task voluntarily as a gesture of devotion for someone of similar or higher social status, no one would expect a person in authority to do this for those beneath him. When Jesus, the Teacher, stooped to bathe the feet of his disciples, he acted contrary to social conventions. Nevertheless, he did not simply invert the usual practice so that teachers became servants and pupils became masters. Jesus reaffirmed that he was Teacher and Lord, and that no servant can be above his master; but, instead of invoking his position as a reason for him not to wash feet, he used it to show that his disciples should wash feet, following their master's example.

The vine is the second symbol associated with the new commandment. The broad appeal of viticulture made it an appropriate image to foster connections between Jesus and "every" or "any" believer (15:2, 6). Across

---

54. On light see pp. 129–36, 142–43; on bread see pp. 96–97; on water see pp. 170, 174–75.

the eastern and northern Mediterranean, vines dotted fields and hillsides, thriving on dew and the occasional rains that moistened the coarse soil in which they took root. Vineyards were a source of joy for many, who delighted in the way a vine "raises itself by its finger-like tendrils and enfolds and embraces the props that hold it up," putting out a bud that ripens slowly amid the foliage that enwraps it, and turning aside "the more ardent glances of the sun."[55] To nurture the productive branches, vinedressers would cut away the dead wood in winter and remove the useless growth in the spring; occasionally the haze of smoke and crackling flames came from the piles of twigs and dry shoots at the edge of the field. The clusters of fruit displayed the quality of the vine and the ability of the vinedresser, who, with the laborers, experienced the proverbial joy of harvest.[56]

The Fourth Gospel uses this familiar imagery to convey the significance of the love commandment and to relate it to the ideal of friendship. Themes in this section intertwine like the tendrils of a vine, but like the other symbols in the Gospel its primary level of meaning is christological. Jesus said, "I am the true vine and my Father is the vinedresser" (15:1). The imagery acknowledges the differences between Jesus and his Father, between the vine and the vinedresser, but it also conveys their unity. Jesus applies to himself the "I Am" expression, whose divine connotations were apparent earlier in the narrative. He is genuine or "true" (*alethinos*), a term appropriate for God (7:28; 17:3) and that which is of divine origin (1:9; 6:32; 8:16; cf. 4:23). Moreover, both the vine and the vinedresser serve the same end: The Father prunes or "cleanses" (*kathairein*) the branches that they might bear fruit, and Jesus makes them capable of bearing fruit, or "clean" (*katharos*), through his word (15:2-3).

Disciples, like the branches of a vine, have the source and norm for their lives in Jesus. A branch must draw nourishment from the vine out of which it grows or it will be barren and wither; in the same way, a disciple's life bears fruit only when nourished by Jesus. Those who remain in Jesus' love obey his commandments just as Jesus remained in his Father's love and obeyed his Father's commandments. One command was that Jesus should speak as the Father told him to speak; accordingly, those who have Jesus' words in their hearts can speak to God with the assurance of being heard (15:7). The other command was that Jesus should lay down his life and take it up again, which Jesus did out of love. Jesus' followers are also called to lay down their lives in love for one another (15:12-13), and as Jesus finds his joy in them, their own joy will be made complete (15:11).

The obedience that is a fruit of discipleship involves Jesus' followers in a community of friends. The model of friendship depicted in John 15

55. Cicero, *De Senectute* 15 §§52–53.
56. Cf. John 4:36; Deut. 16:13-14; Isa. 9:2-3; Ps. 126:5-6; Cicero, *De Oratore* 3.38 §155.

involves reciprocity though not equality with Jesus: They did not choose him, he chose them and commissioned them to bear fruit (15:16). Although the disciples "serve" Jesus, he gives them the dignity of being called his "friends" rather than servants or slaves. A "servant does not know what his master is doing," but Jesus informed his disciples about what his Father told him, so that their relationship might be based on trust (15:15).[57]

As the one "true vine," Jesus displaces anything else that might claim to be the source of a disciple's life. Although this passage makes no reference to the Scriptures, many readers may have known that the vine was a common image for Israel. The vine was most often used in connection with God's judgment upon Israel, the vine that became degenerate even though God had planted it with true seed (Jer. 2:21). Because Israel bore the fruit of idolatry and the "wild grapes" of bloodshed instead of the fruit of righteousness, it was pruned back and burned.[58] Yet because Israel was God's vine, there was hope for its redemption. The Scriptures promised that God would plant and nurture his vineyard, and "Jacob shall take root, Israel shall blossom and put forth shoots, and fill the whole world with fruit" that the Lord might be glorified (Isa. 27:2, 6; cf. 60:21; 61:3).[59]

In other sources the image of the vine was used for the wisdom of God, which was traditionally associated with the Law of Moses. The sages who interpreted the tradition at Jamnia after the temple was destroyed called their academy "the vineyard at Jamnia."[60] Earlier, the book of Sirach said that the divine wisdom found in the law was "like a vine" that "caused loveliness to bud," with blossoms that "became glorious" and "abundant fruit" (Sir. 24:17). Philo also connected the vine with wisdom, which was the source of true joy. In a commentary on the large cluster of grapes the Israelite spies brought back from the land of Canaan (Num. 13:18-21), he said that since these men were "unable to carry the whole main-stalk of wisdom," they "cut a single branch and cluster of grapes and raised it up, a manifest sign of joy" and a "vision of the sprouting and fruit-bearing alike of noble living."[61]

The vine and its fruits also stood as a metaphor for virtue, which was closely related to wisdom. The practice of viticulture was a useful way to describe training in philosophy, which removed vice from a person's soul

---

57. On the difference between a friend and a slave see Philo, *Abraham* 45; *Sobriety* 55–56; Epictetus, *Discourses* 2.4.5.

58. Hos. 10:1; Isa. 5:1-7; Ezek. 15:1-8; Ps. 80:16.

59. Cf. Ps. 80:14-15; *Bib. Ant.* 12:8; 18:10-11; 28:4; 30:4; 4 Ezra 5:23. The connection between the vine of John 15 and Israel is stressed by Rainer Borig, *Das wahre Weinstock: Untersuchungen zu Jo 15,1-10* (SANT 16; Munich: Kösel, 1967) 247–52.

60. *m. Ketub.* 4:6; *m. 'Ed.* 2:4.

61. *On Dreams* 2.171.

in the way a vinedresser pruned useless growth from a vine. Since education was the source and root of goodness, teachers needed to shape the character of their pupils with precepts and exhortations in the way others tend to young plants.[62] Although the vine was a common symbol for Dionysos and for the joy associated with festivals in his honor, philosophical sources insisted that true joy was the product of virtue. Virtue and the joy it produced were part of genuine friendship, the ideal of which is affirmed and redefined in John 15:13. For friendship proceeds not from training in philosophy but from a relationship with Jesus.

Third, an earlier saying of Jesus connected this kind of obedient service with honor. Jesus said, "Unless a grain of wheat falls into the earth and dies, it remains alone; but if it dies, it bears much fruit" (12:24). The primary level of meaning is christological: It conveys the significance of Jesus' glorification through death. In the previous verse Jesus said that the hour had come "for the Son of man to be glorified" (12:23). We have seen that Jesus' actions manifested his own glory and glorified God, from the first sign at Cana (2:4, 11) to the raising of Lazarus (11:4, 8, 40); but we have also seen that these actions were a prelude to his final act of self-sacrifice, through which he glorified God and was glorified by God.

On another level the saying about the seed describes a pattern of discipleship. The implications are presented in two couplets, which must be taken together. Jesus began, "He who loves his life loses it, and he who hates his life in this world will keep it for eternal life" (12:25). The paradox is that love of one's life or "self" (*psychē*) leads to its loss, while renouncing it leads to life everlasting. Some types of self-hatred, like self-love, can result in the kind of self-preoccupation that means the person "remains alone." Here self-hatred is not an end in itself but a prelude to the second couplet, which completes the movement away from self-love into service to Christ: "If any one serves me, he must follow me; and where I am, there shall my servant be also; if any one serves me, the Father will honor him" (12:26). All people will lose their selves and their lives—that is a given—but those who lose themselves in service to Christ enter into a relationship that bears fruit and brings them life.[63]

True honor and glory are given by God to his servants. Jesus laid down his life in an ignominious death out of obedience to God, and God glorified him. Those who lose themselves in the service of Jesus will also be honored by God even if dishonored by other people. The actions of Martha and Mary seem to foreshadow the kind of discipleship envisioned by the parable of the seed. At the beginning of the chapter, it was Martha

62. Plutarch, *Moralia* 4c; 529b; Cicero, *De Oratore* 2.21 §88.
63. Dostoevsky introduced *The Brothers Karamazov* by quoting John 12:24; the novel explores what it means to love, hate, and lose oneself.

who "served" Jesus, the action he later said was characteristic of the disciples who would be honored by his Father (*diakonein*, 12:2, 26). Similarly, Mary anointed Jesus' feet despite the objections raised against her, performing an action very similar to foot washing, which was the example for disciples generally (12:3; 13:14). When read in connection with what Jesus says in the wider literary context, the actions of these women help show readers what it means to be a disciple.[64]

SYMBOL AND THE WORLD

Jesus was not of the world, but God sent him into the world. The world and everything in it was created through God's Word, or *logos* (1:3), yet the world became estranged from its Creator, and God "sent" the Son into the world to save it (3:17-18; 12:44-50). As the one whom God "sent"—and "sent" is the way Jesus is typically described in the Fourth Gospel—Jesus engaged the world, provoking a response by bearing witness to his own divine origin and to the world's sinfulness (7:7; 8:26; 10:36; 18:37). "He was in the world, and the world was made through him, yet the world knew him not," and even his own people "received him not" since they were "of this world" and he was not "of this world" (1:10; 8:23). Nevertheless, Jesus laid down his life to "take away the sin of the world," to "cast out" the demonic ruler of the world, and to "conquer" the world for God (1:29; 12:31; 16:33) by the transforming revelation of divine love (3:16; 14:30-31).

Unlike Jesus, the disciples are creatures rather than creators; but like Jesus, their relationship with the world involves both separation and engagement. The disciples' separation from the world is divinely initiated. They are not "of the world" because God gives them faith to receive Jesus and his words, and to believe that God truly had sent him; the world hates them because Jesus chose them "out of the world" (15:18-19; 17:6-9, 14). The world would not see Jesus after his return to the Father, but the disciples would discern his presence through the Paraclete, or Spirit of truth (14:16-24), who would bear witness to him and the world's sin, creating a community that could engage the world while remaining distinct from it (15:26; 16:8-11). As Jesus had been sent into the world, he sent his followers "into the world" in order that people might believe through their word (17:15-17), and he prayed that their unity might bring the world to know him and the love God has for his disciples (17:20-23).

---

64. See Sandra M. Schneiders, "Women in the Fourth Gospel and the Role of Women in the Contemporary Church," *BTB* 12 (1982) 35–45, esp. 40–42.

The World and the Johannine Context

The Fourth Gospel uses the same term—*world* (*kosmos*)—for the whole creation and for the various groups of human beings that inhabit it. The *kosmos* is the object of God's love and the entity that hates God. The Johannine portrait of "the world" emerges from the interplay between these different uses, and it is helpful to reflect on the relationship of this multifaceted reality to the world experienced by Johannine Christians.

First, we should consider the relationship of human beings to the physical world in which they live. The prologue establishes the created order as the primary context of human life. The narrative allows readers to savor an abundant gift of wine, the taste of bread and fish roasted on hot coals by the lakeshore, and the scent of perfume lavished upon Jesus' feet. The Gospel does not disparage these physical blessings but delights in them.

At the same time, the text is aware that people experience dependency and vulnerability within the created order. The Samaritan woman's daily chores involved trudging to a well outside town, manually hauling water from its depths, and carrying it back home in a jar (4:15). The need for food was so basic, the evangelist observed, that the disciples went into a Samaritan village to buy it even though Jews supposedly had no dealings with Samaritans (4:8-9). A crowd pursued Jesus to demand more bread, reflecting the real and widespread dependence of people on grain (6:26, 34). The disciples fished all night without catching anything (21:3) and were buffeted by winds that churned up the waves and threatened to engulf the boats they rowed (6:18-19). A more serious menace, however, was disease: A fever could threaten a child's life overnight (4:47), congenital blindness could reduce a person to begging (9:1, 9), and other illnesses could incapacitate people for decades (5:5) or result in premature death (11:1, 17).

Along with this vulnerable dependence is the human penchant for judging transcendent realities by material standards. Those who could see physically passed judgment on the beggar who suffered from congenital blindness, yet it was he and not his opponents who proved receptive to the Son of man (9:1-3, 34-41). Crowds were pleased as long as Jesus provided ample food and healed the sick, but they quickly became contentious when he told them about the bread that comes down from above or when he delayed performing a cure (6:34, 41; 11:37). Jesus' adversaries contested the validity of his teaching because he had not studied with a teacher they knew, they disputed his messiahship because he was a Galilean, and they rejected his claim to have come from God because he was a mere man. They judged him on the basis of appearances, not right judgment (7:24).

A second broad area for concern is the way faith relates to ordinary types of human relationships. The Gospel indicates that belief and unbelief cut across family, ethnic, and other social bonds. The most basic relationships are those within families.[65] Like other New Testament writings,[66] John's Gospel attests that in some cases members of the same family did come to faith: Andrew brought his brother Peter to Jesus (1:41-42); Martha, Mary, and Lazarus belonged to the same family (11:1); and the royal official's faith spread throughout his household (4:53). Yet members of the same family sometimes differed sharply in their responses to Jesus. The evangelist contrasts the loyalty of Jesus' mother with the disbelief of his brothers (2:5, 12; 7:5; 19:26-27) and recounts the refusal of the beggar's parents to speak on behalf of their son after his encounter with Jesus, which probably reflects tensions that had been experienced by some Johannine Christians (9:18-23). They faced the prospect of being "orphaned" (14:18) not only by the departure of Jesus but by being alienated from their own kin.

Such divergent responses to Jesus eventually redefined relationships within and between ethnic groups and led to a loss of traditional ethnic identities. The earliest followers of Jesus were Jews who came to believe that Jesus was the Messiah foretold in the Scriptures, yet their most ardent opponents were other Jews who rejected the claims made about Jesus and expelled believers from the synagogue. When disciples were no longer "Jews," their identity needed to be reconceived. Moreover, Jews had often viewed Samaritans with suspicion or contempt for their mixed ethnic background and way of worship, but faith opened a new fault line that left Jews and Samaritans who believed in Jesus on one side and their unbelieving compatriots on the other. If the Romans had demonstrated their opposition to Jesus and his followers by crucifying Jesus and later executing Peter, the fourth evangelist was also cognizant of Greeks who were more open to Jesus, and the Greco-Roman names in the Johannine Epistles suggest that at least some Gentiles had entered these communities, further eroding the significance of older ethnic distinctions.

The social status of these Christians is difficult to measure, but the Gospel suggests that neither belief nor unbelief could be identified with particular social levels. Among the believers depicted in the Gospel, the royal official is at the upper end of the spectrum; his position would have carried some prestige, and his household included servants or slaves. In the middle are Martha, Mary, and Lazarus, who had a house in which to

---

65. On the family and household in the ancient world see Elliott, *A Home for the Homeless,* 170–200.

66. Acts 11:14; 16:15, 31; 18:8.

entertain guests but apparently no servants—Martha served the meal—
and although owning some expensive ointment, they apparently did not
take such luxuries for granted. At the lower end of the scale would be the
servants in the royal official's house, assuming that they came to faith
(4:53), and the man born blind, who was a panhandler. Jesus' opponents
exhibit a similar social range. At one end were the chief priests and Pharisees, who had considerable authority within the Jewish community, and at
the other end is the invalid who collaborated with them; he lay on the
kind of "mat" (*krabbatos*, 5:8-12) used by the lower classes and had no one
to help him into the pool.

These stylized portraits cannot be taken as a direct reflection of the
social status of Johannine Christians, but it seems probable that their
congregations actually included people from various social strata. House
churches like those evidenced in the Johannine Epistles were usually
hosted by someone with a home large enough to accommodate gatherings
of believers, and a number of Johannine households could readily offer
hospitality to travelers. At the same time, some members apparently lacked
"the world's goods" and needed material assistance from others in the
community (1 John 3:17). Studies of other first-century Christian communities suggest that they commonly included a cross section of persons
from various social levels, however these are measured,[67] and Johannine
congregations were apparently not exceptional in this respect.

A third major issue was that the community was challenged to maintain
a boundary with the world that was firm yet permeable. While distinguishing themselves from the world, they needed to allow for the inclusion of
new members. The disputes depicted in the Gospel suggest that there
were a range of opinions about Jesus in the evangelist's own time: While
some insisted that Jesus was a charlatan, others thought he was at least "a
good man" (7:12; 10:19-21), raising the possibility that a favorable disposi-
tion toward Jesus might lead toward faith. The evangelist upbraided Jewish Christians who refused to confess their faith publicly, but he also ap-
pealed to them in the hope that some would openly ally themselves with
Jesus and his followers (12:42-50). And he maintained a cautious interest
in the disciples of John the Baptist, some of whom resented Jesus' popularity, although others were apparently more open to Jesus (1:35-37; 3:26;
10:40-42).

John's Gospel seeks to maintain a boundary between belief and unbelief that is clear but not static. The Gospel is sweeping in its declaration
that people cannot know God on their own yet adamant that God can and

---

67. See Wayne A. Meeks, *The First Urban Christians: The Social World of the Apostle Paul* (New
Haven, Conn.: Yale University Press, 1983) 51–73.

does draw people into faith. Jesus said that *no one* can see or enter the kingdom of God . . . *unless* born from above (3:3, 5); *no one* can come to him . . . *unless* drawn by the Father (6:44); and *no one* comes to the Father . . . *except* through Jesus, who is the way (14:6). In the period after Jesus' departure, the world would hate Jesus' followers, yet people would continue to be drawn to Jesus and so to the Father by the Spirit, which worked through the testimony given by Jesus' disciples.[68]

In sociological terms, this might be called a conversionist response to the world.[69] The fourth evangelist understood that the world was corrupt but believed that change could occur when people were transformed by the power of God. In response to the world's corruption, the community needed to maintain its own separate identity; but because of God's power to bring about change, the community was called to bear witness to the world rather than withdraw from it. The community's distinction *from* the world was the basis for its engagement *with* the world. A religion that is the warp of the social fabric cannot easily confront society with its flaws. It was precisely because the community was different from the world that it could challenge the world on the basis of the love and word of God.[70]

The tension between needing to maintain boundaries with outsiders and allowing for and seeking the inclusion of newcomers was characteristic of Johannine Christianity throughout this period. Although some have argued that Johannine Christianity became increasingly introverted with time, there is strong evidence to the contrary. Chapter 21 was almost certainly added to the Gospel fairly late in the community's history, after the rest of the text had been completed. This chapter alludes to Peter's martyrdom, an incident that manifested the world's hatred for Jesus' followers, but the central action in the passage is the great catch of fish, which is strongly missionary in character. Chapters 15–17 also may have been added at a fairly late stage in the Gospel's composition, and here we find ominous warnings about the world's hatred for the disciples as well as

68. See the beginning of our first chapter. John 14:17 says that the world cannot receive the Spirit, but Bultmann rightly comments that this does not mean an unbeliever cannot become a believer. Rather, the world as world does not receive the Spirit, since to do so it must give up its essential nature, that which makes it the world (*Gospel,* 616).

69. This use of "conversionist" comes from Bryan Wilson, *Magic and the Millennium: A Sociological Study of Religious Movements of Protest among Tribal and Third-World Peoples* (New York: Harper & Row, 1973) 22. Cf. Elliott, *A Home for the Homeless,* 102–4. Johannine Christianity is identified as "introversionist" by Rebell (*Gemeinde als Gegenwelt,* 119) and Rensberger (*Johannine Faith,* 25–29), but the arguments Rensberger provides on pp. 138–50 show that "conversionist" is more appropriate.

70. Rensberger, *Johannine Faith,* 142; Charles H. Talbert, *Reading John: A Literary and Theological Commentary on the Fourth Gospel and the Johannine Epistles* (New York: Crossroad, 1992) 78–79.

the commission to go into the world as witnesses to Jesus (15:18-21, 27; 17:14-19).[71]

The Johannine Epistles manifest the same tension. Sharply distinguishing the community from a world dominated by the evil one and characterized by lust and arrogance (1 John 2:15-17; 5:19), these texts reaffirm that Christ was sent into the world, that he died to take away the sin of the world, and that he was the Savior of the world (2:2; 4:9, 14). The author called believers not to withdraw from the world but to "overcome" or "conquer" (*nikan*) the world's evil through faith (2:13-14; 5:4-5). Although complicated by the rupture in their ranks, missionary work was pursued by both sides in the Johannine schism. The author of 1 John urged readers to test what those who had "gone out into the world" were saying, for the teachings of some negated the significance of Jesus' humanity (1 John 4:1-5). The author of the second letter went further, warning readers not to offer hospitality to those who had "gone out into the world" to propagate false teaching (2 John 7-11). Some apparently went too far in this direction and refused to extend hospitality to missionaries of any sort. Therefore the author of the third epistle commended Gaius for supporting those who had set out in God's service and promised to pursue the issue of hospitality to missionaries and others (3 John 5-8).[72]

Symbols and the World

The symbols in John's Gospel function within this tension between the community's distinction from and engagement with the world (see pp. 30–31). At the physical level, Jesus performed signs that changed scarcity into abundance, sickness into health, and death into life. He worked within the physical world without being resigned to it; situations of deficiency and threat were occasions for Jesus to carry out God's work, transforming matters to accord with God's creative purposes (5:17-29). The signs locate the community that bears witness to them within the world while helping to maintain a dissatisfaction with the world as it is experienced. The signs ally believers with the Creator, who will not allow scarcity, disease, and death finally to triumph.

71. On the literary history of John 15–17 and 21 see Brown, *Gospel*, 2.582–88, 1077–82. Jerome H. Neyrey has tried to argue that Johannine Christianity became increasingly introverted. In his literary analysis he tries to trace developments within the community by making minute distinctions between sources and later redactions, yet he overlooks the evidence of mission in chapters 17 and 21, which most scholars understand reflect a late stage of development (*An Ideology of Revolt: John's Christology in Social Science Perspective* [Philadelphia: Fortress, 1988]).

72. On the issue of missionary support in the Johannine Epistles see Brown, *Epistles*, 738; cf. Schnackenburg, *Das Johannesevangelium*, 4.58–72.

At the same time, the signs do not equate the pursuit of material security with faith or identify health with eternal life. The Gospel shows that not all who are alive in body are alive to God. People may be sated and in full possession of their physical faculties while remaining antagonistic toward God, Jesus, and his followers. Conversely, disciples may be called to risk death or to lay down their lives out of love for others (11:7-10; 15:13; 1 John 3:16). Such courage is manifest not among those whose vision is confined to procuring more bread but among those who, through faith, are brought into a life that is given by God, lived for God, and will endure beyond the death of the body (John 11:25-26; 12:25).

If public profession of belief and baptism altered the social matrix in which people lived, generating conflict with family members and others in the same ethnic group, the Gospel strengthens the distinctive sense of belonging by using familial metaphors and images for the community of faith.[73] On Easter evening Jesus "breathed" the Spirit into his disciples, an action reminiscent of God's breathing the spirit or breath of life into the first human being he created (20:22; Gen. 2:7). The reception of the Spirit gives people a "birth" from above (John 3:3, 5), and those who are "begotten" of God (1:13) receive a new identity as "children of God" (1:12) and have God as their "Father" (20:17). This new relationship with God brings about a new relationship with other people. When Jesus entrusted his mother to the Beloved Disciple, he established a new household centered on a common relationship with Jesus (19:26-27).

Images of light and darkness help define the boundaries of this fellowship, distinguishing the "children of light" (12:36) from the benighted world around them. When considering possible social functions of this motif, we should keep in mind that its primary literary function is to press the distinction between belief and unbelief in ambiguous situations; it does not simply reinforce boundaries that are otherwise apparent. Comments about light and darkness accompany the appearances of Nicodemus—whose relationship with Jesus is perhaps the most stubbornly ambiguous feature of the Gospel (3:2, 19-21; 7:51—8:12; 19:39)—and calls to follow the light and believe in the light are issued precisely when popular opinion about Jesus seems most unsettled (8:12; 12:34-36). Socially the symbols of light and darkness seem to have functioned in a similar way, helping the community maintain a distinctive identity in vague and uncertain situations rather than reinforcing well-established boundaries. This is apparent in 1 John 1:1—2:11, where the author speaks of light and darkness when community has broken down and his readers' relationship to himself and his opponents is in flux.

73. See esp. Elliott, *A Home for the Homeless*, 200–233.

Paradoxically, the symbols that distinguish Jesus and his followers from the world also point to their engagement with the world. Whenever Jesus is portrayed as light, he is a light that comes "into the world" in order to illumine the darkness (1:5, 9; 3:19; 12:46); he is the light "of the world," which means light for the world (8:12; 9:4; 11:9). Similarly, the Gospel sharply contrasts "the bread of life" with the palpable bread the unbeliev-ing crowds craved, yet in the same context Jesus reaffirms that he is the bread that gives life "to the world" (6:33, 51). And the water that Jesus offers cannot be equated with Jewish lustrations or the baptism of John, the water in Jacob's well or the pool of Bethzatha. Yet when Jesus speaks of water, he invites "anyone who thirsts" to come to him and drink (7:37-38).

The representative figures in the Fourth Gospel help to maintain boundaries by showing readers the differences between belief and unbe-lief. Through character portrayal, the evangelist seeks to attract readers to positive exemplars of faith, to alienate them from those who reject Jesus, and to move them beyond responses that seem inadequate. At the same time, the dynamic qualities of characters can help keep boundaries from becoming static. Belief and unbelief are *generated* wherever Jesus is en-countered. The man born blind has a prominent place among Johannine heroes of faith, yet his convictions and audacious loyalty emerged over a period of time (John 9). Similarly, the Pharisees are premier villains, but in this same episode they initially exhibited divided opinions about Jesus and only later hardened in their opposition to him. Elsewhere Nathanael was manifestly skeptical about Jesus at first but he became a disciple (1:46, 49), while others who apparently believed in Jesus for a time ended up abandoning him or even trying to kill him (6:66; 8:31, 59). The lines between the believing community and the unbelieving world are not static.

Groups with convictions as intense as those in John's Gospel may fall prey to the idea that truth is something they "possess." For people to commit themselves to the truth is one thing; for them to equate truth with themselves is quite another. The way representative figures are portrayed in the Gospel provides a vital check on this tendency. In the characters, the most exalted confessions of faith are conjoined with human foibles and limitations. The mother of Jesus followed him to the cross but found Jesus incomprehensible at Cana (2:4-5). Peter rightly declared that Jesus was the Holy One of God yet was confused by the foot washing and even-tually denied Jesus (6:66-69; 13:6-11; 18:15-27). Martha confessed that Jesus was "the Christ, the Son of God," yet she could not understand why he wanted to open up a tomb containing a rancid corpse (11:27, 39). Sim-ilarly, the humorous inability of the Samaritan woman to fathom what Jesus meant by "living water," the disciples' failure to grasp what his "food" was (4:7-15, 31-35), and the brash skepticism of Thomas (11:16; 14:5; 20:25) help Christians develop the capacity for self-criticism.

The paradoxical relationship of the community to the world can be summed up in the symbol of the door (10:7-10), which is a means of both exclusion and inclusion. Using realistic language, Jesus spoke about the fold in which sheep were kept. Sheepfolds usually consisted of a circular wall of stones that could be attached to a house or located out in open country, and several small flocks of sheep could be brought into the fold at night to protect them from predators. Someone remained on watch beside the single door to the fold until morning, when the sheep were taken out to pasture. Traditional descriptions of God's people as his sheep enabled the imagery to be transferred easily to the Christian community.[74]

When Jesus identifies himself as the door of the sheep, he identifies himself as the sole legitimate means of access to God's flock. He sharply distinguishes himself from all who seek entry apart from him, declaring that "all" who have come before him are thieves and robbers (10:1, 8). But if the image of the door separates Jesus and his followers from all others, it also allows for entry and inclusion. The door defines the boundary without sealing the boundary. In broad terms Jesus promises that "anyone [*tis*] who enters by me will be saved" (10:9a). This imagery distinguishes Christians from outsiders without closing them off from their surroundings. The door allows the flock to find protection within the confines of the fold, but it also is the way the sheep are led out to pasture; and it is only by going out as well as coming in that they "have life abundantly" (10:9b-10).

The unity of believers and their love for one another separate them from the world while playing a vital role in their mission to the world. David Rensberger observed that Johannine Christianity confronted the world not only with a message or doctrine but with an alternative society, a counterculture, in which the message of Jesus was realized. "It sought to draw people out of the world and into the messianic community, and it did this not only by its words but by *being* that community."[75] Jesus' unity with the Father and the course of his life and death revealed his love for God and God's love for the world. The corporate life of Jesus' followers bears witness to this, in order that people might come to know the God who loved the world that hated him and the Son he gave to save it (3:16; 13:35; 17:21, 23).

---

74. Pss. 74:1; 79:13; 100:3.
75. *Johannine Faith,* 150; cf. Talbert, *Reading John,* 79.

Postscript:
Johannine Symbolism
and Christian Tradition

The Fourth Gospel was eventually loosed from its moorings among a distinctly "Johannine" circle of believers to take its place in the broader channel of Christian tradition. The journey was sometimes turbulent, as the Gospel caught the variable breezes of conflict and devotion, but its imagery eventually assumed a prominent position in the armada of Christian symbols. To trace the way the Gospel's symbols have been received and understood by various readers is beyond the scope of what we can do here, but reflections on several issues that have engaged interpreters over the centuries may be a useful way to offer an assessment of the course we have taken.

SACRAMENTAL SYMBOLISM

The relationship of the symbols in John's Gospel to Baptism and the Lord's Supper has probably been the most persistent area of dispute. Artists and theologians from ancient times to the present have sometimes interpreted the foot washing and the healings at the pools of Bethzatha and Siloam in terms of Baptism, with the story of the man born blind providing an especially vivid way to depict baptismal enlightenment. The Lord's Supper was associated with the wine at Cana, the meals of bread and fish in Galilee, and the figure of the vine and its branches. The blood and water flowing from Jesus' side were often understood to bind both sacraments to the crucified one.[1] At the same time, the implications of

---

1. See esp. Oscar Cullmann, *Early Christian Worship* (London: SCM, 1953); Paul Niewalda, *Sakramentssymbolik im Johannesevangelium: Eine exegetisch-historische Studie* (Limburg: Lahn, 1958). Brown is open to sacramental interpretations of the symbolism but with greater caution (*Gospel,* CXI–CXIV). Cf. Xavier Léon-Dufour, *Sharing the Eucharistic Bread: The Witness of the New Testament* (New York: Paulist, 1987) 248–77.

these sacramental interpretations for church doctrine and practice have been vigorously debated. Portions of John 6, for example, have been invoked to support opposing positions on withholding the cup versus granting it to the laity and on transubstantiation versus a spiritualized understanding of Christ's presence in the Lord's Supper.[2]

Although it is customary to ask about the Gospel's stance toward "the sacraments" collectively, we should note that Baptism plays a more important role in Johannine symbolism than does the Lord's Supper. Several passages in the Fourth Gospel refer to the baptism administered by John and later by Jesus and his disciples. When baptism is integral to the Gospel's imagery—as in birth "from water and the Spirit"—it is explicitly mentioned in the same episode (3:5, 22). The celebration of the Lord's Supper, however, is not mentioned; five chapters are devoted to Jesus' last meal with his disciples (John 13–17), but there is no reference to the distribution of the bread and cup. Elsewhere the first Cana miracle included wine but not bread; the five thousand were fed with bread and fish but not wine; and the discussion of the vine focuses on fruit bearing, not on drinking or eating. Similarly, the Johannine Epistles almost certainly connect water with Jesus' baptism, but the relationship of his blood to a sacramental meal is less apparent (1 John 5:6-8). This means that readers will find connections between Johannine symbols and Baptism suggested in the Gospel (John 3), but they will discern connections with a sacramental meal only if they are already familiar with the celebration of the Lord's Supper from other sources. And the Gospel's imagery reads quite differently depending on the view of the sacrament the reader supplies.

If we maintain our focus on first-century Christian readers, it seems clear that most understood that Baptism marked a person's entry into the community of faith. The command to baptize people from all nations (Matt. 28:19), the accounts of baptisms in the book of Acts, and references to baptism in Paul's letters and other sources show that it was common Christian practice.[3] The place of the Lord's Supper is more difficult to assess. We do not know how clearly it was distinguished from other meals, what procedures were used, or how often it was celebrated. At Corinth "the Lord's Supper" was an entire meal eaten by the congregation (1 Cor. 11:17-34). The book of Acts says that Christians took bread, gave thanks, and broke it whether eating in the company of other believers (2:42, 46)

2. See my "John Six and the Lord's Supper," *LQ* 4 (1990) 419–37. For a survey of research on the sacraments in John's Gospel see Robert Kysar, *The Fourth Evangelist and His Gospel: An Examination of Contemporary Scholarship* (Minneapolis: Augsburg, 1975) 249–59. My position is similar to that of Kysar as well as to that of Schnackenburg in many cases.

3. See Acts 2:41; 8:12; 9:18; 16:15; 18:8; 19:5; Rom. 6:3; 1 Cor. 1:13-17; 12:13; Gal. 3:27; Eph. 4:5; Col. 2:12; 1 Pet. 3:21.

or pagans (27:35), which suggests that it was common practice for all meals, regardless of their character. Moreover, the Christians in Acts are never said to have shared a cup of wine along with the bread. Although the celebration of the Lord's Supper using bread and wine eventually became a common practice, it is not clear how typical it was at the time John's Gospel and epistles were composed.[4]

A useful way to pursue the question of the relationship of Johannine symbolism to the Lord's Supper is by sketching the history of the interpretation of the bread of life discourse.[5] A sacramental understanding of John 6 may be implicit in the writings of Ignatius of Antioch and Justin Martyr in the second century. It was developed more fully in subsequent centuries by Cyril of Alexandria, John Chrysostom, and others and became a regular feature of Orthodox and medieval Roman Catholic exegesis. These interpreters found it plausible to relate John 6 to the Lord's Supper because Jesus' flesh is identified with bread in 6:51, and references to eating his flesh and drinking his blood are similar to the words Jesus spoke over the bread and cup according to the other Gospels and Paul. Since the exposition of John's Gospel frequently took place in public worship, a sacramental interpretation of the symbolism helped connect the homily with the rest of the service.

Many who read the text sacramentally, however, recognized that it created theological problems. The words "he who eats my flesh and drinks my blood has eternal life" (6:54) seemed to guarantee salvation to everyone who communed, and the warning "unless you eat the flesh of the Son of man and drink his blood you have no life in you" (6:53) seemed to mean that anyone who failed to commune would forfeit eternal life. In response, some Christians, especially in the East, adopted the practice of giving newly baptized infants some of the sacrament, ensuring that they communed at least once. Others, especially in the West, maintained that the elements of the Supper should not be given to infants, since Paul

4. Breaking bread in Acts 20:7 seems to be associated with a gathering for worship; in 20:11 it seems to be an ordinary meal. Luke 22:19 includes the command that Jesus' disciples break bread in memory of him but does not include a similar command for the wine. Christians like those in Acts may have used only bread for the Supper. See Joachim Jeremias, *The Eucharistic Words of Jesus* (New York: Scribner's, 1966) 115. Matt. 26:26-29 and Mark 14:22-25 associate the bread and cup with a new covenant but do not command that these be shared in memory of Jesus in the future. Heb. 6:2 mentions "baptisms," but the author does not connect the bread and wine served by Melchizedek (Gen. 14:18), whose priesthood foreshadowed that of Jesus, with the Lord's Supper (cf. Heb. 7:1-10). On the difficulties pertaining to the evidence regarding the Lord's Supper in the early church, see James D. G. Dunn, *Unity and Diversity in the New Testament: An Inquiry into the Character of Earliest Christianity* (2d ed.; London: SCM; Philadelphia: Trinity, 1990) 161–68. Cf. the survey by Hans-Josef Klauck ("Lord's Supper," *Anchor Bible Dictionary* [1992] 4.362–72), which notes many of the problems but tends to assume greater uniformity.

5. For detailed treatment of primary sources see my "John Six and the Lord's Supper."

urged people to examine themselves before partaking, and insisted that receiving the sacrament did not guarantee salvation, since Paul warned that people could eat and drink judgment upon themselves (1 Cor. 11:27-32). They also maintained that believers who desired the sacrament but were unable to receive it for some reason were not in jeopardy.

Nonsacramental interpretations of John 6, which took eating and drinking as vivid metaphors for faith, are attested in the late second century in the writings of Clement of Alexandria and later in Origen and Eusebius. This was Augustine's primary position and the one considered least problematic by Thomas Aquinas; it was also followed by Erasmus, Luther, Calvin, and others. Theologically, these interpreters argued that if "eating" is a metaphor for faith, the message of John 6 is consistent with the rest of John's Gospel and the New Testament generally, where faith is the way people abide in Christ and receive eternal life. In terms of literary context, they pointed out that the bread of life discourse stressed the importance of faith in Jesus and receiving Jesus' word rather than physical eating (6:28-29, 63-64), and that the parallelism between "he who believes has eternal life" and "he who eats my flesh and drinks my blood has eternal life" (6:40, 47, 54) shows that eating is a synonym for believing. Historically, some also found it odd to discern an allusion to the sacrament so early in Jesus' ministry, since the other Gospels say it was not instituted until later.

Both sacramental and nonsacramental interpretations were deemed viable at the Council of Trent, although most subsequent Roman Catholic exegesis followed the sacramental approach. The nonsacramental interpretation was adopted by Reformed and Lutheran exegetes, with a few exceptions, and it was standard in British exegesis until well into the nineteenth century, when it was challenged on several grounds. (a) Historical critics interpreted the Fourth Gospel as a creative composition by the evangelist, maintaining that an allusion to the sacrament in John 6, which would have been incongruous on Jesus' own lips, must reflect the interests of the early church. (b) They also detached 6:51c-58 from its literary setting by ascribing it to a later editor, whose views resembled those reflected in other late first- and second-century Christian writings more closely than those found elsewhere in the discourse. (c) Theologically, some related the idea that a sacred meal could guarantee eternal life to Ignatius's view that the Eucharist was the "medicine of immortality" (Ign. *Eph.* 20:2). Others discerned sacramental overtones throughout John 6, noting that the feeding of the five thousand was typically interpreted sacramentally in early Christian iconography, that the distribution of bread and fish is reminiscent of Jesus' actions at the last supper according to other sources, and that his command to "gather up" the fragments is similar to a eucharistic prayer found in *Didache* 9.[6]

These interpretations have in turn created new difficulties. Although the Fourth Gospel does allude to the experiences of the postresurrection church, it is difficult to maintain that 6:51c-58 should be ascribed to a later editor, since these verses exhibit the same distinctive literary style as the rest of the discourse; the text should be interpreted in its present literary context. Many who interpret 6:51c-58 sacramentally suggest that it attempts to correct a highly spiritualized view of Jesus and the Lord's Supper similar to that advocated by the opponents of Ignatius. Yet it is hard to see why such a corrective would have been placed in John 6 rather than in the last supper account, since John 6 addresses people who had the opposite problem: They thought Jesus was a mere human being (6:42).

It is theologically problematic to read John 6 in light of Ignatius, since Ignatius often applied Johannine language to the church practices of his own time even when these differed from those of Johannine Christianity. Ignatius connected the flesh and blood of Jesus not only with the bread and cup but with an altar and the oversight of a bishop, elders, and deacons,[7] relating Johannine language to ecclesiastical practices unlike those reflected in the Gospel and epistles. A similar pattern occurs in his other uses of Johannine expressions: He understood Jesus' unity with the Father as analogous to Christian unity with the bishop[8] and invoked the testimony of the Spirit that knows "whence it comes and whither it goes" to validate his appeal to heed the bishop, elders, and deacons.[9] More important, however, the Gospel itself undercuts the idea that the sacrament is the "medicine of immortality." In 6:54-58 Jesus promised that one who "eats" (*trōgein*) would abide in him and live forever, but at the last supper the one specifically said to "eat" (*trōgein*) was Judas, who was united with Satan, not Jesus, and who found destruction rather than life (13:18, 26-27; 17:12).

We noted earlier that Johannine symbols usually have a focused center of meaning with a penumbra of vagueness created by the many associations evoked by the image. The Fourth Gospel mentions Baptism when it

---

6. On the relationship between Ignatius and John's Gospel see Schnackenburg, *Gospel,* 2.452–53 n. 154; Lothar Wehr, *Arznei der Unsterblichkeit: Die Eucharistie bei Ignatius von Antiochen und im Johannesevangelium* (NTAbh 18; Münster: Aschendorff, 1986). Brown stresses the eucharistic features of the entire chapter, noting connections with *Didache* 9 (*Gospel,* 1.246–48); cf. John M. Perry, "The Evolution of the Johannine Eucharist," *NTS* 39 (1993) 22–23. See further my "John and the Lord's Supper," 424–26, 435–36.

7. Ignatius, *Smyrn.* 7:1—8:2; *Phld.* 4:1; cf. *Rom.* 7:3.

8. Ign. *Magn.* 7:1; cf. John 5:19, 30; 8:28.

9. Ign. *Phld.* 7:1; cf. John 3:8.

is integral to the symbolism of a passage (3:5, 22), but the Lord's Supper is not mentioned in the Johannine writings and is not necessary for a cogent understanding of John 6 or other passages. Possible allusions to the sacrament remain in the penumbra and resist being translated into a statement about the Lord's Supper. In our third chapter we tried to show that the references to eating and drinking are vivid metaphors for believing in Jesus incarnate and crucified. Like other symbols in the Gospel, these have an intensely christological center that gives focus to interpretation.

GEOGRAPHICAL SYMBOLISM

The geographical references in the Fourth Gospel, while much less a point of contention, introduce a different set of issues. Many consider the topographical notices to be remnants of tradition and generally accurate, adding a sense of authenticity to the narrative.[10] Others have dismissed the possibility of historical significance in order to stress the symbolic quality of certain places. The gnostic Heracleon, for example, identified Capernaum (2:12) with the lower regions of the cosmos and its inhabitants with those enmeshed in ignorance; when Jesus "went up" from there to Jerusalem (2:13), he ascended to the higher, psychic plane.[11] Origen followed an intermediate course, attributing both historical and symbolic significance to places, often by tracing their etymologies. He maintained that "the names of places agree in their meaning with the things connected with Jesus."[12] The Gospel seems to invite such interpretations: It explains, for instance, that the name *Siloam* means "one who is sent" (9:7). Origen extended this approach to other places, suggesting that Jesus accompanied his mother and disciples to Capernaum to console them (2:12) since the name *Capernaum* means "field of consolation," and that Martha and Mary dutifully attended Jesus at Bethany (12:1-3), which means "house of obedience."[13] The problem is that in most cases the evangelist assumed readers had no knowledge of Hebrew or Aramaic (e.g., 1:38, 41).

Our approach recognizes that physical places can help to convey something of transcendent or representative significance, and that the fourth evangelist does not replace history with symbolism but presents readers with both in the same story (see pp. 8, 38–39). When considering the

10. Chrysostom, *Homilies on the Gospel of St. John* 17.1. Cf. C. H. Dodd, *Historical Tradition in the Fourth Gospel* (Cambridge: Cambridge University Press, 1963) 233–47; Carl Bjerklund, *Tauta Egeneto: Die Präzisierungssätze im Johannesevangelium* (WUNT 40; Tübingen: Mohr/ Siebeck, 1987) 149.

11. See Elaine H. Pagels, *The Johannine Gospel in Gnostic Exegesis: Heracleon's Commentary on John* (SBLMS 17; Nashville: Abingdon, 1973) 67–68.

12. *Commentary on the Gospel of John* 10.10.

13. On Capernaum see his *Commentary* 10.6; on Bethany see 6.24.

significance of particular sites, however, we have not relied on etymology but have tried to connect literary developments in the Gospel with possible allusions to traditions associated with those places.[14] The role of the regions mentioned in the Gospel illustrates the value of this approach. From a literary perspective, chapters 1–5 associate the negative or dubious responses to Jesus with Jerusalem and Judea, and more positive responses with Transjordan, Samaria, and Galilee. In terms of tradition this seems plausible, since various sources attest that Jesus' first disciples came from Galilee, that he was killed in Jerusalem, and that early Christian evangelistic activity met with some success in Samaria. Returning to the narrative, we find that from John 6 on, regional affiliations can be extended to anyone who responds to Jesus in the manner characteristic of the region. For example, Jesus' adversaries in Galilee are called Jews (6:41), and the Roman governor's posture toward Jesus suggests that he too might be Jewish (18:35). Conversely, the tentative openness of the Jewish leader Nicodemus suggests that he might be a Galilean (7:51-52), and people such as the man born blind, Martha, and Mary are not called Jews even though they live in or near Jerusalem, were associated with the synagogue, and voiced the Jewish hope of resurrection.

Specific places also may contribute to the Gospel's symbolism. This happens when Jesus expels the merchants from the temple to foreshadow the time when his crucified and risen body would be the temple (2:13-22). In order to understand the symbolism, readers need to know something about the place. Those who knew that the temple was used for sacrifice and that it was, at least ideally, the place of God's special presence would understand that Jesus assumed these roles through his death and resurrection. Similarly, Jesus' conversation with the Samaritan woman recalls traditions concerning Jacob's well, contrasting Jesus and his living water with the water and worship the woman inherited from her ancestors (4:1-42). And the explanation that Siloam means "one who has been sent" (9:7) identifies the pool with Jesus as the one God "sent" (9:4) and apparently alludes to traditions concerning prophets and the Messiah.

Other topographical notices may contribute more indirectly to the symbolism by reinforcing the significance of the central images, figures, and actions in a passage. Jesus spoke of living water and the light of the world in the vicinity of the temple treasury (8:20), which suggests that the light and water symbolism be related to rituals conducted in the temple during the feast of Booths. The area around Bethany in Transjordan was appar-

14. See the summary of research by Charles H. Scobie, "Johannine Geography," *SR* 11 (1982) 77–84; see also Jouette Bassler, "The Galileans: A Neglected Factor in Johannine Community Research," *CBQ* 43 (1981) 243–57; Robert T. Fortna, *The Fourth Gospel and Its Predecessor: From Narrative Source to Present Gospel* (Philadelphia: Fortress, 1988) 294–314.

ently associated with Elijah, Elisha, Moses, and Joshua and was therefore
an appropriate place for the appearance of the Messiah, who fulfilled all
these roles (1:19-29). Cana was a Jewish community and the home of
Nathanael the Israelite (2:1; 21:2), making it an appropriate place for
Jesus to begin fulfilling and transcending Jewish messianic expectations.
The springs at Aenon were near Salim, a place in Samaria associated with
the field Jacob bought (3:23; 4:5); by baptizing there John seemed to
anticipate Jesus' ministry among the Samaritans. The pool at Bethzatha
seems to have resembled healing shrines found at various places in the
Mediterranean world, and the invalid Jesus met exhibited an attitude toward healing that many associated with such places (5:2-7). The town of
Tiberius was originally settled by people seeking handouts, and the crowds
from that area who pursued Jesus exhibited the same tendencies
(6:23, 34). In none of these instances does interpretation depend on
knowledge of the places involved, but familiarity with these traditions
would enhance the significance of the scene as a whole for the reader.

NUMERICAL SYMBOLISM

The significance of numbers has long fascinated and frustrated interpreters of John's Gospel. The evangelist seems to have structured some, though
certainly not all, aspects of the narrative in groups of seven: seven signs,
seven "I Am" sayings, and sometimes seven scenes in a given episode.[15]
More problematic, however, is the symbolic value of the numbers specifically cited in the text, such as the Samaritan woman's five husbands, the
invalid's thirty-eight-year illness, and a catch of 153 fish. Interpretation is
difficult because even in the ancient world a given number might be given
many different meanings in a single context; Philo's treatment of the
numbers in Genesis 1, for example, shows how easily interpretations could
proliferate.[16] Moreover, larger numbers were usually treated as the sum or
product of smaller numbers; and since various combinations could produce the same result, the interpretive possibilities expanded accordingly.[17]

15. The seven signs begin with the wine at Cana and end with the raising of Lazarus; the
seven "I Am" sayings concern bread (6:35, 48, 51), light (8:12; 9:5), door (10:7, 9), shepherd
(10:11, 14), resurrection and life (11:25), way, truth, and life (14:6), and the vine (15:1, 5).
Episodes with seven scenes symmetrically arranged include John 9:1-41 and 18:28—19:16; see
Paul D. Duke, *Irony in the Fourth Gospel* (Atlanta: John Knox, 1985) 117–37. The most elaborate attempt to discern numerical structuring devices is that of M. J. J. Menken, *Numerical
Literary Techniques in John: The Fourth Evangelist's Use of Numbers of Words and Syllables* (NovTSup
55; Leiden: Brill, 1985).
16. E.g., *Creation* 13–15, 47–52, 89–128.
17. Discussion of modern attempts to formulate a comprehensive approach to numerical
symbolism in John is found in Niewalda, *Sakramentssymbolik im Johannesevangelium*, 24–26. Cf.
Frédric Manns, *L'evangile de Jean à la lumière du Judaïsm* (Studium Biblicum Franciscanum 33;
Jerusalem: Franciscan, 1991) 249–52, 282–84.

The most famous conundrum is the catch of 153 fish (John 21:11), which has spawned more symbolic explanations than any other number in the Gospel. Augustine noted that 153 is the sum of numbers from one through seventeen, and that seventeen is the sum of ten plus seven. Since ten signifies the Ten Commandments and seven corresponds to the seven gifts of the Spirit, the total number of fish marks the fulfillment of the law through the Spirit. Jerome held that it corresponds to the number of species of fish in the sea, so that the catch signifies the universal scope of the church's mission. More recently it has been suggested that the number marks the fulfillment of Ezek. 47:10, which promises that in the age of salvation people will be able to catch fish in the Dead Sea from En-gedi to En-eglaim. When the numerical value of each letter in those names is added, the totals are 17 and 153 respectively.[18]

The interpreter's frame of reference plays a crucial role in the interpretation of numbers. Augustine is a good example, since he explains the numbers in the Gospel with considerable consistency, using the dichotomy between imperfection under the Mosaic law and perfection in faith, love, or the Spirit (2 Cor. 3:6-9). He said that the disciples began following Jesus at "the tenth hour" (John 1:39) since there were Ten Commandments and the time had come for the law to be fulfilled by love.[19] The five books of Moses were signified by the Samaritan woman's five husbands (4:18); by the five porticoes at Bethzatha, which were ineffective for salvation (5:2); by the five barley loaves (6:9); and by the crowd of five thousand people (6:10).[20] Later the disciples rowed for twenty-five to thirty stadia (6:19), a journey from imperfection under the Law of Moses, signified by five times five, to perfection under the gospel, signified by five times six—six was the number of days it took God to complete the world.[21] The invalid at Bethzatha was ill for thirty-eight years (5:5), which is forty minus two. If forty brings work to its perfection—as in the forty-day fasts of Moses the lawgiver, Elijah the prophet, and Jesus the bringer of the gospel, as well as in the proclamation of the Ten Commandments to the four corners of the earth—the law rests on the two commands of love for God and neighbor. Thus the thirty-eight-year illness shows that the law cannot be fulfilled

---

18. See the survey by George Beasley-Murray, *John* (WBC 36; Waco, Tex.: Word, 1987) 401–4.

19. *Homilies on the Gospel of John* 7.10.

20. On the five husbands see the *Homilies* 15.21; these can also be taken as the five senses, with reason as her sixth companion. On the porticoes see 17.2; on the five loaves, two fish, and five thousand people see 24.5–6.

21. *Homilies* 25.6.

apart from the two commands of love.[22] Augustine's interpretation of the 153 fish in terms of law and Spirit follows in the same vein.[23]

Few contemporary interpreters discern symbolism in all these numbers, yet Augustine's relative consistency challenges us to ask about the functions of all the numbers in the Gospel as we try to assess the symbolic significance of any one of them. Our approach has been to distinguish core from supporting symbols, so that if numbers do function symbolically, it is in a supporting capacity. Numbers may acquire significance through association with the central images, persons, and actions in an episode, but the primary meaning of an episode never depends upon a number. As a way of testing the significance of a number, it is useful to ask whether the meaning would change if the text cited a different number or made a more general statement about quantity.

In this interpretive framework, we find that numbers referring to people may occasionally contribute to the symbolism of a scene. On the one hand, the observation about the Samaritan woman's five former husbands and current partner (4:18) has no independent significance but enhances her role as a representative figure by suggesting similarities between her personal and national histories. No other number of relationships would do so. On the other hand, the observation that Jesus fed five thousand people with a bit of bread and fish highlights Jesus' power by showing that there were "so many" (6:9-10), but the effect would be the same if he had fed four thousand, as in Mark 8:6-9.[24]

Numbers referring to specific times occasionally contribute to the symbolic significance of a passage. Jesus was crucified shortly after the sixth hour on the Day of Preparation (19:14), and mentioning the number helps correlate Jesus' death with the time of the slaying of the paschal lambs. The comment that he met the Samaritan woman at the sixth hour (4:6) is more difficult to interpret. From a literary perspective the sixth hour may anticipate the crucifixion, when water like that promised to the woman would flow from his side. From the perspective of Jewish and Samaritan tradition it might strengthen connections with the story of Jacob, who met his future bride beside a well at midday (Gen. 29:7). From a cultural perspective it may help depict the woman as an outcast, who

22. *Homilies* 17.4–6.
23. *Homilies* 122.8–9. See also his treatment of the number six in connection with the jars at Cana (John 2:6) and the hour Jesus met the Samaritan woman (4:6). He identifies six world ages, five of which span the period of the Old Testament, and the sixth is from John the Baptist to the end of time. The advent of Jesus thus fulfilled the prophecies in the Law and the Prophets (*Homilies* 9.6; 15.9). Elsewhere Augustine sometimes interprets numbers in terms of the Trinity or the church.
24. The twelve disciples (6:67-71; 20:24) are associated with the twelve sons of Jacob in some early Christian sources (e.g., Rev. 21:12-14), but this symbolism is not developed in John's Gospel.

came to draw water at an unusual time, when no one else was present. All these meanings are possible, and the number may be useful because it helps maintain a creative interplay between these various aspects of the text. Elsewhere the comment that the wedding at Cana took place "on the third day" (2:1) is suggestive since the sign Jesus performed antici-pates his final glorification, and his resurrection "in three days" is men-tioned in the next scene (2:19). Nevertheless, the meaning does not depend upon the number.

The symbolic quality of other numbered times is less apparent. The first disciples met the Lamb of God at the tenth hour (1:36, 39), a time associated with temple sacrifice and prayer and a number associated with perfection or fulfillment. The problems are that prayer is not mentioned in this context and that Jesus was actually sacrificed at about the sixth hour. The tenth hour could connote perfection, but so could other times, such as the seventh hour, which was when the Galilean official's son was healed (4:52). If Jesus had met his disciples at the seventh hour and healed the boy at the tenth hour, the meaning of these passages would not change.[25]

The numbers indicating quantities of time do not appear to function symbolically in the Gospel. Many are simply descriptive.[26] The observation that it took forty-six years to build the temple helps to show that the temple Jesus would build in three days would be of a different order (2:20). The thirty-eight-year illness of the invalid at Bethzatha confirms the seriousness of his ailment (5:5). Each number illustrates "a long time" (cf. 5:6), and a slightly larger or smaller number would not affect the text in either case. Later, Jesus arrived at Bethany when Lazarus had been in the tomb for four days, which reinforces the finality of Lazarus's death (11:3, 6, 17).[27]

Other numbers in the Gospel seem to function in a similar way, adding vividness to the narrative but not functioning symbolically. The comment that Bethany was "fifteen stadia" from Jerusalem (11:18), like other num-bers giving distances, seems to be purely descriptive, with no symbolic significance.[28] The same is true for quantities of things. At Cana, for exam-ple, there were six stone jars (2:6), which some have suggested point to the imperfection of the old order, since six is one less than seven. Some of the ancients considered six to be a perfect number, however, and in any

25. The risen Jesus appeared on the first day of the week and again eight days later (20:19, 26). This may suggest that Christians traditionally gathered on Sundays, but the numbers one and eight are not significant.

26. See also 4:35, 40; 11:9; 12:1.

27. The Jewish tradition that the soul finally departs on the fourth day is late (third century). See Str-B 2.544-45.

28. For other numbered distances see 6:19; 21:8.

case there were still only six jars there after the water had become wine.[29] The division of Jesus' clothing into four parts is part of a symbolic scene, but its significance is disclosed through its connection with Psalm 22, not through the number four.

Do the 153 fish have symbolic significance? Probably not. There is little reason to think that mentioning this number is any more symbolic than observing that the invalid had been ill for thirty-eight years or that five thousand people were fed with five loaves and two fish. Its function is to emphasize the size of the catch, showing how the net was able to enclose "so many" fish without breaking (21:11). The symbolism of the passage focuses on the missionary connotations of "drawing" in the fish rather than on the specific number in the net (see pp. 118–22). Although chapter 21 was probably added after the rest of the Gospel was completed, its symbolism closely resembles that found in earlier chapters. The author identified this "third" resurrection appearance in relation to those recounted in chapter 20 and followed the typical Johannine movement from Christology (21:1-14) to discipleship (21:15-24). There is no evidence that the symbolism of the catch is an innovation that depends on interpretive techniques not needed elsewhere in John, such as numerology or gematria. If the catch had included somewhat more or fewer fish, the effect would have been the same.

An effective interpretive framework should allow readers to be imaginative yet discriminating. It must be able to identify various possible meanings while distinguishing the plausible from the implausible. Our interpretations of Johannine symbolism can impoverish the meaning by venturing to say too little, and they can empty it of meaning by trying to say too much. The text means many things, but it does not mean just anything. Authentic freedom is enjoyed precisely within limits. This is apparent at the level of faith, where people are set free by love from Christ and are constrained by love for Christ (8:36; 12:26). It is also true at the level of interpretation, as the symbols in the Gospel both awaken and constrain the imagination, guiding the reader to the Christ who is its center.

---

29. Cf. the five porticoes at Bethzatha (5:2).

Bibliography

Aalen, Sverre. *Die Begriffe "Licht" und "Finsternis" im alten Testament, im Spätjudentum und im Rabbinismus.* Oslo: Jacob Dybwad, 1951.

Abrahams, Roger D. "Proverbs and Proverbial Expressions." In *Folklore and Folklife: An Introduction,* edited by R. M. Dorson, 117–27. Chicago: University of Chicago Press, 1972.

Allison, D. C. "The Eye Is the Lamp of the Body (Matthew 6.22-23 = Luke 11.34-36)." *NTS* 33 (1987) 61–83.

Appold, Mark L. *The Oneness Motif in the Fourth Gospel: Motif Analysis and Exegetical Probe into the Theology of John.* WUNT 1. Tübingen: Mohr/Siebeck, 1976.

Ashton, John. *Understanding the Fourth Gospel.* Oxford: Clarendon, 1991.

Auerbach, Erich. *Mimesis: The Representation of Reality in Western Literature.* Princeton: Princeton University Press, 1953.

Aune, David E. "Magic in Early Christianity." *ANRW* 2.23.2 (1980) 1507–57.

Aus, Roger. *Water into Wine and the Beheading of John the Baptist.* BJS 150. Atlanta: Scholars, 1988.

Baldensperger, Wilhelm. *Der Prolog des vierten Evangeliums. Sein polemisch-apologetischer Zweck.* Tübingen: Mohr/Siebeck, 1898.

Barrett, C. K. *Essays on John.* Philadelphia: Westminster, 1982.

————. *The Gospel according to St. John.* 2d ed. Philadelphia: Westminster, 1978.

Bassler, Jouette M. "The Galileans: A Neglected Factor in Johannine Community Research." *CBQ* 43 (1981) 243–57.

————. "Mixed Signals: Nicodemus in the Fourth Gospel." *JBL* 108 (1989) 635–46.

Bauer, Walter. *Das Johannesevangelium.* HNT 6. Tübingen: Mohr/Siebeck, 1933.

Baum-Bodenbender, Rosel. *Hoheit in Niedrigkeit: Johanneische Christologie im Prozess Jesu vor Pilatus (Joh 18,28-19,16a).* FB 49. Würzburg: Echter, 1984.

Beasley-Murray, George. *John.* WBC 36. Waco, Tex.: Word, 1987.

Becker, Jürgen. *Das Evangelium nach Johannes.* Gütersloh: Mohn, 1979–81.

Berger, Klaus. *Exegese des Neuen Testaments: Neue Wege vom Text zur Auslegung.* Heidelberg: Quelle & Meyer, 1977.

Berger, Peter L., and Thomas Luckmann. *The Social Construction of Reality: A Treatise in the Sociology of Knowledge*. New York: Doubleday, 1967.

Bernard, J. H. *A Critical and Exegetical Commentary on the Gospel according to St. John*. ICC. Edinburgh and New York: Scribner's Sons, 1929.

Betz, H. D. "Matthew vi.22f and Ancient Greek Theories of Vision." In *Text and Interpretation: Studies in the New Testament Presented to Matthew Black*, edited by E. Best and R. McL. Wilson, 43–56. Cambridge: Cambridge University Press, 1979.

Betz, Hans Dieter. *Galatians*. Hermeneia. Philadelphia: Fortress, 1979.

————. *Plutarch's Theological Writings and Early Christian Literature*. SCHNT 3. Leiden: Brill, 1975.

Beutler, Johannes. "Greeks Come to See Jesus (John 12,20f)." *Bib* 71 (1990) 333–47.

Bienaimé, Germain. *Moïse et le don de l'eau dans la tradition juive ancienne: targum et midrash*. AnBib 98. Rome: Biblical Institute, 1984.

Bittner, Wolfgang J. *Jesu Zeichen im Johannesevangelium: Die Messias-Erkenntnis im Johannesevangelium vor ihrem jüdischen Hintergrund*. WUNT 26. Tübingen: Mohr/Siebeck, 1987.

Bjerklund, Carl. *Tauta Egeneto: Die Präzisierungssätze im Johannesevangelium*. WUNT 40. Tübingen: Mohr/Siebeck, 1987.

Blank, Josef. "Die Verhandlung vor Pilatus Joh 18,28-19,16 im Lichte johanneischer Theologie." *BZ* 3 (1959) 60–81.

————. *Krisis: Untersuchungen zur johanneischen Christologie und Eschatologie*. Freiburg: Lambertus, 1964.

Blinzler, Josef. *The Trial of Jesus*. Westminster, Md.: Newman, 1959.

Boismard, M. E. "Aenon près de Salem: Jean III.23." *RB* 80 (1973) 218–29.

Borgen, Peder. *Bread from Heaven: An Exegetical Study in the Concept of Manna in the Gospel of John and the Writings of Philo*. NovTSup 10. Leiden: Brill, 1965.

————. "Creation, Logos and the Son: Observations on John 1:1-18 and 5:17-18." *Ex Auditu* 3 (1987) 88-97.

Borig, Rainer. *Das wahre Weinstock: Untersuchungen zu Jo 15,1-10*. SANT 16. Munich: Kösel, 1967.

Braun, F.-M. *Jean le théologian. Sa theologie, I. Le mystère de Jésus Christ*. EB. Paris: Gabalda, 1966.

Broer, Ingo. "Noch einmal: Zur religionsgeschichtliche 'Ableitung' von Jo 2,1-11." In *Studien zum Neuen Testament und seiner Umwelt*, edited by A. Fuchs, 103–23. Linz, 1983.

Brown, Edward K. *Rhythm in the Novel*. The Alexander Lectures, 1949–50. Toronto: University of Toronto Press, 1950.

Brown, Raymond E. *The Birth of the Messiah*. Garden City, N.Y.: Doubleday, 1977.

————. *The Churches the Apostles Left Behind*. New York: Paulist, 1984.

————. *The Community of the Beloved Disciple*. New York: Paulist, 1979.

————. *The Death of the Messiah: From Gethsemane to the Grave*. New York: Doubleday, 1994.

————. *The Epistles of John*. AB 30. Garden City, N.Y.: Doubleday, 1982.

————. *The Gospel according to John*. AB 29–29A. Garden City, N.Y.: Doubleday, 1966-70.

————. "Jesus and Elisha." *Perspective* 12 (1971) 85–104.

Brown, Raymond E., et al. *Mary in the New Testament*. New York/Mahwah: Paulist, 1978.

_____. *Peter in the New Testament.* Minneapolis: Augsburg; New York: Paulist, 1973.

Bultmann, Rudolf. *The Gospel of John.* Philadelphia: Westminster, 1971.

_____. "Zur Geschichte der Lichtsymbolik im Altertum." *Beiträge zum Verständnis der Jenseitigkeit Gottes im neuen Testament,* 7–42. Darmstadt: Wissenschaftliche Buchgesellschaft, 1965.

Burge, Gary M. *The Anointed Community: The Holy Spirit in the Johannine Tradition.* Grand Rapids, Mich.: Eerdmans, 1987.

Cahill, P. J. "Narrative Art in John IV." *Religious Studies Bulletin* 2 (1982) 41–48.

Caird, G. B. *The Language and Imagery of the Bible.* London: Duckworth, 1980.

Carmichael, C. M. "Marriage and the Samaritan Woman." *NTS* 26 (1979–80) 332–46.

Carson, D. A. *The Gospel according to John.* Leicester: Inter-Varsity and Grand Rapids: Eerdmans, 1991.

Coakley, J. F. "The Anointing at Bethany and the Priority of John." *JBL* 107 (1988) 241–56.

Cohen, Ted. "Figurative Speech and Figurative Acts." In *Philosophical Perspectives on Metaphor,* edited by M. Johnson. Minneapolis: University of Minnesota Press, 1981.

_____. "Metaphor and the Cultivation of Intimacy." *Critical Inquiry* 5 (1978) 3–12.

Collins, Raymond F. "The Representative Figures of the Fourth Gospel." *Downside Review* 94 (1976) 26–46, 118–32. Reprinted in *These Things Have Been Written: Studies in the Fourth Gospel.* Louvain: Peeters; Grand Rapids, Mich.: Eerdmans, 1990.

Cosgrove, C. H. "The Place Where Jesus Is: Allusions to Baptism and the Eucharist in the Fourth Gospel." *NTS* 35 (1989) 522–39.

Courtney, E. *A Commentary on the Satires of Juvenal.* London: Athlone, 1980.

Crown, Alan D. *The Samaritans.* Tübingen: Mohr/Siebeck, 1989.

Cullmann, Oscar. *Early Christian Worship.* London: SCM, 1953.

Culpepper, R. Alan. *Anatomy of the Fourth Gospel: A Study in Literary Design.* Philadelphia: Fortress, 1983.

_____. *The Johannine School: An Examination of the Johannine School Hypothesis Based on the Investigation of the Nature of Ancient Schools.* SBLDS 26. Missoula: Scholars, 1975.

Dalman, Gustav. *Sacred Sites and Ways: Studies in the Topography of the Gospels.* London: SPCK, 1935.

Daly, Robert J. "The Soteriological Significance of the Sacrifice of Isaac." *CBQ* 39 (1977) 45–75.

Dauer, Anton. *Die Passionsgeschichte im Johannesevangelium: Eine traditionsgeschichtliche und theologische Untersuchung zu Joh 18,1—19,30.* SANT 30. Munich: Kösel, 1972.

Davies, G. I. "The Presence of God in the Second Temple." *Templum Amicitiae: Essays on the Second Temple Presented to Ernst Bammel,* 32–36. JSNTSup 48. Sheffield: JSOT, 1991.

Davies, W. D. *The Gospel and the Land.* Berkeley: University of California Press, 1974.

Davies, W. D., and Dale C. Allison, Jr. *A Critical and Exegetical Commentary on the Gospel according to St. Matthew.* ICC. Edinburgh: T. & T. Clark, 1988–.

de Jonge, M. *Jesus: Stranger from Heaven and Son of God. Jesus Christ and the Christians in Johannine Perspective.* SBLSBS 11. Missoula: Scholars, 1977.

Deissmann, Adolf. *Light from the Ancient East.* London: Hodder & Stoughten, 1910.

Diel, Paul. *Symbolism in the Bible: Its Psychological Significance.* San Francisco: Harper & Row, 1986.

Diel, Paul, and Jeannine Solotareff. *Symbolism in the Gospel of John.* San Francisco: Harper & Row, 1988.

Dillistone, F. W. *The Power of Symbols in Religion and Culture.* New York: Crossroad, 1986.

Dodd, C. H. "A Hidden Parable in the Fourth Gospel." *More New Testament Studies,* 30–40. Grand Rapids, Mich.: Eerdmans, 1968.

_____. *Historical Tradition in the Fourth Gospel.* Cambridge: Cambridge University Press, 1963.

_____. *The Interpretation of the Fourth Gospel.* Cambridge: Cambridge University Press, 1953.

Duke, Paul. *Irony in the Fourth Gospel.* Atlanta: John Knox, 1985.

Dunn, James D. G. *Unity and Diversity in the New Testament: An Inquiry into the Character of Earliest Christianity.* 2d ed. London: SCM; Philadelphia: Trinity, 1990.

Duprez, Antoine. *Jésus et les dieux guérisseurs.* Cahiers de la *Revue biblique* 12. Paris: Gabalda, 1970.

Edmonds, J. M. *The Greek Bucolic Poets.* LCL. London: Heinemann; New York: Putnam, 1923.

Edwards, William D., Wesley J. Gabel, and Floyd E. Hosmer. "On the Physical Death of Jesus Christ." *Journal of the American Medical Association* 255 (1986) 1455–63.

Eliade, Mircea. "Methodological Remarks on the Study of Religious Symbolism." In *The History of Religions: Essays in Methodology,* edited by M. Eliade and J. M. Kitagawa, 86–107. Chicago: University of Chicago Press, 1959.

Elliott, John. *A Home for the Homeless: A Social-Scientific Criticism of 1 Peter, Its Situation and Strategy.* Minneapolis: Fortress, 1990.

_____. "Social-Scientific Criticism of the New Testament: More on Methods and Models." *Semeia* 35 (1986) 1–33.

Ernst, Josef. *Johannes der Täufer: Interpretation—Geschichte—Wirkungsgeschichte.* BZNW 53. Berlin: de Gruyter, 1989.

Fawcett, Thomas. *The Symbolic Language of Religion: An Introductory Study.* London: SCM, 1970.

Feuillet, André. *Johannine Studies.* Staten Island, N.Y.: Alba House, 1964.

Fitzmyer, Joseph A. *The Gospel according to Luke.* AB 28–28A. Garden City, N.Y.: Doubleday, 1981–85.

Flusser, David. "Paganism in Palestine." In *The Jewish People in the First Century,* edited by S. Safrai and M. Stern, 2.1065–1100. Aasen/Maastricht: van Gorcum; Philadelphia: Fortress, 1987.

Forestell, Terence J. *The Word of the Cross: Salvation as Revelation in the Fourth Gospel.* AnBib 57. Rome: Biblical Institute, 1974.

Fortna, Robert T. *The Fourth Gospel and Its Predecessor: From Narrative Source to Present Gospel.* Philadelphia: Fortress, 1988.

Fox, Robin Lane. *Pagans and Christians.* San Francisco: Harper & Row, 1986.

Freed, Edwin D. *Old Testament Quotations in the Gospel of John*. NovTSup 11. Leiden: Brill, 1965.

Freedman, William. "The Literary Motif: A Definition and Evaluation." *Novel* 4 (1971) 123–31.

Frye, Northrop. *Anatomy of Criticism: Four Essays*. Princeton, N.J.: Princeton University Press, 1971.

Gaechter, Paul. "Zur Form von Joh 5:19-30." In *Neutestamentliche Aufsätze. Festschrift für Prof. Josef Schmid zum 70. Geburtstag,* edited by J. Blinzler, O. Kuss, and F. Mussner, 65–68. Regensburg: Pustet, 1963.

Gallagher, Eugene V. *Divine Man or Magician: Celsus and Origen on Jesus*. SBLDS 64. Chico, Calif.: Scholars, 1982.

Garrett, Susan. *The Demise of the Devil: Magic and the Demonic in Luke's Writings*. Minneapolis: Fortress, 1989.

Geertz, Clifford. "Religion as a Cultural System." In *Anthropological Approaches to the Study of Religion,* edited by M. Banton, 1–46. A.S.A. Monographs 3. London: Tavistock, 1966.

Gerhart, Mary, and Alan Melvin Russell. *Metaphoric Process: The Creation of Scientific and Religious Understanding*. Fort Worth: Texas Christian University Press, 1984.

Girard, M. "Jésus en Samarie (Jean 4,1-42): Analyses des structures stylistic et du process de symbolisation." *Eglise et Théologie* 17 (1986) 275–310.

Goodenough, Erwin R. *Jewish Symbols in the Greco-Roman Period*. New York: Pantheon, 1953–68.

_____. "The Political Philosophy of Hellenistic Kingship." In *Yale Classical Studies,* edited by A. M. Hermon. New Haven, Conn.: Yale University Press, 1928.

Grant, Frederick C. *Hellenistic Religions: The Age of Syncretism*. Indianapolis: Bobbs-Merrill, 1953.

Haenchen, Ernst. *John 1*. Hermeneia. Philadelphia: Fortress, 1984.

Hanson, Anthony Tyrrel. *The Prophetic Gospel: A Study of John and the Old Testament*. Edinburgh: T. & T. Clark, 1991.

Harner, Philip B. *The "I Am" of the Fourth Gospel: A Study in Johannine Usage and Thought*. Philadelphia: Fortress, 1971.

Harsh, Philip Whaley. *A Handbook of Classical Drama*. Palo Alto, Calif.: Stanford University Press, 1944.

Heekerens, Hans-Peter. *Die Zeichen-Quelle der johanneischen Redaktion: Ein Beitrag zur Enstehungsgeschichte der vierten Evangeliums*. SBS 113. Stuttgart: Katholisches Bibelwerk, 1984.

Hegermann, Harald. "Er kam in sein Eigentum: Zur Bedeutung des Erdenwirkens Jesu im vierten Evangelium." In *Der Ruf Jesu und die Antwort der Gemeinde: Festschrift für Joachim Jeremias,* edited by E. Lohse, et al., 112–31. Göttingen: Vandenhoeck & Ruprecht, 1970.

Hengel, Martin. *Crucifixion*. Philadelphia: Fortress, 1977.

_____. "The Interpretation of the Wine Miracle at Cana: John 2:1-11." In *The Glory of Christ in the New Testament: Studies in Christology in Memory of George Bradford Caird,* edited by L. D. Hurst and N. T. Wright, 83–112. Oxford: Clarendon, 1987.

Hinderer, Walter. "Theory, Conception, and Interpretation of the Symbol." In *Perspectives in Literary Symbolism,* edited by J. Strelka. Yearbook of Comparative Criticism 1. University Park, Pa.: Pennsylvania State University Press, 1968.

Holladay, Carl H. *Theios Ane-r in Hellenistic Judaism: A Critique of the Use of This Category in Hellenistic Judaism.* SBLDS 40. Missoula: Scholars, 1977.

Holmberg, Bengt. *Sociology and the New Testament: An Appraisal.* Minneapolis: Fortress, 1990.

Horsley, Richard A., and John S. Hanson. *Prophets, Bandits, and Messiahs: Popular Movements in the Time of Jesus.* Minneapolis: Winston, 1985.

Hoskyns, Edwyn Clement. *The Fourth Gospel.* 2d ed. Edited by F. N. Davey. London: Faber, 1947.

Jacobi, Jolande. *Complex/Archetype/Symbol in the Psychology of C. G. Jung.* Princeton, N.J.: Princeton University Press, 1959.

Jeremias, Joachim. *The Eucharistic Words of Jesus.* New York: Scribner's, 1966.

_____. *Jerusalem in the Time of Jesus: An Investigation into Economic and Social Conditions during the New Testament Period.* Philadelphia: Fortress, 1969.

Juel, Donald. *Messiah and Temple: The Trial of Jesus in the Gospel of Mark.* SBLDS 31. Missoula: Scholars, 1977.

Käsemann, Ernst. *The Testament of Jesus according to John 17.* Philadelphia: Fortress, 1968.

Kee, Howard Clark. *Miracle in the Early Christian World: A Study in Sociohistorical Method.* New Haven, Conn.: Yale University Press, 1983.

Kennedy, George A. *New Testament Interpretation through Rhetorical Criticism.* Chapel Hill: University of North Carolina Press, 1984.

Kittay, Eva Feder. *Metaphor: Its Cognitive Force and Linguistic Structure.* Oxford: Clarendon, 1987.

Klauck, Hans-Josef. "Lord's Supper." *Anchor Bible Dictionary,* 4.362–72. 1992.

Klein, Günther. "'Das wahre Licht scheint schon': Beobachtungen zur Zeit- und Geschichtserfahrung einer urchristlichen Schule." *ZTK* 68 (1971) 261–326.

Klein, Samuel. *Beiträge zur Geographie und Geschichte Galiläas.* Leipzig: Rudolf Haupt, 1909.

Knibb, M. A. "The Date of the Parables of Enoch: A Critical Review." *NTS* 25 (1980) 344–59.

Koester, Craig R. *The Dwelling of God: The Tabernacle in the Old Testament, Intertestamental Jewish Literature, and the New Testament.* CBQMS 22. Washington, D.C.: Catholic Biblical Association, 1989.

_____. "Hearing, Seeing, and Believing in the Gospel of John." *Bib* 70 (1989) 327–48.

_____. "John Six and the Lord's Supper." *LQ* 4 (1990) 419–37.

_____. "Messianic Exegesis and the Call of Nathanael (John 1.45-51)." *JSNT* 39 (1990) 23–34.

_____. "'The Savior of the World' (John 4:42)." *JBL* 109 (1990) 665–80.

_____. "Topography and Theology in the Gospel of John." In *Fortunate the Eyes That See: Essays in Honor of David Noel Freedman,* edited by Andrew H. Bartelt, Astrid B. Beck, Chris A. Franke, and Paul R. Raabe. Grand Rapids, Mich.: Eerdmans, 1994.

Koester, Helmut. *Ancient Christian Gospels: Their History and Development.* London: SCM; Philadelphia: Trinity, 1990.

Kohler, Hebert. *Kreuz und Menschwerdung: Ein exegetisch-hermeneutischer Versuch zur johanneischen Kreuzestheologie.* AThANT 72. Zurich: Theologischer, 1987.

Kopp, Clemens. *The Holy Places of the Gospels.* New York: Herder, 1963.

Kossen, H. B. "Who Were the Greeks of John XII 20?" In *Studies in John Presented to Professor Dr. J. N. Sevenster on the Occasion of His Seventieth Birthday*, 97–110. NovTSup 24. Leiden: Brill, 1970.

Kundsin, Karl. *Topologische Überlieferungstoffe im Johannes-Evangelium: Eine Untersuchung*. FRLANT 22. Göttingen: Vandenhoeck & Ruprecht, 1925.

Kysar, Robert. *The Fourth Evangelist and His Gospel: An Examination of Contemporary Scholarship*. Minneapolis: Augsburg, 1975.

Laato, Antti. *Who Is Immanuel? The Rise and the Foundering of Isaiah's Messianic Expectations*. Åbo: Åbo Academy, 1988.

Leroy, Herbert. *Rätsel und Missverständnis: Ein Beitrag zur Formgeschichte des Johannesevangeliums*. BBB 30. Bonn: Peter Hanstein, 1968.

Léon-Dufour, Xavier. *Sharing the Eucharistic Bread: The Witness of the New Testament*. New York: Paulist, 1987.

————. "Specificité symbolique du langage de Jean." In *La communauté johannique et son histoire*, edited by J. D. Kaestli, J. M. Poffet, and J. Zumstein, 121–34. Geneva: Labor et Fides, 1990.

————. "Towards a Symbolic Reading of the Fourth Gospel." *NTS* 27 (1980–81) 439–56.

Lichtenberger, Hermann. "Täufergemeinde und frühchristliche Täuferpolemik im letzten Drittel des 1. Jahrhunderts." *ZTK* 84 (1987) 36–57.

Lieu, Judith. "Blindness in the Johannine Tradition." *NTS* 34 (1988) 83–95.

————. *The Second and Third Epistles of John*. London: T. & T. Clark, 1986.

Lindars, Barnabas. *The Gospel of John*. NCB. Grand Rapids, Mich.: Eerdmans, 1972.

————. "The Passion in the Fourth Gospel." In *God's Christ and His People: Studies in Honor of Nils Alstrup Dahl*, edited by J. Jervell and W. A. Meeks, 71–86. Oslo: Universitetsforlaget, 1977.

Lütgehetmann, Walter. *Die Hochzeit von Kana (Joh 2,1-11): Zu Ursprung und Deutung einer Wunderzählung im Rahmen johanneischer Redaktionsgeschichte*. BU 20. Regensburg: Pustet, 1990.

MacDonald, J. *The Theology of the Samaritans*. London: SCM, 1964.

MacMullen, Ramsey. *Paganism in the Roman Empire*. New Haven, Conn.: Yale University Press, 1981.

————. *Roman Social Relations 50 B.C. to A.D. 284*. New Haven, Conn., and London: Yale University Press, 1974.

MacRae, George W. "The Ego Proclamation in Gnostic Sources." In *Studies in the New Testament and Gnosticism*, 203–17. Good News Studies 26. Wilmington, Del.: Michael Glazier, 1987.

————. "The Fourth Gospel and *Religionsgeschichte*." *CBQ* 32 (1970) 13–24.

Malherbe, Abraham J. *Social Aspects of Early Christianity*. 2d ed. Philadelphia: Fortress, 1983.

Malina, Bruce J. "Dealing with Biblical (Mediterranean) Characters: A Guide for U.S. Consumers." *BTB* 19 (1989) 127–41.

————. "Is There a Circum-Mediterranean Person? Looking for Stereotypes." *BTB* 22 (1992) 66–87.

————. "Reading Theory Perspective: Reading Luke-Acts." In *The Social World of Luke-Acts: Models for Interpretation*, edited by J. H. Neyrey, 3–23. Peabody, Mass.: Hendrickson, 1991.

Malina, Bruce, and Jerome H. Neyrey. "Honor and Shame in Luke-Acts: Pivotal Values in the Mediterranean World." In *The Social World of Luke-Acts: Models for Interpretation,* edited by J. H. Neyrey, 25–65. Peabody, Mass.: Hendrickson, 1991.

Malmede, Hans H. *Die Lichtsymbolik im neuen Testament.* Studies in Oriental Religions 15. Wiesbaden: Otto Harrassowitz, 1986.

Maloney, Francis J. "From Cana to Cana (Jn. 2:1—4:54) and the Fourth Evangelist's Concept of Correct (and Incorrect) Faith." *Salesianum* 40 (1978) 817–43.

Manns, Frédéric. *L'evangile de Jean à la lumière du Judaïsm.* Studium Biblicum Franciscanum 33. Jerusalem: Franciscan, 1991.

_____. "Le symbolism du jardin dans le récit de la passion selon St Jean." *LA* 37 (1987) 53–80.

Markus, R. A. "Augustine on Signs." In *Augustine: A Collection of Critical Essays,* edited by R. A. Markus, 61–91. Garden City, N.Y.: Anchor, 1972.

Martyn, J. Louis. "Attitudes Ancient and Modern toward Tradition about Jesus." *USQR* 23 (1968) 129–45.

_____. *The Gospel of John in Christian History: Essays for Interpreters.* New York: Paulist, 1978.

_____. *History and Theology in the Fourth Gospel.* 2d ed. Nashville: Abingdon, 1979.

Matera, Frank. "'On Behalf of Others,' 'Cleansing,' and 'Return': Johannine Images for Jesus' Death." *LS* 13 (1988) 161–78.

McFague, Sallie. *Metaphorical Theology: Models of God in Religious Language.* Philadelphia: Fortress, 1982.

Mead, A. H. "The *basilikos* in John 4.46-53." *JSNT* 23 (1985) 69–72.

Meeks, Wayne A. "Breaking Away: Three New Testament Pictures of Christianity's Separation from the Jewish Communities." In *"To See Ourselves as Others See Us": Christians, Jews, "Others" in Late Antiquity,* edited by J. Neusner and E. S. Frerichs, 93–115. Chico, Calif.: Scholars, 1985.

_____. *The First Urban Christians: The Social World of the Apostle Paul.* New Haven, Conn.: Yale University Press, 1983.

_____. "Galilee and Judea in the Fourth Gospel." *JBL* 85 (1966) 159–96.

_____. "The Man from Heaven in Johannine Sectarianism." *JBL* 91 (1972) 44–72.

_____. *The Prophet-King: Moses Traditions and the Johannine Christology.* NovTSup 14. Leiden: Brill, 1967.

Menken, M. J. J. *Numerical Literary Techniques in John: The Fourth Evangelist's Use of Numbers of Words and Syllables.* NovTSup 55. Leiden: Brill, 1985.

Milik, J. T. *The Books of Enoch.* Oxford: Clarendon, 1976.

Millar, Fergus. *The Emperor in the Roman World.* Ithaca, N.Y.: Cornell University Press, 1977.

Moore, Stephen. *Literary Criticism and the Gospels: The Theoretical Challenge.* New Haven, Conn.: Yale University Press, 1989.

_____. "Are There Impurities in the Living Water that the Johannine Jesus Dispenses? Deconstruction, Feminism, and the Samaritan Woman." *Biblical Interpretation* 1 (1993) 207–27.

Moran, Richard. "Seeing and Believing: Metaphor, Image, and Force." *Critical Inquiry* 16 (1989) 87–112.

Mowinkel, Sigmund. *He That Cometh: The Messiah Concept in the Old Testament and Later Judaism.* Nashville: Abingdon, 1954.

Moxnes, Halvor. "Patron-Client Relations and the New Community in Luke-Acts." In *The Social World of Luke-Acts: Models for Interpretation,* edited by J. H. Neyrey, 241–68. Peabody, Mass.: Hendrickson, 1991.

Müller, Theophil. *Das Heilsgeshehen im Johannesevangelium.* Zürich: Gotthelf, 1961.

Müller, Ulrich. "Die Bedeutung des Kreutzestodes Jesu im Johannesevangelium." *KD* 21 (1975) 49–71.

Nadean, Ray. "Hermogenes' *On Stases:* A Translation with an Introduction and Notes." *Speech Monographs* 31 (1964) 361–424.

Neusner, Jacob. *The Idea of Purity in Ancient Judaism.* SJLA 1. Leiden: Brill, 1973.

Neyrey, Jerome H. *An Ideology of Revolt: John's Christology in Social Science Perspective.* Philadelphia: Fortress, 1988.

————. "Jacob Traditions and the Interpretation of John 4:10-26." *CBQ* 41 (1979) 419–37.

Nichol, W. *The Sēmeia in the Fourth Gospel: Tradition and Redaction.* NovTSup 32. Leiden: Brill, 1972.

Nicholson, Godfrey C. *Death as Departure: The Johannine Descent-Ascent Schema.* SBLDS 63. Chico, Calif.: Scholars, 1983.

Nickelsburg, G. W. E. *Jewish Literature between the Bible and the Mishnah.* Philadelphia: Fortress, 1981.

Niewalda, Paul. *Sakramentssymbolik im Johannesevangelium: Eine exegetisch-historische Studie.* Limburg: Lahn, 1958.

Ninck, Martin. *Die Bedeutung des Wassers im Kult und Leben der Alten: Eine symbolgeschichtliche Untersuchung.* Philologus, Supp. 14/2. Leipzig: Dieterich, 1921.

North, John A. "The Afterlife: Rome." In *The Civilization of the Ancient Mediterranean: Greece and Rome,* edited by M. Grant and R. Kitzinger, 997–1007. New York: Scribner's, 1988.

Nötscher, Friedrich. *Zur theologischen Terminologie der Qumran-texte.* BBB 10. Bonn: Peter Hanstein, 1956.

O'Day, Gail R. "'I Have Overcome the World' (John 16:33): Narrative Time in John 13–17." *Semeia* 53 (1991) 153–66.

————. *Revelation in the Fourth Gospel: Narrative Mode and Theological Claim.* Philadelphia: Fortress, 1986.

Okure, Teresa. *The Johannine Approach to Mission: A Contextual Study of John 4:1-42.* WUNT 31. Tübingen: Mohr/Siebeck, 1988.

Olsson, Birger. *Structure and Meaning in the Fourth Gospel: A Text-Linguistic Analysis of John 2:1-11 and 4:1-42.* CB 6. Lund: Gleerup, 1974.

Onuki, Takashi. *Gemeinde und Welt im Johannesevangelium: Ein Beitrag zur Frage nach der theologischen und pragmatischen Funktion des johanneischen "Dualismus."* WMANT 26. Neukirchen-Vluyn: Neukirchener, 1984.

Osiek, Carolyn. "The Social Sciences and the Second Testament: Problems and Challenges." *BTB* 22 (1992) 88–95.

Pagels, Elaine H. *The Johannine Gospel in Gnostic Exegesis: Heracleon's Commentary on John.* SBLMS 17. Nashville: Abingdon, 1973.

Painter, John. "The Farewell Discourses and the History of Johannine Christianity." *NTS* 27 (1980–81) 525–43.

_____. "Johannine Symbols: A Case Study in Epistemology." *Journal of Theology for Southern Africa* 27 (1979) 26–41.

Panackel, Charles. *Idou ho Anthropos (Jn 19,5b): An Exegetico-Theological Study of the Text in the Light of the Term "anthropos" Depicting Jesus in the Fourth Gospel.* Analecta Gregoriana 251. Rome: Pontifica Universita Gregoriana, 1988.

Pancaro, Severino. *The Law in the Fourth Gospel: The Torah and the Gospel, Moses and Jesus, Judaism and Christianity according to John.* NovTSup 42. Leiden: Brill, 1975.

Perry, John M. "The Evolution of the Johannine Eucharist." *NTS* 39 (1993) 22–23.

Petersen, Norman. *The Gospel of John and the Sociology of Light: Language and Characterization in the Fourth Gospel.* Valley Forge, Pa.: Trinity, 1993.

Philonenko, Marc. "Essénisme et gnose chez le Pseudo-Philon: Le symbolism de la lumière dans le *Liber Antiquitatum Biblicarum.*" In *The Origins of Gnosticism: Colloquium of Messina 13–18 April 1966,* edited by U. Bianchi, 401–10. Studies in the History of Religions [Supplements to *Numen*] 12. Leiden: Brill, 1967.

Porsch, Felix. *Pneuma und Wort: Ein exegetischer Beitrag zur Pneumatologie des Johannesevangeliums.* FTS 16. Frankfurt am Main: Josef Knecht, 1974.

Potterie, I. de la. "Jésus roi et juge d'après Jn 19,13: *ekathisen epi bematos.*" *Bib* 41 (1960) 217–47. Cf. "Jesus King and Judge according to John 19:13," *Scripture* 13 (1961) 97–111.

Pryor, John W. "John 4:44 and the *Patris* of Jesus." *CBQ* 49 (1987) 254–63.

Rebell, Walter. *Gemeinde als Gegenwelt: Zur soziologischen und didaktischen Funktion des Johannesevangeliums.* BBET 20. Frankfurt am Main: Peter Lang, 1987.

Reinhartz, Adele. *The Word in the World: The Cosmological Tale in the Fourth Gospel.* SBLMS 45. Atlanta: Scholars, 1992.

Rensberger, David. *Johannine Faith and Liberating Community.* Philadelphia: Westminster, 1988.

Riches, J. K. "Apocalyptic—Strangely Relevant." *Templum Amicitiae: Essays on the Second Temple Presented to Ernst Bammel,* 237–63. JSNTSup 48. Sheffield: JSOT, 1991.

Richter, Georg. *Die Fusswaschung im Johannesevangelium.* BU 1. Regensburg: Pustet, 1967.

_____. *Studien zum Johannesevangelium.* Edited by J. Hainz. Regensburg: Pustet, 1977.

Ricoeur, Paul. "Metaphor and Symbol." *Interpretation Theory: Discourse and the Surplus of Meaning,* 45–69. Fort Worth: Texas Christian University Press, 1976.

_____. "The Metaphorical Process as Cognition, Imagination, and Feeling." *Critical Inquiry* 5 (1978) 143–59.

_____. *The Symbolism of Evil.* Religious Perspectives 17. New York: Harper & Row, 1967.

Rochais, Gerard. *Les recits de resurrection des morts dans le Nouveau Testament.* SNTSMS 40. Cambridge: Cambridge University Press, 1981.

Rohrbaugh, Richard L. "'Social Location of Thought' as a Heuristic Construct in New Testament Study." *JSNT* 30 (1987) 103–19.

Saller, Richard P. *Personal Patronage under the Early Empire.* Cambridge: Cambridge University Press, 1982.

Samain, P. "L'accusation de magie contre le Christ dans les evangiles." *ETL* 15 (1938) 449–90.

Sanders, E. P. *Paul and Palestinian Judaism.* Philadelphia: Fortress, 1977.

Sanders, J. N. *A Commentary on the Gospel according to St. John.* Edited by B. Mastin. HNTC. New York: Harper, 1969.

Sandmel, Samuel. *Philo of Alexandria: An Introduction.* Oxford: Oxford University Press, 1979.

Schein, Bruce E. "Our Father Abraham." Ph.D. diss., Yale University, 1972.

Schnackenburg, Rudolf. *Das Johannesevangelium.* HTKNT 4. Freiburg: Herder, 1965–84.

———. *The Gospel according to St. John.* New York: Herder/Seabury/Crossroad, 1968–82.

Schneiders, Sandra. "History and Symbolism in the Fourth Gospel." In *L'Evangile de Jean: Sources, redaction, théologie,* edited by M. de Jonge, 371–76. BETL 44. Gembloux and Louvain: Duculot and Louvain University, 1977.

———. "Women in the Fourth Gospel and the Role of Women in the Contemporary Church." *BTB* 12 (1982) 35–45.

Schnelle, Udo. *Antidocetic Christology in the Gospel of John: An Investigation of the Place of the Fourth Gospel in the Johannine School.* Minneapolis: Fortress, 1992.

Schottroff, Luise. *Der Glaubende und die feindliche Welt: Beobachtungen zum gnostischen Dualismus und seiner Bedeutung für Paulus und das Johannesevangelium.* WMANT 37. Neukirchen-Vluyn: Neukirchener, 1970.

Schulz, Siegfried. *Die Stunde der Botschaft: Einführung in der Theologie der vier Evangelisten.* Hamburg: Furche, 1967.

Schürer, Emile, Geza Vermes, Fergus Millar, and Matthew Black. *The History of the Jewish People in the Age of Jesus Christ.* Rev. ed. Edinburgh: T. & T. Clark, 1973–87.

Schürmann, Heinz. "Jesu Letzte Weisung: Jo 19,26-27a." In *Ursprung und Gestalt: Eröterungen und Besinnungen zum Neuen Testament,* 13–28. Düsseldorf: Patmos, 1970.

Schwankl, Otto. "Die Metaphorik von Licht und Finsternis im johanneischen Schrifttum." In *Metaphorik und Mythos im neuen Testament,* edited by Karl Kertelge, 135–67. Freiburg: Herder, 1990.

Schweizer, Eduard. "Das johanneische Zeugnis vom Herrenmahl." In *Neotestamentica,* 371–96. Stuttgart: Zwingli, 1963.

Scobie, Charles H. "Johannine Geography." *SR* 11 (1982) 77–84.

Segovia, Fernando F. *The Farewell of the Word: The Johannine Call to Abide.* Minneapolis: Fortress, 1991.

———. "John 13 1-20, The Footwashing in the Johannine Tradition." *ZNW* 73 (1982) 31–51.

Sevenster, G. "Remarks on the Humanity of Jesus in the Gospel and Letters of John." In *Studies in John Presented to Professor Dr. J. N. Sevenster on the Occasion of His Seventieth Birthday,* 185–93. NovTSup 24. Leiden: Brill, 1970.

Smith, D. Moody. *Johannine Christianity: Essays on Its Setting, Sources, and Theology.* Columbia: University of South Carolina Press, 1984.

———. *John among the Gospels: The Relationship in Twentieth-Century Research.* Minneapolis: Fortress, 1992.

Smith, Jonathan Z. "The Influence of Symbols upon Social Change: A Place on Which to Stand." *Worship* 44 (1970) 457–74.

Smith, Morton. "On the Wine God in Palestine (Gen. 18, Jn. 2, and Achilles Tatius)." In *Salo Wittmayer Jubilee Volume on the Occasion of His Eightieth Birthday,* 2.815–29. Jerusalem: Academy for Jewish Research, 1974.

Soskice, Janet Martin. *Metaphor and Religious Language.* Oxford: Clarendon, 1985.

Stauffer, Ethelbert. *Jesus and His Story.* New York: Alfred A. Knopf, 1960.

Stemberger, Günter. *La symbolique du bien et du mal selon Saint Jean.* Paris: Seuil, 1970.

Stibbe, Mark W. G. *John as Storyteller: Narrative Criticism and the Fourth Gospel.* SNTSMS 73. Cambridge: Cambridge University Press, 1992.

Stimpfle, Alois. *Blinde Sehen: Die Eschatologie im traditionsgeschichtliche Prozess des Johannesevangelium.* BZNW 57. Berlin: de Gruyter, 1990.

Stowers, Stanley K. *Letter Writing in Greco-Roman Antiquity.* Philadelphia: Westminster, 1986.

Strauss, David Friedrich. *The Life of Jesus Critically Examined.* Philadelphia: Fortress, 1972; German orig. 1835.

Sylva, Dennis D. "Nicodemus and His Spices (John 19.39)." *NTS* 34 (1988) 148–51.

Talbert, Charles H. *Reading John: A Literary and Theological Commentary on the Fourth Gospel and Johannine Epistles.* New York: Crossroad, 1992.

Theissen, Gerd. *Studien zur Sociologie des Urchristentums.* 3d ed. Tübingen: Mohr/Siebeck, 1989.

Thomas, John Christopher. *Footwashing in John 13 and the Johannine Community.* JSNTSup 61. Sheffield: JSOT, 1991.

Thompson, Marianne M. *The Humanity of Jesus in the Fourth Gospel.* Philadelphia: Fortress, 1988.

Thüsing, Wilhelm. *Die Erhöhung und Verherrlichung Jesu im Johannesevangelium.* NTAbh 21. Münster: Aschendorff, 1960.

Tiede, David L. *Charismatic Figure as Miracle Worker.* SBLDS 1. Missoula: Scholars, 1972.

Tillich, Paul. *Systematic Theology.* Chicago: University of Chicago Press, 1951–63.

Tinh, Tran Tam. "Sarapis and Isis." In *Jewish and Christian Self-Definition,* edited by Ben F. Meyer and E. P. Sanders, 3.101–17. Philadelphia: Fortress, 1982.

Turner, Max. "Atonement and the Death of Jesus in John: Some Questions to Bultmann and Forestell." *EvQ* 62 (1990) 99–122.

Turner, Victor. *The Forest of Symbols: Aspects of Ndembu Ritual.* Ithaca, N.Y.: Cornell University Press, 1967.

Tyndall, William York. "Excellent Dumb Discourse." In *The Theory of the Novel,* edited by P. Stevick, 342. New York: Free Press, 1967.

Vellanickal, M. *The Divine Sonship of Christians in the Johannine Writings.* Rome: Biblical Institute, 1977.

Vermes, Geza. *The Dead Sea Scrolls: Qumran in Perspective.* Rev. ed. Philadelphia: Fortress, 1981.

_____. *Scripture and Tradition in Judaism: Haggadic Studies.* Studia Post-Biblica 4. Leiden: Brill, 1961.

Vermeule, Emily. "The Afterlife: Greece." In *The Civilization of the Ancient Mediterranean: Greece and Rome,* edited by M. Grant and R. Kitzinger, 2.987–96. New York: Scribner's, 1988.

Veyne, Paul. *Bread and Circuses: Historical Sociology and Political Pluralism.* London: Penguin, 1990.

von Wahlde, Urban C. *The Earliest Version of John's Gospel: Recovering the Gospel of Signs.* Wilmington, Del.: Michael Glazier, 1989.

_____. *The Johannine Commandments: 1 John and the Struggle for the Johannine Tradition.* New York: Paulist, 1990.

Vouga, François. *Le cadre historique et l'intention théologique de Jean.* Paris: Beauchesne, 1977.

Webb, Robert L. *John the Baptizer and Prophet: A Socio-Historical Study.* JSNTSup 62. Sheffield: JSOT, 1991.

Wehr, Lothar. *Arznei der Unsterblichkeit: Die Eucharistie bei Ignatius von Antiochen und im Johannesevangelium.* NTAbh 18. Münster: Aschendorff, 1986.

Weiss, Herold. "Footwashing in the Johannine Community." *NovT* 21 (1979) 321.

Wenst, Klaus. *Bedrängte Gemeinde und verherrlichter Christus: Der historische Ort des Johannesevangeliums als Schlüssel zu seiner Interpretation.* 2d ed. Biblisch-theologische Studien 5. Neukirchen-Vluyn: Neukirchener, 1983.

Wheelwright, Philip. "The Archetypal Symbol." In *Perspectives in Literary Symbolism.* Yearbook of Comparative Criticism 1, edited by J. Strelka. University Park, Pa.: Pennsylvania State University Press, 1968.

_____. *Metaphor and Reality.* Bloomington: Indiana University Press, 1962.

Wilson, Bryan. *Magic and the Millennium: A Sociological Study of Religious Movements of Protest among Tribal and Third-World Peoples.* New York: Harper & Row, 1973.

Wink, Walter. *John the Baptist in the Gospel Tradition.* SNTSMS 7. Cambridge: Cambridge University Press, 1968.

Wuellner, W. H. *The Meaning of "Fishers of Men."* Philadelphia: Westminster, 1967.

Index of
Biblical References

OLD TESTAMENT

NEW TESTAMENT

Index of Subjects

Anointing, *See* Foot: anointing
Baptism, 23, 156–67, 180, 184, 257–58, 262
Beloved Disciple, 65, 72–73, 122, 214–19, 229
Bethzatha, Pool of, 51–54, 69, 85–89, 155, 172–73, 193, 257, 264–65, 267
Blind beggar, 14–15, 19, 25, 36, 59, 63–65, 69, 100–104, 144–45, 155, 232, 249–50
Bread, 2–8, 13, 26–27, 55–60, 89–100, 118–19, 186, 194, 234, 249, 255, 257–58. *See also* Lord's Supper
Burial, 204–206
Crucifixion, 185–219
  and community life, 21–22, 223, 234, 236–38
  and Jesus' symbolic actions, 46, 74, 77, 81–85, 89, 98–100, 110–117, 122, 181 83, 238
  and light, 150–52
  and water, 155, 159, 162–64, 177–83, 203–204, 266
Door, 13, 256
Eucharist, *See* Lord's Supper
Exaltation, 29–30, 46, 177, 186, 200, 209–11. *See also* Glorification
Fish, great catch of, 118–22, 152, 264–68
Foot
  anointing, 111–15, 233
  washing, 10, 11, 14, 111, 115–18, 155, 180, 233, 244
Friendship, 240–41, 245–47
Gate, *See* Door
Geographical symbolism, 35, 48–49, 53–59, 80, 103, 141–42, 160, 172–73, 177–78, 180, 262–264. *See also* Burial; Temple

Glorification, 106–107, 162–63, 185, 206, 209–14, 237, 247. *See also* Exaltation
Honor, 241–43, 247–48
Humor, 25, 78, 110, 115, 224, 255–56
Invalid, *See* Bethzatha, Pool of
Irony, 22, 30, 36, 137, 149, 187, 224
Johannine Communities, 18–24, 220–56
Judas, 10, 29, 59, 114, 150–51, 194, 206–208
Lamb, 157–59, 162, 193–200, 232, 267
Lazarus, 58, 65–67, 105–112, 145, 147, 250, 267
"Lifting up" of Jesus, *See* Exaltation
Light and darkness, 2–14, 19–20, 29, 47–48, 59, 123–54, 234–35, 237, 243–44, 254–55
Lord's Supper, 23, 99–100, 257–62
Martha, 58–59, 65–67, 105, 107–108, 233, 247–48, 250, 255, 263
Mary
  sister of Martha and Lazarus, 23, 58–59, 65–67, 105, 112–15, 233, 247–48, 250, 263
Mary Magdalene, 10, 69–70, 216
Mother of Jesus, 77–78, 214–19
Metaphor, 6, 8, 16–18, 29–30, 96, 120, 179, 231–32, 235, 246, 254, 260, 262
Nathanael, 40–41, 68–69, 204
Nicodemus, 2, 5, 7, 9, 12, 29, 45–48, 58, 69, 133–35, 155, 163–67, 204–206, 263
Numerical symbolism, 264–68
Official (Royal, Galilean), 51–52, 58, 69, 85–89, 250, 267
Peter, 39, 71–73, 115–22, 224, 255
Readers, Spectrum of, 18–24. *See also* Johannine Communities

Index of
Modern Authors